Advertising & Sales Promotion

Ken Kaser

SOUTH-WESTERN
CENGAGE Learning

Australia • Brazil • Japan • Korea • Mexico • Singapore • Spain • United Kingdom • United States

© gary18/Shutterstock.com

SOUTH-WESTERN
CENGAGE Learning·

Advertising and Sales Promotion
Ken Kaser

Vice President of Editorial, Business:
Jack W. Calhoun

Vice President/Editor-in-Chief: Karen Schmohe

Executive Editor: Eve Lewis

Senior Developmental Editor: Penny Shank

Editorial Assistant: Anne Kelly

Marketing Program Manager: Linda Kuper

Media Editor: Lysa Kosins

Rights Acquisition Director: Audrey Pettengill

Senior Rights Acquisition Specialist, Text and
Image: Deanna Ettinger

Manufacturing Planner: Kevin Kluck

Senior Art Director: Tippy McIntosh

Internal Designer, Production Management,
and Composition: PreMediaGlobal

Cover Designer: Lou Ann Thesing

Cover Image: © Corbis

Exam*View*® is a registered trademark of eInstruction Corp. Windows is a registered trademark of the Microsoft Corporation used herein under license. Macintosh and Power Macintosh are registered trademarks of Apple Computer, Inc. used herein under license.

© 2013 Cengage Learning. All Rights Reserved.

ISBN-13: 978-1-111-57323-2

ISBN-10: 1-111-57323-9

South-Western
5191 Natorp Boulevard
Mason, OH 45040
USA

Cengage Learning products are represented in Canada by Nelson Education, Ltd.

For your course and learning solutions, visit **www.cengage.com/school**
Visit our company website at **www.cengage.com**

Printed in the United States of America
2 3 4 5 6 7 15 14 13 12

Brief Contents

Contents

Advertising...The Power to Reach Out and Touch People!

Welcome to the exciting world of *Advertising and Sales Promotion* — a comprehensive introduction to its principles and practices. You will learn exciting techniques used in current print, broadcast, and digital advertising.

Let's Get Started!

IMPACT ADVERTISING

You're a Winner!

Nationally recognized companies use sweepstakes to heighten the interest of consumers. A sweepstakes is an effective way to draw attention to a brand. Sweepstakes come in many forms and offer a variety of prizes, including large sums of money.

The letter arrives in the mail, proclaiming, "You're a Winner!" It states that you are among two people vying for a prize of $11 million. All you have to do is send in the attached form, and the money is as good as yours. You may have to subscribe to a few unwanted magazines as a prerequisite to collecting the winnings and becoming a millionaire. The aforementioned letter arrives in the mailboxes of millions of households every year. Most people know offers like this are too good to be true, but there are always those who believe otherwise.

Publishers Clearing House (PCH) is a direct marketing company that offers a magazine subscription service. It has held a sweepstakes since 1967. Over the years, many people, often senior citizens, have received a notice in the mail from PCH declaring them the winner of millions of dollars. Some of these naive customers were so elated with the news that, rather than trust the post office to return the "winning" ticket, they flew it to the PCH headquarters themselves. Unfortunately, upon their arrival at the offices, they were not greeted with a check. It was pointed out that they had not read the fine print of the ticket, which stated that the ticket holder was a winner only if his or her number was the one drawn from millions of other numbers.

Numerous lawsuits have been filed against PCH on behalf of consumers who felt they were duped by false advertising. As a result, PCH has paid out millions of dollars in settlements. In addition, it was ordered to reform its business practices. PCH was banned from using false statements, such as "you're a winner" or "you're guaranteed to win." It must also provide consumers with a sweepstakes fact sheet, which clearly states the odds of winning and explains that purchases do not increase the consumer's chances of winning. PCH also was banned from targeting specific consumer groups, such as senior citizens.

WHAT DO YOU KNOW?
1. Why do you think PCH was found guilty of using deceptive advertising?
2. Why does deceptive advertising frequently target senior citizens?
3. What advice would you give someone who plans to enter a sweepstakes?

349

IMPACT ADVERTISING

an ad campaign case study that introduces the chapter concepts in a real-world context.

WHAT DO YOU KNOW? supplies thought-provoking questions to capture interest.

Each lesson begins with a list of goals and terms to help you focus your reading.

Goals
outline the main objectives of the lesson.

Terms
list the new vocabulary defined in the lesson.

FOCUS ON ADVERTISING
introduces concepts by providing a thought-provoking introduction to each lesson.

2.1 The Consumer Is in Charge

Goals
- Recognize the importance of understanding the customer's wants and needs.
- Identify the five-step consumer decision-making process.

Terms
- consumer behavior, p. 34
- need, p. 35
- want, p. 35
- routine decision making, p. 37
- limited decision making, p. 37
- extensive decision making, p. 38

FOCUS ON ADVERTISING

Staying Connected with Apps

Technology companies are helping consumers solve everyday problems by creating application software, also known as an app, for use with smartphones. People often go to the mall or a sporting event and then forget where they parked their car when they leave. The Android™ smartphone provides the Carr Matey app that uses GPS tracking software to help locate the car. Many people have problems falling asleep at night. The Android Relax and Sleep app provides over 30 realistic sounds that act as soothing background noise to help lull you to sleep. Available iPhone apps turn the smartphone into a currency converter or a ruler. Although these apps help consumers solve simple life problems, smartphone companies look at them as a way to promote their product and brand. Creating highly useful and engaging apps is one way to keep smartphone users connected to the brand. Smartphone companies can also promote their apps as a way to lure new customers.

Work as a Team Have you used any smartphone apps? Did they meet a specific need or solve a problem? Do you think apps are a good promotional tool for smartphone companies? Why or why not?

Understanding the Customer

To succeed, a business must understand its customers, but that isn't always easy. The product and service preferences of customers change frequently. Marketers must study consumer behavior. **Consumer behavior** describes how consumers make buying decisions, choose among alternatives, and use products. Studying consumer behavior is an important factor in creating effective advertising. For example, if a company discovers through research

34   Chapter 2   Consumer Behavior

Special Features Enhance Learning

Sharpen Your
21st CENTURY SKILLS

Communicating in the Technological Age

While technology has opened up numerous opportunities in the world of communication, it has been associated with improper business etiquette. Individuals spend more time communicating using electronic devices than they do using personal, face-to-face communication. The use of cell phones and other text messaging devices has resulted in diminished communication skills. Proper business writing has suffered as a result of text messaging. Abbreviations used for text messages are not acceptable for business communications. Business leaders still expect employees to produce documents that incorporate proper grammar, sentence structure, and flow. Leaders must be able to carry on a formal conversation at a business meeting or lunch.

Individuals who want to make an impact with the top leaders in the business world must practice communication etiquette. Communication etiquette involves respecting the feelings of other people, paying careful attention to a conversation, making eye contact, and turning off electronic devices during meetings. By text messaging or scrolling through information on electronic devices while attending a business meeting, you are sending a message that the other person is not important. Manners do make a big difference when aspiring to leadership positions. Some tips for effective communication include the following:

1. Give your cell phone a break. Turn it off during a business meeting, family gathering, or meal. Show respect for your guest or business associate.
2. Compose written documents using proper grammar and format. Always use the spell check feature and then proof the document to make sure that it is grammatically correct.
3. Practice being a great listener. Give your full attention to the other person through eye contact and respectful feedback. Do not let electronic devices break down the communication process.

Try It Out
For one week, set aside time each day in which you refrain from using your cell phone or other electronic devices. During this time, communicate with someone face to face or by writing a letter. Keep a record of your communications. At the end of the week, describe how your "new" ways of communicating differed from your usual ways of communicating. Did you find that your communication had improved over the past week? Why or why not?

PARTNERSHIP FOR
21ST CENTURY SKILLS

Sharpen Your
21st CENTURY SKILLS

apply valued skills, such as problem solving, critical thinking, and technology use, as defined by the *Partnership for 21st Century Skills.*

PARTNERSHIP FOR
21ST CENTURY SKILLS

Advertising is a very popular competitive event

activities conclude each chapter and help prepare you for BPA, DECA, and FBLA advertising competitive events.

Buying and Merchandising Team Event

This Team Decision Making Event provides an opportunity for you to analyze one or a combination of elements essential to the effective operation of a business in a specific occupational area. Employees in buying and merchandising positions get the product into the hands of the customer. This process includes forecasting, planning, buying, displaying, selling, and providing customer service.

PROBLEM Your team works for a large department store in a city with 500,000 people. Each season your buying team is challenged to select clothing styles that will sell well even without markdowns. A recession has greatly affected consumer spending. Designer brands are not selling until they are marked down 50 percent. Your team must determine a strategy to purchase the appropriate amount of merchandise during slow economic conditions. You must also determine which famous designer brands will sell during this recession. You must explain your purchasing strategy and markdown strategy to move the seasonal clothing. The plan must outline how long the merchandise will be offered at the full retail price and when the percentage discounts will be applied to clear out seasonal merchandise.

Participants must demonstrate the following skills when completing this project:
- communications skills—the ability to exchange information and ideas with others through writing, speaking, reading or listening
- analytical skills—the ability to derive facts from data, findings from facts, conclusions from findings, and recommendations from conclusions
- critical thinking/problem-solving skills
- production skills—the ability to take a concept from an idea and make it real
- teamwork—the ability to be an effective member of a productive group
- priorities/time management—the ability to determine priorities and manage time commitments

Go to the DECA website for more detailed information.

Think Critically
1. Why are promotions so important for a retail business?
2. How can a buyer for a clothing store determine what to purchase for the upcoming fall season?
3. When buying merchandise for a business, what are the main concerns for the buying department?
4. What is a merchandising trend that you have noticed in one of your favorite stores?

www.deca.org

Buying and Merchandising Team Event **89**

Real-World Features

Advertisements and illustrations provide real-world examples that make the content interesting, relevant, and tangible.

SPOTLIGHT ON SUCCESS takes you to advertising success stories of real companies.

SPOTLIGHT ON SUCCESS

MARK ZUCKERBERG
Facebook

Mark Zuckerberg was a 19-year-old sophomore at Harvard when he started a Web service from his dorm in 2004. The Zuckerberg invention was called Thefacebook.com, and it was described as "an online directory that connects people through social networks at colleges." Today Facebook has over 550 million members. One out of every 12 people in the world has a Facebook account, and Facebook's membership currently is growing at a rate of about 700,000 people a day. The Facebook age has arrived.

With Facebook, Zuckerberg has created a social entity almost twice as large as the United States. Social media websites like Facebook have played a significant role in product launches and reviews. The volume of comments posted on Facebook and other social media websites is growing. These comments prove to be a valuable resource for businesses who are trying to launch or revamp their products. Today the fastest-growing market for Facebook is the 25- to 44-year-old-segment, a demographic that is often targeted by businesses. Not only has Facebook changed the way people relate to one another, it has also affected many other aspects of life. There are many Facebook pages dedicated to social and political issues around the world. A posting on Facebook can quickly travel to millions of members and influence social and political changes worldwide.

What started out as a diversion for Mark Zuckerberg has turned him into a multibillionaire. He believes that eventually all businesses will recognize the importance of the social aspects of doing business.

Think Critically

How has Facebook changed the way people communicate? Why do you think people and businesses are embracing this technology?

Making Content Relevant

Reality ✓

© gary718/Shutterstock.com

Digital Advertising Gets Personal

Digital advertising is providing marketers with the opportunity to break through advertising clutter, deliver more targeted messages, and create engaging experiences through interactive billboards, digital projections, and even 3-D images.

Digital marketing has the ability to create a more personally relevant advertising experience. Marketers in Japan began testing facial recognition technology to enhance the digital billboard in 2010. Using billboards with embedded cameras, the passerby is scanned, his or her gender and age are determined, and then a more relevant advertisement is served. Digital technology now has the ability to make public spaces more personalized. Ad placements are being moved from billboards to entire exteriors of buildings.

Digital advertising can use disruptive engagement by catching audiences off guard with unexpected advertising placement and consumer interaction capabilities. Aquafina recently used digital marketing by installing LCD screen mirrors to fill a public bathroom with branded messaging. When a person was ready to use the mirror, the advertisements were simply moved out of the way. Kraft Foods created an iFood Assistant smartphone application. The user can type in three items, and the app will find a recipe using Kraft brands. This form of marketing gets closer to the customer at the point of purchase.

Digital advertising provides personal experiences for consumers and non-static messages. The latest digital advertising trends provide more personal interaction with a brand and builds brand association.

Think Critically
1. What makes digital advertising unique?
2. Could some aspects of the latest digital advertising be classified as invasion of consumer privacy? Explain your answer.
3. How might digital advertising be more cost-effective for a larger target market?
4. Do you think that all age groups will react favorably to interactive digital advertising?
5. What are the advantages and disadvantages associated with using the latest digital technology for advertising?

Assessment

THINK ABOUT IT

1. Briefly describe common pricing objectives used by businesses.

2. What is an advantage and a disadvantage of using a price skimming strategy? What is an advantage and a disadvantage of using a penetration pricing strategy?

3. How do supply and demand affect pricing?

4. Why do retailers offer consumer credit? How is credit related to pricing?

MAKE ACADEMIC CONNECTIONS

5. **MARKETING** Choose a designer brand and a store brand of clothing. Describe the pricing strategy that was likely used to introduce both brands in the market. Explain why this strategy was used.

6. **MATH** You are a retailer who receives a trade discount from one of your largest suppliers. The discount is based upon the dollar amount of merchandise that you purchase each month. The discount for monthly purchases totaling $50,000–$100,000 is 10 percent; $100,001–$150,000, 15 percent; and $150,001–$200,000, 20 percent. What is the dollar amount of your discount for each of the following months' purchases: January, $190,000; February, $105,000; and March, $75,000.

7. **MANAGEMENT** You are opening a furniture store that will offer product lines catering to the middle and high-end markets. Select a pricing objective for your business. You may select more than one objective for the different markets. Explain why you selected the pricing objective(s).

Teamwork

You work for a full-service hotel located in a warm climate that caters to business clients, conventions, and tourists who visit the hotel four to six times each year. Hotel management has asked you to develop pricing strategies for all

End of Lesson Assessment

An abundance of ongoing Lesson Assessments ensure you understand and can apply what you've learned.

Think About It
activities that help you apply what you have learned in the lesson.

Make Academic Connections
integrated curriculum activities that show you how advertising and promotion concepts relate to other courses of study.

Teamwork
opportunities to work with classmates on cooperative learning projects.

Chapter Review and Assessment

End of Chapter Assessment provides a summary of the main points. Questions and activities test your knowledge.

CHECKPOINT

How are psychographics useful to marketers?

enables you to test your understanding of key points before moving on.

activities help students learn the importance of understanding ethics in relation to advertising and sales promotion.

You are the owner of a clothing store that is the sponsor of a new television series that has been highly promoted to teenagers. Since 60 percent of your customer base ranges in age from 12 to 24, you recognize the possible impact on sales from your association with a show that is watched by 2 million teenagers. However, the questionable content of the first show of the new television series has raised a lot of concern from parents. Parents and children's advocacy watch groups have expressed deep concerns about the television show that your company is sponsoring.

As a sponsor, do you have any social or ethical responsibilities? If so, what are they? What actions should your business take in this situation?

Product Family

A Variety of Support

- Adobe PDF Online eBooks
    - Text/Adobe PDF Online eBook (6 year access)   978-1-133-28636-3
    - Adobe PDF Online eBook (6 year access)   978-1-133-28637-0
- Activities and Projects workbook   978-1-133-11021-7
- Annotated Instructor's Edition   978-1-133-56196-5
- ExamView® testing software   978-1-133-36458-0
- Instructor's Resource CD   978-1-133-36546-4
    - PowerPoint® presentations
    - Lesson plans
    - Tests with solutions
    - Activities and Projects solutions
- CourseMate
- Website www.cengage.com/school/advertising

CourseMate helps you make the grade!

You can access interactive study tools in a dynamic, online learning environment. An enchanced eBook provides you with an interactive, online version of the textbook. A Student Learning Pathway features a variety of integrated digital media with a simple, user-friendly interface.

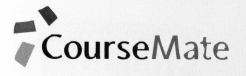

- Interactive eBook
- Simulated Activities
- Video Assessment
- Interactive Quizzes
- Glossary
- Flashcards
- Crossword Puzzles
- Net Bookmarks
- Internet Resources

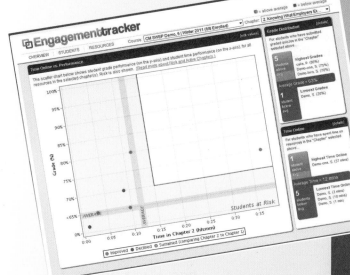

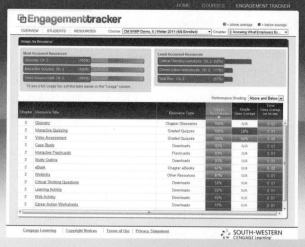

ENGAGEMENT TRACKER allows teachers to assess their students' preparation and engagement. This intuitive, online reporting tool makes it easy to evaluate use of study resources, monitor time-on-task, and track progress for the entire class or for individual students. Teachers can instantly see what concepts are the most difficult for their class and identify which students are at risk throughout the semester.

About the Author

Ken Kaser is Director of the University of Houston Conrad Hilton College at Sugar Land, Texas. He taught marketing education and was a DECA advisor in the Fort Bend ISD in Texas for 15 years. Ken taught business education at Northeast High School in Lincoln, Nebraska for 18 years. He has authored eight books; written local, state, and national curriculum; and served in many professional leadership roles. Ken is the recipient of numerous teaching awards at the state, regional, and national levels.

Reviewers

Michael Crawford
Instructor
GASC Technology Center
Flint, Michigan

Sherry Dockery
Marketing Teacher and
    Coordinator
Evansville Central High School
Evansville, Indiana

Jean Getz
Marketing and
    Business Teacher
Beachwood High School
Beachwood, Ohio

Mechelle Gilles
Marketing Education Teacher
North High School
Evansville, Indiana

Susan E. Hall
Marketing and Real Estate
    Assistant Professor
University of West Georgia
Carrollton, Georgia

Marc W. Hillestad
Marketing Education Teacher
Cedarcrest High School
Duvall, Washington

Rodger Hutley
Teacher
Little Elm High School
Little Elm, Texas

Jayne Johnson
Marketing and
    Entrepreneurship Instructor
Dauphin County Technical School
Harrisburg, Pennsylvania

Julie Lowe
Marketing Teacher,
    CTE Department Chair, and
    Texas DECA Board of Directors
The Woodlands College Park
The Woodlands, Texas

Edward F. McEleney
Business and Technology
    Education Instructor and
    Department Chair
West Branch High School
West Branch, Iowa

Lauren A. Newman
Business Education Teacher
West Deptford High School
West Deptford, New Jersey

Rue L. Ramsey
Marketing and Business Teacher
    and Department Chair
Booker T. Washington High School
Tulsa, Oklahoma

Philip Said
Marketing Teacher
Great Oaks Career
    Development Center
Cincinnati, Ohio

Patricia Wille
Marketing Teacher
Bethel Park High School
Bethel Park, Pennsylvania

1

What Is Advertising?

IMPACT ADVERTISING

Historic Advertising Campaigns

Throughout history, advertising has influenced our shopping habits and culture. Advertising has introduced new products into our lives and created new social norms. Brilliant advertisement ideas have advanced the industry and civilization. Over the years, advertising has used clever headlines, mascots, humor, music, lyrics, and other tactics to make sales pitches.

John Caples was just 25 years old in 1925 when he wrote one of the most successful advertisements in history. His advertising headline that read "They Laughed When I Sat Down at the Piano, But When I Started to Play!" was intended to attract students to the U.S. School of Music. The ad put direct-response advertising on the map. Direct-response advertising urges consumers to respond immediately and directly to the advertiser.

DeBeers is one of the oldest diamond companies in the world. Its advertising campaign, "A Diamond Is Forever," created one of the most recognized slogans of the 20th century. The first ads were launched in 1948 and still run today. The ad successfully created the concept that diamonds are an essential part of a long-lasting, loving relationship. It suggested that diamonds are the only suitable gem for engagement and wedding rings. This advertising campaign revived the diamond market, increasing sales by 55 percent.

Volkswagen used a 1959 advertising campaign that ignored everything that made U.S. car ads successful. This advertising strategy made the German brand a household name. Instead of boasting about power, speed, and luxury, the Volkswagen advertisement focused on great gas mileage and easy parallel parking. The advertisement showed a tiny VW Beetle against a field of white with the headline "Think Small." The advertisement was remarkable for its time, and it holds the number one spot on the *Ad Age Top 100 Advertising Campaigns* list.

Advertising is ingrained in our society. It plays an important role in businesses and the economy by helping spur sales. But successful advertising does more than sell products, services, or ideas. It can touch us, evoke emotions, spark discussions, and educate us. Creative advertising will continue to capture our attention into the next centuries.

© Rob Wison/Shutterstock.com

1. How does advertising influence shopping habits?

2. Why do you think the DeBeers advertising campaign is still successful today?

3. Why do you think creativity is an important factor in advertising?

WHAT DO YOU KNOW?

History of Advertising

Goals
- Explain how advertising has changed to meet the needs of changing times.
- Describe inventions that have impacted advertising.

Terms
- advertising, p. 4
- infomercial, p. 9

FOCUS ON ADVERTISING

Sears Roebuck Catalog

Richard Sears first used a printed mailer to advertise watches and jewelry for the R. W. Sears Watch Company in 1888. Since the postal service classified mail-order publications as aids in the dissemination of knowledge, the postage rate was only one cent per pound. In 1896, then operating as Sears, Roebuck and Company, an enlarged spring and fall catalog was added. For the first time, the company charged 25 cents for the catalog while promising to apply the fee to any orders over $10.

Sears added a color section to the catalog in 1897 and created more specialty catalogs in 1898. The hands-on feel catalog in 1905 featured full-color and texture wallpaper samples, paint samples, and a swatch of material used in men's suits. Testimonials from satisfied customers were eventually added to the Sears catalog to help promote Sears' low prices and exceptional value. Sears stopped publishing its general catalog in 1993 but still produces specialty catalogs.

Work as a Team   Obtain a copy of a Sears specialty catalog. Outline the detail in the catalog. Why have Sears' catalogs been successful for more than 100 years?

The Changing Times in Advertising

Advertising is not an easy term to define. Most people think of advertising as an attempt to persuade them to purchase a good or service. In many cases, advertising is used to promote the sale of products and services. However, a corporation may also use advertising to enhance its image or to educate consumers. **Advertising** is a paid form of communication intended to inform, persuade, and remind an audience to take some kind of action. The roots of advertising can be traced back many years.

First Signs of Advertising

Advertising has been used to promote trade (the sale of goods and services) for centuries. By looking at the evolution of advertising, you can see how its role has changed over the years. Advertising provides a mirror to our social history that reflects values and aspirations of the culture. As historians one day look back at the advertisements of our modern time, they will be able to develop a realistic depiction of the societal values during that era.

Advertising in the Early Centuries Advertising has been around practically since the beginning of time. Advertisements appeared as inscriptions on Egyptian tombs around 3000 B.C. The Greeks engraved theater advertisements in stone around 500 B.C. The ancient ruins of cities like Pompeii and Rome showed evidence of message boards on the lime-whitened walls of buildings displaying political and commercial messages for the public to read. In many parts of South America, Asia, and Africa, stone carvings or paintings displaying commercial advertisements on old walls have been discovered.

Colonial Americans used public message boards in town squares where merchants could advertise the sale of their services and goods. Throughout the 18th century, Ben Franklin greatly influenced advertising. As the owner of the *Pennsylvania Gazette*, he introduced the use of headlines, illustrations, and advertisements placed next to editorial items. He added pictures to advertisements in 1732.

With the onset of the Industrial Revolution in the 19th century, there was a period of economic prosperity and rapidly growing populations and urbanization. The population was referred to as the consumer society because it was shifting away from self-sufficiency and becoming more dependent on the marketplace to meet its needs. As a result of the new consumer society, advertising expanded. In 1848 it was possible to print 10,000 sheets per hour on a printing press, so newspaper advertising grew in popularity. The 1870s techniques in color lithography fueled the poster boom of the 1880s.

Also during the 19th century, circus mogul P. T. Barnum helped spur the growth of outdoor advertising. He created unique advertising in the form of banners for his museum and traveling circus. His banners used attention-grabbing headlines, such as "Caravans of Giant Coursing Elephants and Camels," to draw crowds to the events.

Advertising in the 20th and 21st Centuries Advertising throughout the 20th century was influenced by the changing times. During this period, Americans lived through the Roaring Twenties, the Great Depression, and World War II. Social revolutions occurred in the 1960s and 1970s. The nation struggled with the civil rights movement in the 1960s and the feminist movement in the 1970s.

The advertising agency took on a more prominent role during this time period. By the start of the 20th century, large agencies in London were commissioning artists to produce specific brief, targeted ad campaigns. Advertisements reflected cultural and social changes. In the 1920s, advertising was glamorous and promoted consumption during prosperous times. During the Great Depression in the 1930s, advertising took a no-nonsense approach, and laws were passed to prohibit deceptive advertising practices. In the 1950s, the TV added a whole new dimension to advertising. Typical advertisements focused on families and new technological advances, such as the automatic washer and dryer. Because a social revolution was occurring in the 1960s and 1970s, advertisements became more creative and innovative, reflecting values that were more nontraditional. The economy was robust in the 1980s, and thus advertisements promoted consumption.

In the latter half of the 20th century and the early 21st century, advertising became more visual- and youth-oriented. Advertising also entered the electronic age. Various forms of advertisements began popping up on the Internet. However, it wasn't an easy transition. Technology problems, such as compatibility and bandwidth (data transfer rate) issues, had to be addressed. Also, advertisers found it difficult to measure the effectiveness of online ads. Because of the increasing presence of the Internet, however, advertisers have embraced this media and continue to find creative ways to use it.

Advertising Trends in American History

Advertising has responded to changing business, media, and cultural trends over time. As it evolved, it encouraged Americans to take an active role in a consumer society. With the introduction of advertising agencies, businesses were able to develop more creative and effective advertisements.

How did mass production affect advertising?

Early Advertising Trends Advertisements remained fairly consistent during the early and mid-19th century. Newspapers were commonly used for advertising. Typical newspaper ads were no wider than a single column, and illustrations and special typefaces were generally not used. Magazine advertisers usually reserved the back pages for their ads. Rural America, where the majority of the U.S. population lived until 1920, was also affected by advertising. Sears, Roebuck and Company and Montgomery Ward mail-order catalogs offered rural Americans everything from buttons to kits containing designs and materials for building homes.

Mass Production In the latter half of the 19th century, at the end of the Industrial Revolution, advertisements changed dramatically. New mass production techniques in the 1880s used assembly lines to create standardized products in large quantities. Manufacturers began developing brand names to help consumers clearly identify their products. Mass production industries sought new ways to persuade consumers to purchase branded goods. National advertising of branded goods emerged in response to the dynamic changes in the business environment. Large department stores that cropped up in growing cities in the late 19th and early 20th centuries joined manufacturers to advertise branded goods. Wanamaker's, Marshall Field's, and Macy's implemented new advertising approaches. Advertisements during this period were bolder, more colorful, and more dramatic in an attempt to compete for consumers' attention. The increase in mass-mailed magazines and the growth of radio broadcasting and motion pictures provided new advertising media outlets to reach consumers. Total advertising dollars in the United States grew from about $200 million in 1880 to nearly $3 billion in 1920.

Although mass production increased the availability of products, many consumers were unable to afford them. Consequently, companies began extending credit to their customers. The increased availability of consumer credit during the prosperous 1920s resulted in greater consumer demand for automobiles, appliances, radios, and leisure activities.

Changes in the Advertising Industry Advertising agencies were founded in the late 19th century and became a key component in the advertising process. They grew out of the need to sell branded products that were being mass produced. Advertising helped consumers identify the differences between the branded products. President Calvin Coolidge emphasized the importance of advertising in a 1926 speech by stating, "Advertising ministers to the spiritual side of trade. It is a great power that has been entrusted to your keeping which charges you with the high responsibility of inspiring and ennobling the commercial world."

In later years, advertising agencies that were first used only to sell advertising space in local newspapers and a limited number of magazines were now being called upon to design copy and artwork for advertisements. Society's attitudes toward the advertising industry have fluctuated. Depending on the era, the advertising profession has been characterized by glamour, greed, deception, and creativity. Workers in the evolving advertising industry sought public approval and legitimacy that separated them from the early miracle medicine peddlers.

////// **CHECKPOINT** ◣◥◣◥

What is a consumer society and how does it affect advertising?

Inventions Impacting Advertising

Advertising innovators are constantly searching for new ways to communicate their message to customers. Several inventions over the years have made advertising more effective. Four inventions that have influenced advertising include the printing press, radio, television, and the Internet.

Printing Press

The invention of the printing press made information of all kinds available to the general population. Printing could spread information quickly and provided a platform for advertising. The printing press was used to produce posters and handouts containing information about goods and services for sale during the 16th century. The first newspaper advertisement in the American colonies appeared in the 18th century when a person owning property in New York advertised it in the *Boston News-Letter*. Ben Franklin began placing advertisements in the *Pennsylvania Gazette* in 1729, and the first magazine advertisements for the colonies appeared in Franklin's *General Magazine* in 1742. As the number of publications grew, advertising agencies were born to create selling material for the publications.

Radio

Advertising could be heard for the first time through the use of radio in the 1920s. The first commercial was broadcast in 1922. Radio programming included soap operas, music, and serial adventures that often were sponsored by advertisers. Radio stations and radio advertising grew in the 1930s and 1940s. Radios appeared in virtually every home in America, and the sales of products advertised on the air exploded. Advertisers wrote memorable jingles, an art form that still plays an important role in today's radio advertising. Many radio personalities became well-known for their voices and were sought after to deliver advertisements. Paul Harvey, a pioneer in radio advertising, launched *Paul Harvey News and Comment* in 1951. At one time, his radio show had an audience of 24 million listeners a week, airing on 1,600 radio stations. Harvey refined the art of the radio commercial. Sponsors loved the most listened-to voice in the history of radio. Radio advertising lost some of its appeal when television came onto the scene, but it is still a popular advertising medium today.

Television and Cable Television

The invention of television in the 1920s changed everything. Television became a mass advertising medium in the 1950s when the prices of television sets became more affordable. Print and radio took a back seat to television because, for the first time, commercials were broadcast with sight, sound, and motion. Television had a remarkable impact on the advertising industry and the way products were sold. Advertising agencies were challenged to produce mini movies in units of 30 and 60 seconds. They had to learn how to effectively segment the audience and deliver the appropriate commercial message for the intended audience.

Cable television, developed in the 1970s, was the next great innovation to impact the advertising industry. It offered more channels with specific program offerings. Advertisers could now narrow the demographics of their intended audiences. Before the advent of cable television,

How did the invention of cable television influence advertising?

the networks attempted to reach targeted audiences by airing at different times throughout the broadcast period. For example, to reach women consumers, advertisers would broadcast commercials during the daily soap operas. They would air commercials during the evening news to reach an older audience. Cable television broadcast new channels like MTV that catered to a younger audience and ESPN for (typically) male sports fans. The Food Network catered to people who loved cooking. These new cable television channels enabled advertisers to reach out to target audiences who had specific interests. Cable networks have expanded advertising options but have decreased advertising revenue for the original TV networks.

Television and cable television were also the perfect platforms for infomercials. An **infomercial** is a lengthy paid advertisement that showcases the benefits of a product. Infomercials can range from 5 to 30 minutes, or longer, and often include a product demonstration highlighting the product's features and benefits, testimonials from satisfied customers, and before/after photos for beauty and fitness products. While some products can be successfully pitched to the public using 30-second commercials during primetime programming, other products and services may require a little more explanation or promotion in order to appeal to a selected audience. Instead of producing a standard print ad or 30-second television spot, some companies use the infomercial format. The infomercial includes a call-to-action, which encourages the consumer to place an order.

Internet

In the 1990s, a Web revolution in advertising began. Internet advertising is now a $42 billion industry that has overtaken the conventional methods of advertising. Chat rooms, blogs, e-mails, pop-up advertisements, instant messaging, and web page notices are just a few of the ways advertisers can let people who are surfing the Web know about products and services. Social networking sites, such as Facebook and Myspace, are becoming more popular advertising venues.

© Netfalls/Shutterstock.com

Why was it important for advertisers to embrace the Web revolution?

Advertisements placed on popular search engines allow products and services to be widely promoted. Consumers can use the Internet to access information about a product or service that they want to purchase. Some websites contain product links to web pages where customers can make a purchase. The Internet also allows customers to compare various brands of products and services, sometimes on a single website, such as the Epinions website.

Online advertising has presented a challenge to advertisers. They had to determine the most effective way to deliver their messages on the Web. Online advertising has become more sophisticated over the years, moving from simple, pop-up ads to elaborate Web videos. Because the Internet provides wide exposure for products and services, advertisers will continue to develop innovative online advertising strategies.

///// CHECKPOINT \\\\\

How has the Internet changed advertising?

1.1 Assessment

THINK ABOUT IT

1. What forms of advertising were used by the earliest civilizations?
2. What inventions had the greatest impact on advertising?
3. How is Ben Franklin associated with advertising?

MAKE ACADEMIC CONNECTIONS

4. **SOCIAL STUDIES** Visit the headquarters of your local newspaper (or visit its website) to learn when the newspaper was established and to locate advertisements that were placed in the early editions of the newspaper. Compare those advertisements with the current advertisements in the newspaper and explain how advertising has changed.

5. **RESEARCH** Visit three websites that advertise products and services. Describe each of the websites and rank them for user friendliness and effectiveness. Explain how each website could improve its advertisements.

6. **COMMUNICATION** Watch an infomercial on a television or cable television network. Prepare a report describing the infomercial, including how much time was allotted for the infomercial, what product or service was being promoted, how the product was demonstrated, whether any testimonials were used, and how the call-to-action was handled. Then rate the effectiveness of the infomercial.

Teamwork

Working in a team, design a timeline for the history of advertising. Include pictures of major inventions and people who had an influence on advertising over the years. Be sure to include captions for the images.

Influences on Advertising

Goals

- Describe environmental influences on advertising.
- Describe social and political influences on advertising.
- Describe consumer influences on advertising.

Terms

- green marketing, p. 11
- industry trade groups, p. 15
- consumer, p. 16

Capturing Political Votes in the Digital Age

Political candidates must keep up with the latest technology if they expect to win elections. Facebook, Twitter, and other forms of social media have become very important for successful political campaigns. Candidates can send information in a matter of seconds to millions of prospective voters. Social media can also present challenges that politicians must overcome. One bad political performance or gaff can easily be recorded by the opposition and made available on the Internet in a matter of seconds. Technology provides real-time communication for politicians, but it also can create real-time headaches.

Work as a Team Research the technology being used by current politicians to stay in touch with their constituents. Visit political websites and discuss the positive and negative information you found about prominent national politicians.

FOCUS ON ADVERTISING

© Yuri Arcurs/Shutterstock.com

Environmental Influences

In recent years, protecting the environment has become a top priority for many Americans. Because of increased environmental awareness, businesses are taking notice and making changes to their products and services to help protect the environment. Advertisements are used as public relations tools to present businesses as good stewards of the environment. Protecting the environment from harmful pollutants, conserving nonrenewable resources like coal and oil, disposing of waste responsibly, selling environmentally friendly products, and using environmentally safe and sustainable energy sources to meet business needs are advertising themes that emphasize businesses' responsibility in conserving the environment. The use of advertising to support and improve the environment is known as **green marketing**.

Why is there a green marketing movement in today's businesses?

Because of the growing movement toward environmentally friendly products and processes, businesses that use green marketing have an advantage when introducing their product or service in the marketplace. Advertising can be used to educate consumers on how products or services benefit the earth or conserve resources. Automobile manufacturers are emphasizing electric automobiles and vehicles that are more fuel-efficient. Manufacturers of some household cleaning products advertise that their products are not harmful to the environment.

In addition to offering green products, businesses that use green business practices are often favored by customers. The natural environment influences business in many different ways. The power of the sun and wind to create and conserve energy has created an entirely new industry. Businesses that advertise their use of alternative energy resources are demonstrating their commitment to the environment. Businesses that ignore or underestimate environmental influences will eventually lose market share. When businesses recognize the impact environmental practices have on their business operations and marketing strategies, they are more likely to prosper.

The Environmental Impact of Print Advertising

Print advertising affects the environment through the carbon dioxide emitted into the atmosphere as a result of the production and distribution of print media. On average, over 7 billion metric tons of carbon dioxide greenhouse gases associated with print advertising are emitted into the atmosphere annually by the United States. U.S. advertisers spent over $65 billion dollars on print advertising and created over 250,000 ad pages in a recent year. A single advertising page for a popular consumer magazine can equal as much as seven tons of carbon dioxide emissions created from production, printing, logistics, and landfill disposal or incineration of post-consumer and unsold media.

Victoria's Secret has recently agreed to reduce the environmental impact of its catalogs by using recycled paper and not using paper from endangered forests. John Hardy, a manufacturer of jewelry and accessories, began the Sustainable Advertising program in 2006. The pilot program was a bamboo reforestation project on Nusa Penida, an island southeast of Indonesia where the company's workshops are located. The objective of the project was to sequester the carbon dioxide associated with the company's print advertising by planting bamboo, a long-lasting woody perennial grass. The program continues today.

Advertising When Environmental Disaster Strikes

Companies associated with environmental disasters are faced with major public relations nightmares. The British Petroleum Deepwater Horizon explosion on April 20, 2010, killed 11 people and was declared to be one of the worst oil spills in the world. The three-month oil spill caused major damage to wildlife and Gulf Coast industries. BP's reputation and stock prices took a major hit due to the environmental disaster. Every day that the oil spill continued, BP found a greater need to present itself as a responsible citizen that would resolve the environmental disaster and compensate the thousands of Gulf Coast residents whose businesses were shut down by the oil spill.

BP's advertisements before the Gulf Coast oil spill focused attention on the company's commitment to the environment. The advertisements highlighted new inventions used by BP to conserve energy and the environment. Frequently the BP commercials highlighted the company's commitment to communities and individuals. In the months following the Gulf of Mexico oil spill, BP tripled its advertising budget. The company also increased the number of markets where it purchased newspaper advertising from just 2 states in 2009 to 17 states in 2010. According to the House Energy Committee, BP spent $93.4 million—about $5 million per week—on newspaper advertisements and TV spots between April and the end of July in 2010. A U.S. Congressional investigation forced BP to defend its increased spending for advertising when the businesses of so many Gulf Coast citizens were shut down during the oil spill clean-up. BP claimed that the advertising campaign was needed to inform

How is advertising used when environmental disasters occur?

the public about clean-up efforts and the compensation claims process. Advertising plays an important role when environmental disaster strikes. Businesses must carefully develop advertising strategies that promote a sense of responsibility.

▰▰▰▰▰ **CHECKPOINT** ◤◤◤◤◤◤

How can companies use advertising as a public relations tool?

- -

Social and Political Influences

Advertising is highly influenced by social and political issues. Because advertising related to these issues can have both positive and negative results, advertisers must carefully plan their strategies.

Social and Ethical Responsibility

Two goals of advertising include selling a product and maintaining a high public perception of the company or product. Most companies or industries want to relay an image of being committed to the well-being of the community. Their advertisements frequently focus on the company's or industry's contributions to the community or society.

Social responsibility is the principle that businesses should contribute to the welfare of society. Many businesses now view social responsibility as an opportunity for growth. In a recent survey, 55 percent of consumers indicated they are more likely to choose a product that supports a certain cause when choosing between similar products. By advertising its social responsibility efforts, a business can increase profits. Oftentimes a business will advertise that a portion of its profits will be donated to a charitable cause. Consumers who support this cause may be more likely to support the business. For example, in recent years, L.L.Bean has contributed over $6 million to national conservation organizations, such as the National Park Foundation. For those consumers who value conservation and outdoor recreation activities, shopping at L.L.Bean may be a way to contribute to these efforts.

Today, doing "what is politically correct," or ethical, has become the theme for many advertisements. When Toyota faced massive recalls of its vehicles because of a manufacturing defect, it acted ethically by releasing advertisements that communicated its commitment to fixing the problem and restoring consumers' faith in the safety and quality of its vehicles.

Political Advertising

While advertising is important for political campaigns, there is no clear agreement on the effects of political advertising on electoral outcomes. During an election year, unregulated political advertisements on television and radio are predominant in the United States. Great Britain prohibits the purchase of broadcast advertising by political candidates and regulates their television advertisements. The number of negative advertisements in U.S. election campaigns has increased over the years. Negative campaign advertisements involve criticism of a candidate, a policy position, or past performance. Some of the advertisements question the character of political candidates. Exposure to advertisements does influence public perceptions of the candidates. The debate continues over the effectiveness of negative political advertising. Some individuals believe that "going negative" actually discourages people from going to the polls to vote and diminishes confidence in the political system. Most consumers are relieved when the elections are over and the political commercials are no longer airing day and night.

What role does advertising play in political campaigns?

Influence of Industry Trade Groups

Industry trade groups, referred to as *trade associations*, are founded and funded by businesses operating in a specific industry and are responsible for public relations activities such as advertising, education, political donations, lobbying, and publishing. The main focus of trade associations is collaboration between companies to develop industry standards. One of the primary purposes of trade groups in the United States is to influence public policy in a direction favorable to the group's members. Trade groups exert their influence by contributing to the campaigns of political candidates and parties through Political Action Committees (PACs), producing advertising to influence public sentiment, and lobbying legislators to support or oppose particular legislation. Trade groups also attempt to influence the activities of governmental regulatory agencies.

Industry trade groups produce advertisements to promote the views of an entire industry. Advertisements also are used to improve the industry's image. The advertisements mention the industry's products as a whole, painting the industry in a positive light to gain approval from the public and to form positive associations with the industry and its products. The USA advertising campaign "Beef, it's what's for dinner" is used by the National Cattlemen's Beef Association to promote a positive image of beef to consumers.

Some advertisements are developed to shape opinion on a specific issue. Ads against domestic violence, smoking, and drinking and driving use dramatic scenes to make a point. Some industries that manufacture controversial products, such as alcoholic beverages, produce ads to promote responsible use of the products.

CHECKPOINT

How do industry trade groups influence advertising?

Consumer Influences

The **consumer** is the end user of a product or service. The overall consumer market consists of all buyers of goods and services for personal or family use. More than 310 million people spend trillions of dollars annually for goods and services in the United States. *Consumer behavior* describes how and why people make purchase decisions. Advertising is highly influenced by consumer needs and purchase patterns.

Analyzing Consumer Motivation

To effectively sell a product or service, marketers need to determine the major needs being satisfied by a good or service purchased by consumers. Two principal ways to evaluate the motivation behind consumer purchases are by *direction* (what they want) and *intensity* (how much they want it). Direction refers to what the customer wants from a product. For example, although a customer who is selecting a pain reliever may like the idea that one pain reliever is priced lower than another similar alternative, what the customer really wants is fast pain relief. The consumer will probably pay more if he or she thinks the more expensive brand can relieve pain more effectively. Marketers need to understand the principal motivation behind the purchase of a product to develop advertisements that correctly target potential customers.

Intensity is used to determine whether a customer's interest in a product is compelling enough to motivate them to make the purchase. Burger King's "Aren't You Hungry for Burger King Now?" campaign that aired on late-night television was compelling enough for people to leave their homes late at night to buy hamburgers, leading to increased sales. Understanding consumer motivation is the best way to learn how to increase buyer incentive through effective advertising.

Why is it important for advertisers to study consumer behavior?

Getting the Message to Consumers

Historically, advertisers used mass media—television, radio, magazines, and newspapers—as a one-way channel of communication to consumers. The latest technology has given consumers greater control over how they get information about products and product brands. Rather than relying on advertisements, consumers can visit websites to view product information or make purchases. Consumers are in control of the disbursement of product information when they use *blogs*, which are websites frequented by individuals with common interests. The facts, opinions, and personal experiences posted by individuals on blogs are emerging as new, sophisticated sources of product and brand information. Many consumers choose to receive targeted advertisements through text messaging.

Consumers also exert control over the messages they receive by using digital video recorders (DVRs) and controllers that have ad-skipping capabilities. Because consumers now can easily ignore advertisements, advertisers must adapt to consumer control by using more entertaining and informative advertising. To counter the effects of DVRs, advertisers are now running advertising messages along the bottom of the screen during television programs. As new technology emerges, advertisers will need to continue to find new ways to get their messages to consumers.

Why do today's consumers have more power over advertising?

1.2 Assessment

THINK ABOUT IT

1. Describe a recent advertisement that had an environmental message. How did the advertiser benefit from this advertisement?

2. What does it mean for an advertisement to be "politically correct"? Describe an advertisement you've seen or heard that is politically correct.

3. Why must advertisers pay attention to the latest technology being used by consumers?

4. What is the purpose of an industry trade group? Give an example of an industry trade group and the advertisement campaign used by it.

MAKE ACADEMIC CONNECTIONS

5. **MATH** A company that suffered an image problem due to a defective product spent $6.5 million each week for television and magazine advertising during the first six months of the year in an attempt to sway public opinion about the company. What is the total amount that the company spent on the public relations campaign?

6. **ECONOMICS** Sales of products and services are directly affected by the economy. Conduct research to determine how fast food restaurants have used advertising to maintain sales during tough economic conditions. Report your findings in a PowerPoint presentation.

7. **MARKETING** You work for the advertising agency for an automobile manufacturer that has had the top sales of all auto manufacturers for the last eight years. The manufacturer's automobiles have experienced major mechanical defects, forcing the recall of millions of vehicles. Some of the defects have resulted in tragic accidents. What advertising strategy would you use to regain a favorable image for the company and to regain lost market share?

8. **RESEARCH** Your school wants to start a recycling awareness program to encourage students to increase their recycling efforts. Conduct research to learn more about the recycling options available in your community and school. Then create a print ad that raises awareness and encourages students to recycle. Assume the print ad will be posted on bulletin boards around the school.

 Teamwork

The U.S. government has become increasingly concerned about the obesity problem. Companies that produce sodas have taken a direct hit as one of the causes for obesity. Your team has been hired by a major soda manufacturer to develop an advertising campaign that emphasizes the company's commitment to the health of consumers. Prepare a PowerPoint presentation to describe your advertising campaign for the soda manufacturer.

The Advertising Industry and Careers

Goals
- Explain how the advertising industry works.
- Describe the participants (careers) in the advertising industry.

Terms
- product advertising, p. 20
- brand, p. 20
- brand advertising, p. 20
- corporate advertising, p. 20
- advertising agency, p. 21
- advertiser, p. 21
- boutique advertising agency, p. 23

FOCUS ON ADVERTISING

Using Creativity to Get the Job

Applying for a job usually involves sending a cover letter and resume by mail or e-mail or posting them on career websites. The job recruiter will probably receive hundreds of e-mails or online submissions for the advertised job. This means that job seekers may need to think outside the box when trying to get hired. Because advertising is a creative field, creative tactics may be what it takes to stand out from the crowd. For example, some job seekers have rented billboards to launch their own public relations campaign. Others have created websites to market their skills and work experience. Some have produced a video version of their resumes and mailed it on a CD or DVD to prospective employers. Not all companies appreciate such gimmicks and may consider them unprofessional. So job seekers should learn as much as possible about the company to gain a sense of how much it values originality.

JOB OPENING AHEAD

© Gary Paul Lewis/Shutterstock.com

Work as a Team What are some unique ways to get an interview with a company in the creative industry?

How the Advertising Industry Works

Advertising is the most effective way to reach consumers and create product/service awareness. Advertising has become increasingly important as more and more companies compete for consumer dollars. Companies rely on advertising to drive demand for their products and services. Developing the most effective advertisements is a time-consuming, expensive process. Successful advertising requires more than a strong understanding of the product or service being promoted.

How does this advertisement represent product and brand advertising?

It also requires knowledge about psychology, consumer behavior, cultural trends, technology, the competition, and many more marketing elements.

Types of Advertising

Advertisers include large for-profit corporations that sell products or services, nonprofit groups, politicians, and other types of organizations. Among these various types of advertisers, there are three common types of advertising.

Product Advertising
Most companies use some form of product advertising. **Product advertising** uses rational arguments to communicate why consumers need a specific product by highlighting the benefits associated with the use of that product. Product advertising presents at least one product characteristic as a reason for purchasing a product. For example, Hyundai advertisements may emphasize the 100,000-mile warranty for its automobiles.

Brand Advertising
A brand is an important component in many advertisements. A **brand** is the combination of unique qualities of a company, product, or product line. The name, logo, slogan, and design are important elements of the brand. McDonald's is a well-known brand throughout the world. The McDonald's brand may be described by popular menu items, price, or the golden arches. A less tangible attribute of the McDonald's brand could be the emotional connection it creates with consumers, such as through its "I'm lovin' it" advertisements.

Brand advertising is used to build an image based on the set of values held by the company. Nike is known for its competitive edge and can-do attitude, which has been communicated through its "Just Do It" slogan. Through brand advertising, Nike has created a personality in the minds of consumers. Individuals look for brands that match their personalities.

Brand advertising and product advertising sometimes overlap. For example, Slim-Fast uses product advertising to promote its delicious chocolate shakes that can help people lose weight. But the name itself, Slim-Fast, helps promote the brand. As the name implies, the company's mission is to supply diet supplements to help people lose weight quickly.

Corporate Advertising
Some companies use **corporate advertising,** which is intended to enhance a company's reputation or build goodwill. It is also known as *institutional advertising.* Corporate advertising does not ask consumers to take a specific action, such as to buy a product. Instead, it promotes a positive attitude toward the company.

When GE ran an advertisement about capturing and using wind energy through the use of windmills, it was not promoting a product. Instead, it was attempting to associate its name with energy conservation. Corporate advertising can also be used by companies to take a stand on important social issues.

The Advertising Agency

Many companies obtain the outside services of an advertising agency to develop advertising strategies. The **advertising agency** is a marketing business that plans, creates, and manages the advertising for other businesses (clients). The primary role of the advertising agency is to analyze a company's goals and help it achieve those goals through well-planned, result-oriented advertising strategies. Advertising agencies are also assigned with the tasks of building campaigns to increase sales of the company's products, to reaffirm the brand image, to attract new customers, and to retain current customers. They are challenged to find ways to present a business's product and service offerings in a positive light.

Many companies decide to work with advertising agencies because of the knowledge, expertise, and talent they can provide. Representatives of the advertising agency create, strategize, and plan advertising messages to reach targeted audiences. The first task of the advertising agency is to develop a thorough understanding of the product to be advertised and the target audience for the product so that an overall advertising strategy can be developed. Then an advertising campaign is created, and the advertising agency searches for the most effective types of media to use to promote the product. The agencies must do all of this while staying within their client's budget.

///////// CHECKPOINT \\\\\\\\\

Why would a company decide to hire an advertising agency instead of creating its own advertisements?

Participants in the Advertising Industry

The **advertiser** is the client (persons, organizations, companies, and manufacturers of products and services) that needs creative messages (advertisements) and advertising campaigns to reach target markets. Advertisers hire advertising agencies to create the most effective advertisements for target markets. Advertising agencies handle a broad range of marketing tasks, requiring people with experience and specialized skills. They offer creative services, media services, marketing research services, account management services, and production services. Various careers can be found within each of these service categories.

Advertising Agency Services and Careers

Account management in the advertising agency begins with the *account executive* who serves as the main link between the client and the advertising agency. Account executives communicate the client's objectives to the other team members and ensure that strategies are carried out on schedule and within budget.

An *account planner* directs the marketing research efforts involved in an advertising campaign. The account planner helps the creative team understand what "turns the consumer on." Research may be conducted in various ways. In *focus groups*, a moderator leads a discussion about an advertising campaign with a small group of people. Surveys and telephone calls are also used to gather important information from the target market. The feedback collected is used to develop or improve the advertising campaign.

Many advertising agencies employ *media planners* who explore media options to determine the most effective way to deliver the client's message at the lowest cost. Media planners create a *media plan* that outlines when and where advertisements will run and how often.

An advertising agency has many employees who provide creative services. The artistic look of the advertisement is the responsibility of the *art director*, while the words used in the advertisement are the responsibility of the *copywriter*. The art director and copywriter work as a creative team to produce attractive advertising with captive wording. A *creative director* oversees and helps guide the creative process to ensure that team members deliver an advertisement that conveys the client's message.

The production department for an advertising agency is led by a *producer* who manages everything that happens after an advertisement is developed. The producer ensures that the TV ad, print ad, or radio ad gets produced. Producers coordinate the efforts of editors, directors, photographers, and others needed in the production of the finished advertisement.

Media Services and Careers

Although the larger advertising agencies have their own media departments, many of the smaller agencies outsource this task. *Outsourcing* occurs when individual tasks are assigned to companies that specialize in planning, designing, and creating advertisements.

Because communication and media options are constantly changing and becoming more complex, advertising agencies may choose to work with a company that specializes in media services. A media planning and buying company has the expertise of placing advertising where it will reach the right people at the right time in the right place in a cost-effective way.

There are many more positions within a media company than just the media planner. *Executive media directors* oversee management of media planning, including budgets, costs, resource allocation, and strategic leadership.

NETBookmark

Do you think you have what it takes to work in advertising? Though there are many different career paths in advertising, there are several key skills and talents required by anyone who hopes to succeed in the field. Access www.cengage.com/school/advertising and click on the link for Chapter 1. Based on the article, which skill is the most important for someone working in advertising? What three adjectives do you think best characterize a successful advertising professional?

www.cengage.com/school/advertising

What kind of media services are provided in the advertising industry?

They play a lead role in acquiring new business and act as a consultant to top corporate officers. *Group media directors* lead overall management of one large client and/or multiple clients. They provide strategic direction and drive long-term business. *Associate media directors* are responsible for the overall service of assigned accounts and media teams. They approve the development and execution of media strategies for advertising plans while maintaining cost controls.

Executive media buying directors are responsible for management of the media buying and operations. They handle sensitive company/agency negotiations with suppliers and are involved in policy-making decisions. *Media buying directors* represent agency's senior management on a day-to-day basis and are involved with negotiations.

Support Organizations and Careers

Just as many advertising agencies outsource their media services, they may also rely on support organizations for other services, such as defining the brand for products and services, performing market research, and planning social media strategies. A **boutique advertising agency**, also referred to as a *virtual ad agency*, is a small, specialized advertising company that outsources many of its services. The primary objective of a boutique advertising agency is to create brand identification for a product or service through the use of nontraditional creativity. Boutique advertising agencies typically serve one particular market exclusively. They focus on what they are good at—the creative aspect of advertising—and then outsource the other work, such as media planning and buying, to those with more expertise. By doing so, they are able to produce the best product at the most reasonable price.

Brand specialists may act as consultants to advertising agencies. They are called upon to identify what makes a company unique in a market flooded with consumer choices. The brand specialist creates an identity for a product that is to be used throughout the advertising campaign. The brand specialist might be a leader in the industry, a high performer, or a trendsetter.

Because marketing research plays such an important role in creating an effective advertising strategy, advertising agencies often outsource this function to companies that have proven strategies for collecting data. This saves the advertising agency valuable time and money. Marketing research companies can supply data about target markets and product trends.

Social media has provided new opportunities for communicating advertising messages. Advertising agencies that want to incorporate this new technology trend into their advertising strategies may outsource projects to social media marketers who have expertise with Facebook, Twitter, and YouTube. Marketers in this field look for ways to use social media to create buzz about a product. They also help clients track the effectiveness of their social media efforts.

///// CHECKPOINT \\\\\

Why might an advertising agency outsource certain tasks?

1.3 Assessment

THINK ABOUT IT

1. How do product advertising, brand advertising, and corporate advertising differ?
2. What role does the advertising agency play in the advertising industry?
3. Name and describe three types of positions typically found in an advertising agency.
4. Why might a business prefer to work with a boutique advertising agency instead of a larger, more traditional advertising agency?

MAKE ACADEMIC CONNECTIONS

5. **MARKETING** Choose one of your favorite products and describe how you would use product advertising and brand advertising to promote it. Create a collage using pictures, words, colors, symbols, or other elements that you associate with the product and brand you selected.

6. **TECHNOLOGY** Explain why social media is playing a bigger role in advertising today. Using the product you selected above, describe how you could use social media as part of the advertising strategy.

Teamwork

Not all advertising involves the promotion of products and services. Some corporations use advertising to enhance their image, promote a philosophy, or support a cause. Select a high-profile corporation that you think could benefit from corporate advertising. Develop an ad and present it to the class, using visual aids.

Sharpen Your
21st CENTURY SKILLS

PARTNERSHIP FOR
21ST CENTURY SKILLS

Creating an Effective Resume

Your resume has to be your best sales pitch when you are searching for a job. The resume should sufficiently highlight your achievements, carefully cover your job experience and skills, and provide a clear picture of who you are and how you can enhance the company. Most employers are willing to look at a resume for only 60 seconds or less, which means every bold heading and bulleted word counts.

Job seekers must know how to create the perfect resume. Employers want to see how you can summarize information. Before you prepare the resume, it is important to take notes about the job for which you're applying and consider how your skills, past work experience, and education fit the job description.

The *header* on your resume should begin with your name centered at the top of the page followed by your contact information. Include all ways of getting in touch with you, such as telephone numbers and e-mail addresses. Do not include websites unless they are necessary for the job. Effective resumes are one page in length and should not be more than two pages.

The *career objective* is a sentence of 10–20 words that shares your ambitions and career goals. Many recruiters have no desire to read your aspirations and only want to know how you can help them. Thus, a *positioning statement*, which is a sentence that offers a clear summation of your skills and what you have to offer, is often preferred.

The *qualifications* and *career highlights* sections of your resume should list skills and achievements in three to five bulleted action phrases. An example of a good bulleted item would be "Acted as president of the Math Club." When you describe work experience, it is important to use action verbs and buzz words. You should highlight accomplishments instead of responsibilities.

Most potential employers are more concerned with your professional experience than your education. You should keep the *education* section of the resume simple, unless you are low on work experience.

A *professional development* section can also be included. It should list all of your professional organization memberships and volunteer experiences. Volunteer work speaks volumes about your character.

Do not include hobbies or references at the end of your resume. Bring a printed list of your references with you to the interview in case the interviewer requests them.

Try It Out
Search for various resume styles online. Select one that will showcase your qualifications, work experience, and education in the best manner and prepare your own resume.

SUMMARY

1.1 History of Advertising

- Advertising is a paid form of communication intended to inform, persuade, and remind an audience to take some kind of action.
- Advertising has been around for many centuries. It has changed to reflect the times. It has gone from message boards in town squares in colonial times, to ads in newspapers and magazines in the 18th and 19th centuries, with radio and TV ads making an appearance in the 20th century. The Internet is playing a big role in advertising in the 21st century.
- Trends that had a big impact on advertising included the introduction of mass production to produce mass quantities of branded products. Advertising agencies grew out of the need to sell the mass-produced products.
- Four inventions that have influenced advertising include the printing press, radio, television/cable television, and the Internet.

1.2 Influences on Advertising

- Because of increased efforts to protect the environment, advertisements attempt to present businesses as good stewards of the environment.
- Advertising is greatly influenced by social and political issues. Advertisements can be used to promote a charitable cause and "politically-correct" views. Advertising is a major component of political candidates' campaigns.
- Consumer behavior refers to how and why people make purchase decisions. Marketers need to examine consumer motivation and choose the best media to deliver the message.

1.3 The Advertising Industry and Careers

- There are three common types of advertising—product, brand, and corporate advertising.
  - Advertisers are clients that need creative messages (advertisements) and advertising campaigns to reach target markets.
  - The advertising agency is a marketing business that plans, creates, and manages the advertising for other businesses (clients).
- Workers in an advertising agency provide many services, including creative, media, marketing research, account management, and production services.
- Advertising agencies often outsource tasks to media companies and other support organizations, such as brand specialists, market researchers, and social media marketers.

WHAT DO YOU KNOW?

Read *Impact Advertising* on page 3 again to review the historic advertisements discussed. Use the Internet to conduct research about the latest advertising campaigns used by DeBeers and Volkswagen. Have their advertising messages or target audiences changed? Explain how.

Vocabulary Builder

Match each statement with the term that best defines it. Some terms may not be used.

1. A lengthy paid advertisement that showcases the benefits of a product
2. The use of advertising to support and improve the environment
3. A client that needs creative messages and advertising campaigns to reach target markets
4. Advertising that uses rational arguments to communicate why consumers need a specific product
5. Advertising used to build an image based on the set of values held by the company
6. Associations that are founded and funded by businesses operating in a specific industry to handle public relations activities
7. A paid form of communication intended to inform, persuade, and remind an audience to take some kind of action
8. The end user of a product or service
9. Advertising intended to enhance a company's reputation
10. The combination of unique qualities of a company, product, or product line

a. advertiser
b. advertising
c. advertising agency
d. boutique advertising agency
e. brand
f. brand advertising
g. consumer
h. corporate advertising
i. green marketing
j. industry trade groups
k. infomercial
l. product advertising

Test Your Knowledge

11. A(n) _____ is a paid-for advertisement ranging from 5 to 30 minutes that includes a product demonstration and customer testimonials.
    a. infomercial
    b. commercial
    c. blog
    d. brand
12. _____ measures how much a consumer wants a product.
    a. Direction
    b. Motivation
    c. Inspiration
    d. Intensity
13. The invention of the _____ has greatly influenced advertising.
    a. radio
    b. Internet
    c. printing press
    d. all of the above
14. Boutique advertising agencies
    a. are large advertising agencies
    b. complete all tasks for the advertising campaign
    c. are small, specialized companies
    d. have many specialized departments

15. The _____ directs the marketing research efforts involved in an advertising campaign.
    a. account executive   c. account planner
    b. media planner   d. copywriter
16. The _____ manages everything that happens after an advertisement is developed.
    a. copywriter   c. account planner
    b. producer   d. brand specialist
17. The _____ is called upon to identify what makes a company unique in a market flooded with consumer choices.
    a. art director   c. account planner
    b. brand specialist   d. copywriter
18. One of the biggest impacts on advertising agencies was the introduction of
    a. radio   c. mail-order catalogs
    b. the Internet   d. mass production
19. The Internet has presented challenges to advertisers because
    a. there have been compatibility issues among different operating systems
    b. large file sizes created bandwidth problems
    c. it is difficult to measure ad effectiveness
    d. all of the above
20. Who was responsible for spurring the growth of outdoor advertising?
    a. Ben Franklin   c. P. T. Barnum
    b. Paul Harvey   d. John Hardy

Apply What You Learned

21. Search online for information about a product that you would be interested in purchasing. Browse the Internet for 15 minutes and keep track of the number of advertisements you see, product-related or otherwise. What can you conclude about the importance of using the Internet for advertising? Did some ads catch your attention more than others did? Explain why.
22. You are working closely with a local professional baseball team to organize a career day/baseball game for high school students in a city that has a population of 4 million people. What is the best strategy for getting the message out to all prospective students in the surrounding area? Explain your answer.

Make Academic Connections

23. **RESEARCH** Choose a popular business that has had success with its advertising campaign. Prepare a one-page report describing the advertising campaign. Explain why you think the advertising campaign has been so successful.
24. **HISTORY** Select an era in time (such as the early 1920s, 1950s or 1960s) and conduct research to learn more about important events and social perceptions that helped shape that era. Then

prepare a two-page report describing how these events and perceptions influenced advertising during that time.

25. **MATH** Companies want to make the most effective use of their advertising dollars. A recent survey of 250 successful companies polled them about the methods they use to measure the effectiveness of their promotions. The responses are summarized in the following table. (Respondents could select more than one evaluation method.) What is the percentage of each of the response types? Create a bar graph to illustrate the results. Use spreadsheet software if available.

Evaluation Method	Number of Respondents
Coupon redemption	180
Toll-free customer line	115
Focus groups	120
Customer survey	40
Rebate redemption	50
Recognition tests	30

26. **COMMUNICATION** Advertising agencies are often the driving force behind a successful advertising campaign. Search for a successful advertising agency online and browse its website. Prepare a flyer that could be used to attract clients to the agency. Describe the agency's mission, explain how it is structured, and list some of its top clients and advertising campaigns. Include anything else that you think would help "sell" the agency to potential clients.

27. **HISTORY** Learn more about the early days of advertising. Conduct research about an individual that had an early influence on the advertising industry. Prepare a 5- to 7-minute oral presentation on what you learned. Use visual aids to enhance your presentation.

28. **GOVERNMENT** Political campaigns rely heavily on advertising. Assume you are running for your city council. Outline the issues you want to address while in office. Then develop an advertisement for your campaign. Will you run any negative ads? Why or why not?

You are the owner of a clothing store that is the sponsor of a new television series that has been highly promoted to teenagers. Since 60 percent of your customer base ranges in age from 12 to 24, you recognize the possible impact on sales from your association with a show that is watched by 2 million teenagers. However, the questionable content of the first show of the new television series has raised a lot of concern from parents. Parents and children's advocacy watch groups have expressed deep concerns about the television show that your company is sponsoring.

As a sponsor, do you have any social or ethical responsibilities? If so, what are they? What actions should your business take in this situation?

Reality ✓

Digital Advertising Gets Personal

Digital advertising is providing marketers with the opportunity to break through advertising clutter, deliver more targeted messages, and create engaging experiences through interactive billboards, digital projections, and even 3-D images.

Digital marketing has the ability to create a more personally relevant advertising experience. Marketers in Japan began testing facial recognition technology to enhance the digital billboard in 2010. Using billboards with embedded cameras, the passerby is scanned, his or her gender and age are determined, and then a more relevant advertisement is served. Digital technology now has the ability to make public spaces more personalized. Ad placements are being moved from billboards to entire exteriors of buildings.

Digital advertising can use disruptive engagement by catching audiences off guard with unexpected advertising placement and consumer interaction capabilities. Aquafina recently used digital marketing by installing LCD screen mirrors to fill a public bathroom with branded messaging. When a person was ready to use the mirror, the advertisements were simply moved out of the way. Kraft Foods created an iFood Assistant smartphone application. The user can type in three items, and the app will find a recipe using Kraft brands. This form of marketing gets closer to the customer at the point of purchase.

Digital advertising provides personal experiences for consumers and non-static messages. The latest digital advertising trends provide more personal interaction with a brand and builds brand association.

Think Critically

1. What makes digital advertising unique?
2. Could some aspects of the latest digital advertising be classified as invasion of consumer privacy? Explain your answer.
3. How might digital advertising be more cost-effective for a larger target market?
4. Do you think that all age groups will react favorably to interactive digital advertising?
5. What are the advantages and disadvantages associated with using the latest digital technology for advertising?

The Emerging Business Issues Event provides you with an opportunity to research and present an emerging business issue. The event will be completed by your team, consisting of two or three members.

FBLA provides you with a topic to research. Your team must then present an affirmative or negative argument about the topic, based upon random selection. Facts and working data should be secured from reliable sources. After drawing an affirmative or a negative argument, your team will have five minutes to finalize your preparations. Your presentation must represent only your team's work and will last no longer than five minutes. Following each oral presentation, the judges have three minutes to ask questions.

TOPIC   The use of the Internet, cell phones, and other communication technology devices has increased dramatically in the last ten years. Some business leaders believe that technology has decreased the social and communication skills of employees. Text messages use abbreviations and codes, and tweeting or conversing on the Internet does not require any formal language skills. Be prepared to argue the affirmative, that yes, technology has had a negative impact on social and communication skills; or be prepared to argue the negative, that the use of technology has added a whole new layer of communication and in turn has improved the way individuals interact and connect with others.

Performance Indicators Evaluated

- Understand how a current issue affects business profitability and image.
- Communicate an opinion based upon facts and figures.
- Work as a team to persuade the audience to support a certain viewpoint.
- Manage time effectively to research, outline, and present a viewpoint.
- Demonstrate effective teamwork and align ideas into a persuasive argument.

Go to the FBLA website for more detailed information.

Think Critically

1. Why must business professionals have effective writing, listening, and other communication skills?
2. How has the latest technology impacted the writing and communication skills of individuals?
3. Why is social etiquette important in the business setting?
4. Describe a balanced approach of using communication technology and traditional communication and social skills to improve workplace performance.

www.fbla.org

2

Consumer Behavior

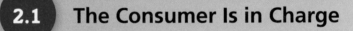

2.1   The Consumer Is in Charge

2.2   Consumer Purchase Classifications

2.3   Influences on Consumer Behavior

Using Emotional Appeals to Reach Customers

Parents fret about their teenager driving the car for the first time alone. Subaru of America taps into this emotional moment in a television commercial called "Baby Driver." The commercial shows a father leaning into the passenger side window to give driving instructions to what appears to be his 6-year-old daughter, who is sitting behind the wheel. After giving his safety talk, the father hands the car keys to his daughter, who now appears to be 16 years old. To add to the realism, Subaru chose a real father and his two daughters as the actors in the commercial. As is the case with many fathers, this one still sees his older daughter as his "little girl." "We knew this day was coming, that's why we bought a Subaru," says the father.

The advertisement highlights two of the top reasons why people buy Subarus—high safety and reliability ratings. Safety is one of Subaru's core brand values, but the company chose not to drill viewers with a list of its top ratings from the National Highway Traffic Safety Administration or the Insurance Institute for Highway Safety. Instead, Subaru created an ad that tugs at the heartstrings of parents. Many parents can identify with this commercial because they someday will be handing over the car keys to their son or daughter for the first time. In the ad, Subaru also emphasizes that many owners pass down their Subarus to their children because they are so highly dependable. The Subaru commercial is based upon the theme that Subaru owners have like-minded "values."

The commercial also addresses teen and distracted driving issues, which are frequent topics in the news. Motor vehicle accidents are the leading cause of death among 15- to 20-year-olds, and 16-year-olds have higher crash rates than drivers of any other age. Parents have a real reason to be concerned. The Subaru advertisement attempts to get parents thinking about the importance of selecting a vehicle that can increase teens' safety while driving.

Subaru's message seems to be working. Its sales increased 30 percent compared to previous years' sales. If an advertiser can appeal to the consumers' emotions, it may make a connection that leads to sales!

WHAT DO YOU KNOW?

1. What core values does Subaru present in the advertisement with the teen driver and her father?

2. Why is this commercial more intriguing than a commercial that cites Subaru's national safety record?

3. Why do you think advertisements that make an emotional connection with consumers are successful?

Goals

- Recognize the importance of understanding the customer's wants and needs.
- Identify the five-step consumer decision-making process.

Terms

- consumer behavior, p. 34
- need, p. 35
- want, p. 35
- routine decision making, p. 37
- limited decision making, p. 37
- extensive decision making, p. 38

Staying Connected with Apps

Technology companies are helping consumers solve everyday problems by creating application software, also known as an app, for use with smartphones. People often go to the mall or a sporting event and then forget where they parked their car when they leave. The Android™ smartphone provides the Carr Matey app that uses GPS tracking software to help locate the car. Many people have problems falling asleep at night. The Android Relax and Sleep app provides over 30 realistic sounds that act as soothing background noise to help lull you to sleep. Available iPhone apps turn the smartphone into a currency converter or a ruler. Although these apps help consumers solve simple life problems, smartphone companies look at them as a way to promote their product and brand. Creating highly useful and engaging apps is one way to keep smartphone users connected to the brand. Smartphone companies can also promote their apps as a way to lure new customers.

© cobalt88/Shutterstock.com

Work as a Team Have you used any smartphone apps? Did they meet a specific need or solve a problem? Do you think apps are a good promotional tool for smartphone companies? Why or why not?

Understanding the Customer

To succeed, a business must understand its customers, but that isn't always easy. The product and service preferences of customers change frequently. Marketers must study consumer behavior. **Consumer behavior** describes how consumers make buying decisions, choose among alternatives, and use products. Studying consumer behavior is an important factor in creating effective advertising. For example, if a company discovers through research that price is the most important factor in a consumer's buying decision for its product, the company's advertisements can promote its "low prices."

Identifying Consumer Needs and Wants

All consumers have needs and wants. A **need** is anything you require for survival. Some needs are basic, while others are higher-level. Abraham Maslow was a psychologist who identified five areas of personal needs, which are referred to as *Maslow's Hierarchy of Needs*. The five levels of needs in the hierarchy include physiological, security, social, esteem, and self-actualization.

Basic physiological needs (food, sleep, water, shelter, air) must be satisfied first before individuals can focus on higher-level needs. Once basic needs are covered, security becomes a high priority for individuals. After people have a sense of physical and economic security, their attention turns to social needs. Friends, love, and a sense of belonging are all part of social needs. Gaining

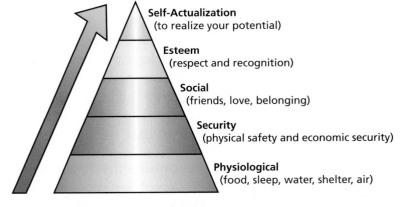

Maslow's Hierarchy of Needs Pyramid

respect and recognition from others satisfies esteem needs. Running for president of a student organization might be an attempt to satisfy esteem needs. Self-actualization involves intellectual growth, creativity, and accomplishment. Earning a college degree or taking gourmet-cooking lessons are examples of ways to meet self-actualization needs.

A **want** is something that is desired. Wants are not essential for living, but they are important for maintaining a desired lifestyle. Good marketing and advertising create wants. Flashy advertisements often create an image that attracts consumers. For example, many perfume and cologne advertisements use celebrities to create images of beauty, independence, and power. These ads inspire consumers who desire these same qualities to buy the perfume or cologne.

Scarcity

Personal needs and wants are never ending, but the resources used in the production of products and services are limited. This is the concept of *scarcity*. Resources include natural resources (raw materials), human resources (labor), and capital resources (money, buildings, and equipment). Scarcity may result in the production of fewer products and services at higher prices. A consumer's financial resources are limited by his or her income. Scarcity affects the way consumers make buying decisions. They must decide how to use their limited income to buy all the things they want and need, while choosing among the alternatives available in the marketplace.

CHECKPOINT

What is the difference between a need and a want?

So Many Different Decisions

Every day consumers are faced with buying decisions. Some decisions require little or no thought while others are time consuming. Borrowing more than $10,000 to buy a car that you are likely to keep for several years requires different decision-making skills than purchasing a $2 bottle of ketchup.

Consumer Decision-Making Process

Consumers usually follow a formal *consumer decision-making process* when buying products or services, especially new or expensive items. By understanding the decision-making process that customers use to purchase products and services, advertisers can assist customers in making the most appropriate choices. There are five steps in the decision-making process: (1) recognize the problem, (2) search for information, (3) evaluate alternatives, (4) make the purchase, and (5) evaluate the purchase.

Recognize the Problem   The first step in the decision-making process (problem recognition) occurs when the consumer recognizes a need, desire, or problem. Advertising can play a big role in this step by triggering a need. The urgency to satisfy the need plays an important role in the decision-making process. If your car has broken down and you have no other mode of transportation, you will try to find a car repair shop or buy a new car as soon as possible. An urgent need may result in less comparison shopping and a quicker decision. If you want to buy a camera before you go on vacation next year, you may take more time to evaluate your options.

Search for Information   Once the need or problem has been identified, the consumer gathers information about alternative solutions. The extent of the search for information depends on your past experiences. When the need is one you have satisfied before, identifying alternatives may be relatively easy. If you face a new problem that you have not encountered in the past, identifying possible solutions is more difficult.

The information search may occur internally or externally. Internal information comes from past experiences with products or services. External information comes from several sources, including family and friends and public sources such as advertisements.

Evaluate Alternatives   After alternatives have been determined, the consumer must evaluate them and narrow down the number of choices. This may involve summarizing information, comparing the benefits of each choice, and ranking the alternatives. For example, you may select a product feature that is important to you and then exclude all alternatives that don't have this feature. After evaluating the alternatives, the consumer may discover that he or she doesn't have enough information or adequate resources to make a purchase. When this happens, the consumer may search for more information.

Make the Purchase The next step of the consumer decision-making process is to make the purchase when an appropriate option has been identified. An option is appropriate if it will satisfy the need or solve the problem at an affordable price. In addition to price, other considerations during the purchasing process include when and where to buy and what payment method to use.

Evaluate the Purchase The final step in the consumer decision-making process is the post-purchase evaluation. During this stage, the consumer decides whether the purchase met his or her expectations and satisfied the need. Marketers are paying more attention to post-purchase satisfaction. Many businesses now offer money-back guarantees to customers who are not fully satisfied with a product. They are also making an effort to communicate with customers after a sale to reinforce the buying decision and to ensure satisfaction. Businesses that follow up with customers can learn how to improve customer relations and win repeat business.

Types of Consumer Decision Making

When making purchases, consumers use three types of decision making: routine, limited, and extensive. **Routine decision making** is used for frequently purchased, low-cost products that require little thought. The consumer is familiar with the products available for routine purchases and spends little time searching and selecting them. The consumer often chooses the same brand because it has satisfied his or her needs in the past. Snacks, personal hygiene products, and basic necessities are often purchased using routine decision making.

Limited decision making takes a moderate amount of time to collect and compare information about an unfamiliar product or brand. Products that are more expensive and purchased less frequently often require limited decision making. Buying a new flat-screen television will require comparison shopping to determine prices, picture clarity, and warranty. After you identify and complete a reasonable comparison and evaluation of several brands of televisions, you will make a choice. Sometimes even low-cost purchases can involve limited decision making. If you prefer one brand of shampoo, but it's not available, you most likely will spend some time looking at the alternatives to determine which one best meets your needs.

When is a consumer more likely to use limited decision making?

Extensive decision making occurs when the consumer uses a methodical decision-making process to buy an infrequently purchased product. This type of decision making is commonly used to buy automobiles and homes. Consumers are willing to spend time and effort evaluating alternatives to ensure they make the right decision. They carefully review their needs to match them with the best possible choices.

Marketers must understand the level of decision making the consumer uses when making purchases. Customers do not want to be overwhelmed with information for a routine decision; however, they will appreciate more product information when making extensive decisions. For products that involve routine decision making, in-store advertising or coupons may be appropriate. For products that require higher-level decision making, a television or online advertising campaign that provides details about the product may be effective.

▰▰▰▰ CHECKPOINT ◤◤◤◤◤

Why should marketers be concerned about the consumer decision-making process?

2.1 Assessment

THINK ABOUT IT

1. Do you think advertising influences consumer needs and wants? Explain your answer.
2. Give an example of a personal purchase that required limited decision making. Explain the process you used before making the purchase.
3. Write a post-purchase evaluation for a recent purchase. The evaluation should describe your product expectations and your satisfaction or dissatisfaction with the purchase.

MAKE ACADEMIC CONNECTIONS

4. **COMMUNICATION**   Many businesses use customer feedback cards to learn more about customers' wants and needs. Assume you work for a local restaurant. Create a customer feedback card to identify what customers like and dislike about the restaurant. Explain how customer feedback can be used to improve customer satisfaction.
5. **RESEARCH**   Extensive decision making is used when buying an automobile. Use the Internet to prepare a comparative analysis of three new competing cars. Prepare a three-column table containing information about each car that would help you choose among them.
6. **VISUAL ART**   Create a collage that shows Maslow's Hierarchy of Needs. Use pictures or other images to represent each level of the hierarchy.

Teamwork

Working in a team, conduct research to determine the natural resources in your area. Then prepare a report that explains how these natural resources are used to satisfy consumer needs and wants.

Consumer Purchase Classifications

Goals

- Distinguish between types of consumer purchases and recognize the level of consumer involvement in buying decisions.
- Describe different types of consumer products.

Terms

- convenience products, p. 42
- shopping products, p. 43
- specialty products, p. 44
- unsought products, p. 44

From iPod to iWatch

Consumers who desire the latest electronic gadgets often line up for the newest versions of Apple's iPhones and iPods. Apple is well known for it product innovations and has had a large impact on consumer buying trends. Just when it seemed like the watch was becoming obsolete, ADR Studio came up with a concept design for a new product called the iWatch. ADR envisioned an innovative timepiece with an aluminum casing, 16GB of internal storage, and connectivity to iPhones or iPads by Wi-Fi or Bluetooth. Although ADR's version of an iWatch was only a concept, other companies acted on this idea and created their own watch conversion kits for use with the iPod nano. These kits contain a watchband that enables you to wear an iPod nano on your wrist and have access to the time as well as to all of your favorite tunes. Many popular products today are created and marketed as accessories to enhance the use of other successful products.

© elwynn/Shutterstock.com

Work as a Team Name other products or services that are marketed as accessories. Why do you think building a company based on the success of another company is a common marketing strategy?

The Buying Decision

Consumers are faced with buying decisions ranging from routine to complicated. Buying decisions that require little or no thought involve a low level of risk while other decisions that require extensive thought involve higher risks.

Why is a new purchase the most complex type of purchase?

Types of Purchases

Generally, consumers are confronted with three types of purchases—new purchases, modified purchases, and repeat purchases. Purchase types are closely associated with the three levels of consumer decision making—extensive, limited, and routine.

New Purchase A *new purchase* involves buying a product or service for the first time. New purchases tend to be infrequent. Consumers may be inexperienced with the product or service, making it the most challenging type of purchase. Extensive decision making will likely be used when consumers are purchasing an unfamiliar, expensive item or an infrequently purchased item. This complex type of consumer buying decision requires the most consumer involvement. Consumers check out all possible choices to make the best decision. Extensive decision making can involve lengthy research because there are so many products or services to consider. Internal and external information is collected before making new purchase decisions.

Modified Purchase Sometimes consumers realize that products purchased in the past do not totally meet their current needs. After consumers identify the product changes or improvements needed, they will make a modified purchase to meet their new specifications. A *modified purchase* occurs when consumers must make new decisions about a product or service that they have previously purchased. Limited decision making is often involved in modified purchases. The consumer has previous product experience but is unfamiliar with the current product updates and available brands, so he or she likely will compare the various alternatives. For example, when a consumer goes to the store to purchase his or her favorite brand of paint and discovers that the brand has been discontinued, the consumer will expend moderate effort to search for information about a substitute product. A consumer who is loyal to a particular make and model of an automobile may decide that more options and features are needed to meet his or her needs. When it is time to buy a new car, the consumer will do some research to determine the features needed and make a modified purchase.

Repeat Purchase Purchasing the same products and services over and over again is known as a *repeat purchase*. This is the most common type of purchase and involves routine decision making. The buyer has identified a product or service that meets his or her needs and habitually purchases it with little or no thought. Even though buyers are familiar with several different brands in the product category, they stick with one brand. Repeat purchases are usually associated with low-cost products and services that involve low risk.

Why does the level of consumer involvement in buying decisions increase with high-priced items?

Consumer Involvement in Buying Decisions

The level of involvement, or time and effort, consumers apply to their buying decisions varies for different products and services. Several factors influence the level of consumer involvement in buying decisions, including past experience, interests, perceived risk, circumstances, and self-image. Knowing the level of consumer involvement associated with various products and services is helpful to advertisers.

- When consumers have had a past experience with a product or service, there is a lower level of involvement in making the buying decision. When a consumer has a favorite brand of soda, he or she will not spend a lot of time deciding between the competing brands of soda offered at the supermarket.

- Consumers' specific interests can increase the level of involvement in buying decisions. Consumers who are interested in technology products will spend more time shopping before purchasing items in this product category. A car enthusiast will spend considerable time researching the price, horse power, gas mileage, warranty, and available features and options of different cars.

- When consumers perceive risk associated with a purchase, they will become more involved in the buying process. High-priced items can result in financial risk. Thus, a higher level of consumer involvement is associated with higher-priced items. Psychological risk occurs if consumers experience anxiety about making the right decision. To help lessen this anxiety, consumers will put more time and effort into their buying decision.

- Circumstances also can influence the level of consumer involvement in making a purchase. A consumer may put more thought into buying a product or service if it is for a special occasion. If a shopper is caught outside in the rain unexpectedly and needs to buy an umbrella, he or she will quickly make a purchase without any planning.

- Higher consumer involvement is often associated with purchases that enhance self-image. If a consumer wants to make a statement or reinforce his or her image by purchasing a certain product, the buying decision becomes more relevant. Designer clothing and luxury cars are often purchased to make a personal statement about the buyer.

▨▨▨▨▨ CHECKPOINT ◣◣◣◣◣

What are some reasons for a modified purchase?

Types of Products

Each day consumers make purchases ranging from routine to unique products. Convenience, shopping, specialty, and unsought products are four common product categories. Advertising for each product category differs because each one has a different target market.

Convenience Products

Convenience products are purchased regularly without much planning. Consumers want to purchase convenience products as quickly and easily as possible. They do not spend much time shopping and comparing products and brands that seem to be similar. Businesses must emphasize product location (convenience) for these types of products. Convenience products should be widely available at retail outlets, including supermarkets, discount stores such as Walmart, pharmacies such as CVS, and mini markets at gas stations.

Convenience products can be further categorized as staple products, impulse products, and emergency products. *Staple products* are routine purchases. Consumers do not put much thought into

What factors are important to consumers when purchasing convenience products?

purchasing staple products like milk and paper towels. Consumers often have a brand preference for staple products. However, prices charged for staple products cannot be higher than similar products in the same location, or the consumer will switch brands. When promoting staple products, marketers emphasize the brand.

Impulse products are purchased with no advanced planning. Since consumers purchase impulse products on a whim, they are less concerned about the price. Impulse products are often the ones displayed at the end of aisles or near the checkout counter in stores. So marketers are likely to focus on in-store displays for impulse products.

Emergency products are purchased because of an urgent need. For example, if your roof springs a leak, you are likely to hire the first available roofer to make the repair without shopping around. Price is a minor consideration for emergency products that are needed now to solve a problem. Businesses that market emergency products emphasize quick availability, such as by advertising 24-hour service.

Shopping Products

Shopping products consist of products that consumers want to own after they meet personal needs. They are more expensive than convenience products. Automobiles, homes, furniture, televisions, and clothing are examples of shopping products. Consumers are willing to spend extra time shopping and comparing before making a buying decision. Shopping considerations could include style, price, and lifestyle compatibility.

Shopping products do not have to be available in the most convenient locations. Advertisements for these products emphasize the qualities of the product or service that are most important to consumers. Consumers focus on the best combination of features, options, services, and uses. Effective promotions for shopping products help consumers compare brands.

© Losevsky Pavel/Shutterstock.com

How are shopping products different from convenience products?

If consumers believe there is little difference among the products or brands, they will search for the best possible price. Furniture, clothing, and automobile retailers must demonstrate that they have the lowest price or the best financing terms.

Specialty Products

Specialty products are those that have a strong brand loyalty. Consumers are reluctant to buy substitutes because of their positive past experiences with the product. Vacation destinations, restaurants, luxury automobiles, and designer clothing are examples of specialty products. Advertising campaigns for specialty products must emphasize why consumers believe the product or service is unique, which could include factors such as quality, location, or price. Brand names and quality of service are also highly promoted. An innovative advertising campaign can be used to create an image of superiority, giving the impression that the product is a specialty product.

Unsought Products

Unsought products are not actively sought out by consumers. This could be because the consumer is unaware of the product or service. Advertising is used to increase awareness of new products. The advertising must communicate how the new product will satisfy consumer needs and where it can be purchased. Without awareness, there will be no demand, and the product will not succeed.

Other unsought products include those that consumers do not want to buy. Insurance and funeral planning are examples of unsought products and services for most people. Two things that are certain in

SPOTLIGHT ON SUCCESS

© Whataburger Restaurants L.P.

HARMON DOBSON, Whataburger

Harmon Dobson, an adventurous and determined entrepreneur, opened the world's first Whataburger in Corpus Christi, Texas. Dobson wanted to serve a burger so big that it took two hands to hold and that made customers say, "What a burger!" Mr. Dobson succeeded. The little burger stand took on legendary status throughout Texas and the South, and now there are over 700 Whataburger restaurants in ten states.

Every Whataburger is made to order based on each customer's taste, resulting in a fresher, more satisfying product. Burgers are made with 100% pure American beef and served on a toasted five-inch bun with all the extras, including grilled jalapenos, bacon, cheese, tomatoes, pickles, and other favorite toppings—just the way the customer likes it. Customers can get their Whataburger 24 hours a day 7 days a week.

In addition to traditional advertising methods, Whataburger uses a more unconventional method on its website through its Whatastore link. Website visitors can buy Whataburger t-shirts, hats, mugs, and postcards. But customers can also design their own t-shirts by choosing the icons representing their favorite Whataburger toppings. The t-shirt advertises a customer's favorite menu selections. In essence, when a customer buys a customized t-shirt, he or she is paying Whataburger to advertise the restaurant!

Think Critically

Is Whataburger a specialty product? Explain your answer. Do you think Whataburger's customized t-shirt is a good advertising strategy? Why or why not?

life—death and taxes—are not popular topics for consumers. Funerals can cost from $3,000 to more than $10,000. A preplanned funeral arrangement service offered by a funeral home is not a desirable purchase. Marketing this type of product or service often requires personal selling and persuasive advertising. Salespeople seek out potential customers. Advertisements may make an emotional claim to convince consumers of the need for this type of product or service.

///// CHECKPOINT \\\\\\

What is an effective strategy for selling shopping products?

2.2 Assessment

THINK ABOUT IT

1. Give an example of a new purchase you recently made. Did you use extensive decision making to make the purchase? Explain why or why not.

2. List some examples of unsought products and services in addition to those described in the chapter.

3. When preparing an advertising strategy for impulse products, what factors should be considered?

4. What factors could influence the level of consumer involvement in the buying decision for a product or service?

MAKE ACADEMIC CONNECTIONS

5. **MATH**   Life insurance is an unsought purchase for many people. The purpose of life insurance is to cover personal and funeral expenses when someone dies and to provide financial support for dependents. A 30-year-old father purchases a $100,000 whole life insurance policy that costs $120 per month. If the father lives until age 80, how much will he have paid for the life insurance policy?

6. **ECONOMICS**   Special financing terms are sometimes offered for the sale of shopping products, such as a house. In past years, the federal government loosened the credit restrictions for obtaining a home loan. Often down payments from first-time homebuyers were not required. Using the Internet, research the effects that the looser credit restrictions had on the housing market. Describe your findings in a one-page report.

7. **PROBLEM SOLVING**   An upscale clothing store sells designer clothing predominantly to young people, ages 15 to 25. The manager of the store wants to broaden the customer base by changing the perception of the merchandise from a specialty product to a shopping product. How will the store's merchandise need to change? What type of advertising will be necessary to change the customers' perception?

Teamwork

Your team has been hired by a retailer to set up displays that will increase the number of impulse purchases made by customers. Choose a popular department store, home improvement store, or supermarket and describe the displays you will create.

2.3

Influences on Consumer Behavior

Goals
- Discuss consumer buying motives.
- Describe individual, social, and marketing influences on consumer behavior.

Terms
- buying motives, p. 47
- emotional motives, p. 47
- rational motives, p. 48
- patronage motives, p. 48
- culture, p. 50
- reference group, p. 50
- advertising campaign, p. 51

FOCUS ON ADVERTISING

Supermarkets Go Hi-Tech

Supermarkets have created numerous in-store advertising and promotional campaigns to increase sales. Video screens throughout supermarkets remind shoppers about items they need to take home. These videos are especially effective when shoppers are hungry. The dairy refrigeration department and produce departments in supermarkets now include sound effects of cackling chickens or mooing cows. Sounds are activated by motion sensors when consumers walk past the coolers. These sounds grab the attention of shoppers and entice them to check out the items in the coolers. Large supermarkets offer customer loyalty cards. When the cards are scanned by the cashier, customers get special prices on their purchases. Tracking software is used to issue personalized coupons based on the types of purchases being made.

Work as a Team Why are supermarkets now using high-tech, in-store advertising and promotional strategies? Do you think these strategies are effective? Why or why not?

Buying Motives

The actions of individuals are influenced by *motivation*, which is an incentive or a reason for doing something. Consumer purchases are influenced by short- and long-term motivation. When you are hungry, you might be motivated to go to a restaurant and buy a sandwich. After graduating from high school, you may be motivated to attend college to obtain a degree that will help you land a good career and

How does the Virgin America advertisement appeal to emotional buying motives?

salary. There are also positive and negative motivators that influence your actions. You may have a negative motivation to watch TV for an hour instead of exercising. Earning a pay increase is an example of a positive motivator that could encourage you to increase your savings.

Motivation has a direct influence on consumer buying behavior. **Buying motives** are the driving forces that cause consumers to buy products and services. Three categories of buying motives that influence consumer decisions include emotional motives, rational motives, and patronage motives.

Emotional Motives

Reasons to make a purchase based on feelings, beliefs, or attitudes are called **emotional motives**. Consumer purchases may be influenced by such things as love and affection, guilt, fear, protection, appearance, prestige, and popularity. Emotional advertising spends more time creating a special experience than describing product features. Folgers Coffee commercials emphasize the importance of family gatherings. Campbell Soup ads promote their soups as a comfort food that is "good for the body and the soul." Advertising for technology products, such as cell phones, shows people staying in touch with loved ones. Advertisements for security systems and environmentally friendly household products use fear and protection as emotional motivators. By focusing on how a product or service makes customers feel, marketers appeal to consumers' emotional buying motives.

Rational Motives

Not all buying decisions are based on emotions. Purchases that are based on facts or logic are influenced by **rational motives**. Quality, reliability, convenience, value, and cost are examples of rational buying motives. Rational motives are very important for expensive purchases like homes and automobiles. Shopping for a home can involve emotional motives, but rational motives should preside when considering price, financing, and maintenance needs of the home. Rational motives also influence less expensive purchases. When buying a pair of shoes, you need to consider the purpose of them. If they will be used for work, fit and comfort will be more important than style.

Patronage Motives

Purchases that are based on loyalty are driven by **patronage motives**. Consumers may be loyal to a particular business or a specific brand. Loyalty results from previous positive experiences or personal identification with the product or business. A patronage motive is likely the reason a consumer purchases Coca-Cola instead of Pepsi. Consumers can also develop loyalty because of reasonable prices, high quality, friendly customer service, or a convenient location. A consumer may always choose to shop at a local neighborhood business because it is nearby. If you have had a positive experience with a retailer's website, you probably will return to that website. Some patronage motives are the result of family preferences. If your family has always purchased the same brand of soft drinks or shopped at the same store, you are likely to do the same.

 CHECKPOINT

How do buying motives affect consumer purchases?

Factors Influencing Consumer Buying Decisions

Understanding what influences consumer buying decisions is essential for the success of a business. When marketers are equipped with this knowledge, they can create effective marketing campaigns to increase the sale of products and services.

Individual Influences

Many buying decisions are influenced by personal characteristics that are unique to an individual. The characteristics and character that make a person unique form that person's *personal identity*. Personality, gender, age, culture, and ethnicity all play a role in a person's identity.

Personality No two people are alike because they have different personalities. *Personality* is the set of emotions, traits, and behaviors that define an individual. Personalities influence consumer purchases. The types of clothing, cars, hobbies, and social activities preferred by consumers are based on their personality.

An individual's personality is comprised of his or her attitude, self-concept, and lifestyle choices. An *attitude* is a state of mind or point of view. Values, beliefs, and feelings contribute to a person's *attitude*. Consumers hold different attitudes about such things as brand-name products, luxury items, eco-friendly business practices, and the use of credit. These attitudes shape buying decisions. *Self-concept* is how a person perceives him or herself. It consists of self-image and self-esteem. An individual may choose to buy a sports car instead of a family sedan to project a youthful image.

Lifestyle examines how a person lives as identified by material goods, activities, interests, and relationships. Lifestyle decisions involve housing choices, family size, leisure activities, and community involvement. Lifestyle characteristics can be used to categorize and target consumers. For example, General Mills Nature Valley® granola bars target busy, active consumers who want a healthy on-the-go snack.

© StockLite/Shutterstock.com

How are some purchases, such as jewelry, related to a person's self-concept?

Gender Men and women have different needs, resulting in a variety of gender-specific products, such as health and beauty products. Many TV networks target men or women. ESPN airs sporting events primarily watched by men, while the Lifetime Movie Network airs movies about topics that interest women. Advertisements that specifically target men or women are broadcast on these networks. Men and women also have different decision-making processes. Men tend to be more single-minded and focused and are more willing to take risks. Women have many purchasing criteria and prefer to consider several alternatives. Emotions play a bigger role in decisions made by women. Based on this, marketers need to use different advertising strategies when marketing to men versus women.

Age Consumer behavior is highly influenced by a person's age. Wants and needs of individuals change as they grow older. A person's age influences the types of products and services that he or she will buy and the product features that are important. As a person's maturity, experience, and income levels change, so does his or her shopping habits. Marketers often categorize their target markets by age groups, such as under 25, 25–34, 35–44, 45–54, and so on. Age is a consideration when creating advertisements and choosing the advertising media.

Culture and Ethnicity **Culture** can be described as the shared attitudes and behaviors of a specific social group. The history, beliefs, values, customs, and language of a group make up its culture. Culture is passed on from generation to generation. *Ethnicity* is a shared identity with a group of people who have a common heritage or culture. Cultural and ethnic views and values have a strong influence on individual choices and decisions. They influence dress, social activities, and food choices. Ethnic markets are growing in the United States. Advertisers must be aware of the best marketing strategies to use when targeting various ethnicities, including Hispanic Americans, African Americans, and Asian Americans. Many advertisements now portray people from various ethnic backgrounds.

Social Influences

The buying behavior of an individual is influenced by his or her social environment. A *social environment* consists of other individuals or groups with whom you interact on a regular basis. School is part of a teenager's social environment.

An organization or group of people that an individual identifies with and admires is called a **reference group**. Informal reference groups may include friends, family, coworkers, and social organizations. Formal reference groups could include clubs and professional organizations. To join a reference group, an individual may change his or her behavior and image to meet perceived group expectations. For example, teens may start wearing a certain style or brand of clothing to fit in with a peer group. Successful marketing encourages individuals to purchase and use the same products and services used by their reference group.

© William Perugini/Shutterstock.com

How do reference groups affect consumer buying behavior?

Marketing Influences

Consumers have many choices of products and services they can purchase to meet their needs. Companies rely heavily on advertising and promotion to build and strengthen product and brand awareness.

Advertising Influences An **advertising campaign** is a series of related advertisements with a common theme or idea that focuses on a specific product, service, brand, or message. "Sell the sizzle, not the steak" refers to selling the benefits of a product, not its attributes (features). A successful advertising campaign combines creativity with a convincing message that appeals to a strong need or want within the target audience. Advertisements that succeed in making a personal connection with the consumer can influence that consumer's buying decisions.

Advertising must be a continuous process. When advertising becomes stagnant, even valuable brands lose consumer interest and market share. Companies must reinvent their messaging and image if their advertisements begin to lose effectiveness. Geico, an insurance company, is well-known for its original advertising. The company manages to keep its advertising fresh by using humorous concepts and mascots (such as the Gecko and the Cavemen) and catchy slogans, such as "calling Geico for a quote is so simple that even a caveman could do it" and "15 minutes could save you 15 percent or more on car insurance."

Why are advertisements and promotions important marketing tools?

Marketing also provides a channel to raise awareness about the serious problems facing our society. Advertising campaigns have encouraged people to change their diets, quit smoking, use eco-friendly products, and contribute money to help fund medical research. Consumers make purchases to support their change in lifestyle as a result of increased public awareness.

Promotional Influences *Promotion* is any form of communication that a company uses to create a favorable image of its products or services. Promotions are used to introduce products and services, stimulate consumer demand/action, and increase repeat sales. Coupons and samples may be handed out to encourage consumers to try a new product. Contests and giveaways may attract new customers. Customer loyalty and frequent-buyer programs reward repeat customers with special deals and pricing. CVS has had success with its ExtraCare Rewards Program. It is the largest retail loyalty program in the United States with more than 66 million members.

Promotional strategies can be used to match demand with supply. Automobile dealerships need to sell the remaining inventory of new cars at the end of the year to make room for the new models. Special promotions offered by automobile dealerships include deep discounts, special financing, low interest rates, no down payment, and delayed payment plans. Furniture and electronics stores have special promotions that allow qualified customers to purchase on credit and pay no interest for up to three years. Retailers offer special discounts to move seasonal merchandise, such as clothing, patio furniture, and plants. Although promotions are frequently used to stimulate demand when quantities of products are high, promotions can also be used to make consumers aware of a limited supply of a highly demanded product, such as tickets to a popular concert or football game.

///// ◢ CHECKPOINT ◣ \\\\\

What personal characteristics might influence a consumer's buying decision?

2.3 Assessment

THINK ABOUT IT

1. Describe a purchase you made based on an emotional motive. Were you satisfied with the purchase? Why or why not?
2. Describe a cultural influence that impacts your buying decisions.
3. Describe one of your reference groups and explain how your purchases have been influenced by that group.
4. Why do new products need advertising campaigns and/or promotions?

MAKE ACADEMIC CONNECTIONS

5. **MARKETING** Give an example of an advertisement that increases awareness for a product, brand, business, or special cause. How would you rate the effectiveness of the advertisement?
6. **ECONOMICS** Which type of buying motive (emotional, rational, patronage) is the most prevalent when the economy is bad? Why is this a common buying motive during a slow economy? How might the other buying motives be a factor when making purchases in a slow economy? Provide examples.

Teamwork

Design an advertisement to increase public awareness about an important social issue. Design a print advertisement and create a 30-second radio commercial for your special cause. Explain how your advertisements could influence consumer buying behavior.

Sharpen Your 21st CENTURY SKILLS

Digital Vision/Getty Images

PARTNERSHIP FOR
21ST CENTURY SKILLS

Appreciating Diversity

Diversity recognizes the uniqueness of individuals based on race, ethnicity, gender, socio-economic status, age, physical abilities, and religious beliefs. Each person brings his or her own background, beliefs, values, talents, and behavior standards to the classroom, workplace, and community. Respecting diversity involves recognizing each individual for his/her unique traits. Diversity is about learning from others who are not the same.

As you live and work in a multicultural environment, it is important to embrace diversity. To help overcome the barriers associated with diversity, follow the tips below.

- Create opportunities for people to get to know one another and to learn about similarities they share.
- Recognize differences among people as diversity, not as inappropriate behavior.
- Confront prejudices and stereotypes that demean or exclude people.
- Respect others' values, beliefs, and feelings.
- Be an advocate for others.
- Be sensitive about the impact you have on others.
- Never harass or accept the harassment of others.
- When working together, provide equal opportunities for each group member and recognize each other's accomplishments.

Dealing with diversity can be challenging. Following the practices described above is a good start. To further increase diversity awareness, you can participate in diversity activities such as the following:

- Attend diversity training to learn about diversity issues and ways to approach them.
- Set up a school or workplace diversity day by choosing a culture and preparing presentations and displays about the culture.
- Attend a cultural event or celebration and compare the similarities and differences to your culture.
- Read an article or book or watch a movie about another cultural group.

Try It Out

You are hosting a diversity day at your school. Choose a country or culture and develop a PowerPoint presentation about it. Describe its language, customs, traditions, food, dress, and other unique traits. Conclude your presentation by explaining the benefits of embracing and supporting diversity.

© iofoto/Shutterstock.com

SUMMARY

2.1 The Consumer Is in Charge

- To succeed, a business must study consumer behavior to learn how consumers make buying decisions.
- All consumers have wants and needs. There are five levels of needs in Maslow's Hierarchy of Needs, including physiological, security, social, esteem, and self-actualization needs.
- Consumers typically use a five-step consumer decision-making process: (1) recognize the problem, (2) search for information, (3) evaluate alternatives, (4) make the purchase, and (5) evaluate the purchase.
- Generally, consumers use three types of decision making: (1) routine, (2) limited, and (3) extensive.

2.2 Consumer Purchase Classifications

- A new purchase involves buying a product or service for the first time. New purchases tend to be infrequent.
- A modified purchase occurs when the consumer must make new decisions about a product or service that they have previously purchased.
- A repeat purchase occurs when the same products or services are purchased over and over again.
- Factors that affect the level of consumer involvement in buying decisions include past experience, interests, perceived risk, circumstances, and self-image.
- Consumer purchases can be classified as convenience products, shopping products, specialty products, and unsought products.

2.3 Influences on Consumer Behavior

- Motivation is the driving force behind consumer purchases. Consumers make purchases based on emotional, rational, and patronage motives.
- Individual influences on consumer buying decisions include a person's personality, gender, age, culture, and ethnicity.
- Social influences on consumer buying decisions consist of reference groups, which are organizations or groups of people that the consumer identifies with or admires.
- Marketing influences on consumer buying decisions can take the form of advertising and promotion. Both forms of marketing try to increase demand for a product or service.

WHAT DO YOU KNOW? Now

Read *Impact Advertising* on page 33 again to review how emotional appeals are used in advertising. List one other advertisement you have seen that seems to use emotion as a selling tactic. Describe it and explain why it is or is not effective.

Chapter 2 **Assessment**

Vocabulary Builder

Match each statement with the term that best defines it. Some terms may not be used.

1. How consumers make buying decisions, choose among alternatives, and use products
2. Anything you require for survival
3. Something that is desired
4. The decision-making process used for frequently purchased products that require little thought
5. A series of related advertisements with a common theme or idea
6. The shared attitudes and behaviors of a specific social group
7. Products that consumers want to own after they meet personal needs
8. The methodical decision-making process used to buy an infrequently purchased product
9. Organization or group that a person identifies with and admires
10. Reasons to make a purchase based on feelings, beliefs, or attitudes

a. advertising campaign
b. buying motives
c. consumer behavior
d. convenience products
e. culture
f. emotional motives
g. extensive decision making
h. limited decision making
i. need
j. patronage motives
k. rational motives
l. reference group
m. routine decision making
n. shopping products
o. specialty products
p. unsought products
q. want

Test Your Knowledge

11. _____ is the concept that personal needs and wants are never ending, but the resources used in the production of products are limited.
    a. Consumer behavior
    b. Promotion
    c. Scarcity
    d. Advertising

12. _____ products are the most difficult to sell.
    a. Specialty
    b. Shopping
    c. Unsought
    d. Convenience

13. The highest level of need in Maslow's Hierarchy of Needs is
    a. esteem
    b. physiological
    c. security
    d. self-actualization

14. Snacks, personal hygiene products, and basic necessities require _____ decision making.
    a. extensive
    b. limited
    c. routine
    d. emotional

15. Buying a $50 bouquet of roses for Valentine's Day is an example of a(n) _____ purchase.
    a. patronage
    b. convenience
    c. rational
    d. emotional
16. The final step in the consumer decision-making process is to
    a. make the purchase
    b. evaluate alternatives
    c. evaluate the purchase
    d. search for information
17. The level of consumer involvement in the buying decision is lower for purchases involving
    a. favorite brands
    b. risk
    c. self-image
    d. special occasions
18. Which of the following is an example of a staple product?
    a. automobile
    b. clothing
    c. television
    d. milk
19. When searching for information about a product, internal information could include which of the following?
    a. advice from a friend
    b. past experiences
    c. a magazine article
    d. none of the above
20. An individual's state of mind or point of view is his or her
    a. personality
    b. attitude
    c. self-concept
    d. identity

Apply What You Learned

21. List the five steps involved in the consumer decision-making process. Then explain how you would use each step of the process to purchase a product or service that interests you.
22. List the five levels of Maslow's Hierarchy of Needs. Then explain how you will personally satisfy each type of need.
23. You own a beauty salon and spa. Describe how you would market it to appeal to various consumer characteristics, such as a person's lifestyle, gender, and age. Would you use different marketing strategies for each characteristic? Why or why not?
24. Work with a partner to develop a newspaper advertisement for a cooking class being offered at the local community center. The advertisement should appeal to a consumer's social needs and self-actualization needs.
25. Select a product or service that would require a consumer to use extensive decision making before making the purchase. As a marketer, describe what product or service information you could include in an advertisement to help a consumer in the decision-making process.

Make Academic Connections

26. **MARKETING** A new restaurant plans to open in a neighborhood that already has many successful competing restaurants with strong customer bases. The general manager for the new restaurant has asked you to develop a promotional plan to help her

compete with the other restaurants. Prepare a PowerPoint presentation of your promotional plan.

27. **ECONOMICS**   Life insurance is commonly an unsought product for many consumers. Conduct research to determine common reasons for purchasing life insurance. Based on your research, how could you persuade an individual to buy a life insurance policy from your company?

28. **MATH**   You work for a music store that sells CDs for the following music categories: Pop, Rock, Country & Western, and R&B. Last year your store reported the sales shown below. Compute the total sales and the percent of the total sales for each music category. How can you use this information to meet consumer demand?

Pop	$32,000
Rock	28,000
Country & Western	25,000
R&B	19,000

29. **RESEARCH**   You are considering the purchase of a new smartphone. Conduct online research to evaluate three different brands of phones. Use a word processing or spreadsheet program to create a table listing the features, benefits, and price of each phone. Based on your research, determine which phone you would buy. Justify your choice.

30. **SOCIOLOGY**   Interview someone of a different ethnicity to learn about his or her culture, customs, and traditions. Write a one-page report describing the other culture and explain how it differs from your culture.

31. **HISTORY**   Conduct online research to learn how advertising based on gender has changed over the years. Describe how the changing roles of men and women have made it necessary for companies to develop new advertising strategies.

32. **ETHICS**   When companies use advertising to increase public awareness about social issues, they often make emotional appeals to persuade consumers to take some kind of action, such as to make a donation. Do you think these kinds of advertisements are ethical? Present your point of view to the class.

A local department store advertised an incredible price for designer jeans. The excellent prices inspired you to visit the store so you could stock your closet with high-end clothing. You arrived at the store when it opened to ensure you would have a better selection of the popular designer jeans. Upon entering the store, you were surprised to learn that it did not have any of the advertised jeans. When you asked the store manager about the advertised special, she responded that the store would not be getting an additional shipment of the designer jeans. She then showed you some other designer jeans sold by the store at a higher price.

What would you do? Do you think the store's advertising was deceptive? Why or why not? How can you help prevent the store from using the same advertising tactic again?

Reality ✓

The Marketing Guilt Trip

Advertisements are frequently used to raise the consumer's level of concern about health, security, finances, savings, and numerous other issues. Spend an entire day watching television and you will soon feel insecure about your weight, lack of insurance, home security, household odors, facial wrinkles, and numerous other deficiencies.

One goal of marketing is to increase public awareness. This has been particularly effective in relation to the environment. Products from cars to household cleansers are promoted as being environmentally friendly. The implication is that by using these products you will cause less harm to the environment. In advertisements for prescription drugs, pharmaceutical companies often depict people living happier, more active lives with friends and family after taking the medication. In both cases, the message being communicated is that by taking the action promoted in the advertisements, consumers are doing something good for themselves as well as others, thus relieving their guilty consciences.

As a result of the obesity epidemic in the United States, companies in the snack food industry often promote their healthy, guilt-free snacks. Fitness and exercise equipment companies advertise frequently during the holidays, playing on people's guilty consciences about overeating during this time. Advertisements encourage consumers to battle the bulge after the holidays.

Using guilt as a way to convince consumers to make a purchase is a common marketing strategy. Marketing can provide valuable information to improve the lives of consumers; however, many people have become skeptical with hyped-up marketing campaigns that exploit the most vulnerable people.

Think Critically

1. Describe some advertisements you have seen that use guilt to promote products or services.
2. Why should consumers be skeptical about advertisements that use guilt as a tactic to sell products and services?
3. Do you think advertising that uses a guilt appeal has any benefits for consumers? Explain your answer.
4. Another advertising tactic closely related to guilt is fear. Provide some examples of advertisements that use fear as a selling tactic. Do you think these advertisements are effective? Why or why not?
5. *Caveat emptor* means, "let the buyer beware." How is this phrase related to marketing and advertising?

Fashion Merchandising Promotion Plan

The purpose of the Fashion Merchandising Promotion Plan is to provide an opportunity for you to demonstrate promotional competencies. You must develop a seasonal sales promotion plan for a retail store. The parts of the Fashion Merchandising Promotion Plan include the following:

I. Executive Summary (one-page description of the plan)
II. Description of the Store
III. Objectives (what the promotional campaign is to accomplish)
IV. Schedule of Events—Promotional activities must include the following:
    A. Special events (example: fashion shows, demonstrations)
    B. Advertising (example: paid/co-op advertisement in various types of media)
    C. Display (example: interior and exterior)
    D. Publicity (example: press releases sent to various types of media)
    E. Other in-store activities (example: involvement of sales employees, etc.)
V. Responsibility Sheet (assigned positions and activities)
VI. Budget (detailed projections of actual cost for Section IV, Parts A–E)
VII. Statement of Benefits to the Retail Establishment
VIII. Bibliography
IX. Appendix

You must demonstrate skills needed to address the components of the project as described in the content outline as shown above as well as learn/understand the importance of the following:

- communications skills—the ability to exchange information and ideas with others through writing, speaking, reading, or listening
- analytical skills—the ability to derive facts from data, findings from facts, conclusions from findings, and recommendations from conclusions
- critical thinking/problem-solving skills
- production skills—the ability to take a concept from an idea and make it real
- priorities/time management—the ability to determine priorities and manage time commitments and deadlines
- promotional budgeting skills

Go to the DECA website for more detailed information.

Think Critically

1. Why must a business outline its promotional plan?
2. Why should the business prepare a budget for each phase of promotion?
3. Why should a business look at last year's promotional plan when developing the new plan?
4. What promotional activities will stimulate buyer behavior for fashion merchandising?

www.deca.org

3

The Basics of Marketing

© gary718/Shutterstock.com

Starbucks' Target Market Strategy

The success of Starbucks has not been based upon sleek advertising campaigns promoting the business. Instead, Starbucks has chosen to focus its marketing efforts on the customer's in-store experience. The average Starbucks' customer visits the store six times a month. Starbucks' top 20 percent of customers visit the store at least 16 times a month. Customers go to Starbucks not only to order their favorite coffee drink but also to use the Internet, listen to music, and hang out with friends.

The success of Starbucks has attracted the attention of an unlikely competitor—McDonald's. McDonald's created a series of advertisements to promote its new McCafé coffee drinks. The McDonald's advertisements identify Starbucks as a stuffy store overrun with brooding intellectuals. McDonald's has a website called unsnobbycoffee.com that describes its coffee as simple, easy, and unpretentious when compared to Starbucks. It encourages people to kick the "snobbish habit."

Starbucks insists that it is not losing coffee drinkers to McDonald's as a result of the head-to-head competition. The company emphasized that customers were cutting back on espresso drinks in an attempt to save money in a slow economy. Starbucks' senior vice president of marketing, Terry Davenport, believes that the competition is trying to genericize coffee by taking it to a level where all coffee is the same. Starbucks does not buy into "the coffee is coffee" concept.

To stay in touch with Generation Y, Starbucks' strongest customer base, Starbucks has planned more communication through social media. Twitter is used to answer questions and to promote open communication with the public. Its Facebook page contains videos, blog posts, photos, and invitations to special events. Thousands of people subscribe to Starbucks' YouTube Channel. Subscribers can upload informational videos about the origins of different coffee blends. Starbucks' blog, titled "Ideas in Action," is written by Starbucks' employees. Employees keep customers in the loop by updating them on how Starbucks incorporates customer ideas into the operation of the business. Starbucks' social media strategy is creating customer loyalty as well as a competitive advantage.

WHAT DO YOU KNOW?

1. To help fight off competitors that want to enter the lucrative retail coffee market, what do you think Starbucks should emphasize in its marketing efforts?

2. Why is the use of social media a popular advertising strategy?

3. McDonald's advertisements compare McDonald's coffee to Starbucks' coffee. For McDonald's, what are the advantages and disadvantages of using this strategy?

61

3.1

The Marketing Concept

Goals
- Explain the marketing concept.
- Define the functions of marketing.

Terms
- marketing, p. 62
- marketing concept, p. 63
- marketing mix, p. 64
- marketing functions, p. 66
- marketing plan, p. 68

FOCUS ON ADVERTISING

The Super Bowl Advertising Bonanza

Every year the Super Bowl is watched by millions of people throughout the world, providing a grand stage for advertisements. Because the television audience for the Super Bowl is so huge, the price charged for airing a 30-second commercial during this sporting event ranges from $2 million to $3 million. Many people who are not fans of professional football watch the Super Bowl just to see the advertisements. Companies spend millions of dollars to develop creative commercials to reach the expansive television audience. Humor and shock are frequently used to capture attention. Some of the most prevalent advertisers during the Super Bowl include food and beverage companies, automobile manufacturers, delivery companies such as UPS, and technology companies. Clever advertisements capture and hold the attention of viewers, giving them a reason to stay tuned instead of change channels.

Work as a Team Discuss some well-known Super Bowl commercials. Why are these commercials appropriate to show during the Super Bowl? Who are the target audiences of these commercials?

What Is Marketing?

Marketing means different things to different people. Some people think of advertising when they hear the term *marketing*. Others may think of the selling process. Although these are components of marketing, it is a much broader activity. **Marketing** involves all of the processes used to identify, create, and maintain exchange relationships that satisfy individuals and organizations. An *exchange* occurs when people give up something in return for something else. When a customer pays money for a product, an exchange has occurred.

Marketing has not always been viewed as an important business function. During the early 1900s, businesses were product-oriented. They were more concerned about producing products efficiently and profitably and less concerned about producing products that would meet the needs of customers. Marketing became an important business function during the last half of the 20th century. As consumers' standard of living and income increased so did the demand for new and improved products. Because of improved production processes, consumers had more choices of products and services. Businesses had to compete for customers. They realized that having a good product would not guarantee success. Businesses became more market-oriented by focusing on how to deliver products and services that would have value for customers. More emphasis was placed on basic marketing activities.

The Marketing Concept

As selling products became increasingly more difficult and expensive for businesses, business leaders realized the importance of understanding the needs of customers. The **marketing concept** focuses on identifying and satisfying the needs of customers during the development and marketing of a product or service. Successful implementation of the marketing concept involves the following:

- Focusing on customer needs and wants to develop and market products or services that are considered better than competitors' products or services
- Applying the marketing concept to the planning, production, pricing, distribution, and promotion of products and services
- Satisfying customer needs and wants while operating profitably

Successful businesses identify and respond to customers' needs. Banks have branch offices in grocery stores and offer online services for the convenience of their customers. Colleges offer courses at night, online, and on the weekends to meet the special needs of students. Some grocery stores and restaurants are open 24 hours a day to cater to the needs of a population that works different shifts. During a bad economy, many fast food restaurants offer $1 menus, making meals more affordable. Automobile manufacturers added air bags and antilock brakes to address consumer safety concerns.

Businesses must conduct research, watch consumer trends, and listen to customer feedback to produce products and services that will sell. Those businesses that do not apply the marketing concept will have to cut prices, increase advertising, and resort to other strategies to persuade customers to buy unneeded or unwanted products or services.

Why is it important for businesses and organizations, such as colleges, to follow the marketing concept?

The Marketing Mix

An important step in implementing the marketing concept is to develop a marketing mix that meets the needs of the market. The **marketing mix** is the combination of four marketing elements—product, price, distribution, and promotion—used by a business. Sometimes the marketing mix is referred to as the *four P's of Marketing*, with *place* used as the alternate term for *distribution*.

Product The *product* is a good or service produced to meet consumer demand. It is the central focus of the marketing mix. Having a great idea for a new product or service does not guarantee success. The product or service has to satisfy consumers' wants and needs to generate a demand for it. Entrepreneurs and marketers must pay close attention to consumer preferences in order to produce products and services that will sell.

Consumer demand is influenced by many factors, including quality, perception, price, promotion, trends, and the economy. Products that are known for their high quality are often in high demand. Toyota had a reputation of producing high-quality automobiles and was the leading brand in automobile sales for many years. Its sales slipped when manufacturing defects and related accidents tarnished the company's image. Companies are continually improving products to maintain consumer interest and stimulate sales. Fast food restaurants frequently introduce new menu items because of healthful diet trends.

Producers must also predict the amount of goods and services that consumers will demand. When consumer demand exceeds the quantity of goods and services available, sales and revenue potential are lost. A *surplus* exists when the amount produced is greater than the demand. If a surplus occurs, retailers may mark down merchandise to clear out excess inventory.

Price The amount customers pay for a good or service is the *price*. It plays a major role in what will be produced and consumed. Many factors help determine the price. The availability of a product can affect prices. A limited supply of a highly demanded product often results in higher prices. Product perception also influences price. High-end clothing brands like Ralph Lauren Polo™ and Lacoste™ project an image of high quality and status and, thus, can command higher prices. Consumers often associate a higher price with a high-performance company or product. BMW's automobiles have landed in the top ten of J.D. Power and Associates vehicle dependability study for nearly 20 years. BMW's proven track record helps justify its higher prices. A weak economy can be a challenge to both businesses and consumers. During economic downturns, businesses must provide products and services that consumers can afford.

Distribution Also referred to as place, *distribution* involves having the product in the right place at the right time. Offering plenty of hot drinks at a cold football game will result in high sales. Tickets for sporting events and concerts can be sold online, through ticket agencies, at department stores, directly at the entertainment venue, and through a toll-free number. Numerous forms of distribution for the concert tickets increase the likelihood of a sold-out concert. When a product is not available when consumers want it, they will shop for alternatives.

Distribution also involves the packaging, storage, handling, and transportation of products. As products move

What activities are involved during the distribution of a product?

from the manufacturer to the customer, they may travel hundreds of miles, needing to be stored at various points. The product packaging and storage facilities must provide adequate protection so that the product arrives to the customer in usable condition.

Promotion Businesses use promotion strategies to build relationships with customers. *Promotion* involves all communications used by a business to create a favorable impression of its products or services. Promotions must communicate the tangible and intangible benefits offered by products and services. Tangible benefits, which can be seen or measured, are easier for customers to understand. Saving money on the purchase of an automobile by taking advantage of a special promotion is a tangible benefit. Intangible benefits are those that are not as obvious. Promoting the intangible benefits of an automobile, such as its safety features or eco-friendly features, is also important in creating a favorable impression.

There are many forms of promotion, including advertising, publicity, public relations, personal selling, and even word of mouth from satisfied customers. Automobile manufacturers, technology manufacturers, restaurants, retailers, and numerous other businesses spend large sums of money on various forms of promotion to generate sales and increase profits. Every day consumers are bombarded with messages, commercials, advertisements, and other forms of promotion encouraging them to buy products and services.

CHECKPOINT

Why is marketing an important business function?

Marketing Functions

There are many marketing activities that need to be completed before a product or service is ready to be advertised and sold. **Marketing functions** are related activities that must be completed to accomplish an important marketing goal. Each of the marketing functions described below plays a role in the development and sales of products and services. When carried out effectively, they increase the chances of customer satisfaction and company profitability.

- *Market planning* involves identifying target markets (consumers or businesses that a company wants to serve) and developing an effective marketing strategy and marketing mix that will produce a satisfying exchange relationship.
- *Product and service management* involves creating products and services that meet the needs of customers. Researching, testing, and gathering customer input are essential activities of the product and service management function.
- *Distribution* involves determining the best methods and procedures to use so that customers can locate, obtain, and use a product or service. *Supply chain management* is used to coordinate the activities of all the companies involved in the flow of products and services from the manufacturer to the consumer.
- *Pricing* involves establishing and communicating the value of products and services to customers. Consumers often relate the price to the satisfaction they expect to receive from a product or service.
- *Promotion* is the communication of information about products and services to potential customers. Businesses may create a promotional blend by using a mix of advertising, sales promotions, publicity, and personal selling.
  - *Selling* is direct, personal communication with prospective customers that involves assessing needs, explaining how the business's products and services can satisfy those needs, and following up to ensure satisfaction. Well-qualified salespeople are good listeners and problem solvers.
  - *Marketing-information management* involves collecting and managing the information needed to make marketing decisions. Accurate and current information about changes and trends in the market are vital to a business's success.
  - *Financing* has two components. First businesses must budget to ensure they have the financial resources needed to carry out their marketing strategies. Second, businesses may need to provide financial assistance to customers to enable them to buy products and services. Payment plans offered by a store may include cash, layaway, credit, and special financing terms such as 90 days same as cash.

© iofoto/Shutterstock.com

Why is personal selling an important marketing function for many businesses?

- *Risk management* involves identifying potential risks associated with marketing decisions and activities and developing a strategy for dealing with and reducing the risks. Businesses must consider the risks associated with each marketing mix element—product, distribution, price, and promotion—during the marketing planning process.

Putting the Marketing Functions into Action

You can see the marketing functions at work in many well-known businesses. VIZIO, a consumer electronics company, uses *product/service management* by incorporating the latest technologies to produce a variety of high-definition and 3D televisions. Netflix gained success through its *distribution* strategy, first by delivering DVD movie rentals through the mail and later by delivering them via the Web or on game consoles such as Xbox and Wii.

The use of the *marketing-information management* function can be seen at grocery checkout lines. The Kroger Plus card gives customers the opportunity to save money, but Kroger uses it to collect data about customers. When the card is scanned, Kroger is able to track what customers buy, how much they spend, and how often they visit the store. This data helps Kroger offer the products and services that are most demanded by its customer base.

Many *pricing* strategies are used to sell products and services. Walmart promotes its stores as having everyday low prices and often advertises price rollbacks. Companies that sell expensive products usually offer special *financing* to enable customers to make purchases. Automobile manufacturers arrange low-interest or no-interest loans for creditworthy customers.

Promotion is developed for different target markets. Motel 6 airs promotions emphasizing "keeping the light on" for price-conscious customers looking for limited-service motels. Luxury automobile dealerships target higher-income markets by sending out well-designed, eye-catching brochures. *Personal selling* has always been important, and an increasing number of businesses are requiring that employees complete sales training and development to effectively obtain new clients and handle their needs.

Fast food franchises such as McDonald's and Subway used the *market planning* function to expand globally. They had to carefully research and plan which markets to enter based on a country's political and economic environment as well as the population's customs and culture. Market planning gives the restaurants a better chance of success.

The *risk management* function is evident in many ways. A business buys product liability insurance to protect against financial loss in the event that its product causes injury or death. Retailers install surveillance equipment to prevent shoplifting. Packaging is designed to protect the product from damage while being shipped and stored. Marketers develop pricing strategies to avoid pricing a product too low or too high.

COOL FACT

A child is exposed to an estimated 40,000 television commercials each year. Over $15 billion is spent annually on advertising directected at children.

The Marketing Plan

The marketing functions play a big role in the development of the marketing plan. The **marketing plan** is a written description of the marketing objectives and the planned marketing strategies and activities required to meet those objectives. A marketing plan contains detailed information about how the marketing functions will be carried out. For example, the marketing plan should describe the product or service; target markets; pricing, promotional, distribution, and selling strategies; marketing budgets; and risk analysis and management plans.

Action plans and timelines for completing the activities are included in the marketing plan. Activities are assigned to specific individuals or groups. By specifying action plans and timelines, the effectiveness of the marketing plan can be evaluated. Marketing plans will vary among businesses depending on the type of business and its marketing objectives. However, all marketing plans should address the implementation of marketing function activities.

CHECKPOINT

What are some of the activities related to the product and service management function?

3.1 Assessment

THINK ABOUT IT

1. What is the marketing concept? How is this concept different from how marketing was viewed by businesses in the early 1900s?

2. What is the marketing mix and why is it important?

3. Describe how the nine marketing functions might be utilized by a business where you shop?

MAKE ACADEMIC CONNECTIONS

4. **CAREERS**   Use the Internet to research a marketing job that relates to one of the nine marketing functions. Prepare a PowerPoint presentation describing the job title(s), job responsibilities, training and qualifications required, salary, and job outlook. (*Hint:* The *Occupational Outlook Handbook* is a good online resource.)

5. **HISTORY**   Businesses have not always considered marketing necessary. Research the history of marketing and write a one-page report on how it has evolved and grown in importance over the years.

6. **VISUAL ART**   Select a business and design a poster that illustrates its marketing mix. Make sure to cover all four elements of the marketing mix—product, price, distribution, and promotion.

Teamwork

Working in a team, design a three-minute PowerPoint presentation about the importance of marketing for businesses, other organizations, and consumers. Provide examples that demonstrate the benefits of marketing for each group.

Goals
- Define *target market*.
- Explain the process for selecting target markets.

Terms
- target market, p. 69
- niche market, p. 71
- integrated marketing communication (IMC), p. 74

Kia Targets Young Drivers

In recent years, the automobile industry has had sluggish sales. Kia Motors America, which is owned by Hyundai Group, is going against that trend by reporting strong sales of its Kia® Soul. While many auto manufacturers were decreasing marketing efforts because of the slow economy, Kia did the opposite. Kia made an aggressive effort to get to know its target market—young drivers and the 20-something set. It added features to the Soul that would appeal to the target market— glowing speakers, iPod hookups, Bluetooth hands-free phone connections, and many other options. Then Kia developed a crafty advertising campaign featuring furry hamsters. The debut ad titled "A New Way to Roll" made the driving experience look "cool." This ad was followed by an even more popular one titled "This or That." The ad featured hamsters in hooded sweatshirts rapping about the Kia Soul. The ads were such a hit with the target market that sales surged 45 percent. Kia dealers reported that customers would come in and ask to drive the "hamster car."

Work as a Team Do you think a business is more likely to succeed if it focuses its marketing efforts on a target market? Why or why not?

What Is a Target Market?

Every business has a **target market**, which is a specific group of consumers to whom the business wants to sell its products or services. The target market may be defined in terms of age, gender, income level, ethnicity, religion, location, or lifestyle. To identify the target market, a business creates a profile of the typical customer who is likely to purchase its products or services.

Introducing our new running & training apparel for men & women

DESIGNED BY CITY SPORTS

designed by athletes for athletes.

Who is the target market represented in this City Sports advertisement? How does the ad try to appeal to its target market?

Building Success Using Target Markets

A business's marketing and sales initiatives are based upon identified target markets. It is very difficult to take steps to connect with potential customers without a clear understanding of who is likely to be interested in the products and services offered by the business. Building a customer base becomes much easier by defining the basic characteristics of a given target market and then developing a marketing mix that will meet the market's needs and wants.

Businesses spend a lot of time and money on research to identify target markets and the products and services demanded by those target markets. Based on the market research data, a business can make changes or improvements to its product before it is offered in the marketplace. It can also develop new product lines to increase the size of its customer base. For example, a company that produces sporting equipment may create and market a line of energy snacks for athletes. Consumers who already purchase the sporting equipment may also purchase the energy snacks because they know and trust the products they previously purchased from the manufacturer.

The task of identifying a target market is an ongoing process for businesses of all sizes. Even businesses that have a strong presence in several markets will be on the lookout for emerging markets where they can reach new customers. By exploring the appeal of their products in various target markets, businesses can determine if expansion into other markets would be successful.

Target Market Strategies

While some businesses focus on reaching and maintaining one target market, other businesses work on establishing relationships with consumers in several different target markets. There are various target market strategies businesses can follow.

Businesses may use an *undifferentiated strategy* by viewing the market as one big market rather than as segmented markets. One marketing mix is used for the entire market. This strategy lowers marketing costs but increases the dangers of competition. A *concentrated strategy* is used for a **niche market**, which is a smaller market that has a unique set of needs. A business concentrates on satisfying the needs of a narrowly defined market segment by using one highly specialized marketing mix. Competition among businesses serving a niche market is reduced because it would not be profitable for many businesses to serve it. A concentrated strategy allows a business to better meet the needs of a market, but it puts the business at risk if the market shrinks or changes.

Businesses that use a *multiple-segment strategy* choose to serve two or more target markets. A business may offer different products for different target markets. For example, a department store may sell clothing, sportswear, shoes, cookware, and cosmetics. A business may also offer the same product or service to different target markets. In both cases, the business will develop different marketing mixes to reach the distinctly different target markets. By focusing on more than one target market, a business can offset unforeseen drops in sales in one target market with a growth in sales in the other target market. The multiple-segment strategy helps protect businesses from sudden changes in customer tastes or financial conditions that affect an entire target market. However, creating multiple marketing mixes will increase marketing costs.

What type of target market strategy do you think a motorcycle shop would use? Why?

Selecting a Target Market

Because a business's target market includes customers who are most likely to buy its products and services, careful consideration must be given to selecting the target market. The target market should be described in as much detail as possible based upon the product or service offered by the business. Some questions that should be addressed about the target market include the following:

- Are the target customers male or female?
- How old are the target market customers?
- Where do they live? (Is geography a limiting factor for any reason?)
- What do they do for a living?
- How much money do they earn? (Can they afford the product or service? This question is very relevant for expensive or luxury items.)
- What other aspects of their lives matter? (What lifestyle characteristics could be targeted?)
- What needs or wants will the product or service satisfy?
- What price are they willing to pay for the product or service?

By answering these questions, a business can define the target market, develop a product or service that will meet the needs of the market, and create a marketing mix that appeals to customers. The target market must be reevaluated periodically to ensure that the product or service and marketing mix still meet the changing needs of customers.

Effective Target Markets

Business owners used to treat all potential customers as one big market. For example, businesses would market their products or services to the "18- to 49-year-old" category. This strategy is no longer as effective because the consumer marketplace has become extremely differentiated. The marketplace cannot be described in generalized terms. Instead, most businesses today target one or more markets.

Effective target marketing can help a business grow by bringing in new customers and retaining current ones. An effective target market has the following characteristics:

1. People in the target market have common, important needs and will benefit from the use of the business's product or service.

How can occupations be used to help define a target market?

© Goodluz/Shutterstock.com

2. People in the target market can afford the product or service.
3. The demand for the product or service by the target market is high enough to produce a profit.
4. There is adequate data available about the target market that can be used to create an effective marketing mix.

Target Market Examples

The importance of target markets is evident in some of today's most well-known products. Businesses have built success on selecting the right target market.

The Youth Market PepsiCo used target market analysis to broaden the audience for its Mountain Dew® brand. From its early beginnings in Tennessee, Mountain Dew acquired a "hillbilly" image through the use of its hillbilly mascot pictured on the bottle and its slogan "Yahoo Mountain Dew!" Entering new markets was a challenge. In 1990 Mountain Dew sponsored the X-Games, which is an annual event focusing on action or extreme sports that are popular with youth. It was during this time that the slogan "Do the Dew" was introduced. Advertising campaigns began targeting urban youth by featuring hip-hop music artist Busta Rhymes in a variety of extreme-sports antics. The

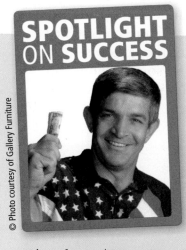

SPOTLIGHT ON SUCCESS

© Photo courtesy of Gallery Furniture

JIM "MATTRESS MACK" McINGVALE

Gallery Furniture

Jim "Mattress Mack" McIngvale is the powerhouse behind Houston-based Gallery Furniture, which is the most productive single-site retail furniture store in the world with sales of over $200 million a year. McIngvale turned an ordinary business into an all-American success story. He also has earned a reputation as a skillful promoter and civic contributor.

For a time, Mattress Mack advertised so much it was nearly impossible to turn on any television or radio station for more than 15 minutes without seeing a Gallery Furniture commercial. McIngvale is known for his fast-talking commercials that promise customers they can save money and get same-day delivery without enduring back orders for furniture. The "Mattress Mack" nickname was born when McIngvale appeared in a series of ads wearing a mattress. The advertisements became a family affair

when his young son (Mattress James) strapped on a mattress and joined his father in the commercials. Even though McIngvale hasn't worn a mattress in some time, the name has stuck. Everyone in town still calls him "Mattress Mack."

McIngvale is a marketer extraordinaire and a devoted philanthropist. His story contains a basic philosophy of success that can be understood and used in business and other areas of life. Every Christmas, McIngvale gives away households of furniture to needy families. For several years, he was the high bidder (spending close to $1 million dollars each year for local scholarships) for the grand champion animals raised by high school students and sold at the Houston Livestock Show. McIngvale gives several hundred speeches a year to numerous organizations, telling his inspiring story of going from rags to riches. McIngvale understands the value of free publicity associated with community service.

Think Critically

What methods has Jim McIngvale used to help grow his business? Why do you think he has been such a success?

campaign was a hit, and sales increased in inner-city markets. Mountain Dew continues to target the active youth market by airing action-packed, high-energy commercials and using online ad campaigns and contests.

The Luxury-Auto Market BMW is an automobile manufacturer that sells a wide range of vehicles, ranging in price from $38,000 to well over $100,000. BMWs are classy, stylish, comfortable, luxurious vehicles sold to an exclusive target market. In 2005 the vice president of marketing for BMW of North America was alarmed to learn that, despite record sales in the United States, research indicated a whopping 75 percent of luxury-auto buyers weren't even considering purchasing a BMW. There were many consumers, specifically luxury-auto buyers, who still associated BMW with the yuppies of the 1980s.

To increase its target market, BMW decided to target the "creative class," which includes scientists, engineers, architects, educators, writers, and entertainers. To do this, BMW changed the focus of its advertising campaigns from car performance to car design. Every new BMW model was associated with human attributes. For example, the BMW Formula M was described as having a "soul." These human traits helped create an image and personality for the vehicle with which the consumer could identify.

BMW marketers decided to use an integrated marketing communication strategy to promote the brand. **Integrated marketing communication** (IMC) is a strategy used to plan, execute, and monitor all promotional messages about a product to ensure consistency among all those messages. A wide range of promotional tools—advertising, sales promotions, public relations, personal selling, and interactive media—work together to create widespread exposure. An

What are some of the promotional tools that could be used to reach BMW's target market?

IMC strategy was used to increase interest in and traffic to the BMW website. At the website, prospective customers could watch short films to view the cars before purchasing them. Website visitors also had the option of creating a customized version of a vehicle based on their preferences and tastes. An online magazine was made available to website visitors considering a purchase.

CHECKPOINT

What are two identifying characteristics of an effective target market?

3.2 Assessment

THINK ABOUT IT

1. Why should businesses spend time and money on research to learn more about their target markets?

2. List three products and describe the target market for each product.

3. Choose a product or service that you buy frequently. Answer the questions on p. 72 about the target market for the product or service you selected. Do your answers indicate that you are part of the target market for this product or service? Why or why not?

4. Compare and contrast the concentrated target market strategy and the multiple-segment target marketing strategy.

MAKE ACADEMIC CONNECTIONS

5. **MATH**   A luxury automobile costs $42,000. Creative marketing accounts for 3 percent of the price being charged for the auto. How much money was spent to market the luxury auto? What would be the price of the auto if marketing costs weren't applied to the final price?

6. **MARKETING**   The rapidly rising price of fuel has increased consumer interest in fuel-efficient automobiles. However, many consumers associate fuel-efficient models with unappealing and unattractive designs. Conduct research to learn more about some of the latest models of fuel-efficient autos. Make suggestions to auto manufacturers about how they could make the car more attractive to their target markets.

7. **TECHNOLOGY**   Visit the website of two popular clothing retailers. View the site's advertisements, promotions, images, links, and other features. Which retailer do you think does a better job of targeting teen customers? Explain why.

Teamwork

Your marketing team has been hired by a sporting goods store that sells athletic shoes and apparel, fitness equipment, and camping supplies. The store's owner would like your help in implementing a multiple-segment target market strategy. Select two target markets for the store. Describe the target markets and develop a marketing mix for each one.

Market Segmentation

Goals

- Differentiate between market segmentation and mass marketing.
- Describe market segmentation categories.
- Explain how to select market segments that have market potential.

Terms

- market segmentation, p. 77
- mass marketing, p. 77
- customer profile, p. 78
- geographic segmentation, p. 78
- demographics, p. 79
- psychographics, p. 79
- product usage, p. 80
- benefit segmentation, p. 80
- market share, p. 82

FOCUS ON ADVERTISING

Humor Reaches the Mass Market

An increasing number of companies are incorporating humor into their advertising. This tactic doesn't always work because everyone has a different sense of humor. Some consumers may find it insulting. While using humor in ads is risky, if done right, it can be quite effective. When using humor in advertising, it works best for products and services to which everyone can relate. CareerBuilder.com used humor effectively in its advertising campaign that showed a young businessman who was stuck in a job he didn't like working with "monkeys," who represented incompetent coworkers. Many people can relate to this situation. Humor also worked well in the Snickers® advertising campaign that stressed, "you're not you when you're hungry," and reminded viewers that Snickers satisfies hunger. Again, all consumers know what it's like when hunger suddenly strikes. Humorous advertising that resonates with the mass market can improve brand recognition.

Work as a Team

Discuss three humorous commercials you have seen on television. Was humor used effectively? Why or why not?

© Knartz/Shutterstock.com

Market Segmentation vs. Mass Marketing

A *market segment* is a subgroup of individuals within a larger market who share one or more characteristics. Because individuals in a market segment share similar characteristics, they tend to purchase similar products and services. All individuals are members of multiple market segments based on the type of music they listen to, the type of clothing they wear, the type of sporting events they enjoy, and where they live. Some businesses use the opposite approach to market segmentation—mass marketing.

Market Segmentation and Target Markets

Market segmentation is the process of dividing a large group of consumers into meaningful subgroups based on identifiable and similar characteristics and needs. Businesses rely on market research and marketing information to identify market segments. The market segments are analyzed, and a target market is selected. Market segmentation enables a business to develop marketing strategies that meet the needs of one or more target markets.

As an example, an automobile insurance company could use the market segmentation process to identify a target market. First, the insurer should consider all drivers as potential customers. Segments then can be identified based on the location of the drivers, their driving records, their age, and the types of coverage needed. After identifying several segments, the insurer should study needs, attitudes, and trends related to the different market segments. After all information is analyzed, the insurer can identify the segment(s) offering the best market opportunities. The identified segments become the target markets for the insurer.

There are many advantages of market segmentation. By customizing a marketing mix based on the needs of a specific market, customer satisfaction rises, leading to increased profits. This helps offset the higher marketing costs associated with the market segmentation process. Businesses that focus on a specific market have a competitive advantage over larger businesses that use a mass marketing approach.

Mass Marketing

Mass marketing is an attempt to appeal to a large, general group of consumers. A company that uses market segmentation focuses its efforts on a specific group of consumers with unique needs. A company that uses mass marketing directs its efforts to the whole market in order to reach the largest number of consumers. Businesses that are unable or unwilling to spend the time and money required to conduct research and analyze data to identify market segments may choose to use mass marketing. Mass marketing is more commonly used for products and services that everyone tends to buy, such as soap, snacks, and household cleaners.

There are some benefits of mass marketing. The business can reach a larger audience, gain

When might a business use mass marketing to sell its products or services?

wider exposure, increase sales volume, and lower marketing costs. However, success for a business using mass marketing becomes more difficult because there are numerous businesses competing for the same consumers' dollars. Mass marketing involves developing one marketing mix for all consumers, which can by risky when trying to appeal to a diverse group of customers with different needs.

Mass marketing can be effective for large companies that have high volumes of production and that sell to domestic and international markets. Smaller or more specialized businesses have better success using market segmentation.

CHECKPOINT

What is the difference between market segmentation and mass marketing approaches?

Customer Profile: Types of Segmentation

A market segment consists of individuals with similar characteristics. Characteristics marketers use to segment markets include one or more of the following: geography, demographics, psychographics, product usage, and benefit expectations. Marketers can examine various segmentation data to build a customer profile. A **customer profile** is a description of the characteristics exhibited by an individual who is likely to buy a business's products or services. By learning as much as possible about the customer, a business can develop a product or service that will meet specific wants and needs. This helps build customer relationships and customer loyalty.

Geographic Segmentation

Geographic segmentation is based on where consumers live. Market segments could consist of a particular zip code, section of the country, or part of the world. This form of segmentation believes that individuals who live in the same geographic area might have the same wants and needs. The climate of a region has a major impact on buying behavior. Consumers who live in Montana are more likely to be interested in snowmobiles than those who live in Florida. Food choices and recreational activities are other aspects that vary by region of the country. Politicians campaign based on particular topics of interest in certain cities and states. Marketers

How does geography affect the sale of products and services?

adjust their marketing and product mixes based on geographical preferences of customers.

Demographic Segmentation

Demographics include consumer characteristics such as age, gender, race, marital status, income, education level, and occupation. Types of music, housing, restaurant menus, and automobiles are developed to meet the needs and wants of different demographics. Demographics offer an abundance of useful information about consumers.

Today marketers commonly segment markets by age. *Generational marketing* defines consumers by age but also considers their social and economic backgrounds and lifestyles to create a more accurate picture of the target market. Age categories used for marketing purposes include tweens, teens, Generation Y (young adults), Generation X (adults), baby boomers, and seniors. *Cohort marketing* takes generational marketing a step further by targeting people who underwent the same experiences and events while growing up. The theory is that people will have similar characteristics because of shared experiences. For example, people who grew up in the 70s may be more free-spirited and open to change than other generations.

Gender and income are other important influences on marketing decisions. In the typical American family, women handle the family's finances and make most of the purchases. Businesses have responded by placing more focus on women when developing and marketing products. Income level determines buying power. Businesses use marketing strategies that appeal to low-income, middle-income, or high-income consumers.

Psychographic Segmentation

Psychographics describe consumers based on their interests, attitudes, opinions, and lifestyles. Psychographics focus attention on the way people spend their time and the motives behind their actions. Lifestyles and social interests influence the types of products and services offered to a market segment. An indoor rock climbing facility caters to adventure-seeking enthusiasts. Downtown housing developments market to young professionals who want to live and work in the heart of the city.

Product brand and performance are critical issues when considering psychographic segmentation. Starbucks is a highly recognized brand that is associated with a certain lifestyle. When customers go to Starbucks, it's not just about coffee. Customers go there to relax, work, and socialize.

NETBookmark

When marketers know the demographic and psychographic characteristics of their target audience, their messages can be targeted more effectively. Marketing-information resources company Claritas provides demographic and psychographic information for any residential zip code in the United States. Access www.cengage.com/school/advertising and click on the link for Chapter 3. Click on the *Zip Code Look-Up* link and enter the zip code 40472. (Use the PRIZM segmentation system.) Describe the demographic and psychographic characteristics of the people in that community.

www.cengage.com/school/advertising

Information about the lifestyle of a target market is valuable for creating advertisements that connect with consumers. Very different marketing and advertising strategies are needed to appeal to different psychographic segments.

Product Usage Segmentation

Product usage refers to the amount of a product purchased and used. Product usage information can help determine the value of a market segment. Consumers may be first-time users, light users, or heavy users. Marketers focus their attention on heavy users and try to change first-time and light users into heavy users. Heavy users are often loyal to the brand, which is encouraged in product advertising. In addition to how frequently a product is purchased and used, businesses need to consider the quantity of the product used at one time. There may be a need for different package sizes. Laundry detergent is sold in a variety of sizes based on the number of loads that can be washed per container.

Product usage is rewarded through customer loyalty programs that offer special pricing and deals only to loyalty program members. Airlines and hotels often design special marketing mixes that appeal to frequent flyers or hotel guests.

Benefit Segmentation

Benefit segmentation groups consumers based on specific benefits they expect to receive from a product or service. Benefit segmentation focuses on the consumers' needs and wants more than any other type of segmentation. Think of the wide variety of toothpastes. Each brand of toothpaste meets different consumer expectations, from whiter teeth, to fewer cavities, to fresher breath. Benefit segmentation can be used to create effective advertisements that focus on the benefits desired by selected target markets.

CHECKPOINT

How are psychographics useful to marketers?

Selection of Market Segments

Although there are differences among consumers, they often have similar needs, preferences, and buying behaviors. Market segmentation groups consumers based on these similarities. This allows a business to gain a better understanding of a specific market and its potential customers, which results in the development of a more effective marketing mix. Because of the importance of market segmentation, a business must make an effort to identify market segments and analyze their potential.

Identifying Market Segments

A business must identify market segments and target markets before it can create an effective marketing mix that will reach customers. Steps for identifying market segments are as follows:

1. *Select a market or product category to study.* The *market* is a large group of consumers who have an interest in a particular product or service. It may be a market or product category in which the business already has experience, or it could be a new one that the business wants to explore.

2. *Choose a basis for segmenting the market.* Determine the needs of the consumers in the market identified in Step 1. Think about the factors that would influence a buying decision. Consider why consumers would buy your product or service.

3. *Collect and analyze data.* This stage will require extensive marketing research about consumer buying behavior and buying motives.

4. *Identify market segments.* Based on your research, begin narrowing the market into market segments. Group consumers who have similar characteristics and needs based on geography, demographics, psychographics, product usage, or benefit expectations.

5. *Select the market segments with the most potential.* Conduct further research and analysis on the market segments having the highest potential and then select the target market(s).

What basis or bases could a restaurant use for segmenting the market?

© Creatas/Jupiter Images

Analyzing Market Potential

Although there are many market segments that a business could target, it must identify the one that offers the most potential. *Market potential* is based on profitability. Factors that determine whether a market segment has strong potential include the following:

1. The market segment is measurable. Geographic, demographic, and psychographic data are readily available for analysis.

2. The business is capable of producing a product or service at a price that meets customers' wants and needs.

3. The market segment must have many potential customers and the potential for growth.

4. The market segment is accessible. There are specific advertising media, such as magazines or websites, that the target audience likes to use, making potential customers easy to reach.

5. The business can serve the market segment more effectively than competitors can.

Even if a business determines that it can serve the market more effectively than its competitors can, it is highly unlikely that the business will capture all the customers in the market. Businesses must estimate their market share. **Market share** is a business's portion of the total sales generated by all of the businesses operating in the same market. For example, if data indicate that total sales for lawn care services in your city are $1,650,000 a year and a new lawn care company estimates that it can capture 15 percent of the market, it would earn $247,500 ($1,650,000 × 15%). Based on this estimate, the lawn care company would have to determine whether it would make a profit. Would sales exceed expenses? Company goals often include market share projections because they provide an effective way to measure how well the business is performing in the market.

 **CHECKPOINT**

What steps are involved in identifying a market segment?

3.3 Assessment

THINK ABOUT IT

1. What product or service could use a mass marketing strategy? Explain why.
2. Why should businesses pay attention to the demographics of an aging population?
3. If you are going to open a new business in your community, why should you consider market potential and market share?
4. What is a customer profile and why is it important?

MAKE ACADEMIC CONNECTIONS

5. **ECONOMICS**   Choose your favorite automobile. Then conduct research to determine what market share this automobile (or the automobile manufacturer) has in the United States. Write a paragraph explaining how you think the automobile manufacturer could increase its market share.
6. **MARKETING**   You are opening a new bowling alley in your neighborhood. Identify two specific market segments based on demographic and psychographic characteristics that you will target in your marketing efforts. Using visual aids, present your marketing plan to the class.

 Teamwork

Conduct research to determine the psychographic characteristics of students who attend your school. Create a short survey to collect this data. Then prepare a Power-Point presentation that explains your research findings. Describe the most common psychographic characteristics shared by the group of students you surveyed.

Sharpen Your 21st CENTURY SKILLS

Communicating in the Technological Age

While technology has opened up numerous opportunities in the world of communication, it has been associated with improper business etiquette. Individuals spend more time communicating using electronic devices than they do using personal, face-to-face communication. The use of cell phones and other text messaging devices has resulted in diminished communication skills. Proper business writing has suffered as a result of text messaging. Abbreviations used for text messages are not acceptable for business communications. Business leaders still expect employees to produce documents that incorporate proper grammar, sentence structure, and flow. Leaders must be able to carry on a formal conversation at a business meeting or lunch.

Individuals who want to make an impact with the top leaders in the business world must practice communication etiquette. Communication etiquette involves respecting the feelings of other people, paying careful attention to a conversation, making eye contact, and turning off electronic devices during meetings. By text messaging or scrolling through information on electronic devices while attending a business meeting, you are sending a message that the other person is not important. Manners do make a big difference when aspiring to leadership positions. Some tips for effective communication include the following:

1. Give your cell phone a break. Turn it off during a business meeting, family gathering, or meal. Show respect for your guest or business associate.
2. Compose written documents using proper grammar and format. Always use the spell check feature and then proof the document to make sure that it is grammatically correct.
3. Practice being a great listener. Give your full attention to the other person through eye contact and respectful feedback. Do not let electronic devices break down the communication process.

Try It Out

For one week, set aside time each day in which you refrain from using your cell phone or other electronic devices. During this time, communicate with someone face to face or by writing a letter. Keep a record of your communications. At the end of the week, describe how your "new" ways of communicating differed from your usual ways of communicating. Did you find that your communication had improved over the past week? Why or why not?

PARTNERSHIP FOR 21st CENTURY SKILLS

© Chris_Granados/Shutterstock.com

Chapter 3 Review

3.1 The Marketing Concept

- Marketing involves all of the processes used to identify, create, and maintain exchange relationships that satisfy individuals and organizations.
- The marketing concept is used by businesses today to focus on how to deliver a product or service that has value for customers. At one time, businesses were product-oriented, meaning they were more concerned about producing products efficiently and profitably and less concerned about customers' needs.
- The marketing mix is the blending of the product, price, distribution (place), and promotion used by a business to sell products and services.
- Marketing functions include market planning, product and service management, distribution, pricing, promotion, selling, marketing-information management, financing, and risk management.

3.2 The Target Market

- Every business has a specific group of consumers (target market) to which it wants to sell its products or services.
- Businesses can follow several target market strategies, including the undifferentiated strategy (one big market), concentrated strategy (niche markets), and multiple-segment strategy (two or more markets).
- Effective target markets have common needs that can be satisfied with a product or service, are able to afford the product or service, and have a high demand for the product or service.

3.3 Market Segmentation

- Market segmentation involves dividing a market into subgroups of individuals who share one or more characteristics. Mass marketing focuses on the whole market and aims to reach the largest number of consumers.
  - Five common categories for segmenting markets include geography, demographics, psychographics, product usage, and benefit expectations.
  - Market segments must be identified and analyzed for market potential (profitability). Steps involved in identifying market segments include: (1) select a market to study, (2) choose a basis for segmenting, (3) collect and analyze data, (4) identify market segments, (5) select market segments that have the most potential.

Read *Impact Advertising* on page 61 again to review the marketing strategies used by Starbucks. Conduct research to learn more about Starbucks' latest marketing strategies. Is the company using more social networking strategies? How is Starbucks competing with competitors like McDonald's that want a larger market share of the coffee business?

Vocabulary Builder

Match each statement with the term that best defines it. Some terms may not be used.

1. Related activities that must be completed to accomplish an important marketing goal
2. A strategy used to plan, execute, and monitor all promotional messages to ensure consistency
3. A written description of the marketing objectives and the planned marketing strategies and activities required to meet those objectives
4. Specific group of consumers to whom the business wants to sell products or services
5. An attempt to appeal to a large, general group of consumers
6. Dividing a large group of consumers into meaningful subgroups based on identifiable and similar characteristics and needs
7. A smaller market that has unique needs

a. benefit segmentation
b. customer profile
c. demographics
d. geographic segmentation
e. integrated marketing communication (IMC)
f. market segmentation
g. market share
h. marketing
i. marketing concept
j. marketing functions
k. marketing mix
l. marketing plan
m. mass marketing
n. niche market
o. product usage
p. psychographics
q. target market

8. A description of the characteristics exhibited by an individual who is likely to buy a business's product or service
9. Product, price, distribution, and promotion
10. Consumer characteristics based on interests, attitudes, opinions, and lifestyles

Test Your Knowledge

11. _____ involves all of the processes used to identify, create, and maintain satisfying exchange relationships.
    a. Marketing
    b. Promotion
    c. Distribution
    d. Customer service
12. The marketing concept uses the needs of _____ for the planning, production, pricing, distribution, and promotion of products and services.
    a. government
    b. business
    c. customers
    d. society
13. Consumer demand is influenced by which of the following factors?
    a. price
    b. promotion
    c. economy
    d. all of the above

14. Which of the following marketing functions involves identifying target markets and developing an effective marketing strategy?
    a. financing
    b. promotion
    c. market planning
    d. risk management
15. ____ marketing targets consumers who underwent the same experiences and events while growing up.
    a. Cohort
    b. Generational
    c. Mass
    d. Target
16. Consumer characteristics that include age, gender, race, marital status, income, education level, and occupation are classified as
    a. geographics
    b. demographics
    c. psychographics
    d. none of the above
17. A business that concentrates on meeting the needs of a narrowly defined market segment is using which target market strategy?
    a. undifferentiated strategy
    b. multiple-segment strategy
    c. concentrated strategy
    d. IMC strategy
18. Product usage focuses on
    a. how frequently a product is purchased
    b. how many features a product has
    c. the amount of product used
    d. both a and c
19. ____ can be based upon zip codes throughout the country.
    a. Geographics
    b. Demographics
    c. Psychographics
    d. Product usage
20. ____ is a business's portion of the total sales generated by all of the businesses operating in the same market.
    a. Market opportunity
    b. Market strategy
    c. Market potential
    d. Market share

Apply What You Learned

21. Choose a product that you purchase frequently. Using each of the five market segmentation categories (geography, demographics, psychographics, product usage, benefit expectations) develop a customer profile for the product.
22. The marketing concept uses the needs of customers as the primary focus during the planning, production, pricing, distribution, and promotion of a product or service. Select either a restaurant, supermarket, or airline and outline the best strategy for the business to use to learn about the needs of its customers.
23. For each of the three target market strategies (undifferentiated, concentrated, and multiple-segment), describe a business or product that uses it. Explain how the strategy used could affect the marketing mix of the business.

Make Academic Connections

24. **RESEARCH** Conduct Internet research to learn about popular retirement communities in the United States (examples: Sun City and Robson Ranch in Arizona). List five major benefits

that the retirement communities are promoting to their target markets.

25. **MATH**   A city has a population of 1.5 million people with average annual auto sales of $95 million. An automobile dealership in the community wants to direct its marketing efforts to 30 percent of the population. How many people is the automobile dealership trying to reach with its marketing campaign? If the auto dealer gains 22 percent of the market share, how much will it make in sales?

26. **ECONOMICS**   Conduct research to determine the average annual income that you would earn for a selected career. What types of businesses would target individuals in your profession? What types of products or services would they try to sell you? How might businesses target your income level?

27. **GEOGRAPHY**   Describe how geographic segmentation could be used by businesses that want to sell products and services in the part of the country in which you live. Compile a list of products and services that you think would sell well based on the geographical needs and preferences of consumers in your area.

28. **ETHICS**   Many businesses target young children with their marketing and advertising campaigns. For example, McDonald's and Burger King often market their products to children by airing advertisements that promote toys linked to popular movies. Why do you think this type of marketing has raised concerns? Specifically, what are the ethical issues when the food industry targets children?

29. **PSYCHOLOGY**   Some consumer purchases are based on psychographic characteristics—interests, attitudes, opinions, and lifestyles. Survey five people and ask them to identify three purchases they made based on psychographic characteristics. Were there any similarities among the purchases? Describe them.

You are the marketer for a home security business that sells a variety of home security devices, such as surveillance systems, alarms, and motion detector lighting systems. The owner of the business would like you to develop a new advertising campaign that targets senior citizens in affluent neighborhoods. He wants the ads to suggest that the city's crime rate is at an all-time high. The business owner explains to you that fear tactics should be used to persuade senior citizens that their only line of defense against rising crime rates is a complete home security system. He even suggests creating an ad based on a fictitious story about a senior citizen who was attacked in her home in a nearby neighborhood. The ad's tagline would be "Don't let this happen to you!"

What Would YOU DO ?

As the marketer for this business, what would you do? Do you agree with the business owner's methods for targeting senior citizens? Why or why not? What marketing strategy do you think would be more appropriate?

Reality ✓

The Mass Marketing of Valentine's Day

Valentine's Day is a dream come true for retailers. Consumers are willing to spend large sums of money on jewelry, flowers, candy, clothing, spa visits, and fine dining to celebrate Valentine's Day. As a marketing ploy, supermarkets set up tents in the parking lot to sell floral arrangements, making it quick and easy for customers to buy last-minute gifts. Even products that are not traditionally associated with Valentine's Day may be heavily promoted during this holiday in hopes of capturing some of the market share. For example, a golf course sent out advertisements to club members promoting "a Valentine of a golf deal." Mars, Inc., promotes a romance gift box containing personalized M&Ms® for the special day.

According to a recent survey conducted by Price Grabber®, the most popular Valentine's Day purchase for 62 percent of female shoppers was greeting cards. Forty-two percent of female shoppers spent money on an evening out, and 26 percent bought candy on Valentine's Day. The most popular purchase on Valentine's Day for 53 percent of male shoppers was an evening out. Forty-five percent of male respondents purchased greeting cards, 45 percent purchased flowers, and 18 percent bought candy on Valentine's Day. Products in these categories are heavily advertised to remind consumers of the important day. Businesses reap the benefits as customers rush out to buy gifts, often at inflated prices.

Many people argue that the romance of Valentine's Day has been damaged by mass marketing. They believe the holiday is now dominated by stores and advertisements. Because of expansive advertising campaigns, many people now feel obligated to buy expensive gifts for their loved ones. Advertising has also encouraged consumers to buy gifts and cards for friends, not just for loved ones. There's no question that Valentine's Day presents market opportunities for businesses that can persuade consumers to buy their product for that special someone.

Think Critically

1. Describe three market segments for Valentine's Day gifts.
2. Explain how psychographics influences purchases for Valentine's Day.
3. Why is the marketing mix important for products that are traditionally sold as gifts for holidays?
4. How can businesses benefit from the mass marketing of holidays?

Buying and Merchandising Team Event

This Team Decision Making Event provides an opportunity for you to analyze one or a combination of elements essential to the effective operation of a business in a specific occupational area. Employees in buying and merchandising positions get the product into the hands of the customer. This process includes forecasting, planning, buying, displaying, selling, and providing customer service.

PROBLEM Your team works for a large department store in a city with 500,000 people. Each season your buying team is challenged to select clothing styles that will sell well even without markdowns. A recession has greatly affected consumer spending. Designer brands are not selling until they are marked down 50 percent. Your team must determine a strategy to purchase the appropriate amount of merchandise during slow economic conditions. You must also determine which famous designer brands will sell during this recession. You must explain your purchasing strategy and markdown strategy to move the seasonal clothing. The plan must outline how long the merchandise will be offered at the full retail price and when the percentage discounts will be applied to clear out seasonal merchandise.

Participants must demonstrate the following skills when completing this project:

- communications skills—the ability to exchange information and ideas with others through writing, speaking, reading or listening
- analytical skills—the ability to derive facts from data, findings from facts, conclusions from findings, and recommendations from conclusions
- critical thinking/problem-solving skills
- production skills—the ability to take a concept from an idea and make it real
- teamwork—the ability to be an effective member of a productive group
- priorities/time management—the ability to determine priorities and manage time commitments

Go to the DECA website for more detailed information.

Think Critically

1. Why are promotions so important for a retail business?
2. How can a buyer for a clothing store determine what to purchase for the upcoming fall season?
3. When buying merchandise for a business, what are the main concerns for the buying department?
4. What is a merchandising trend that you have noticed in one of your favorite stores?

www.deca.org

4

Product and Price Planning

4.1 Product Development

4.2 Product Life Cycle

4.3 Price Planning

"Just for the Taste of It"

Diet Coke® was launched in 1982. After only one year on the market, it grew to become the largest-selling, low-calorie soft drink in the United States. Diet Coke was introduced in many other countries as Coca-Cola Light. By 1986, Diet Coke was the most popular low-calorie beverage in the world. Almost 30 years later, Diet Coke is still going strong.

By 1980, research indicated that nearly 20 percent of the population was drinking diet soft drinks. At the same time, fitness and diet fads were on the rise. Coca-Cola recognized an opportunity to break into the sugar-free soft drink market. Diet Coke was introduced with a $100 million advertising campaign and a launch party at Radio City Music Hall in New York.

Since its inception, Diet Coke has expanded its product line by introducing many other flavors, including Diet Cherry Coke, Diet Vanilla Coke, Diet Coke with Lemon, and Diet Black Cherry Vanilla Coke. After learning that consumers liked the taste of SPLENDA® Brand Sweetener, which is a no-calorie sweetener that tastes like sugar, Diet Coke with SPLENDA® Brand Sweetener was launched in 2005. Customers were offered another alternative in 2007 when Diet Coke Plus hit the market. It contains vitamins B3, B6, and B12 and the minerals zinc and magnesium. Coca-Cola continues to offer diet colas to satisfy consumers' refreshment needs.

Diet Coke advertising campaigns have been associated with memorable themes and celebrities. In 1987, Diet Coke ads encouraged people around the world to drink Diet Coke "just for the taste of it." Paula Abdul and Elton John teamed up in popular television commercials in the 90s to sing about their love of Diet Coke.

More recently, Diet Coke has partnered with Heidi Klum and the National Heart, Lung, and Blood Institute (NHLBI) in a national heart health awareness campaign called The Heart Truth®. The Heart Truth campaign has helped raise awareness about heart disease in women. The Heart Truth campaign celebrates healthy lifestyle choices, which have become increasingly important to Diet Coke consumers. One of the tips from NHLBI is to maintain a healthy weight. Since Diet Coke has zero calories and tastes great, Coca-Cola believes that it is an excellent choice for managing calorie intake. The Heart Truth's Red Dress logo appears on more than 6 billion packages of Diet Coke throughout the year.

Coca-Cola continues to develop advertising strategies that differentiate Diet Coke from all of the other diet soft drinks on the market. By doing so, it aspires to remain the leader in the diet soft drink industry.

1. **What has contributed to the success of Diet Coke?**

2. **Why do you think Coca-Cola continues to invest heavily in advertising when Diet Coke is already ranked as the number one diet soft drink?**

3. **How does it benefit Diet Coke to be involved with a major health awareness campaign?**

WHAT DO YOU KNOW?

Product Development

Goals
- Identify the stages of new product development.
- Explain the various levels of products and the components that make up the product mix.

Terms
- product mix, p. 95
- product line, p. 96
- trademark, p. 97
- licensed brand, p. 98

FOCUS ON ADVERTISING

Getting Product Ideas from Customers

One of Baskin-Robbins' newest ice cream flavors was not developed in the ice cream icon's test kitchen. It was invented by a 62-year-old grandmother of four, Diana Sroga, who entered her idea in an online contest. Sroga was one of 40,000 consumers who competed in the online contest to create the chain's newest flavor. Her Bunches of Crunches, which was renamed Toffee Pecan Crunch, was the winning entry. Marketers are finding ways to involve consumers in the product planning process. Because usage of the Internet is at an all-time high, marketers are developing online product promotions that tap into the talents of social-media-savvy consumers. Mountain Dew let consumers get involved in the design of its new bottles and cans. Recently, Lands' End let kids design T-shirts that it sold online. By giving consumers a say in the product, companies are building customer relationships while learning about consumer interests.

© M. Unal Ozmen/Shutterstock.com

Work as a Team Why are companies willing to give consumers some control over the product planning process? Do you think this is a good strategy? Why or why not?

It Starts with a Product

When creating a marketing mix, a business usually starts with the product. A *product* is a good or service produced and sold to consumers or other businesses. The product must be useful to customers and satisfy their needs. There are many existing products on the market. Successful products are the result of careful research and study of target markets. The product development process often starts with a new product.

New Products

A "new product" can mean different things to different people. A product can be brand new, meaning it is the first of its kind. For example, when first introduced, the television set was a brand new product. Nothing like it had existed before. There are very few brand new products. Most new products involve changes and improvements to existing products. However, the change must be significant to be classified as a "new product." Laundry detergents once were sold only in powdered form. Eventually, "new" laundry detergents were offered in liquid and concentrated forms.

When products that have been sold in specific markets enter new markets, they are often classified as "new." A business that has had success with a product in its home country may decide to sell the product globally. Microfiber cleaning products had achieved success throughout Europe and Asia before finally being introduced in the United States. Now microfiber cleaning products, such as the Swiffer® line of mops and cloths, are popular among consumers.

Finally, discovering a new use for an existing product can result in a "new product" for new markets. Baking soda has been used throughout history as an ingredient in baked goods. ARM & HAMMER® baking soda has been manufactured since the mid 1800s. In 1972, ARM & HAMMER began promoting its baking soda as a deodorizer to combat odors and keep foods fresh in the refrigerator and freezer. In 1999, it started selling Fridge-n-Freezer® boxes of baking soda. Since then, ARM & HAMMER has developed many new products that use baking soda as the active ingredient, including carpet and cat litter deodorizers, toothpaste, and laundry detergent.

Stages of New Product Planning

Companies understand the importance of identifying and developing new products. Because the introduction of a new product to the market is expensive, it is important to filter out products that are unlikely to succeed. When developing a new product, the business must specify the characteristics of the product and identify how those characteristics will meet the needs of the target market. Typically, there are six stages in the product development process.

Generate Ideas Finding ideas for new products is the most difficult stage in new product planning. Ideas come from many sources. They often originate from problems that customers have that cannot be solved with products that are currently on the market. New products are developed to meet consumer needs. Businesses must gather information from consumers and involve them in the development process. Many businesses organize consumer panels that meet regularly to generate ideas for new products. Social networking sites are being used more frequently to encourage customer feedback.

Other sources of ideas include employees. Attentive salespeople often get ideas for products through their interactions with customers. Many businesses reward their employees for new product ideas. Brainstorming sessions with employees can produce an unlimited number of ideas. Competitors are another source of ideas. Monitoring competitors' products can provide valuable product information.

How are new product ideas screened?

Screen Ideas After new product ideas have been identified, the second stage of the product planning process involves carefully screening the ideas. Businesses must reject ideas that are not workable for any reason. They should determine which ideas have the greatest potential for success. Factors to consider during the screening process include the following:

- sales and profit potential
- production costs and time
- legal and safety issues
- competition

The screening process may also involve getting consumer reactions to proposed products. The feedback can be used to rate alternative ideas.

Prepare a Business Analysis Product ideas that survive the screening process will move on to the next stage—the business analysis. The business analysis is a much more detailed study of some of the factors examined in the product screening process. It is used to determine the size of the market, costs of production and marketing, and sales and profit projections. Market research plays an important role in this stage because markets, competition, and costs must be studied. A business must determine if it can manufacture a product at an acceptable cost that will enable it to make a profit. Computer models and spreadsheets are used by businesses to analyze best-case and worst-case scenarios for the launch of a new product. After the analysis is performed, the business must decide if the new product fits with the company's overall goals and profit objectives.

Develop a Marketing Strategy When a business determines that a product idea is realistic, a sample marketing strategy is created. Research is conducted during this stage to identify a target market and to ensure there is a demand for the product. Marketers should decide on the product's packaging, branding, and labeling. They should also develop a strategy for the other marketing mix components—promotion, price, and distribution. The marketing mix must be evaluated to determine if it meets the needs of the proposed target market and if the company can implement the mix effectively.

Develop and Test the Product If research and analysis indicate that a product idea has a good chance of success, it will enter the development stage. The development stage can take many years and can be very expensive. The production process often involves many team members, including researchers, marketers, engineers, and production employees. All team members lend their knowledge and expertise throughout the various product development stages.

A business faces a great deal of risk if the product is poorly designed. If the product does not perform as expected, consumers will return it for a refund and lose confidence in the business. Businesses must study how consumers will use the product to meet their expectations. They must also design the product to avoid any risk of injury to those who use the product.

Businesses may develop a prototype or model for products. The prototype can alert a business to potential risks such as quality and cost issues before full-scale production of the product begins. Businesses also use a test market to determine if the product will be successful. A limited quantity of the new product is introduced to potential customers, and their reactions are recorded and evaluated. Based on the test marketing, businesses may choose to end production or change the product.

Market the Product Introduction of the new product into the market is the final stage of the product planning process. This stage requires extensive preparation. All of the marketing mix components must be carefully planned. Manufacturers must produce the product, transportation companies must ship the product, wholesalers must store the product, advertising agencies must promote the product, and retailers must sell the product. The activities and schedules of all of these participants must be coordinated. Marketers must continually study the market. Changing economic conditions, competitors' products, and consumer trends can make it necessary to adjust the marketing strategy.

▨▨▨▨▨ CHECKPOINT ◤◤◤◤◤

What are the six stages in the new product planning process?

Product Mix

Most businesses sell more than one type of product. The **product mix**, or product assortment, includes all of the different products a business sells. For example, Paul Mitchell® sells a wide array of shampoos, conditioners, and other hair care products. Together, all of these products make up Paul Mitchell's product mix.

Product Levels

A business's product mix often begins with a *basic product*. Consumers are familiar with the basic product and know how it meets their needs. The basic product is very similar to products offered by competitors. A computer is an example of a basic product.

A business may try to meet the needs of several target markets by enhancing its basic product. An *enhanced product* includes features and options that increase the usefulness of a product. A computer can be manufactured with more gigabytes of memory, faster processing

Is there a difference between a basic MP3 player and an iPod? Millions of satisfied iPod users would answer with a resounding, "Yes!" Access www.cengage.com/school/advertising and click on the link for Chapter 4. View Apple's iPod page. How many different kinds of iPods does Apple sell? How are they different from one another? (*Hint:* Try the *Compare iPod models* link.) Which iPod would you characterize as the "basic product"? Why? If you were buying a new iPod, which would best meet your needs? Explain.

www.cengage.com/school/advertising

speeds (gigahertz), and a larger monitor to meet the various needs of consumers. Other types of enhancements may involve levels of quality, design, and colors.

A business may try to increase customer satisfaction by offering an *extended product*. An extended product may be in the form of services or complementary products. Guarantees, warranties, product usage recommendations, and additional products that improve the use of the primary product can help the customer get the most value from his or her purchase. Special financing offers, free delivery and installation, and repair services can make a purchase more enhancing. When selling a laptop computer to a customer who makes numerous PowerPoint presentations, the sales associate might suggest the purchase of a remote mouse that enables the speaker to move around the room while changing PowerPoint slides during the presentation. Free technical support might also be very appealing to customers.

Product Mix Components

Whether a business offers only one product or an assortment of products, there are three things it must consider when developing its product mix—the product line, package and label, and brand.

How can a business that produces only one product offer a product line to consumers?

Product Line As a business grows, it likely will expand into other markets and develop a product line to attract more customers. The **product line** is a group of closely related products with slight variations developed by the same business. A business that manufactures dinnerware may offer a wide array of colors, levels of quality, and prices. A soup manufacturer offers different kinds of soups and sizes of soups in its product line. By adding items to their product line, businesses are able to meet more consumer needs, thus increasing their number of potential customers.

Product lines are developed in different ways. For a business that offers only one product, offering different product sizes is an easy way to expand its product line. A shampoo manufacturer could offer a travel size, economy size, or family size bottle of its shampoo. Offering different levels of quality is another way to develop product lines. Carpet is classified as good, better, and best. Consumers who want carpet for high-traffic areas can purchase the high-quality carpet for longer wear. Other consumers who are more concerned about price may purchase the lower-quality carpet.

Product lines can have width and depth. The width refers to the number of product lines a business offers. A shampoo manufacturer may have three product lines—shampoo, conditioner, and styling products. The depth of a product line refers to the number of product items within the product line. The shampoo product line may have shampoos for dry, normal, or oily hair. By increasing the width and depth of its product lines, a business can potentially increase sales and profits by targeting different market segments. On the other hand, offering a wider product line adds to the cost of manufacturing, distribution, inventory control, and other related marketing activities.

Package and Label Most products are sold in a package. The two main functions of the package are protection and promotion. There is a risk of damage to the product as it is shipped and stored. Packages should protect the product. Packages also should use designs, colors, and shapes to attract consumers' attention and differentiate products from competitors' products.

Improving the use of a product is another function of product packaging. Consumers prefer easy-to-open packages with pour spouts, screw-on tops, zipper tear strips, and hinged lids. Safety and protection factors have led many businesses to switch from glass containers to plastic containers. Pharmaceutical companies package their products in childproof containers.

Another function of packaging that has become more essential is protecting the environment. Environmental concerns have resulted in eco-friendly packaging. Many manufacturers are using recycled and biodegradable packaging materials.

The label, which contains information about the product, is an important part of the package. The label has two functions—promotion and distribution of information. The product's brand name and logo are prominently displayed on the label. But the label also contains product information such as ingredients and care instructions. This information helps consumers make better buying decisions.

Brand A *brand* is the combination of unique qualities of a company, product, or product line. It is the main way businesses differentiate their products from competitors' products. Individuals are loyal to clothing, automobiles, soft drinks, restaurants, and a wide array of other brands. **A trademark** grants a business the exclusive right to use a brand

© Michal Skowronski/Shutterstock.com

Do you have a favorite brand of gym shoes? Why do you prefer this brand?

name, symbol, or design. Others cannot use the elements of a brand without permission. A **licensed brand** is a well-known brand owned by one company that is sold for use by another company. Universal Studios licenses the use of character names and images for products ranging from toys to clothing. Celebrities license their names for use on perfumes and colognes.

Businesses use brands to help create awareness of their products and to increase the likelihood of a sale. Consumers often consider the brand when making a buying decision. Branding helps consumers identify the products they want to buy again. Building brand loyalty among consumers is important to the success of a business.

CHECKPOINT

Describe the three different levels of a product.

4.1 Assessment

THINK ABOUT IT

1. Why would a business license the use of its brand to another business? Give an example of a licensed brand.

2. Why is it important to perform a business analysis when planning a new product?

3. Select a product that you regularly purchase and recommend ways to improve the packaging and labeling.

MAKE ACADEMIC CONNECTIONS

4. **CONSUMER RESEARCH**   TV home improvement shows have contributed to the success of home improvement stores like Home Depot and Lowes. Survey people who regularly shop at home improvement stores to find out what products they believe have simplified DIY (do-it-yourself) projects around the home. Then describe a new product idea that you believe would have good potential in the DIY market.

5. **COMMUNICATION**   List a basic product that you use frequently. Describe the enhanced version(s) of this product. Recommend two additional enhancements that could be made to this product to meet your needs. Write a letter to the product manufacturer describing your product enhancement recommendations.

6. **HISTORY**   Conduct research on a well-known business that offers several product lines. Create a chart that lists the company's product line width and depth. For each product in the product line, describe how it is unique from the others in the product line.

Teamwork

Working as a team, brainstorm ideas for a new product for teenagers. After the brainstorming session, screen the ideas and narrow them down to one. Present your new product idea to the class and explain why you think there will be a demand for it among teenagers.

4.2

Product Life Cycle

Goals

- Explain the stages of the product life cycle.
- Describe real-world applications of the product life cycle.

Terms

- product life cycle, p. 99
- brand extension, p. 100
- intensive distribution, p. 101
- obsolescence, p. 102

FOCUS ON ADVERTISING

Shifting to Online Advertising Strategies

Traditionally, advertisements for high-end designer clothing have appeared in magazines such as *Vogue*, *GQ*, and *Elle*. Today many clothing designers are turning to the Internet to advertise. French-brand Lacoste™, known for its crocodile logo and polo shirts, is dropping print ads and switching completely to an online strategy in the United States, spending $12 million a year for online advertisements. Making the switch to online advertising is a big shift for a company that relied on traditional advertising for more than 30 years. Lacoste realized that its largest market segment (18- to 34-year-olds) no longer relies on magazines to learn about the latest fashion trends. By placing ads on Facebook and Hulu, Lacoste is reaching tech-savvy customers. In addition, during a recession when budget cuts are necessary, premium brands like Lacoste are recognizing the cost advantages of online advertising. Only 33 percent of luxury brands advertised online in 2008. That number increased to 66 percent in 2009.

Work as a Team Why have luxury brands changed their attitude about online advertising? Do you think this is a good move? Why or why not?

The Stages of a Product

A new product goes through a sequence of stages, known as the **product life cycle**, during its time on the market. There are four stages—introduction, growth, maturity, and decline. The time spent in any one stage varies among products. Fads or trendy items move quickly through all four stages. Other products, such as microwaves, stay in the maturity stage for years. A different marketing mix is needed in each stage of the product life cycle.

© Arcady/Shutterstock.com

How can a business build product awareness for a new product?

Introduction Stage

When a new product is launched, it enters the introduction stage. A new product that is quite different from existing products will face low competition. The business must build product awareness. To do so, some businesses announce a product before it is introduced to the market. Because consumers are not familiar with the product and its benefits, sales are low during this stage. Initially, the product is distributed only to selective markets where consumers are more likely to buy the product. Because of low-sale projections, widespread distribution would be too expensive. Generally, the price of a new product is high because the business will attempt to recover its research and development costs.

Promotion costs are also typically high. Advertising is used to increase product and brand awareness. It also educates consumers about the product. Advertising may encourage consumers to be the first to own the new product. The advertising media used to communicate the message must be selected carefully. Marketers should consider the type of media (print, television, radio, or the Web) most likely to reach the target market. Promotion strategies used to create demand for the product include giving out samples or trial products.

Brand Extension Brands are often a barrier for new products trying to enter the market. Many businesses could make a new cola, but none of them would have the brand recognition that Coca-Cola has, making it difficult to gain market share. Thus, having a well-known, existing brand name can benefit a business that is trying to enter the market with a new product. **Brand extension** is a marketing strategy that allows a business to use one of its well-known brand names in a new product category. This provides immediate brand awareness for a new product. Consumers who have a favorable impression of a "parent" brand are more willing to try the brand extension than an unfamiliar brand in the same product category.

Iams™, a pet food company, successfully launched pet insurance as its brand extension. Antiques Roadshow used the brand extension strategy to introduce a line of furniture. Kellogg's®, known for its cereals, has many brand extensions, including Pop-Tarts® and Nutri-Grain® bars.

Benefits and Risks of Brand Extensions There are many benefits of brand extensions. By introducing a product under an established brand name, the business reduces its risk of failure. Brand extensions save companies money. A business can introduce new products to the market at a significantly lower cost. Advertising for the new product reinforces the consumers' perception of the parent brand. It is not uncommon for sales of the business's other products to rise after the launch of a successful brand extension.

Although brand extensions have many benefits, there are risks in using this strategy. The brand loses its identity when it is over-extended. When too many unrelated brand extensions are introduced, the brand can be damaged. Although Virgin airlines is successful, its brands of cola and blue jeans were not.

Growth Stage

If a product survives the introduction stage, it enters the growth stage. Two goals during the growth stage include gaining consumer preference and increasing sales. Sales should grow rapidly as consumers become more aware of the product and its benefits. Early users like the product, and more consumers start buying it. Product distribution is expanded to meet demand. Competitors are attracted by the sales opportunities, and they enter the market with similar products. The business and its competitors add new features and options to improve the quality and usefulness of the product. New models, multiple sizes, and different flavors are offered to enhance the basic product.

Two different pricing strategies are used during the growth stage. One strategy is to maintain high prices due to the increased demand for the product. Another strategy is to reduce prices to capture additional customers. Businesses must consider economic conditions. During a slow economy, it may be difficult to convince consumers to purchase the higher-priced original brand instead of lower-priced competitor brands.

More money is spent on promotion and advertising during the growth stage as the focus shifts from product awareness to product preference. Additional market segments are targeted to attract customers who have not tried the product. Increased promotional efforts are used to convince consumers that the original product is superior to the products offered by competitors. Advertising is also used to remind current product users why buying the business's product is a "smart choice."

Maturity Stage

Typically, maturity is the longest stage in the life cycle of a product. During the maturity stage of a product, sales continue to increase but at a slower pace than sales in the growth stage. The main goals during the maturity stage are to maintain market share and extend the product life cycle. Decreased market share is often the result of additional competition in the market. Competing products may be very similar to the original product at this point, increasing the difficulty of differentiating the product. During this stage, style modifications such as color and design are more common than function modifications such as technology upgrades.

In the maturity stage, businesses may use **intensive distribution**, which is a marketing strategy to sell a product at as many locations as possible. Consumers can find the product almost everywhere they go, including supermarkets, drug stores, and gas stations. Soft drinks are generally made available through intensive distribution.

Because of increased competition, price is an important factor during this stage. Prices among businesses are very competitive. Businesses start offering discounts and sale prices to persuade customers to buy their brand.

COOL FACT

According to a recent study by BuyingAdvice.com, the median life span of a passenger car in the United States is 9.2 years.

Heavy advertising and promotion are required during the maturity stage. Advertising and promotion emphasize product differentiation and try to build brand loyalty. Advertising encourages competitors' customers to switch to the original brand. Fast food restaurants in the maturity stage, such as McDonald's and Burger King, often run commercials to persuade consumers that their prices, portion sizes, freshness, and value are better than the competitors'.

Decline Stage

Sales drop rapidly in the decline stage of a product. This occurs because the product is no longer meeting customers' needs or consumers have found a better product. The rate of decline varies among products. Fads in the clothing industry often are short-lived and quickly reach the decline stage. Some automobile models have loyal customers and remain popular for years.

The market is shrinking during the decline stage, reducing the number of sales that can be shared among the remaining competitors. Because of low sales, businesses are unwilling to incur additional costs to make product improvements. Distribution of the product is reduced to only those markets that remain profitable. Prices are often lowered to reduce inventory of the product. Advertising and promotion efforts are reduced to a level that helps retain loyal customers.

Businesses must carefully monitor the supply of goods on hand during the decline stage. Companies must decide if products are profitable enough to continue producing them.

Marketing Strategies for the Decline Stage During the decline stage, businesses must decide whether to keep or eliminate weak products. There are several strategies businesses can follow. A business may decide to broaden the market by adding new features or by finding new uses for the product. Another option is to reduce inventory by selling the product at lower prices through secondary markets like Stein Mart®, Marshalls®, T.J. Maxx®, and outlet malls. A business may decide to reduce production and marketing costs and continue to offer the product to a loyal niche market. Other strategies include discontinuing the product or selling it to another business that is willing to continue production of the product.

Obsolescence One reason products reach the decline stage is obsolescence. **Obsolescence** occurs when a product is out of date, no longer wanted, or unusable. There are many forms of obsolescence.

When a new product or technology surpasses the old one, *technical obsolescence* occurs. Computers and cell phones become technically obsolete when a new, improved version of the product enters the market. Although the older computers

What factors can make a product obsolete?

and cell phones may still work, the technology used in the new ones is technically superior. Some products become obsolete because supporting technologies are no longer available to produce or repair a product.

When a product does not function in the same way that it did when it was purchased, *functional obsolescence* occurs. If a cell phone no longer works because it is not compatible with the provider's new, upgraded service, the cell phone is functionally obsolete because it cannot get phone service. Products that naturally wear out or break down may become obsolete if replacement parts are no longer available.

Sometimes businesses intentionally introduce obsolescence into their marketing strategy. The objective of *planned obsolescence* is to generate more sales by reducing the time between purchases. For example, a computer printer is manufactured to have a short life span, meaning consumers have to purchase new printers more frequently.

When a product is no longer desirable because it has gone out of fashion, *style obsolescence* occurs. Although flared leg jeans may be perfectly functional, they no longer may be desirable if skinny leg jeans are the current style trend. Because of the "fashion cycle," stylistically obsolete products may eventually regain popularity. "Acid-wash" jeans, which were popular in the 1980s, became stylistically obsolete in the mid to late 1990s but returned to popularity in the early 2000s.

▰▰▰▰▰ CHECKPOINT ◣◣◣◣◣
What are the stages of the product life cycle?

Real Strategies Using the Product Life Cycle

The product life cycle is an important marketing tool. It can be used to help predict and forecast sales. It can also help identify the type of marketing mix needed as the product moves through the various stages. There are many real-world examples of the implementation of the product life cycle concept in today's businesses.

Kinko's

The first Kinko's opened in 1970 near the University of California, Santa Barbara. Since students could make copies only at the school's library, Paul Orfalea, Kinko's founder, recognized an opportunity to meet the demand for copy services. During the introduction stage, the store specialized in selling supplies and photocopying services for college students. Kinko's mission was to provide customers with consistent, high-quality services in a timely and reliable manner at a reasonable price. Copies could be made for just four cents a page. Orders were taken and delivered personally. The 24-hour service offered by Kinko's was a good fit for the college population. Promotion consisted of flyers stuffed in mailboxes. Kinko's attributed its early success to location, convenient services, lack of competition, good customer service, and the development of long-term relationships.

What changes did Kinko's make during its growth stage?

During its growth stage, Kinko's added sophisticated color copiers, high-speed printers, and fax machines. Kinko's main target market was no longer college students. Large and small companies accounted for the majority of its customers. The business eventually changed from full-service to self-service, allowing customers to swipe credit cards and make their own copies. FedEx delivery services were also added. During Kinko's maturity stage, FedEx purchased Kinko's in 2004, created a new name for the company (FedEx Office), and adjusted the brand to maintain market share. New technology and consumer demands require companies like Kinko's to monitor markets and adjust strategies for survival.

BMW

BMW does not always implement strategies for all four stages of the product life cycle. Instead of developing a strategy to deal with a declining product, BMW would prefer to withdraw the product from the market. In other words, maturity and decline stages usually do not exist in BMW's product life cycle. Before a product reaches the maturity stage, characterized by a decreasing sales rate and a drop in profits, BMW pulls the product from the market. BMW wants to keep its automobiles in the introduction and growth stages to keep sales high. It does this by regularly introducing new models and modifying existing models to help differentiate them from competitors' automobiles. BMW automobiles typically have a product life cycle of seven years, with a new model introduced each year.

PepsiCo and Coca-Cola

While in its maturity stage, PepsiCo faces the challenge of competing with Coca-Cola, which is ranked number one in the soft drink world. PepsiCo's soft drinks (Pepsi®, Mountain Dew®, and Sierra Mist®) make up about one-quarter of its sales. Aquafina®, Tropicana®, and Lipton® are also part of the Pepsi brand. PepsiCo also owns Frito-Lay®, the world's number one producer of snack foods, including Doritos®, Fritos®, and Ruffles®. PepsiCo's mission is to be the world's premier consumer products company focused on convenient foods and beverages.

To help meet its lofty goal, PepsiCo has entered into agreements with restaurants, schools, and the NFL. Restaurants like Applebee's® now offer Pepsi instead of Coke. NFL fans who prefer Coke will have to settle for Pepsi now that Pepsi is the official soft drink of the NFL. Pepsi is also going head to head with Coke in its advertising campaigns. Pepsi commercials promote the cola wars. Pepsi positions itself as "the choice of a new generation." There's no doubt that Pepsi will continue advertising heavily throughout its maturity stage to try to beat the competition.

Blockbuster and Netflix

During the late 1980s and early 1990s, video rental stores such as Blockbuster were extremely popular. Consumers could rent their favorite movie videos for several days and then return them to the video store. Blockbuster even sold popcorn and other snacks commonly available at the movie theater to help enhance the customers' movie rental experience. Blockbuster entered its growth stage with an innovative business model. It offered a larger selection of videos, had computerized inventory, provided a quick video check-out process, and stayed open until midnight. Blockbuster began widespread distribution by expanding its operations from coast to coast. However, in the late 1990s, Blockbuster hit the decline stage when Netflix introduced its new online mail-order movie rental service. The convenience of renting movies without having to leave their homes was a big hit with consumers. The success of Netflix coincided with the introduction of DVDs, which soon made video tapes obsolete. DVDs were inexpensive to ship. Netflix now gives consumers the option of downloading movies via the Internet. Blockbuster soon realized that it would need to make adjustments to its marketing strategy or go out of business. In 2004 Blockbuster launched its own online rental service to try to

SPOTLIGHT ON SUCCESS

© THOMAS COEX/AFP/Getty Images

MARK ZUCKERBERG
Facebook

Mark Zuckerberg was a 19-year-old sophomore at Harvard when he started a Web service from his dorm in 2004. The Zuckerberg invention was called Thefacebook.com, and it was described as "an online directory that connects people through social networks at colleges." Today Facebook has over 550 million members. One out of every 12 people in the world has a Facebook account, and Facebook's membership currently is growing at a rate of about 700,000 people a day. The Facebook age has arrived.

With Facebook, Zuckerberg has created a social entity almost twice as large as the United States. Social media websites like Facebook have played a significant role in product launches and reviews. The volume of comments posted on Facebook and other social media websites is growing. These comments prove to be a valuable resource for businesses who are trying to launch or revamp their products. Today the fastest-growing market for Facebook is the 25- to 44-year-old-segment, a demographic that is often targeted by businesses. Not only has Facebook changed the way people relate to one another, it has also affected many other aspects of life. There are many Facebook pages dedicated to social and political issues around the world. A posting on Facebook can quickly travel to millions of members and influence social and political changes worldwide.

What started out as a diversion for Mark Zuckerberg has turned him into a multibillionaire. He believes that eventually all businesses will recognize the importance of the social aspects of doing business.

Think Critically
How has Facebook changed the way people communicate? Why do you think people and businesses are embracing this technology?

gain back some of its market share. Blockbuster experienced success through 2007 in its battle with Netflix, adding customers to its online rental service at a faster rate than its competitor; however, the competition was too great and Blockbuster declared bankruptcy in 2010. It was purchased by satellite-TV provider Dish Network in 2011. With the backing of Dish Network, Blockbuster is attempting a comeback by offering competitively priced DVD and Internet video packages.

▟▟▟▟▟▟ CHECKPOINT ◣◣◣◣◣◣

How is the product life cycle concept useful to businesses?

4.2 Assessment

THINK ABOUT IT

1. If sales are increasing during the growth stage of a product, why do businesses continue to spend heavily on advertising?

2. Why is the maturity stage difficult for many businesses?

3. Based on Kinko's history, what were some of the contributing factors to its success during the introduction stage?

MAKE ACADEMIC CONNECTIONS

4. **COMMUNICATION**   Create a table with five columns. In the first column, list a product representing each of the four stages of the product life cycle. Create four more columns for each of the marketing mix components (product, distribution, price, and promotion). Complete the table by describing the marketing mix elements for each product.

5. **MATH**   Each year Coca-Cola pays a large school district $40,000 to be the official soft drink for that school district. Only Coca-Cola products are offered at the school district's sporting events and in its vending machines. The school district has 12 high schools with a total student population of 62,000. What is the Coca-Cola cost per student in the school district? Is this a wise investment for Coca-Cola? Explain your answer.

6. **RESEARCH**   Vizio, a consumer electronics company, is now the sponsor of college football bowl games and other high-profile sporting events. Conduct research to determine Vizio's current stage in the product life cycle. Provide examples of Vizio's marketing mix that are indicators of the product life cycle stage.

 Teamwork
Prepare a PowerPoint presentation about a once-popular product that is in the decline stage or that has already been eliminated. If the product is currently in the decline stage, describe the business's marketing strategy to continue with the product or to eliminate it. If the product has already been eliminated, describe the marketing strategy used by the business to phase out the product.

4.3

Price Planning

Goals

- Discuss pricing objectives used by businesses when setting prices.
- Compare and contrast pricing strategies.

Terms

- price skimming, p. 109
- penetration pricing, p. 109
- markdown, p. 110
- price competition, p. 110
- nonprice competition, p. 110
- price equilibrium, p. 110
- elastic demand, p. 110
- inelastic demand, p. 111
- consumer credit, p. 111
- trade credit, p. 111

FOCUS ON ADVERTISING

Competing on Price

Priceline.com is a search engine that helps consumers find the best travel deals and discounts. Its business model is based on price. It uses price to distinguish its services from other competing travel websites. Priceline's advertising has helped it build its well-known, strong brand. The advertising campaign features cleverly named characters such as the Priceline Negotiator, Big Deal, and Naomi Pryce. These amusing characters help demonstrate how Priceline is the home of the "Big Deal" for hotel rooms and airline tickets. William Shatner has been the Priceline celebrity spokesman for 13 years, helping build continuity and brand recognition. Priceline's website has online promotions that complement its TV ads. Its price competition strategy and successful advertising campaign have helped Priceline maintain its dominant market share.

Work as a Team How has brand recognition helped Priceline succeed? What are the advantages and disadvantage of competing on the basis of price?

© Kayros Studio "Be Happy!"/Shutterstock.com

Pricing Objectives

The amount customers pay for a good or service is the *price*. Consumers make many buying decisions based on price. The price consumers are willing to pay is based on the satisfaction they expect to receive from a product or service. Consumers want to get value for their money.

Prices are also important to businesses. A business's revenues and profits are closely related to prices. *Revenue* is the money earned from

How can a business maximize profits?

the sale of products and services (price × number of units sold). *Profit* is the difference between the revenues earned and the expenses of operating a business. If the revenues are not high enough to cover expenses and generate a profit, the business likely will fail. To earn a profit, businesses must carefully select a price for their products and services. The price cannot be too high or too low. Setting pricing objectives is the first step in the price planning process. Pricing objectives help a business meet its overall financial, marketing, and strategic objectives. Pricing objectives change throughout a product's life cycle, so businesses must make price adjustments periodically.

Maximize Profits

A common pricing objective is to maximize profits. If a business wants to maximize profits, it will set prices as high as consumers are willing to pay. The business wants to earn high revenues to cover its expenses and earn a profit. To do this, the business will have to study the target market and the competition closely. If a business is the only seller of a product, it can charge much higher prices than a business operating in a highly competitive environment.

A business can maximize revenue and profits by increasing customer satisfaction. For example, the business might offer excellent customer service or build strong customer relationships through loyalty programs. It can also maximize revenue and profits by reducing production costs.

Earn a Return on Investment

When setting prices, businesses often use return on investment as their main pricing objective. The *return on investment (ROI)* measures a business's profits against the money invested in the product. ROI is usually expressed as a percentage. A business can use a target ROI to determine whether a particular price will help it achieve a profit. For example, if a business invests $10,000 in its product and wants a 12 percent ROI, it would need to price its product so that it earns a profit of $1,200 ($10,000 × 0.12). Businesses can compare their ROI to the industry average ROI to see how they are performing.

Increase Sales or Market Share

Some businesses set prices to maximize sales. In doing so, the price may cover expenses, but it may not result in a profit. Prices will usually be low to encourage customers to buy. Businesses that have excess inventory want to increase sales to clear out old models and make room for the new ones. Holiday and seasonal items often are deeply discounted after the holiday or season has ended. Businesses that want to increase their market share may also choose this pricing objective. Sales maximization cannot be a long-term objective because little or no profit is earned.

Create a Price-Quality Image

Consumers often associate high price with high quality. They assume that higher-priced products or services are made with better materials and better workmanship. Businesses may use *prestige pricing* by charging higher prices for their products to create a higher-quality image. This pricing objective is used for various products, including coffee, hair-care products, designer clothing, furniture, and perfume. Some businesses try to establish a low-price image. Walmart and Dollar General promote their low prices to appeal to cost-conscious consumers.

CHECKPOINT

Why is it important for a business to set pricing objectives?

Pricing Strategies

Businesses face two risks when setting prices for their products. If the price is set too high, product demand will be low. If the price is set too low, the business will be unable to make a profit. Businesses must develop pricing strategies to avoid these risks. There are many factors to consider when setting prices, including the stages of the product life cycle, the competition, and supply and demand. Businesses must also decide whether credit is a necessary part of their pricing strategies.

Product Life Cycle Pricing Strategies

Since products have a high rate of failure during the introduction stage, the pricing strategy for new products is very important. A business can control the price of a product during the introductory phase if only one brand of a new product is available. Two pricing strategies commonly used during the introduction stage are price skimming and penetration pricing. **Price skimming** involves setting a high price to emphasize the uniqueness of a product and to recover the product development costs quickly. Businesses must carefully analyze the target market to determine if it is willing to pay high prices. Businesses earn higher profits when using the price skimming strategy, but they also attract more competition to the market. **Penetration pricing** involves setting a low price for new products to gain a larger market share rapidly. This strategy might also be used if a business determines its target market is more price-conscious. Penetration pricing results in lower profits, but it discourages competition.

Coupons and rebates that reduce the price paid for a product also are commonly used during the introduction stage. These act as incentives to encourage consumers to try the new product. Businesses continue to offer coupons and rebates during the growth and maturity

Why might a company choose to use a price competition strategy?

stages to encourage repeat purchases. In the growth and maturity stages, the emphasis often is on price competition because of the growing number of competitors.

During the decline stage of the product life cycle, businesses may offer discounts or markdowns. Discounts could include quantity discounts for buying large quantities of a product and seasonal discounts for buying products at certain times of the year. A **markdown** is a reduction from the original selling price.

Competition Pricing Strategies

When setting product prices, businesses need to be aware of the competition. When consumers view competing products as being very similar, businesses will set similar prices. If a business chooses to use a **price competition** strategy, it tries to distinguish its product or service from competing products based on low price. When emphasizing low prices, a business must always strive to keep prices as low as possible. A **nonprice competition** strategy tries to distinguish a product or service from competing products based on factors other than price, such as design, quality, and workmanship. Businesses use a nonprice competition strategy because it is usually more profitable than selling products at a lower price. Nonprice competition will increase advertising and promotional costs.

Supply and Demand Pricing Strategies

The concept of supply and demand can affect prices. *Supply* is the quantity of a product or service that a business is willing to produce at different prices. *Demand* is the quantity of a product or service that consumers are willing to buy at different prices. For example, if a consumer electronics company can sell a calculator at a price of $50, it may be willing to produce (supply) 200 calculators. However, at this price consumers may be willing to buy (demand) only 50 calculators. If the price is lowered to $25, 100 customers may want to buy the calculator, but the company may be willing to produce only 25 calculators at this price. The point at which demand and supply are equal is known as the **price equilibrium**. If a product is priced above the equilibrium price, fewer people will buy it, meaning supply exceeds demand. This often leads to price reductions. If a product is priced below the equilibrium price, more people will buy it. This could lead to shortages, meaning demand would exceed supply. Shortages lead to price increases.

Demand is an important concept to consider when pricing products. As the price drops, consumer demand usually rises. When the demand of a product is affected by its price, the product has **elastic demand**. Consumers will buy more or less of a product when the price changes. Elastic demand is common among products that have good substitutes. If the price of corn chips has increased, a consumer may buy potato chips or pretzels instead. If concert tickets are priced too high, consumers may choose a less expensive form of entertainment, such as going to the movies. Products that have elastic demand experience an increase in revenue when prices are decreased.

When a change in price has very little effect on demand, the product has **inelastic demand**. Inelastic demand is common among products that do not have good substitutes, such as eggs, milk, and certain medications. Consumers will continue to buy these products even if their prices increase. For products with inelastic demand, price decreases will result in decreased revenue.

Using Credit as Part of the Pricing Strategy

Businesses often extend credit to their customers to help them make purchases. Without credit, consumers would not be able to afford high-priced items. Credit is offered by homebuilders, automobile dealerships, and appliance and consumer electronics retailers. In addition, department stores, home improvement stores, and gas stations offer credit cards to creditworthy customers. **Consumer credit** is made available by retailers to assist consumers in making purchases. **Trade credit** is offered by one business to another business. Businesses must determine if credit should be used as part of their pricing strategy.

Although offering credit can increase sales volume, poorly managed credit may end up being more costly than profitable to a business. Businesses must establish credit procedures and policies. After deciding to extend credit to customers, businesses must decide if they will offer their own store credit or extend credit through other financial institutions, such as banks, financing companies, or credit card companies like MasterCard®. Credit terms must be developed that outline the amount of credit that will be extended to customers, the rate of interest to charge, and the length of time customers have to make a payment.

Businesses must also have a plan for identifying creditworthy customers. A business must look at a customer's character, capital, and collateral to determine if he or she is a good credit risk. Character is examined by reviewing the customer's credit history. Capital would include a customer's income, such as wages or salary and checking and savings accounts. Collateral refers to assets that a customer owns that could be sold to help pay off debts.

Businesses need collection procedures to ensure customers are billed and payments are collected on time. Even with the best credit policies in place, there will be

Why do businesses need to establish credit policies?

times when customers do not pay their debts. Credit policies should include procedures for handling overdue accounts. Some accounts will never be collected, and most businesses budget for this. However, too many uncollected accounts can result in a price increase for all customers.

 **CHECKPOINT**

What factors should a business consider when setting prices?

4.3 Assessment

THINK ABOUT IT

1. Briefly describe common pricing objectives used by businesses.
2. What is an advantage and a disadvantage of using a price skimming strategy? What is an advantage and a disadvantage of using a penetration pricing strategy?
3. How do supply and demand affect pricing?
4. Why do retailers offer consumer credit? How is credit related to pricing?

MAKE ACADEMIC CONNECTIONS

5. **MARKETING** Choose a designer brand and a store brand of clothing. Describe the pricing strategy that was likely used to introduce both brands in the market. Explain why this strategy was used.
6. **MATH** You are a retailer who receives a trade discount from one of your largest suppliers. The discount is based upon the dollar amount of merchandise that you purchase each month. The discount for monthly purchases totaling $50,000–$100,000 is 10 percent; $100,001–$150,000, 15 percent; and $150,001–$200,000, 20 percent. What is the dollar amount of your discount for each of the following months' purchases: January, $190,000; February, $105,000; and March, $75,000.
7. **MANAGEMENT** You are opening a furniture store that will offer product lines catering to the middle and high-end markets. Select a pricing objective for your business. You may select more than one objective for the different markets. Explain why you selected the pricing objective(s).

 Teamwork

You work for a full-service hotel located in a warm climate that caters to business clients, conventions, and tourists who visit the hotel four to six times each year. Hotel management has asked you to develop pricing strategies for all three markets. Be sure to consider factors such as the product life cycle, the competition, and supply and demand. You should also consider credit as part of your pricing strategies. Prepare a PowerPoint presentation that describes your recommended pricing strategies.

Sharpen Your
21st CENTURY SKILLS

PARTNERSHIP FOR
21ST CENTURY SKILLS

Getting the Best Price When Buying a New Car

Purchasing a new car is a major investment. Buying a car from a car dealership can be intimidating. But you can get the best price for your new car by following a few tips.

1. *Do your homework before shopping for a new car.* Being uninformed is the fastest way to lose money. Gathering key facts and pricing information beforehand gives you more control over the buying process. If you have a trade-in, find out what it is worth. Websites such as Edmunds.com and Kelley Blue Book provide car appraisals.

2. *Know the car's invoice price, which is how much the dealer paid the manufacturer for the car.* This price can be found on websites such as Edmunds.com or Kelley Blue Book. The invoice price will not be the same price as the *sticker price*, which is the manufacturer's suggested retail price. The sticker price is almost always higher than the car dealer expects you to pay for the car. Expect to pay about 4 to 8 percent more than the invoice price. Also factor in dealer rebates and other incentives when determining a fair price for the car.

3. *Negotiate one thing at a time.* Salespeople like to mix financing, leasing, and trade-in negotiations together. By doing so, they may offer you a good price in one area while inflating the price in another. Do not discuss financing, leasing, or a trade-in until you have agreed on the price.

4. *Arrange financing in advance.* Compare interest rates at several banks, credit unions, and loan organizations before checking the dealer's rates. If you are preapproved for a loan, you can keep financial arrangements out of the negotiations.

5. *Shop during the week.* Car dealers have fewer customers during the week, making them more willing to negotiate a better deal.

6. *Don't pay for extras you don't need.* Dealers often try to sell you unnecessary options such as rustproofing, fabric protection, and paint protection. Add-ons increase the price of the car. If add-ons are listed on the sales contract, put a line through them.

Try It Out

Using the websites listed above or other online sources, research the price for a new car that interests you. If there are any extra options you want, be sure to include those in the price. Find out if there are any promotions, such as rebates or dealer incentives that could lower the price. Finally, research the best interest rates for a car loan. Write a plan of action for shopping and getting the best price for the car you selected.

© Local Favorite Photography/Shutterstock.com

4.1 Product Development

- When creating a marketing mix, a business usually starts with the product. A new product must be entirely new or changed in an important and noticeable way. Most new products involve changes and improvements to existing products.
- The six stages of new product planning include (1) generating ideas, (2) screening ideas, (3) preparing a business analysis, (4) developing a marketing strategy, (5) developing and testing the product, and (6) marketing the product.
- The product mix may include various levels of a product, including a basic product, an enhanced product, and an extended product. Additional components of the product mix to consider are the product line, package and label, and brand.

4.2 Product Life Cycle

- During the introduction stage of the product life cycle, there is little competition, sales are low, prices are generally high, distribution is selective, and promotion is used to create product awareness.
- During the growth stage of the product life cycle, competition is increasing, sales are growing, prices may remain high or be reduced, distribution is expanded, and promotion is used to build brand preference.
- During the maturity stage, competition is high, sales are increasing at a slower pace, products are priced competitively, distribution is widespread, and promotion emphasizes product differentiation and brand loyalty.
- During the decline stage, sales are shrinking, prices are lowered to reduce inventory, and distribution and promotion efforts are reduced while the business decides whether to continue production of the product.

4.3 Price Planning

- A business sets pricing objectives on the basis of maximizing profits, earning a return on investment, increasing sales or market share, or creating a price-quality image.
- When setting prices, factors to consider include the stages of the product life cycle, the competition, and supply and demand.
- Businesses often extend credit to customers to help them make purchases, especially high-priced purchases.

WHAT DO YOU KNOW?

Read *Impact Advertising* on page 91 again to review the history of Diet Coke. Conduct online research to learn about recent Diet Coke advertising campaigns. What is Diet Coke promoting in its new ads? Do you think the ads will help Diet Coke maintain its market share?

Chapter 4 Assessment

Vocabulary Builder

Match each statement with the term that best defines it. Some terms may not be used.

1. All of the different products a business sells
2. Setting a low price for a new product to gain a larger market share
3. Selling a product at as many locations as possible
4. Setting a high price for a new product to emphasize its uniqueness and to recover development costs quickly
5. A group of closely related products with slight variations developed by the same business
6. A strategy by which a company distinguishes its product or service from competing products based on factors other than price, such as design, quality, and workmanship
7. The exclusive right to use a brand name, symbol, or design
8. Made available by retailers to assist consumers in making purchases
9. A marketing strategy that allows a business to use one of its well-known brand names in a new product category
10. A reduction from the original selling price

a. brand extension
b. consumer credit
c. elastic demand
d. inelastic demand
e. intensive distribution
f. licensed brand
g. markdown
h. nonprice competition
i. obsolescence
j. penetration pricing
k. price competition
l. price equilibrium
m. price skimming
n. product life cycle
o. product line
p. product mix
q. trade credit
r. trademark

Test Your Knowledge

11. The second step of new product planning involves ____.
    a. generating ideas
    b. testing the product
    c. screening ideas
    d. marketing the product
12. Product mix components include all of the following *except*
    a. price
    b. product line
    c. brand
    d. package
13. A(n) ____ includes features and options that increase the usefulness of a product.
    a. basic product
    b. enhanced product
    c. extended product
    d. product line
14. A(n) ____ is a well-known brand owned by one company that is sold for use by another company.
    a. licensed brand
    b. trademark
    c. new product
    d. none of the above

15. Which of the following stages of the product life cycle experiences the highest increase in sales?
    a. introduction
    b. growth
    c. maturity
    d. decline
16. In which of the following stages of the product life cycle is the pricing the most competitive?
    a. introduction
    b. growth
    c. maturity
    d. decline
17. If a washing machine breaks down and replacement parts are unavailable, _____ has occurred.
    a. technical obsolescence
    b. functional obsolescence
    c. planned obsolescence
    d. style obsolescence
18. The typewriter is an example of _____.
    a. technical obsolescence
    b. functional obsolescence
    c. planned obsolescence
    d. style obsolescence
19. If consumer demand for a product exceeds the quantity of the product producers supply, all of the following likely will occur *except*
    a. there will be a shortage of the product
    b. producers will decrease prices
    c. consumers will be willing to pay higher prices
    d. producers will increase prices
20. The point at which demand and supply are equal is known as _____.
    a. elastic demand
    b. inelastic demand
    c. price competition
    d. price equilibrium

Apply What You Learned

21. Describe how an existing product has been changed or improved and introduced to the market as a "new" product. What consumer needs are met with the new product?
22. Using an automobile as an example, describe the difference between the basic product and the enhanced product. Then describe extended products that could be offered as part of the sale of the automobile.
23. Some businesses use planned obsolescence as part of their marketing strategy. Explain what planned obsolescence is and why businesses would choose to use this strategy. Does the clothing industry use planned obsolescence? Explain your answer.
24. Many products fail during the introduction stage. List products throughout history that have failed in the following product categories: snacks, automobiles, consumer electronics, and beauty.

Make Academic Connections

25. **LANGUAGE ARTS** Many businesses get new product ideas from customers. Think about a product you purchased with which you were dissatisfied. Write a letter to the manufacturer of the product describing your reasons for dissatisfaction. Explain why the

product did not meet your needs. Then provide suggestions for improving the product.

26. **HISTORY** There have been many innovative products throughout history. Select one and conduct research to learn more about the planning and development processes for the product. Give a presentation about the product. Describe how it changed the lives of consumers.

27. **LAW** Businesses trademark their products so that no other company can use their brand name, symbol, or design without their permission. Even so, trademark violations still occur. Conduct research to find a case of trademark violation. Write a one-page report describing the case. Explain how the trademark violator was penalized.

28. **MANAGEMENT** You own a pizza restaurant that has been in business for several years. It has reached the maturity stage of the product life cycle, so sales are slowing as competition increases. Outline a plan for increasing sales. Describe what changes you will make to your marketing mix (product, price, distribution, and promotion) to boost sales.

29. **GOVERNMENT** Pricing is a major factor among competitors. Competition helps keep prices lower for consumers. The government tracks mergers and acquisitions between companies that could result in reduced competition. Conduct research to learn about a merger in which the government intervened. Write a one-page report describing the merger and why it caused concern.

30. **CONSUMER ECONOMICS** Select three different brands from the same product category that have a wide range of prices (for example, three brands of gym shoes). Create a table listing each brand and its price. List the unique characteristics of each product. Do you think these characteristics justify the price differences? Why or why not?

31. **FINANCE** Select a credit card that you would like to have. Gather information about the credit card and credit card company, such as the credit application process, credit policies and procedures, credit terms, interest rate, rewards and bonuses, and penalties. Report your findings to the class and state whether you would recommend the credit card to others. Explain why or why not.

Tom Johnson owns and operates Stop-n-Go Oil Change, which offers oil changes and other minor auto maintenance services such as tire rotations and air filter replacements. Lately, because of higher operation costs, Tom is having difficulty competing with the two other local oil change companies in the same neighborhood. Tom decides to cut his prices below cost with the intention of luring in more customers and driving the other oil change companies out of business. Then, when there is less competition, Tom will raise his prices to increase profits. You are the assistant manager of Stop-n-Go, and Tom recently shared his pricing strategies with you.

What problems do you see with Tom's plan? What would you do to try to convince him to use another strategy, such as nonprice competition?

Reality ✓

Weak Real Estate Market

Purchasing a home is one of the largest investments many people will ever make. Most individuals buy a home as an investment, which they expect to grow in value. However, in recent years, a recession, high unemployment, and uncertain economic conditions have had a major impact on the housing industry.

Builders are now using sales tactics similar to those that traditionally have been part of the new car industry. New homebuilders are pricing houses higher to leave room for negotiation. This pricing strategy allows room for builders to offer special incentives like $30,000 in upgrades (granite countertops, hardwood floors, a three-car garage, and others) for free.

Homebuilders are also adjusting to our multicultural environment. Some cultures believe in the right to negotiate prices paid for most products and services. By setting high prices for their houses, homebuilders are more willing to negotiate, making it easier to work with customers in other cultures.

New neighborhoods advertise houses in price ranges from $200,000 to $500,000. Usually there are very few houses for sale in the lower price range. The lower price is a form of psychological pricing. It lures consumers into the neighborhood. When prospective homebuyers walk through the model homes that feature many upgrades, they often desire the same features. Adding upgrades can increase prices by an additional $50,000 to $100,000.

Some individuals feel that the pricing strategies used by new homebuilders are deceptive. They believe that it is better for the builder to be honest and upfront about its prices. Others just consider the pricing strategies a way of doing business.

Think Critically

1. Why do most people consider the purchase of a home an investment?
2. Why do homebuilders include upgrades in the model homes that prospective customers tour?
3. Why do you think the pricing strategies being used by homebuilders are successful?
4. Do you think the homebuilders' pricing strategies are deceptive? Explain why or why not.

Impromptu Speaking Event

Expressing your thoughts without prior preparation is a critical business skill. Poise, self-confidence, and organization of facts are also important in delivering an effective speech. The Impromptu Speaking event gives you an opportunity to demonstrate the qualities of business leadership by combining quick and clear thinking with conversational speaking.

TOPIC   Your speech topic is about advertising strategies and the product life cycle. Your speech should describe appropriate advertising strategies for each of the four stages of the product life cycle for a popular soft drink. You must explain why you would budget more or less money for advertising during each product life cycle stage. During your speech, you should describe your proposed advertising campaigns and explain why they will be effective. You are trying to convince the CEO of the soft drink company to use your advertising strategies and campaign.

You have ten minutes to prepare this impromptu speech. You can use two 4" by 6" note cards to write down any notes to be used during your speech. Your speech must be four minutes in length. Your grade will be lowered by five points for a time under 3:31 and over 4:29. Your speech will be evaluated for content, presentation, knowledge, and examples.

Performance Indicators Evaluated

- Understand the advertising campaign for different product life cycles.
- Communicate your opinion based upon facts and figures.
- Persuade management to spend a certain dollar amount on an advertising campaign.
- Manage time effectively to outline and present a viewpoint.
- Demonstrate the ability to align ideas into a persuasive argument.

Go to the FBLA website for more detailed information.

Think Critically

1. Why does the advertising budget for a product change during different product life cycle stages?
2. How should the advertising strategies change as the product moves through the different life cycle stages?
3. Why is the introduction stage so important for a new soft drink?
4. Why must companies continually create fresh advertising campaigns even when the product is well known?

www.fbla.org

5
Distribution Planning

© gary718/Shutterstock.com

IMPACT ADVERTISING

Evolution of the Online Market

The first attempt at online sales simply mimicked the traditional retail shopping experience. Some individuals assumed that the online environment would never be a legitimate alternative or addition to traditional retailing. In the beginning, the Web was used mostly to conduct product research. Times have changed dramatically, and now online advertising and e-commerce outperform the offline alternatives. According to studies conducted by Forrester Research, online sales totaled $172.9 billion in 2010 and are projected to grow to $248.7 billion in 2014, growing an average of 7 to 8 percent each year.

© Andresr/Shutterstock.com

Retailers are using more innovative strategies to coax people to shop online. Online video technology is being used on many retail websites to create a new customer experience. For example, Netflix has added movie trailers to entertain and entice its members to rent movies. Netflix uses personalization techniques to determine which movie trailers would be of interest to each individual. American Eagle teamed up with the CW Network to sponsor some of its shows targeting teens. It launched a website that showed clips of the TV shows with characters wearing American Eagle's clothing. Build-A-Bear's website has many videos and games to entice its target market of 8- to 12-year-old girls. Website visitors can become a member and earn rewards for free merchandise. J&R Electronics offers product and seminar videos to promote and demonstrate various products. The website also has event videos, which feature live performances by well-known recording artists sponsored by J&R Electronics.

Another approach taken by many online retailers is the addition of customer reviews on their websites. On the PETCO.com website, visitors can click on the Ratings & Reviews link, choose a pet product to review, give it a rating between 1 and 5 paws, and write a review. Research has shown that 60 percent of online shoppers find customer product reviews helpful in making buying decisions.

Some online retailers have formed partnerships with other branches of the media to help promote their products. JCPenney has teamed up with People magazine. JCPenney's website showcases fashion items handpicked by People StyleWatch editors. Website visitors can click on the item to order it. Online retailers continue to add features to encourage customers to shop at their sites.

WHAT DO YOU KNOW?

1. **Why do you think more consumers are now shopping online?**

2. **Do you think special features such as online videos make a website more appealing? Why or why not?**

3. **Are your friends' opinions about products important to you? Why do you think some websites include customer reviews of their products?**

5.1

Channel of Distribution

Goals
- Explain the functions of the channel of distribution and channel members.
- Identify various distribution channel options.

Terms
- distribution, p. 122
- channel of distribution, p. 123
- direct channel, p. 125
- indirect channel, p. 126
- kiosk, p. 127

FOCUS ON ADVERTISING

Costco's Low-Profile Advertising Strategy

A product is moved through various channels from the time it is produced until the time it is consumed. One of the common stops along the way is with a wholesaler. Although wholesalers don't always sell directly to consumers, one business has been successful in doing just that. Costco Wholesale Corporation has a chain of membership warehouses throughout the world. It is known for carrying high-quality, brand-name merchandise at low prices. Although Costco's primary target market is

small businesses, it also sells to individual consumers. Costco is able to save its customers money by reducing its costs, including advertising and promotion costs. Costco has no public relations department, and its stores have very few, if any, salespeople. Costco puts most of its selling efforts into persuading businesses to purchase memberships. Its promotion strategies are simple and largely consist of in-store product sampling. Costco relies on word-of-mouth advertising to attract new members. In Costco's case, it believes less is more. Less advertising results in more cost savings for customers.

Work as a Team What do you think of Costco's advertising (or lack of advertising) strategy? Would you prefer to shop at Costco's no-frills store or a store that offers numerous customer services? Why?

The Function of Distribution Channels

If the advertising of a product is effective and results in consumer demand, a business must ensure that its product is available where and when customers want it. **Distribution** involves the methods used by businesses to get their products to customers. If a product isn't available, the business will miss out on a sale. The earliest product exchanges involved consumers buying goods and services directly from producers. Today, products move through the channel of distribution. The **channel of distribution** is the path on which products and services flow from the producer to the final consumer. The simplest distribution channels involve only the producer (manufacturer) and the final consumer. Most distribution channels are more complex and involve many businesses or channel members.

After a new BMW automobile is manufactured in Germany, it is shipped to the U.S. BMW distribution center. The U.S. distribution center ships BMW automobiles to dealerships throughout the United States. If a dealership doesn't have the specific car model selected by a customer, it will contact other BMW dealerships to locate the car. Once located, the car will be transported in the most efficient manner to the appropriate dealership and delivered to the customer.

Channel Members

Businesses involved in the distribution of products from producers to consumers are referred to as *channel members*. While channel members may not be directly involved in the production of products, they are responsible for having the products when and where customers want them. Channel members may include the following:

- producers—manufacturers that make products and sell them to other businesses or consumers
- retailers—businesses that sell products directly to consumers
- wholesalers—businesses that buy products from producers and then sell the products to other businesses, often retailers
- transportation companies—businesses that move products by airplane, railroad, ship, truck, pipeline, or a combination of methods
- warehouses—storage facilities used to store products as they move through the channel of distribution
- agents and brokers—businesses that work to bring producers and buyers together in exchange for a fee
- consumers—final end user of a product

Each channel member specializes in various marketing activities. Marketing activities performed by channel members could include order processing, inventory control, handling and shipping, storage, pricing, display, promotion, and selling. For example, wholesalers purchase an assortment of products from many manufacturers and allow retailers to purchase the products they need in the quantity they need. Wholesalers also help manufacturers analyze sales data to

What channel members do you think were involved in getting these products to customers?

determine appropriate inventory levels. Retailers must price products and develop promotional strategies that will result in sales. All channel members work closely together to make sure the marketing mix is satisfactory to all participants.

The channel of distribution for a service is very short. The service provider, such as an electrician, a restaurant owner, or a doctor, deals directly with the customer. Generally, services are performed and received at the same time. Distribution planning must ensure that the service can be provided when the customer needs it. Otherwise, the customer will find another service provider.

Distribution Channels at Work

Consumers have varying needs when it comes to products. These needs relate to the quantity, assortment, and location of a product. In addition, consumer demand for certain products varies throughout the year. Products are moved through the channel of distribution to meet consumer needs and demand in the most efficient way.

Although producers make large quantities of a product, individual consumers typically buy small quantities. To overcome the discrepancy between the amount of product produced and the amount an individual consumer wants to buy, a business can use a wholesaler or warehouse to store its product and distribute it as needed to meet consumer demand. Consumers also need a wide assortment of products to meet their needs. A wholesaler can buy different products from different producers and distribute them to various retailers, such as supermarkets, that offer an assortment of products to consumers.

Because consumers live throughout the country and around the world, they need products at different locations. Channel members, such as wholesalers and transportation companies, can move the product from the place where it is produced to numerous locations where it will be purchased.

Although producers manufacture products year-round, consumers may want to purchase the product only at specific times. For example, consumers usually want to buy winter coats only during the winter months. The coat manufacturer can use a wholesaler and warehouse to store the coats in anticipation of consumer demand. On the other hand, consumers want to buy fruits and vegetables throughout the year. Farmers in southern states have a limited season to grow fresh produce and fruits. To meet consumer demand for these products outside the growing season, supermarkets purchase fruits and vegetables from other parts of the country.

NETBookmark

Small manufacturers can expand the distribution of their products by branching out from smaller, specialty stores to more mainstream retailers. Steaz is a beverage company that produces certified organic teas and energy drinks. Access www.cengage.com/school/advertising and click on the link for Chapter 5. In what types of stores are Steaz's products sold? How might a wider distribution strategy benefit Steaz? How might it benefit consumers? Read about Steaz's various products, and then determine other channels of distribution that you think might be a good fit for Steaz. Explain your reasoning.

www.cengage.com/school/advertising

They are transported by refrigerated airplanes and trucks to reach the store within days of being harvested.

Distribution Channels Provide Efficiency

The exchange of goods and services between producers and consumers without using other channel members would be time consuming and expensive. Having numerous distribution channels makes it easier and more efficient for consumers to purchase the products they want. The retailer tracks consumer demand. It then works closely with the producer or wholesaler to get the products consumers need. The producer or wholesaler arranges transportation and storage of the products as they are distributed to department stores, supermarkets, and shopping malls. This process saves time for consumers, producers, wholesalers, and retailers. In addition, because channel members specialize in certain marketing functions, they are more efficient in providing the services needed, which reduces marketing costs for businesses and consumers.

///////// CHECKPOINT \\\\\\\\\

Who are the participants in the channel of distribution?

Channel Options

Efficient distribution systems must be carefully planned. There are many routes that a product can take before reaching the consumer. The type of product influences the channel of distribution chosen. For example, the distribution channels for baked goods would be very different from the distribution channels for a luxury automobile. Effective distribution occurs when all channel members cooperate with each other and apply the marketing concept by focusing on the customers' needs.

Direct and Indirect Channels

Products can be moved to consumers through direct channels or indirect channels, as shown in the illustration on the next page. When producers sell directly to final consumers, they are using a **direct channel**. When a direct channel is used, the producer or consumer is responsible for completing all of the marketing functions (market planning, product and service management, distribution, pricing, promotion, selling, marketing-information management, financing, and risk management). Examples of direct channels include telemarketing, mail-order and catalog shopping, online shopping, television home-shopping networks, factory outlets, and farmers' markets. The Internet has made it easier for businesses to use direct channels of distribution. Many businesses that sell products over the Internet use sales, distribution, and customer service specialists to give customers more personalized attention.

How is telemarketing a direct channel of distribution?

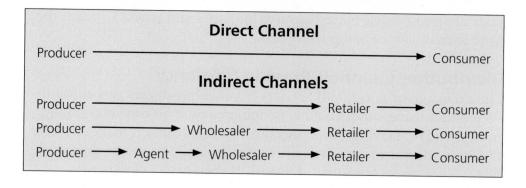

An **indirect channel** involves *intermediaries*, or individuals and businesses that move a product from the producer to the consumer. Intermediaries may include retailers, wholesalers, and agents. Indirect channel members buy the product from the producer or other channel members to sell to consumers or other businesses.

Selection of Distribution Channels

Several factors must be considered when deciding upon a direct channel or an indirect channel of distribution. Indirect channels are typically used for the distribution of consumer products, while direct channels are commonly used for business and industrial products. Manufacturers often buy raw materials, equipment, and supplies that must meet technical specifications directly from other manufacturers. However, manufacturers with large domestic and international markets rely on other agents or brokers to help them sell, distribute, and provide financing for their products.

Certain market conditions make direct channels of distribution a better choice. If there are a small number of customers or the customers are located in a small geographic area, direct channels may be more efficient. In addition, complex products that are customized to meet specific customer needs or require a lot of service can be marketed effectively through direct channels of distribution. Some businesses choose a direct channel because they want more control over the marketing mix.

Multiple and Nontraditional Channels

A producer may select *multiple channels* of distribution to market the same product to several target markets. Each target market may have different needs and purchasing behaviors. A riding lawn mower manufacturer may have customers that range from individual consumers to large lawn service companies. To reach all prospective customers, the lawn mowers may be sold at lawn equipment dealers, home improvement centers, specialty stores, and department stores. Some of the lawn service businesses will be contacted directly by the manufacturer's salespeople. Other businesses will buy from a wholesaler or another business that sells lawn mowers from several manufacturers. Retailers often use multiple channels of distribution by selling their products in-store, online, and through catalogs.

Nontraditional channels of distribution, such as vending machines and kiosks, are becoming more popular. Vending machines, which were once used to sell only snacks and beverages, now have many offerings, including t-shirts, ball caps, books, DVDs, and small electronics such as iPods. Vending machines are popular with consumers because they are quick and easy. A **kiosk** is a small, free-standing booth containing a computer or display screen that distributes product information. Kiosks are popping up at department and furniture stores to help customers locate and order products.

 **CHECKPOINT**

What is the difference between a direct channel and an indirect channel of distribution?

5.1 Assessment

THINK ABOUT IT

1. Why is the channel of distribution an important part of marketing products and services?

2. How is the channel of distribution used to meet the product quantity, product assortment, and product location needs of consumers?

3. What factors make it more likely that a business will use direct channels of distribution instead of indirect channels?

MAKE ACADEMIC CONNECTIONS

4. **SOCIAL STUDIES** Today, there are many educational options for K-12 (Kindergarten through 12th grade) students. An increasing number of channels of distribution exist to provide education for students. Conduct research and list the educational options available for students. Describe the channels of distribution for each option. Write a two-page report discussing the various alternatives and describing the advantages and disadvantages of each one.

5. **RESEARCH** Conduct research to determine the distribution channels used for designer clothing. List the various channel members. Can any retailer sell a designer brand or does the retailer need to meet specific requirements to do so? If so, describe them.

6. **MARKETING** Select a business that uses a direct channel of distribution. Design a flyer or newspaper advertisement that emphasizes the benefits that the direct channel of distribution provides to the consumer.

 Teamwork

Vending machines are being used to distribute unique products. As a team, compile a comprehensive list of all the various products currently being distributed and sold in vending machines. Then brainstorm ideas for other products that could be sold successfully through vending machines. Select one of the products and create a unique name and logo for the vending machine.

Supply Chain Management

Goals
- Describe the processes involved in supply chain management.
- Identify factors that can influence supply chain decisions.

Terms
- supply chain, p. 128
- business-to-business marketing, p. 129
- purchase order, p. 130
- invoice, p. 130
- electronic data interchange (EDI), p. 130
- point-of-sale (POS) system, p. 131
- imports, p. 132
- exports, p. 132

FOCUS ON ADVERTISING

McDonald's Takes Advertising on the Road

Truckside advertising uses the sides of delivery trucks as billboards for advertisers. McDonald's realizes that much of its store sales come from impulse purchases, and the big, bold food images on trucks and other mobile forms of transportation are making a significant impact. McDonald's has a series of advertisements on their trucks that are seen frequently on the busiest highways in the United States. Advertisements include large pictures of the most popular McDonald's menu items that appear to be flying off the restaurant chain's delivery trucks. French fries and Big Macs appear to be struggling against the wind in a "moving billboard" campaign. McDonald's also uses the backs of their trucks to relay messages to drivers. The advertising message for McCafé shakes tells drivers to "Whip through traffic."

One study found that 91 percent of people do notice words and pictures on mobile advertising vehicles.

Work as a Team Why are more companies using truckside advertising? Do you think it's effective? Why or why not?

Supply Chain Activities

Distribution is part of a larger process known as supply chain management. A **supply chain** includes all of the businesses involved in the flow of products, services, resources, and information from the producer to the consumer. *Supply chain management* is the coordination and

How does effective supply chain management benefit consumers?

implementation of supply chain activities in a way that maximizes customer satisfaction. When members of a supply chain cooperate and share information, they are able to respond quickly to changes in the supply and demand of a product. Supply chain managers are responsible for making decisions about purchasing raw materials and supplies, processing orders, managing inventory, transporting and storing supplies and finished products, and performing various other customer service activities. A number of procedures and processes occur throughout the supply chain to ensure that products are delivered to consumers.

Purchasing Materials

In order to function, businesses need a variety of products and services. They need raw materials, component parts, and equipment to produce products. They also need equipment and supplies that are used in the daily operations of the business, such as office furniture, computers, and paper. Businesses also require services that support the production, sales, or maintenance of their products and services. Attorneys and accountants are hired by businesses to perform specialized business services. Advertising agencies create promotional strategies for businesses.

Since a producer or manufacturer does not have everything it needs to develop the products it sells, it purchases these resources from other businesses. Many of the components needed to manufacture automobiles, computers, televisions, and other products are produced by other businesses. The essential components are purchased, incorporated into the production process, and then resold as part of the finished product. **Business-to-business marketing** occurs when businesses purchase products or services from other businesses.

Some businesses do not actually manufacture the products they sell. Instead, they purchase products for direct resale to other customers. A manufacturer may not want to handle the marketing and sale of its products, so it sells its finished products to businesses that will complete all of the marketing functions.

Because many of the products they purchase are unique and complex, businesses have purchasing specialists who manage the purchasing process. Common job titles for purchasing specialists include buyer and purchasing agent. Their job responsibilities include creating a buying plan, identifying and selecting suppliers, communicating specifications, and managing the paperwork. Once the buyer has determined what materials are needed, he or she will complete a **purchase order**, which is a form listing the types, quantities, and prices of products ordered. The top priority for buyers is to reduce the costs of raw materials and supplies. Buyers must negotiate the price and terms of the sale.

After the purchase order is processed, the seller ships the products to the buyer and sends an **invoice**, which is an itemized bill for products and services that states the terms of payment. Buyers evaluate or inspect the products to determine if they meet the business's and its customers' needs.

Processing Orders

A customer's order is often what sets the supply chain in motion. A customer commonly places an order with a sales associate, but the order may also be placed by telephone, fax, or electronically, such as through the Internet. Once received, the order works its way through the order processing system.

The order processing system involves many departments within the business, including the sales department, warehouse and shipping departments, and the accounting department. The sales department communicates the order to the warehouse department where an employee checks to see if the product is in stock. If the product isn't in stock, a backorder is placed so that the product can be delivered to the customer when it's available. If it is in stock, the product is packaged and prepared for shipment. Before the order is shipped, it is checked for accuracy. Shipping incorrect merchandise results in customer dissatisfaction. The shipping department determines the transportation methods and costs involved in getting the package to the customer on time. The accounting department prepares an invoice that contains the terms of the sale, method of payment, and cost of the products. Customers are then notified that the order has been processed and shipped. Product inventory records are updated to reflect the change in inventory levels.

Today, order processing is becoming more automated. **Electronic data interchange (EDI)** allows for the electronic exchange of information between the purchaser and supplier. Orders can be read and processed by computers, speeding up the ordering process. EDI replaces paper records.

Managing and Controlling Inventory

Businesses must maintain an adequate level of inventory to meet customers' demands. Several types of information must be maintained in an inventory control system, including the types of products in inventory, the quantity of each product on hand, and the length of time each product has been in inventory. Inventory systems must also have a method of determining what products to order, when to order them, and how many to order. Using EDI allows businesses to quickly replenish inventory when it is low.

Many retail businesses use a computerized **point-of-sale (POS) system**, which updates inventory records as each sale occurs. As products with bar codes are scanned at the cash register, adjustments to inventory are automatically made. Thus, inventory managers have access to up-to-date inventory records. POS systems can be used in combination with EDI to trigger orders of merchandise automatically. As products are sold and scanned by the retailer, the supplier can view the electronic inventory records. When the retailer's inventory falls below pre-established levels, the supplier automatically processes and ships an order for more merchandise.

Warehousing and Shipping

Many businesses need to store their products until the buyer wants or needs them, or they simply may have excess product that needs to be stored. Businesses also may need to store the raw materials or components that are used in the production of products. In all of these cases, products likely will be stored at a warehouse. Warehouses are designed to facilitate shipping and receiving in the most efficient manner. Computerized systems automate the warehousing process. Scanners track bar codes on products that are entering and leaving the warehouse. Customer orders are often processed and shipped directly from the warehouse. Businesses must decide which mode of transportation to use to ship the product.

Managing Supply Chain Risks

To prevent supply chain disruptions, all potential risks must be identified. Supply chains face many risks involving safety, security, distribution, and inventory control. Safety risks apply to products, buildings, equipment, employees, and customers. Procedures must be established to reduce the risk of damage or injury when shipping products from one location to another. Insurance can be purchased to help protect against financial loss due to damage or theft. Employees must be trained how to use equipment safely. Inventory theft by burglars, customers, and employees is a common problem. Surveillance systems and security procedures are used to prevent theft. Computerized inventory systems must have built-in security features to keep out computer hackers.

Supply chains also face external threats, including natural disasters, widespread technology

© Baloncici/Shutterstock.com

What role does the warehouse play in the supply chain?

failures, political instability, economic uncertainty, terrorism, and worker strikes. These threats can result in a temporary shut down of the supply chain. In the event of an emergency, businesses should have contingency plans for getting systems back up and running as quickly as possible.

///////// CHECKPOINT \\\\\\\\

What activities are involved in supply chain management?

Supply Chain Management Considerations

Changes in the business environment are having an effect on supply chain management. Trends in international markets, outsourcing, digital distribution, and eco-friendly business practices can influence supply chain decisions.

International Markets

More businesses are buying and selling products in international markets. **Imports** are products and services purchased from another country, while **exports** are products and services sold to another country. One of the biggest challenges faced by importers is understanding the international trade laws in other countries. Businesses may have to obtain permits, licenses, and registrations for imported products. Some countries may set *quotas*, which are limits on the amount of a product that can be imported into a country. Other countries set *tariffs*, which are taxes placed on imported products. Businesses must consider the additional costs associated with importing and exporting products. Transportation costs will also be higher. International transportation can be dangerous and unreliable. Government regulations require inspections of products moving across borders, which slows things down. Even with all of the restrictions and regulations, international trade is on the rise because it can be quite profitable.

Do you own clothing that has been imported into the United States? Check the labels.

Outsourcing

Outsourcing is becoming an important part of the distribution process. *Outsourcing* occurs when the manufacturer or supplier hires a third party (another company) to perform specific supply chain management functions, such as order processing, warehousing, or shipping. By relying on third-party companies for their expertise in specific areas, businesses can increase overall efficiency and customer service and lower the cost of providing the services to customers. Many businesses outsource the shipping function to delivery companies like FedEx and UPS that offer specialized transportation services. The special tracking systems offered by these delivery companies allow businesses to track deliveries to their final destinations. ARAMARK provides food and beverage outsourcing services and facilities management for sports arenas and convention centers. By allowing ARAMARK to handle the purchasing, delivery, and management of food and food services, the sports arenas and convention centers can focus on what they do best—entertainment and hospitality.

Digital Distribution

Some products can be distributed electronically through the Internet or a satellite transmission. Many software programs can be downloaded from the Internet. Tickets to sporting events and concerts can be purchased online and printed out at home. ESPN offers iPhone users comprehensive sports coverage, including breaking news and the latest scores. Songs and TV shows can be delivered directly to MP3 Players. Digital distribution offers several advantages. For businesses, it lowers distribution costs and provides access to more potential customers. Customers love its convenience.

SPOTLIGHT ON SUCCESS

© Bettmann/CORBIS

RAY, KROC
McDonald's

When Ray Kroc was 15 years old in 1917, he lied about his age to join the Red Cross as an ambulance driver. He never finished his training and went on to work other jobs, including as a piano player, paper cup salesman, and multimixer milkshake salesman. It was during his time as a multimixer salesman in 1954 that Kroc discovered a highly successful restaurant run by the McDonald brothers in San Bernardino, California. As Kroc watched a rapidly moving line of customers buy bags of hamburgers and fries, he came up with the vision of expanding this concept to other locations throughout the United States. The McDonald brothers were not interested in overseeing the expansion of their restaurant, so Kroc became their exclusive franchising agent and began selling the McDonald's name and concept across the nation beginning in 1955. The restaurant chain sold its 100 millionth hamburger by 1958, and Kroc bought the exclusive rights to the McDonald's name in 1960.

To achieve success, Ray Kroc knew it was important to consistently offer high-quality food and use uniform methods of preparation in all McDonald's restaurants. The burgers, buns, fries and beverages had to taste the same no matter in which state they were served up. To achieve this goal, Kroc persuaded franchisees and suppliers to buy into his vision—"in business for yourself, but not by yourself." He used the image of a 3-legged stool to describe his philosophy—one leg was McDonald's; the second, the franchisees; and the third, suppliers.

McDonald's has gone on to be one of the most successful franchises in history. McDonald's menu items are now distributed in more than 32,000 restaurants serving more than 60 million people in more than 100 countries each day. Individuals wishing to operate a McDonald's franchise must pay 40 percent as a down payment for a new restaurant or 25 percent as a down payment for an existing McDonald's restaurant. McDonald's distribution strategy now goes beyond free-standing restaurants to include locations in service stations, stores, and airports.

Think Critically

Why do you think the McDonald's business concept found success worldwide? How has McDonald's distribution strategy helped the business grow?

Eco-Friendly Practices

Businesses are recognizing the advantages of eco-friendly practices. Efforts to protect the environment are evident throughout the supply chain. Recyclable or reusable packages and packing materials are designed to prevent excess pollution and waste. Hewlett-Packard (HP), a computer manufacturer, has a recycling program for printer supplies and computers. HP makes recycling easy for customers by providing postage-paid shipping labels in printer cartridge boxes and by offering an online ordering tool to request recycling services. Businesses also use energy-efficient and pollution-free equipment and processes in their production facilities. Many businesses now use biodiesel delivery trucks to reduce carbon dioxide emissions.

CHECKPOINT

What factors influence supply chain decisions?

5.2 Assessment

THINK ABOUT IT

1. What are the responsibilities of a purchasing specialist?
2. How can a retailer manage its inventory efficiently?
3. Why is risk management an important part of supply chain management?
4. What are some of the considerations for a business that conducts international trade?

MAKE ACADEMIC CONNECTIONS

5. **VISUAL ART**   Design a flowchart that describes the supply chain management process. Within the flowchart, include a brief description of each process.

6. **ECONOMICS**   Outsourcing of various business functions is very popular among businesses. There are two types of outsourcing—onshore and offshore. Conduct research to learn about both types of outsourcing. Learn about the advantages and disadvantages of outsourcing and the effect it has on the economy. Write a one- to two-page report on your findings.

7. **MANAGEMENT**   You operate a department store that sells a variety of merchandise. You have determined that 5 percent of your inventory is lost to shoplifting. Items that are commonly shoplifted include clothing and small electronics such as cell phones, cameras, and MP3 players. Outline a plan to prevent shoplifting of these items.

 ### Teamwork

Select a product that is imported to the United States. Conduct research to determine the supply chain through which the product moves to get from the manufacturer to the final consumer. Prepare a PowerPoint presentation that describes the supply chain. Also, describe any restrictions or regulations, such as permits, licenses, tariffs, or quotas, that apply to the imported product.

5.3

Distribution Logistics

Goals

- Define logistics and explain its role in distribution.
- Explain the importance of product storage, handling, and packaging in the distribution process.

Terms

- logistics, p. 135
- warehouse, p. 138
- distribution center, p. 139

FOCUS ON ADVERTISING

UPS and Logistics

Logistics is the main focus of UPS. UPS performs logistics management every day when it links millions of organizations and individuals together by delivering an average of 15 million packages and documents in more than 220 countries and territories. UPS promoted that in its "That's Logistics" advertising campaign. UPS used the tune from one of the most recognizable songs in the world, "That's Amoré," to create a memorable theme song that described its role in the supply chain. The definition for "amoré" is "love," and UPS wanted to explain why all customers involved in the supply chain love the on-time delivery it provides. In one of the UPS commercials, a delivery person declared that, "UPS makes the world work better." UPS commercials emphasized how the latest technology used in combination with different modes of transportation keeps the continuous link of delivery in sync. UPS continued this theme on its website. Visitors could click on the "share the love for logistics" link to watch videos in which actual customers described how UPS helped them meet logistic challenges.

Work as a Team What processes do you think are involved in logistics? Why is this an important part of doing business?

Moving the Product

Logistics is the physical distribution process that involves transporting, storing, and delivering products throughout the supply chain. Logistics requires careful planning to ensure products are moved through the distribution channel efficiently. Several modes of transportation may be required as products are moved from the manufacturer to the consumer.

How many different modes of transportation do you think are required to move automobiles from the manufacturer to the consumer?

Products are frequently grouped into large units to lower transportation costs. Additional handling and packaging are required to separate the larger shipments into smaller units for display, sale, storage, or use.

Modes of Transportation

Logistics planning must determine the best method of transportation for moving products from the producer to consumers. The most common forms of transportation for product distribution include railroads, trucks, airplanes, ships/boats, and pipelines. Many products reach their final destination through the use of a combination of transportation methods.

Railroads Heavy, bulky items can be transported by railroad. The next time you stop for a flashing railroad crossing, take note of the products loaded on the railcars. Coal, iron ore, and automobiles are likely candidates to move by rail. Raw materials, industrial equipment, and large quantities of consumer products are often shipped by rail. The cost of shipping by rail is reasonable for large quantities but more expensive for only one or a few carloads of a product. Transportation by rail is slow as is the loading and unloading of materials from rail cars. Some parts of the country do not have rail service, so other forms of transportation are needed to move products from the closest rail site to the final destination. To accommodate this, manufacturers can use a *piggyback service* by packing products into large containers or truck trailers, which are then shipped on flatbed rail cars. This makes it quicker and easier to transfer the shipments to trucks.

Trucks Flexibility and low cost are common reasons businesses use trucks to transport products. Trucks can accommodate small or large

© Ulrich Mueller/Shutterstock.com

shipments, durable or fragile products requiring special handling, and short- or long-distance deliveries. Small companies frequently own a delivery truck. Large manufacturers, wholesalers, and retailers own fleets of trucks to move products easily. The cost of transportation by truck is low for short distances and easy-to-handle products. The cost increases for long-distance deliveries and products that are difficult to move. The rising cost of fuel has a major impact on the trucking industry. The increased costs of transportation associated with higher fuel costs are passed on to consumers in the form of higher prices for products.

Airplanes For rapid delivery of products, many businesses rely on airplanes. Small items can be transported on commercial flights, and large items or large quantities of an item can be transported on cargo planes. Although the cost of transportation by air is high, other cost savings can be realized. The speedy delivery may reduce the need for product storage and handling, which could result in less product spoilage, damage, and theft. Airplanes may be used by businesses or other organizations for emergencies or special deliveries. Timing is extremely important for medical emergencies. Special medicines and internal organs must be shipped by airplane for speedy delivery.

How does FedEx promote its shipping service as a good choice for businesses?

Ships and Boats The growth of international trade has increased the transportation of products by ship or boat. Ships can move large quantities and large products at relatively low prices. The biggest drawback for transporting products by ship is the time it takes. It could take several weeks for a product to arrive at its destination. Products can be damaged by weather or other conditions while traveling by ship. Because ships are limited to travel between major ocean ports that have product-handling capabilities, they are used in combination with trucks and railroads to complete product deliveries. Barges and other cargo-handling boats travel on lakes and large rivers to move raw materials (coal, grain, cement, and other bulky, nonperishable items).

Pipelines Gas, oil, and water that must be moved over long distances are transported through pipelines. Building and maintaining a pipeline is expensive. Once the pipeline is in operation, however, it is an inexpensive way to move large quantities of a product from one location to another.

Transportation Considerations

Because transportation is an important function of the supply chain, businesses must carefully plan all aspects of it. The mode of transportation used depends on the needs of the shipper. Factors to consider when selecting the mode of transportation include the following:

Why are reliability and capability important factors when choosing a mode of transportation?

- *Cost*—The amount charged to move a product from one location to another
- *Travel time*—The amount of time it takes for a product to arrive at its destination after leaving the shipper's location (includes the time for pickup, delivery, handling, and transit)
- *Reliability*—The transporter's record of making on-time deliveries in acceptable condition
- *Capability*—The ability of the transporter to move specific kinds of products, such as those requiring refrigeration or other special handling
- *Accessibility*—The ability of the transporter to access specific routes
- *Traceability*—The ease with which the location of a shipment can be tracked

//////// CHECKPOINT \\\\\\\\

What role does logistics play in the supply chain?

Product Storage, Handling, and Packaging

Businesses use storage facilities to store products at various times throughout the distribution process. Products are stored until they need to be moved to the next channel member. Storage facilities must be designed to protect the product during handling and to facilitate the shipping process. Another important part of product handling is packaging.

Warehouses

Large amounts of raw materials or finished products are often stored in warehouses until they can be used or sold. A **warehouse** is a building designed to store large quantities of products safely. Any of the businesses along the channel of distribution, such as the manufacturer, retailer, or wholesaler, may own a warehouse. By owning its own warehouse, the business can conveniently locate it and design the building as needed to house its products. Other businesses may choose to rent public warehouses because they need only limited storage space for limited periods of time, such as for seasonal inventory.

Warehouse districts can be found in many cities. In the past, warehouse districts consisted of multistory buildings located near the center of the city to be close to the retail businesses that needed storage space. Today, warehouse districts are typically large one-story buildings located on the edge of town near major highways and/or airports. The one-story buildings can be used more efficiently for product storage and distribution than can multiple-story buildings. Conveyor belts, computer-controlled robots, and forklifts are used to move products throughout the warehouse. Bar codes on shelves and products are used to keep a computerized inventory of the contents of the warehouse.

Distribution Centers

Large retailers like Walmart and the Dollar Tree use distribution centers to move products efficiently to thousands of stores located throughout the country. A **distribution center** is a large facility that offers a variety of supply chain services to help move a product to the marketplace more efficiently. While the main function of a warehouse is storage, a distribution center offers other services in addition to storage, including order processing and fulfillment, packaging and labeling, and shipping and receiving. Warehouses are focused on providing a cost-effective way to store products. Although cost-effectiveness is also an important consideration for distribution centers, their main focus is on providing excellent customer service. Distribution centers for large retailers like Walmart are located throughout the country to better serve all Walmart stores.

Packaging

Although product packages are designed to help promote products, they are also designed to help protect the product as it moves through the channel of distribution. Products often are shipped, stored, and handled many times between production and consumption. Businesses

What roles do distribution centers play in the supply chain?

suffer a financial loss on damaged or destroyed products. Today, environmentally friendly packaging is also a concern. More companies are packaging products in cans, bottles, and plastic containers that can be recycled.

The type of product and the quantity of the product are factors when choosing a packaging method for shipping. Shipping a small quantity of a product by truck across town will require different packaging than shipping a large quantity of the same product around the world. Products must be packaged in a way that enables them to be easily stacked on shelves in stores and in storage facilities as well as in trucks, railroad cars, ships, and airplanes for shipping.

CHECKPOINT

Why are product storage, handling, and packaging important components of the distribution process?

5.3 Assessment

THINK ABOUT IT

1. What types of products are more likely to be shipped by airplane? What are the advantages and disadvantages of shipping by air?

2. What types of products might use a combination of shipping methods?

3. What are some differences between a warehouse and a distribution center?

4. Look on the label of a product you purchased recently to learn where it was manufactured. Describe the logistics that you think were involved in getting the product to you, the consumer.

MAKE ACADEMIC CONNECTIONS

5. **VISUAL ART**   Design a poster to illustrate the advantages and disadvantages of shipping goods by air, rail, truck, water, and pipeline.

6. **RESEARCH**   The U.S. Postal Service (USPS) is a government agency. UPS and FedEx are privately owned companies that compete with the post office. Conduct research to determine the market share of delivery services held by each organization. How do their services and costs differ? Under what circumstances would it be better for a business to use the USPS to deliver a package? When would it be better to use UPS or FedEx? Write a report about your findings.

7. **TECHNOLOGY**   Research the types of technology being used by warehouses and distribution centers to improve their storage, handling, and distribution processes. Report what you learn to the class.

Teamwork

Your company sells soft drinks and spring water packaged in plastic bottles. Environmentalists are complaining about plastic bottles that take up space in landfills. Devise a new environmentally friendly packaging strategy for the soft drinks and water. Present your strategy to the class.

Sharpen Your
21st CENTURY SKILLS

PARTNERSHIP FOR
21ST CENTURY SKILLS

Effective Organizational Skills

Organization plays an important role in supply chain management. People and processes must be coordinated to ensure products get from the manufacturer to the consumer. People who work as supply chain managers need good organizational skills. Those who have good organizational skills tend to be efficient, punctual, and reliable because they use a systematic approach to manage their time, space, and tasks. Being well organized saves time and reduces the stress associated with looming deadlines.

Everyone can develop better organizational skills by taking note of their current habits and then implementing some important new routines. Incorporating the following steps can lead to better personal organization skills.

1. Evaluate your current organizational strategies. Make a list of areas in which you feel you are unorganized. Get advice from others. There are many organizational tips available online.

2. Make a To Do list for daily, weekly, and monthly tasks. Prioritize the list in the order that each task is to be completed. Check off tasks as they are completed. Add new tasks to the list as needed.

3. Write yourself notes as reminders and put them in places where they will catch your attention, such as on your computer monitor, on your doors, or on mirrors.

4. Maintain a calendar of events that includes contacts, telephone numbers, and e-mail addresses to avoid the frustration of missing important appointments, meetings, deadlines, and events.

5. Keep your computer files organized. Create electronic folders to store files in their proper place. Delete files that are no longer needed. Make backups of important files.

Strong organizational skills are required for most careers. Many of these steps can be completed using a software program or a smartphone application.

Try It Out

Make a To Do list of tasks that you must complete today and this week. Rank the tasks according to order of importance and then set deadlines for the completion of each task. Check off all completed tasks throughout the week. Also, write notes to yourself to remind you about important tasks you must complete. As an alternative, use a computer program to perform these tasks. At the end of the week, rate your organizational skills. Did keeping a To Do list and writing notes help you get more organized? Did they save you time?

IKO/Shuttertock.com

SUMMARY

5.1 Channel of Distribution

- The channel of distribution is the path on which products and services flow from the producer to the final consumer.
- Channel members include producers (manufacturers), retailers, wholesalers, transportation companies, warehouses, agents and brokers, and consumers.
- Products can be moved to consumers through direct channels and indirect channels. Direct channels involve the producer selling directly to the consumer. Indirect channels involve intermediaries that move the product from the producer to the consumer. Multiple channels of distribution may be used to market the same product to several target markets.

5.2 Supply Chain Management

- Supply chain activities include purchasing materials, processing orders, managing and controlling inventory, warehousing, shipping, and managing supply chain risks.
- Many of the supply chain processes are computerized. Electronic data interchange (EDI) and point-of-sale (POS) systems make the processes more efficient.
- Factors that must be considered when making supply chain decisions include international markets, outsourcing, digital distribution, and eco-friendly practices.

5.3 Distribution Logistics

- Logistics is the physical distribution process that involves transporting, storing, and delivering products throughout the supply chain.
- The most common modes of transportation for product distribution include railroads, trucks, airplanes, ships/boats, and pipelines.
- When choosing a mode of transportation, factors for businesses to consider include, cost, travel time, reliability, capability, accessibility, and traceability.
  - Finished products must be stored until they need to move to the next channel member. Warehouses and distribution centers help facilitate the storage and handling processes. Packaging helps protect the product as it moves through the channel of distribution.

WHAT DO YOU KNOW Now?

Read *Impact Advertising* on page 121 again to review online promotion strategies used by various retailers. Visit the website of one of the retailers discussed in the feature or another retailer to learn more about online strategies being used to win over consumers. Describe an online strategy that appeals to you and explain why.

Chapter 5 Assessment

Vocabulary Builder

Match each statement with the term that best defines it. Some terms may not be used.

1. A small, free-standing booth containing a computer or display screen that distributes product information
2. A distribution method in which the producer sells directly to the consumer
3. A building designed to store large quantities of products safely
4. All of the businesses involved in the flow of products, services, resources, and information from the producer to the consumer
5. A distribution method in which intermediaries are used to help move a product from the producer to the consumer
6. A form which lists the types, quantities, and prices of products ordered
7. Occurs when a business purchases products or services from other businesses
8. A computerized system that updates inventory records as each sale occurs
9. A large facility that offers a variety of supply chain services to help move a product to the marketplace more efficiently
10. Products or services purchased from another country

a. business-to-business marketing
b. channel of distribution
c. direct channel
d. distribution
e. distribution center
f. electronic data interchange (EDI)
g. exports
h. imports
i. indirect channel
j. invoice
k. kiosk
l. logistics
m. point-of-sale (POS) system
n. purchase order
o. supply chain
p. warehouse

Test Your Knowledge

11. The earliest product exchanges involved consumers buying goods and services
    a. from distributors
    b. from other consumers
    c. directly from producers
    d. from retailers
12. Which of the following is *not* a channel member?
    a. producers
    b. wholesalers
    c. retailers
    d. advertisers
13. Supply chain risks include all of the following *except*
    a. employee injuries
    b. competition
    c. inventory theft
    d. natural disasters
14. _____ are taxes placed on imported products.
    a. Tariffs
    b. Logistics
    c. Quotas
    d. EDI

15. Product packaging is used to
    a. promote products
    b. protect products
    c. protect the environment
    d. all of the above
16. Outsourcing is used
    a. to distribute products electronically
    b. to manage supply chain risks
    c. when another company can perform the activity better
    d. none of the above
17. Which of the following channels of distribution is likely to be used in international markets?
    a. producer to consumer
    b. producer to retailer to consumer
    c. producer to wholesaler to retailer to consumer
    d. producer to agent to wholesaler to retailer to consumer
18. Railroads and boats are good modes of transportation for
    a. perishable products
    b. small parcels
    c. large, bulky items
    d. emergency medications
19. Trucks are a popular method for shipping products for all of the following reasons *except*
    a. they easily accommodate heavy, bulky items
    b. they can accommodate small or large shipments
    c. they can be used for short and long distances
    d. they are a low-cost option
20. The ability to move specific kinds of products, such as those requiring special handling, refers to the transporter's
    a. reliability
    b. capability
    c. accessibility
    d. traceability

Apply What You Learned

21. Describe the packaging for three different foods or beverages. Explain how the package protects the food or beverages as they travel through the channel of distribution.
22. The marketing concept focuses on identifying and satisfying the needs of customers. Explain the role of the distribution process in implementing the marketing concept.
23. Select a product that you believe has more than one target market. Describe how the manufacturer of the product could use multiple channels of distribution to reach the different target markets.

Make Academic Connections

24. **MATH**   A company pays an average of $2,000 each year to insure against possible losses associated with exporting products around the world. The business has been in operation for 10 years and has paid the same insurance premium every year. How much has the company paid for insurance? The company recently filed an insurance claim for damage to shipped products valued at $50,000. The insurance company paid only 80 percent of the claim. How much did the company receive? How much of the loss was not covered?

25. **RESEARCH**   Conduct research to learn more about distribution centers. Prepare a one-page report describing the various services provided by distribution centers. Describe how retailers and consumers benefit from the use of distribution centers.

26. **INTERNATIONAL**   Prepare a PowerPoint presentation that describes all of the channels of distribution involved in the sale of an imported automobile of your choice to a customer in the United States. The presentation should include a description of supply chain activities, including the purchasing, ordering, warehousing, and shipping processes. Also, explain the supply chain risks involved with this purchase.

27. **COMMUNICATION**   Interview people about bad shopping experiences related to supply chain management. Experiences may involve out-of-stock products, shipping errors, or delayed shipments. How did the shoppers react to the problem? Did it affect their image of the business? What can you conclude about the importance of an effective supply chain?

28. **GOVERNMENT**   Research some of the trade restrictions and regulations that the United States imposes on imported products. Also, research U.S. legislation related to international trade, such as the North American Free Trade Agreement (NAFTA). Prepare a chart listing the restrictions, regulations, and legislation along with the pros and cons of each one as it relates to the U.S. economy. Discuss your chart in class.

29. **MATH**   You are the buyer for Sports Action, which sells sporting and fitness equipment and apparel. Select five products typically sold at this type of store and research their prices. Assume you need to order more of these products to restock your inventory. Create a purchase order form containing the name of your company, its address (use a fictitious address), and the types, quantities, and prices of products you want to order. Be sure to include the total price of the purchase order.

You order a piece of exercise equipment from an online retailer. The website indicates that the exercise equipment is currently out of stock but will be available for shipment in 7 days. You choose to have the exercise equipment shipped overnight. Overnight delivery costs you an additional $25. You pay for the exercise equipment and shipping fees with your credit card. When you don't receive the exercise equipment after 14 days, you track your order online and learn that the exercise equipment will be out of stock for another 7 days. Because you got such a good deal on the price of the exercise equipment, you decide to wait another 7 days. In the meantime, you receive your credit card bill containing the charge for the exercise equipment and pay it. It has now been 30 days, and you have not received the exercise equipment. The website still indicates it is out of stock. You research the company online and discover there are numerous customer complaints about this retailer.

What should you do now? What will you do differently the next time you shop online?

Reality ✓

Using eBay to Distribute Products

Sellers and buyers are brought together on eBay, an online auction service that allows users to sell a wide variety of merchandise by accepting bids from prospective buyers. Bids are accumulated throughout the duration of the auction, and the highest bidder is awarded the item at the end of the auction.

Over 150 million people in over 30 countries buy and sell products through eBay, making it the largest marketplace in the world. It has become a valuable distribution channel for individuals and businesses selling new and used items. It began as a place for people to sell collectibles but has expanded to include over 45,000 different product categories, ranging from trading cards to automobiles. The fastest-growing categories on eBay include business and industrial sales.

Like all other marketplaces, the marketing functions must be carried out on eBay. With the help of search engines, eBay performs much of the promotional tasks for eBay sellers. Keyword searches for products often provide direct links to the products being sold on eBay. Sellers can help promote their products by giving detailed descriptions and using enticing photos. The buyers and sellers are responsible for many of the other marketing functions. To gauge demand and determine pricing for a product, sellers can comparison shop for similar products on eBay. To help with the financing function, sellers and buyers can use PayPal, which is a global online payment system similar to using a credit card. The distribution function involves shipping, handling, and packaging. Although buyers pay for shipping, sellers typically select the shipping method. They must determine the best way to package and ship small and large items. The risk management function is left to the buyers. They must be cautious and knowledgeable and use common sense when purchasing products.

As the distribution of products through eBay continues to grow, so do the opportunities for sellers and buyers. As buyers become more educated, eBay sellers will have to find smarter ways to perform the marketing functions.

Think Critically
1. How can you become a seller on eBay? (Conduct online research.)
2. Why is eBay such a popular way to buy and sell products?
3. How does the eBay marketplace differ from traditional marketplaces?
4. What kinds of research should a customer do before making a purchase on eBay?

You are to assume the role of distribution coordinator for SUPERMART, a large retailer that has 3,000 locations throughout the country. SUPERMART recently added 20 new stores in the central part of the United States due to high consumer demand. SUPERMART's annual sales for the 20 new stores totaled $20 billion. The nearest distribution center is located 600 miles from the new stores. Inventory management at the new stores has become increasingly difficult. The store wants to add an additional distribution center in the middle of the United States that will be located within 150 miles of each of the new stores. The distribution center will employ approximately 500 employees. Total yearly income for all employees is estimated at $19.2 million. The owner of SUPERMART has asked you to explain the need for an additional distribution center.

You will have up to ten minutes to determine how you will handle the role-play situation and demonstrate the performance indicators of this event. During the preparation period, you may make notes to use during the role-play situation.

Performance Indicators Evaluated

- Apply information to accomplish a task.
- Explain the nature and scope of channel management.
- Coordinate channel management with other marketing activities.
- Explain the relationship between customer service and channel management.
- Define the purpose of a distribution center.
- Explain the importance of location in relation to distribution centers and retailers.

Go to the DECA website for more detailed information.

Think Critically

1. Why must large retailers have nearby distribution centers?
2. What factors should be considered when determining a new location for a distribution center?
3. How does the location of a retailer's distribution center affect its sales?
4. How is customer service affected by the location of a distribution center?
5. What are the benefits to a city in which a distribution center is located?

www.deca.org

6

Promotion Planning

© gary718/Shutterstock.com

Promotional Products

Promotional products containing a company's name and logo have been used successfully for many years to increase business and maintain relationships with customers. Displaying a company or brand name and logo on a product is a good way to advertise. The types of promotional products and their costs are wide ranging.

The Parker Pen Company has one of the most recognized fine-writing pen brands in the world. Its pens are known for their craftsmanship. Certain Parker pens can cost hundreds of dollars. Companies that have large clients may choose to give Parker pens as a promotional tool. The company's name or logo is discreetly printed on the pen. Although there are many fine pens on the market at a fraction of the cost, companies choose to give out Parker pens because their clients are more likely to use them, meaning the company's name and logo are always on display.

T-shirts and caps are great promotional products because they are a walking billboard. Companies increase their exposure when individuals wear the t-shirt or cap bearing the company's logo. Magnets, bottle openers, calendars, and a wide array of other products can also reap great promotional results. These inexpensive promotional items are very effective because they are useful. Consumers often use magnets to display things on their refrigerators. The magnets act as mini-billboards every time the consumer opens the refrigerator door. Calendars imprinted with a company's name and logo are often hung in homes and offices.

Grocery stores are offering promotional products that are in line with the eco-friendly trend. They provide reusable fabric shopping bags containing the store's name and logo as a way to replace the plastic shopping bags that clog landfills and contribute to the litter problem.

Because of the popularity of digital devices, technology-related promotional products imprinted with company names and logos are a big hit. Items such as laptop or iPad sleeves, flash drives, mouse pads, and USB laptop lights are more likely to be used and kept by customers, making them a more effective promotional tool.

When it comes to promotional products, businesses should do research to learn what would be relevant to their target market. For example, a sporting goods company who targets physically active adults might want to give away imprinted golf tees, golf balls, or golf umbrellas as a promotion. The key is to create a memorable message.

© aroas/Shutterstock.com

WHAT DO YOU KNOW?

1. **Why are promotional products an effective way to maintain customer relations?**

2. **Why is it important to carefully select the promotional product based on the target market?**

3. **Describe any promotional products you or your family has received. Do you think they were effective? Why or why not?**

Promotion

Goals

- Define *promotional mix* and explain its importance.
- Identify the steps in developing the promotional plan.

Terms

- promotion, p. 150
- promotional mix, p. 151
- promotional plan, p. 152

FOCUS ON ADVERTISING

Promotion Sells Products

Promotion is used by businesses to inform, persuade, and remind consumers about products and services. Procter & Gamble, a consumer goods company, uses promotion very effectively. P&G is the world's number one advertiser, with an advertising budget of over $8 billion in a recent year. It was inducted into the Advertising Hall of Fame in 2010 for its global reputation as an advertising leader. In addition to advertising, P&G uses sales promotions to help sell its products. Consumers can go online to order a P&G sampler to have the latest coupons and product samples delivered to their door. P&G also runs numerous sweepstakes offering consumers free trips and other prizes. Public relations and publicity are important promotion tools for P&G. It sponsors events, such as the "Clean Sheet Week" challenge where someone lived and slept in a window display at Macy's for a week to help promote Downy® fabric softener. P&G also receives publicity through its numerous Best of Beauty awards given by Allure magazine for P&G's products, such as Olay® lotions. P&G has developed a promotional mix that has made it one of the most successful companies in the world.

Work as a Team Name another business that uses several forms of promotion to help sell its product. Describe the promotions and explain why they are effective.

The Promotional Mix

Consumers do not automatically buy products. They must obtain information about a product or service before they make a purchase. **Promotion** involves all communications used by a business to create a favorable impression of its products or services. Businesses use a **promotional mix**, which is a combination of advertising, public relations, personal selling, and sales promotion, to reach their target market. An effective promotional mix can help a business introduce products and services to the market, increase sales, raise public awareness, and even develop a good-citizen reputation.

Why Is the Promotional Mix Needed?

Every day consumers are bombarded with thousands of messages trying to convince them to buy products and services. Only a few of the messages actually make an impact with the target market, and even a smaller percentage of the messages persuade consumers to take action and make a purchase. A well-planned promotional mix can deliver the message in the most effective manner.

Different types of promotions are better suited for different products and different target markets. For example, appliances usually require a higher level of decision making on the part of the consumer. Thus, appliance manufacturers rely on personal selling to persuade customers to buy their products. However, advertisements or sales promotions, such as coupons, would work more effectively to sell toothpastes. A business that sells a product that is used by more than one target market may use different promotional mixes for each target market. An exercise equipment manufacturer may sell its treadmill to consumers and businesses. It may use infomercials to attract consumers. When selling to fitness companies, the exercise equipment manufacturer may send out advertisements and then have salespeople follow up to promote the benefits of the equipment.

A business must decide which promotional mix will meet its objectives. Each type of promotion has its strengths when used appropriately. When more than one type of promotion is used, they must complement each other and deliver a consistent message about the product.

The AIDA Concept and the Promotional Mix

The main objective of any promotion is to get someone to buy a product or service. Many marketers use the *AIDA concept* to help accomplish this goal. AIDA is an acronym that stands for *attention*, *interest*, *desire*, and *action*, which are the four stages of promotion. Promotion must attract the attention of the consumer, create an interest, turn the interest into a desire, and then persuade the consumer to take action.

How can promotions be used to catch consumers' attention?

1. *Attention*: To sell a product or service, a business must first capture the attention of consumers and create awareness. This can be done in advertisements in many ways, such as by using interesting visuals and powerful words. Salespeople can catch the attention of consumers by using a friendly greeting. A public relations event, such as a concert sponsored by a business, is a good way to create awareness.
2. *Interest*: Product awareness does not always lead to a sale. Marketers must gain the consumers' interest.

Advertisements should communicate the benefits of the product to let people know what's in it for them if they purchase the product. Salespeople can give product demonstrations to generate interest.

3. *Desire*: Interest and desire are closely related. As marketers build interest in their product or service, they should try to appeal to consumers' buying motives (emotional, rational, and patronage). Salespeople can promote the safety features of a car to appeal to families with children. Restaurant advertisements can show pictures of freshly prepared burgers with all the toppings to entice TV viewers.

4. *Action*: Finally, promotions must motivate consumers to take action. A restaurant may invite customers to use a coupon on certain menu items. A retailer may promote discounts on selected merchandise. Salespeople can offer special financing to help consumers afford purchases of high-priced items.

Marketers must determine which stage applies to most of its target market. If a product has been on the market for a while, market research may show that consumers are past the attention and interest stages. For example, research may indicate that although many consumers have a high desire for a 3D television set, consumers haven't bought one yet. Manufacturers of 3D televisions could develop a promotional mix that would create a desire and persuade consumers to take action and buy one.

///////// CHECKPOINT \\\\\\\\\

Why do businesses need to develop a promotional mix?

The Promotional Plan

By delivering a message in many different ways, a business increases its odds of reaching its target market. To increase the effectiveness of its promotions, a business should create a **promotional plan**, which outlines how all of the elements in the promotional mix will work together to reach the target market. Creating an effective promotional plan takes time and involves a step-by-step process.

Determine the Target Market

Using market research, businesses must first identify their target market(s) before planning a promotional mix. Understanding the attitudes and behaviors of the target market will help the business design the best message and select the best form of promotion to reach the target customers. A company that sells farm equipment should run advertisements on rural radio stations that carry livestock and grain market reports and in print publications that are read by the target market—farmers.

Identify Promotional Objectives

Businesses must determine the response that they want to elicit from the target market. Promotional objectives identify what the business wants to achieve with its promotional mix. The objectives should be realistic and measurable. Some common examples of company objectives include introducing a new product to the market, correcting false impressions of a brand, creating greater brand awareness, communicating new product features, generating more buzz or word-of-mouth business, building a new image, or retaining the current customer base.

Set the Promotional Budget

After the promotional objectives are set, marketers must determine what it will cost to meet those objectives. Previous promotional budgets are a good starting point. Some businesses simply set their promotional budgets based on a percentage of sales. For example, a business that sold $1.5 million in equipment last year might allocate 7 percent of sales to promotion, for a promotional budget of $105,000.

Another common method of budgeting involves matching what competitors are spending for promotion. Marketers can monitor competitors' advertisements, promotions, and special events and estimate their costs. Although this does not provide a precise budget, it provides an overall estimate. A better strategy for budgeting is to compile a list of promotional methods that a business feels will meet its objectives, assuming money is not a factor. Then actual and estimated costs for each promotional activity can be researched. Marketers must then begin scaling down the list to achieve a reasonable budget.

Most companies test a variety of promotional mixes. It will take time to determine the most cost-effective promotional mix for a company. The budget will need to be reevaluated, and adjustments will need to made periodically.

How does a business determine the promotional budget?

Determine the Promotional Mix

Based on the budget, marketers can determine the best methods to convey their message. They need to choose the appropriate mix of advertising, public relations, sales promotion, and personal selling. Advertising is good for introducing new products to target markets, persuading potential customers to select one brand over another brand, and reminding customers of the product's benefits. Public relations can enhance a business's image and build goodwill. Sales promotions provide extra value or incentives for consumers. Personal selling works well for expensive, technical, or highly specialized products. Often, the various promotional tools will be coordinated to work together. For example, a newspaper advertisement for a product might also promote a contest being sponsored by the same business or include a coupon for the product.

Implement and Evaluate the Promotional Plan

After a promotional mix is determined, the budget will be spread among the promotional mix activities. A schedule is created that shows when the various promotional activities will occur. Promotion activities may run simultaneously or be staggered throughout the year.

The effectiveness of the promotional mix is usually measured by the amount of increased sales. The results of various promotional activities are also compared to the promotional objectives. Advertisements that include coupons can be tracked to see how many coupons were redeemed. The attendance at a public relations event sponsored by a business can be tracked. The number of phone calls registered after an infomercial can be counted. The promotional mix must be evaluated so that ineffective promotions can be adjusted. Evaluation also provides information for future promotional efforts.

CHECKPOINT

What are the steps in developing a promotional plan?

6.1 Assessment

THINK ABOUT IT

1. What is the AIDA concept?
2. Provide an example of when each of the promotional mix elements (advertising, sales promotion, public relations, personal selling) might be used by a business.
3. Why might a company have different promotional mixes for the same product?

MAKE ACADEMIC CONNECTIONS

4. **MATH**   Your company has decided to budget 5 percent of its net sales for promotion. Net sales for the year totaled $1.2 million. The promotional budget will be allocated as follows: 60 percent for advertising, 25 percent for sales promotions, 12 percent for public relations, and 3 percent for personal selling. How much money will be spent on each element of the promotional mix?

5. **RESEARCH**   Visit the websites of three online clothing retailers that are popular with teenagers. What promotional items are included on the websites? Do they offer coupons or other special incentives for shopping at the websites? How can the retailers track the effectiveness of their online advertising? What other types of promotion would you suggest for the online retailers?

6. **PROBLEM SOLVING**   Write three promotional objectives for a business where you frequently shop. Remember, the objectives should be realistic and measurable.

Teamwork

Select a business in your community and develop a promotional mix for it. Describe the product or service sold by the business. Prepare a PowerPoint presentation to describe the promotional mix elements you have chosen. Include a projected budget that estimates the cost for each element of the promotional mix.

6.2

Advertising and Public Relations

Goals

- Discuss the advantages and disadvantages of advertising.
- Explain the need for public relations.

Terms

- public relations, p. 157
- publicity, p. 157
- press release, p. 157

FOCUS ON ADVERTISING

Careers in Public Relations

The public relations career field is a popular one. It traditionally attracts more job applicants than there are job openings. Work in this industry is fast-paced and exciting, but it can also be stressful because tight schedules and long hours, including evenings and weekends, are common. Those working in this profession have to like interacting with other people and must have lots of energy. Most public relations projects require a team effort. The top priority of the public relations professional is to get the company's name out to the public. The job duties are wide ranging and could involve speaking publicly about the company, acting as the company's spokesperson, doing TV and radio interviews about new products, attending conferences or exhibitions where the company's products will be displayed and demonstrated, organizing company-sponsored events, and coordinating the efforts of photographers and the media. Public relations is an important part of the promotional mix for a company, so effective public relations professionals are a highly valued asset.

Work as a Team Why do you think public relations careers are so popular? Besides the characteristics described here, what other characteristics do you think someone would need to succeed in this field?

Advertising for Results

Advertising is a paid form of communication intended to inform and persuade an audience to take some kind of action. The money budgeted for advertising by companies like Verizon, Procter & Gamble, Johnson & Johnson, and General Motors is well over $2.5 billion each. Industries that

What are some common methods of advertising used by businesses?

spend high dollars on advertising include automotive, telecom, financial services, retail, and food and candy industries. Advertising is responsible for some of today's most successful brands, like Coca-Cola. Effective advertisements sell a business, its message, or its product. The winning combination combines creativity with a message that appeals to a strong need or want within the target market. Successful advertisements are convincing. They engage prospective customers in a personal manner, as if the business was speaking directly to them. When a business succeeds in making this connection, brand recognition is built.

Advertising is used more commonly than any other form of promotion to introduce new products to the market. Advertisements give new products the high level of exposure needed to create product awareness and to influence purchasing decisions. When a product hits the maturity stage, advertising is used to remind customers about the product to help maintain market share.

Businesses must decide what form of advertising will be the most effective at increasing sales. An advertising campaign may include print ads in magazines and newspapers, audio campaigns for radio, commercials on television, streaming messages on the Internet, or ads on outdoor billboards. Since most campaigns use several advertising options, marketers must ensure that all strategies complement one another and present a unified message to consumers.

Advantages of Advertising

When businesses advertise, they bring a sense of credibility to their products. Consumers' opinions about a product's legitimacy and quality are more favorable when the product is advertised. In addition, the advertisements can be repeated many times, reinforcing the advertising message through repetition. For businesses that operate nationally, the same advertisement can be used to reach people around the country. Because advertising reaches a large audience, the cost-per-viewer is relatively low compared to other promotional methods.

One of the biggest advantages of advertising, particularly television advertising, is the ability to make an emotional connection with the target market through the use of actors, music, images, and other production factors. Emotional connections help build strong brands. Businesses can establish a competitive advantage when consumers associate favorable images with a brand name.

Disadvantages of Advertising

Even though advertisements seem like a cost-effective way to reach a large audience, the overall cost to produce and run advertisements in various types of media can be very expensive. Professionally produced television commercials can cost between $350,000 and $400,000 to produce. Running a 30-second advertisement on television can cost between $500,000 and $3 million during the Super Bowl. Airing advertisements during some of the more popular primetime television shows can cost between $700,000 and $800,000 for a 30-second commercial.

Although, advertising can attract consumers' interest initially, it can become stale over time, causing consumers to block it out. In most cases, advertisements cannot be modified or updated quickly. Advertising is also impersonal because it doesn't allow for face-to-face communication or provide ways for the consumer to give feedback. Finally, just due to the sheer volume of advertisements, which is referred to as *advertising clutter*, consumers have a tendency to tune out.

▰▰▰▰ CHECKPOINT ◥◥◥◥◥◥

Why is advertising the most common form of promotion for new products?

Public Relations and Publicity

All businesses and brands want to have a good reputation and positive image with consumers. Activities and events that create goodwill for a business or other organization are referred to as **public relations** (PR). Public relations involves writing press releases, organizing news conferences, producing company newsletters, sponsoring events, and exhibiting at trade shows.

Public relations campaigns help the public develop a better understanding of a company, its products, and its philosophies. A business may donate money to a local charity or sponsor the local baseball team. It could donate resources including money and volunteers to help construct a local playground or actively participate in local schools. Marketers plan public relations campaigns that enhance the business's image and focus on target markets. Timberland, an outdoor clothing and shoe company, has developed a climate strategy to help tackle global warming. Timberland plans to reduce its carbon emissions and increase its use of renewable energy. It sponsored the "Plant One on Us" campaign in which Timberland planted trees on behalf of customers who made purchases. These public relations activities aim to preserve the lifestyle of Timberland's target market—outdoor enthusiasts.

Publicity often goes hand-in-hand with public relations. **Publicity** is any nonpaid form of communication designed to arouse public interest about a product, service, business, or event. Publicity occurs when a newspaper, television news show, or other media outlet reports about donations made by a business or special events sponsored by a business. Businesses may write a **press release**, which is a written statement to inform the media about a new product or special event. Press releases are often posted on a company's own website.

Why Is There a Need for Public Relations?

Why would an individual or company develop a public relations campaign? A good PR campaign highlights company-sponsored events or community activities as a way to build a positive image in the minds of consumers. New businesses count on public relations to make the public aware of their existence. A mature business may use public relations to gain greater visibility, publicize its growth, or promote recent product innovations or product launches. New employees and employees who have had major accomplishments can be recognized in the local media to generate positive public relations. Public relations can also attract new employees who have similar viewpoints.

Responding to unfavorable publicity or a negative event is also part of the public relations function. In 2011 a lawsuit alleged that Taco Bell's taco filling was made of a meat mixture and did not meet federal requirements to be labeled as "beef." Taco Bell fought the negative publicity by running full-page ads in major newspapers, airing television commercials, and launching a YouTube campaign defending the quality of its product. It spent between $3 and $4 million in advertising. Taco Bell managed to overcome the bad press with its aggressive response, and the lawsuit was eventually dropped.

Advertising vs. Public Relations

Many people do not know the difference between advertising and public relations. Advertising uses creative and edgy techniques to communicate a message. Because the advertiser is paying for the advertisement, it has control over what the ad will say and when and where it will be aired or published. The goal of public relations is to get free publicity for a business and its products or services. This usually involves reporting just the facts without any hype. The media has control over whether it will report on the event or publish the press release. Advertising has a longer life span than a public relations event. An advertisement can run over and over again. The exposure a business receives from a sponsored event or a press release about a new product happens only once.

Advantages and Disadvantages of Public Relations

Most people perceive publicity as more credible than an advertisement. Consumers are more likely to believe a third-party source, such as a reporter, because he or she can speak freely about a company or product. Favorable product reviews on a newscast or by a celebrity are more enticing to consumers than product claims made by an advertiser in a commercial. When a trusted talk-show host recommends a product, the sales of that product quickly grow. Many companies try to get endorsements on popular talk shows and newscasts.

Publicity is often considered to be free advertising. The cost of public relations is relatively inexpensive. When the release of a new product becomes the topic of big news stories, it can be worth millions of dollars in free publicity. Apple frequently makes the headlines when it releases highly demanded products like the iPhone. The media

How can publicity benefit a company?

buzz about the release of a new *Harry Potter* book or movie helps generate big sales. On the other hand, although a business does not pay for the publicity directly, some sponsored events, such as concerts, can be costly to stage.

The biggest disadvantage of public relations is the lack of control. Third-party media outlets, not the company, have control over what is said about the company or product. Companies cannot accurately predict or control the amount and kind of coverage a product will receive. A newscast can run a story about a product when fewer viewers are watching. Information could be improperly reported or important details could be omitted. If negative reviews of a product are reported, it could be disastrous for the company.

▰▰▰▰▰ CHECKPOINT ◣◣◣◣◣◣

How does public relations differ from advertising?

6.2 Assessment

THINK ABOUT IT

1. What are some advantages of using advertising as a form of promotion? What are some disadvantages?
2. Why is it easy to develop an emotional connection through advertising?
3. Provide some examples of why a business might need public relations.
4. Why is it difficult to control public relations?

MAKE ACADEMIC CONNECTIONS

5. **MATH**   Assume 106 million people watched the most recent Super Bowl. If a company spends $3 million for one commercial during the Super Bowl, what was the advertising cost per person reached by the commercial? Assume that advertising costs for the commercial represent 8 percent of the projected sales revenue of the product. What is the amount of the projected sales revenue? If the advertised product sells for $12.50, how many products will have to be sold to meet the projected sales revenue amount?

6. **COMMUNICATION**   Conduct research to find a local business that has had a positive role in the community. Write a press release that describes the business's most recent community or charitable efforts.

7. **RESEARCH**   Learn about a public relations campaign implemented by a company that has experienced an image problem due to a defective product, bad business practices, or other issues. Write a one-page report that describes the PR strategy used by the company. Did the company recover from the bad publicity?

Teamwork

Select a company that has successfully used advertising to build a well-known brand. Describe some of the company's most successful advertisements. Explain how the advertisements made a connection with the target market and built brand identity.

Personal Selling and Sales Promotion

Goals

- Explain the steps involved in the sales process.
- Describe reasons why sales promotion is needed.

Terms

- personal selling, p. 160
- approach, p. 161
- preapproach, p. 161
- demonstration, p. 162
- close, p. 162
- suggestion selling, p. 162
- follow-up, p. 163
- sales promotion, p. 164

Coupons Are Serious Business

Coupons are one of the most popular forms of sales promotion. They were used as early as the late 1800s, when C. W. Post Company issued penny-off coupons to try to get people to try its Grape-Nuts cereal. About 350 billion coupons are distributed annually. Traditionally, coupons have been distributed as inserts in newspapers. Today, coupons also are distributed online. At websites such as coupon.com, consumers can print free coupons for their favorite brands. Kroger, a popular grocery store, is offering digital coupons that can be used in combination with its Kroger Plus card. Card members can go to Kroger's website, click on the coupons they want, and have them loaded on their Kroger Plus card, where they can be redeemed at the checkout line when the card is scanned. Groupon is an online subscription service that offers daily deals to members. It negotiates huge discounts with businesses in over 44 countries and extends those savings to subscribers. Consumers purchase "groupons" and redeem them at businesses.

Work as a Team Do you think coupons are effective sales promotion tools? Do you think the online coupon sites will increase the usage of coupons? Why or why not?

Making the Sale

Personal selling is face-to-face communication between the buyer and seller that attempts to influence the buying decision. In certain situations, personal selling may work better than other forms of promotion in obtaining the sale. Salespeople that are trained and knowledgeable are more effective at informing customers and persuading them to buy than an advertisement is. Personal selling is often used for products that are complex or relatively expensive, such as automobiles, homes, insurance, furniture, and computers. The biggest disadvantage of personal selling is the cost. Salespeople make one sale at a time, making the cost per customer high.

Steps in the Sales Process

The sales process will vary for different types of products, depending on the product features and customer needs. Some sales take only minutes, while other sales can take days or even months. A salesperson is responsible for helping customers satisfy their needs. The sales process involves several steps.

Generate Sales Leads In some cases, customers seek out salespeople when they want to buy a product. This commonly occurs in retail settings. In these instances, the first step in the sales process—generating sales leads—is not always necessary. However, in other types of businesses, salespeople must identify prospective customers. This is more common in business-to-business selling. Sales leads can be obtained in many ways. A *referral* is a recommendation from a customer or another business. Networking is another valuable way to obtain sales leads. *Networking* involves establishing informal ties with a group of people, including friends, business contacts, coworkers, acquaintances, and fellow members of professional and civic organizations, who can provide valuable business advice. Online networking sites, such as LinkedIn, are becoming a popular way to connect with prospective customers.

Approach Customers The first contact that the salesperson makes with the customer is called the **approach**. During the approach, salespeople can introduce themselves, their company, and their products. In a retail setting, sales associates should greet customers when they enter the store and determine if the customer wants assistance. Salespeople can help customers who are in the early stages of the consumer decision-making process by providing basic product information and directing them to several product choices that could meet the customers' needs. When the customer is closer to making a buying decision, the sales associate can review product features, payment options, and other important factors.

In business-to-business selling, sales associates can introduce themselves through telephone calls, letters of introduction, and other promotional materials. The first meeting is used to get acquainted with the customers and their needs and to introduce them to the business's products. Information is collected for use in follow-up meetings.

Effective salespeople will use a **preapproach** process, which involves researching prospective customers before initially contacting them. This could involve visiting a company's website or contacting others who may have information about

Why is the approach an important step in the sales process?

the individual or company. The preapproach process enables salespeople to create a customized sales presentation for each customer.

Determine Customer Needs During the approach, the salesperson's top priority is to assess the customer's needs. The salesperson can do this by asking the customer questions. After learning about the customer's wants and needs, the salesperson must determine the best way to satisfy those needs based on the company's product options. If a preapproach is used, customer needs can be uncovered through the use of surveys, questionnaires, e-mails, and telephone calls.

Present the Product Salespeople should be very familiar with the products and services they are selling. They often need to demonstrate a product to show customers how it can meet their needs. A **demonstration** is a personalized presentation that shows how a product can benefit and provide value to the customer. The demonstration should be tailored to the customer's needs. When communicating product features and benefits, salespeople should use descriptive language that customers understand. Allowing customers to handle and test the product will engage them more effectively than simply demonstrating the product. At the end of the presentation, salespeople should review the benefits that are most important to the customer.

Overcome Objections After the sales presentation, most customers will have questions or raise objections. Salespeople should view objections as an opportunity to supply more information. Questions and objections help salespeople identify what is most meaningful to the customer. As the salesperson answers each of the customer's questions or addresses his or her objections, the customer will be less resistant to making the purchase. Good salespeople anticipate questions and objections and have responses prepared in advance.

Close the Sale The best sales presentations spark the customer's interest and build a strong desire. The **close** is the step in the sales process when the customer decides to buy a product or service. Customers may provide signals during the presentation that indicate they are ready to buy. The salesperson should respond immediately by asking for the sale and reinforcing the customer's decision. Reminding a customer that the car she just bought gets 42 miles per gallon will reinforce her smart buying decision.

Customers do not want to be pressured to make a purchase. First-time purchases and expensive items may require more time to close the sale. If the buyer is hesitant, the salesperson may need to repeat the product benefits. To overcome a price objection, the salesperson could offer customers financing options, such as 12 months same as cash. Negotiations may be required to close the sale. A *negotiation* is an attempt to arrive at a sales agreement by making trade-offs. Automobile sales often involve negotiations.

After the sale is closed, the salesperson may recommend the purchase of additional products. **Suggestion selling** occurs when the salesperson offers related products and services that could enhance the use of the purchased product. The idea is to increase customer satisfaction. When a customer buys a new suit, the salesperson may suggest accessories (belt and shoes) to match the new suit.

Follow Up A salesperson's responsibility does not end after the sale is closed. One of the most important steps in the sales process is the **follow-up**, which involves contacting the customer after the sale to ensure satisfaction. Was the product delivered on time? Was it installed properly? Did the product meet the customer's expectations? Does the customer have any additional needs with which the salesperson can assist? Following up after the sale helps build loyal customer relationships and repeat business. Follow-up may be in the form of a telephone call, a visit, an e-mail, or a survey.

Improving Sales Performance

Increasing sales is always a top goal for businesses. A business sets sales goals for itself as well as for each of its salespeople. To meet these goals, businesses will use a combination of methods, such as incentives for salespeople and sales promotions for customers. Salespeople are more motivated when they feel their efforts are recognized and appreciated by the business. Some businesses provide special incentives, including bonuses and gifts, to those salespeople who improve their

SPOTLIGHT ON SUCCESS

© Photo courtesy of Suzette Peoples

SUZETTE PEOPLES
Peoples Properties

Suzette Peoples started her real estate career as a full-time agent in 1988. In 2001, Suzette was ranked #16 in Houston, Texas, as the Top Individual Agent for RE/MAX. Suzette also earned RE/MAX Platinum Club status for several years. Over 100 monthly awards for Top Producer, Top Sales, and Top Lister in real estate in the greater Houston area have been given to Suzette during the last 21 years. In 2009, she decided to start her own full-service real estate and property management company, Peoples Properties, to promote her own brand, name, and reputation.

Suzette Peoples' philosophy is "putting people first." She is a highly respected professional who provides full service to all of her real estate clients. Making clients' wants and needs her top priority is the formula for Suzette's success. Eighty percent of Suzette's business is from referrals or past customers. She is constantly raising the bar to deliver the highest-quality real estate experience for customers. Successfully networking with lenders, inspectors, builders, title companies, and other real estate professionals has increased the value that Suzette provides to her customers. She also stays current on marketing, advertising, zoning, and builder trends.

Suzette is focused on the quality, not the quantity, of real estate transactions. She utilizes the latest technology and marketing tools to ensure that the customer receives the best value. Suzette's negotiating skills have contributed to her top 1 percent ranking in the real estate field. Suzette wants her customers to be clients for life. She accomplishes this goal through her honest approach and VIP treatment of all clients.

Think Critically

Why does the real estate field require excellent personal selling skills? How do you think Suzette approaches each of the steps in the sales process? Provide examples.

sales performance. Customer incentives such as special promotions and sales events may also increase sales.

A well-informed, motivated sales staff can help businesses reach their sales goals. Most businesses try to incorporate new products into their product mix to meet customer needs. Salespeople should be aware of new, incoming merchandise. They need time to become familiar with it so that they can confidently sell it to customers. Sales staff meetings are a good place to explain and demonstrate the new merchandise. Developing sales strategies for the new merchandise will result in more sales.

Sales managers should monitor on-floor selling activities to ensure that salespeople are presenting merchandise to customers in an appealing manner. Sales managers should also encourage the sales staff to build relationships with customers to put them at ease. Salespeople should greet all customers who enter the business and offer their assistance. Asking a customer's name and then addressing him or her by name makes the encounter more personal. Small talk that indicates the salesperson's interest in the customer provides a good launch into the sales process.

////////// **CHECKPOINT** \\\\\\

What are the steps in the sales process?

Sales Promotions

Businesses frequently use short-term incentives to increase consumer sales, with the expectation that consumers will continue to make the purchase later without the incentive. **Sales promotion** involves the use of marketing activities that provide extra value and buying incentives for customers. Common types of sales promotions include price discounts, coupons, rebates, giveaways, contests, sweepstakes, product displays, free product samples, and loyalty marketing programs.

Reasons for Sales Promotions

Sales promotion accomplishes things that other components in the promotional mix cannot. Advertising tries to influence consumers' attitudes by building brand awareness and preference over the long term. Sales promotion tries to influence consumers' behavior by giving them an incentive to make an immediate purchase. Sales promotions can be used to introduce a new product, increase short-term consumer demand, strengthen brand loyalty, and influence consumer behavior.

Sales promotions are commonly used to get consumers to try new products. Coupons, rebates, and free samples help reduce the consumer's risk of trying a new product. Coupons and rebates lower the price of a product. Supermarkets may offer freshly prepared samples of the newest pizza or other food item, allowing customers to taste the featured item before buying.

When a business decides that it wants to generate an immediate response from customers, it will use sales promotions. When prices are reduced, short-term consumer demand usually increases. Once a holiday has passed, the prices of holiday-related products are reduced

How can sales promotions entice consumers to buy a product or service?

drastically to sell the merchandise. Consumer demand also increases with special promotional incentives like coupons, rebates, and sweepstakes. Consumers may be offered a free product with the purchase of another product. Cosmetic companies may offer a free tote bag or umbrella with the purchase of a perfume or cologne. The demand goes up when consumers feel like they are receiving more value for their money. These types of offers are good for a limited time only, so they encourage consumers to act fast. After trying the product, businesses hope consumers will continue buying it and become loyal customers.

Sales promotions can strengthen brand loyalty by rewarding consumers for repeat purchases. Airlines, car rental companies, hotels, grocery stores, and department stores have special loyalty marketing or frequent-buyer programs that reward customers who buy a company's products or services regularly. The rewards can range from free travel to special discounts on merchandise.

Effective sales promotions are designed to influence consumer behavior. Consumers who normally do not shop at a certain store may change their shopping habits when they receive a 15 percent coupon. McDonald's popular Monopoly game awards prizes for game pieces given away with purchases at the restaurant. Big prizes may entice consumers to eat at McDonald's more frequently.

Advantages and Disadvantages of Sales Promotion

Sales promotions offer many benefits to businesses. They result in short-term sales that can increase a business's revenue. These sales can lead to loyal customers. Consumers enjoy contests and sweepstakes, and these kinds of sales promotions provide an incentive to make a purchase. The effectiveness of sales promotions can be measured. When customers use rebates and coupons, businesses can count the number redeemed. When a store or restaurant runs a contest, it can calculate the increase in sales during the promotion. When customers use frequent-buyer cards, businesses can track their buying patterns.

Although generating short-term sales is an advantage of sales promotion, it is also a disadvantage. Sales will decrease when the promotion ends, and there is no guarantee that customers will return. Customers may shift their loyalty to products associated with other special promotions. Another disadvantage of sales promotions is that customers may grow dependent on them. Customers may withhold or even modify their purchase if there isn't some kind of price discount or rebate. Businesses that give out coupons or use price discounts risk undermining the image of their product. Consumers may ignore product benefits because they view the product as being cheap.

Reaching Customers with Sales Promotions

Historically consumers became aware of sales promotions when they received coupons and other promotions randomly in the mail. Today, businesses realize that effective sales promotions are based on an understanding of what motivates prospective customers. Frequent travelers may be looking for ways to earn free travel and hotel room upgrades. Teenagers on a limited budget are looking for fast food restaurants offering value menus, while retirees may be looking for restaurants that give special senior citizen discounts. A couple buying a new car may be convinced to make the big purchase because of special interest rates or cash-back promotions. Businesses should plan sales promotions based on the needs of their target markets.

Sales promotions may be directed to customers by mail, in-person, or through print, radio, or television media outlets. Technology is changing the way sales promotions reach consumers. Websites offer access to coupons. Members of social networking sites share details about sales promotions. The combination of mobile cell phone devices and geographic positioning technology will soon allow marketers to target promotions to a customer's physical location. Businesses will be able to issue sales promotions, such as electronic coupons, to a customer's mobile device when he or she is near the location where the coupon can be used. Marketers are challenged to find creative sales promotions that will help increase sales.

CHECKPOINT

What is one of the main purposes of sales promotion?

6.3 Assessment

THINK ABOUT IT

1. What is an advantage and disadvantage of personal selling?
2. Why is the demonstration so important in the sales process?
3. What is follow-up and why is it important in the sales process?
4. Provide two examples of when a sales promotion might be used.

MAKE ACADEMIC CONNECTIONS

5. **MARKETING** Prepare a PowerPoint presentation describing three types of sales promotions you will use to attract customers to your new restaurant that serves meals ranging from $8 to $25. Describe the type of restaurant you own and your target market.
6. **MATH** A restaurant earns 30 percent profit on all hamburgers. The hamburgers normally sell for $6, but the restaurant is offering 20 percent off the price of hamburgers this week only. If the restaurant typically sells 800 hamburgers a week, how many discounted hamburgers will the restaurant have to sell during the promotion to match the profit normally earned?
7. **SALES** Select a product to demonstrate to the class. Explain and demonstrate the product's features and benefits. At the end of your presentation, answer any questions your classmates may have about the product.

Teamwork

Working with a partner, assume you own a department store that sells a variety of products. Select three products and determine how you will use suggestion selling in coordination with these three products. Then role-play a salesperson and customer to demonstrate the suggestion selling process.

Other Types of Promotion

Goals
- Describe other types of promotion that businesses use.
- Explain the purpose of visual merchandising.

Terms
- endorsement, p. 168
- direct marketing, p. 169
- visual merchandising, p. 170

Product Placement

As competition among companies becomes more intense, businesses look for unique ways to promote their products. Product placement is the practice of placing a business's product, service, or name into a movie, television show, video game, or other form of entertainment. One of the most famous product placements was for Reese's Pieces in the movie *E.T. the Extra-Terrestrial*. The lovable alien had a sweet tooth for the candy. In some cases, the product placement may be more subtle, such as when actors in movies and TV shows drive Ford or Chevrolet automobiles. Apple products have a heavy presence in many movies. Characters can be seen using iPhones and MacBooks. Including a real product adds a sense of realism to a movie and provides valuable product exposure for the business. Product placements are very common in reality TV shows, since the shows are supposed to represent real life. In video games, characters can be seen using Visa credit cards, wearing Nike basketball shoes, and driving BMWs. Businesses must carefully match the product placements with the movies, TV shows, and video games most likely to be viewed by their target markets.

Work as a Team Why do you think product placement is becoming a popular way to promote products? How can product placements be used in coordination with the other promotional mix elements?

FOCUS ON ADVERTISING

© Nils Z/Shutterstock.com

Promotional Tools

In addition to the types of promotion already discussed, there are several other promotional tools that businesses can use to reach customers. Three types include endorsements, word-of-mouth promotion, and direct marketing. These elements are often used in conjunction with some of the more traditional promotional methods.

To learn how the protein in milk helps build muscle, visit bodybymilk.com/albertpujols

Want muscle? got milk?®

Why do you think celebrity endorsements work so well for the milk industry?

Endorsements

An **endorsement** is a public expression of approval or support for a product or service. Endorsements are also known as *testimonials*. Although ordinary citizens, doctors, and other professionals can endorse products, most endorsements are associated with celebrities. A celebrity is paid handsomely to be the spokesperson or endorser for a product or business. There are an endless number of athletes who endorse sports-related products.

Certain restrictions apply to endorsements. The person making the endorsement must state factual information. Exaggerations and misleading statements are not allowed. Endorsers must actually have used the product that they are endorsing. If a product is updated or changed, the endorser must continue to use and believe in the merits of the modified product.

Celebrity Endorsements LeBron James and Nike, Queen Latifah and Cover Girl, Katy Perry and Proactiv—what do they all have in common? Companies like Nike, Cover Girl, and Proactiv use celebrities to endorse their products. These advertisements can be seen on television and in magazines and heard on the radio. Can consumers really be persuaded by the charm and looks of celebrities? Celebrity endorsements or testimonials are defined by the Federal Trade Commission as an advertising message that consumers are likely to believe reflects the opinions, beliefs, findings, or experience of a party other than the sponsoring advertiser. Opinions vary when it comes to the effectiveness of celebrity endorsements. Celebrity Endorsement Network, an agency that assists advertisers in getting celebrity endorsers, believes that the effectiveness of endorsements depends on proper celebrity casting. Celebrity endorsements transfer the traits of the celebrity to the product. Queen Latifah's beauty and personality are a good match for Cover Girl cosmetics. Her endorsement suggests that others can be beautiful too. However, using celebrity endorsements can be tricky. Celebrities may fall out of favor with the public due to inappropriate behavior. This decreases their value as an endorser for a business or product.

Endorsement Considerations Teenagers look up to celebrities because they want to be like them. When teenagers see their favorite celebrity endorsing a product, they often develop a strong desire for that product. Celebrity endorsements may not be as effective for older generations because they are more concerned about the quality and affordability of a product or service, characteristics most celebrities do not promote. Educated consumers also are less likely to be swayed by celebrity endorsements because they have done their homework and know what they want to buy. Older generations and educated consumers may be more influenced by testimonials from everyday citizens or professionals such as doctors who are considered more trustworthy.

Word-of-Mouth Promotion

Word-of-mouth promotion is one of the most effective ways of spreading the news about products and services. Many new, small businesses rely completely on word-of-mouth promotion because they do not have the funds available for other expensive forms of promotion. Consumers consider information from friends and family members to be very credible. Recommendations and referrals from happy customers can help boost a business's sales.

For the most part, businesses do not have control over word-of-mouth promotion. People will have positive and negative comments about a business. Unfortunately, dissatisfied customers are more likely to communicate their feelings than satisfied customers are. It can be nearly impossible for a business to overcome negative word-of-mouth promotion. Thus, businesses need to consistently offer a good product or service.

Businesses can provide a forum for word-of-mouth promotion on their websites. They can also set up a Facebook page and build a fan base for the company and its products. Customers can post comments and share their thoughts with others online.

Direct Marketing

Direct marketing uses techniques to get consumers to buy products or services from a nonretail setting. A nonretail setting could include the consumer's home or office. Direct marketing techniques include direct mail, catalogs, telemarketing, and e-mail. Direct mail can be a very efficient way of targeting customers. Mailing lists group prospective customers based on demographic, geographic, and psychographic characteristics. Consumers are added to mailing lists when they perform certain activities, such as subscribe to a magazine, place a catalog order, submit a warranty card, redeem a rebate, and apply for credit. Businesses can buy mailing lists containing the names of customers who fit

NETBookmark

Have you ever asked a friend's opinion about a product or business? Online review sites such as Yelp—one of the most popular local review directories—allow consumers to post, read, and comment on opinions about all kinds of products and services. Businesses can even respond to reviews on Yelp to create a dialog with their customers. Access www.cengage.com/school/advertising and click on the link for Chapter 6. Read some of the reviews on the Yelp site. Would a favorable review on Yelp influence your decision to patronize a business? Can you think of some ways businesses might use review sites to put their businesses in a positive light?

www.cengage.com/school/advertising

their customer profile. Targeted direct mailings are much more effective than mass mailings, which are often considered junk mail.

Many types of products are now available for purchase through catalogs. Consumers like the convenience of shopping from home. Telemarketing is a sales technique in which a salesperson directly contacts a prospective customer by phone. As with direct mail, telemarketing allows businesses to target specific customers. Because many consumers consider it intrusive, telemarketing strategies must be planned carefully. Another direct marketing technique is to send out targeted e-mail advertisements. Consumers can sign up to receive e-mails about sales and other special promotions. The e-mails contain direct links to the retailers' websites, where consumers can make purchases. Unsolicited e-mail advertisements are referred to as *spam*. Spam is usually treated as junk e-mail and ignored by the consumer.

CHECKPOINT

Other than traditional forms of promotion, what other types of promotion can a business use?

Visual Merchandising

For a retail business, visual merchandising is an important part of promoting the sale of products. **Visual merchandising** is the process of displaying products in a way that makes them appealing and enticing to customers. It is used to catch the attention of shoppers and persuade them to buy the product. Consumers who can see, taste, or feel the merchandise are more likely to make a purchase.

How do retailers use visual merchandising to promote products?

Components of Visual Merchandising

Visual merchandising includes window displays, interior displays, and signs. Most retailers have an in-house team of visual merchandisers to design product displays. One of the top reasons for display windows in a store is to attract the attention of people walking by and draw them into the store. Customers give only three to five seconds of their attention to window displays. Retailers must convey the image of the product and reflect the personality of its target market within that short time period. Imaginative displays use color, lights, space, mannequins, furniture, smells, and sounds to showcase products attractively. Hi-tech displays may use digital technology and interactive elements. The most effective window displays create a theme, mood, or "lifestyle" with which the target market can identify. Too many retailers make the mistake of cramming too much merchandise in the display to represent the variety of items the store offers. Window displays must be changed frequently and should always showcase the newest or best-selling items.

In-store displays must make an impact. Effective displays often turn the "just looking" customer into one who makes a purchase. The main focus of the display should be the product. Displays for products that require touch and feel should be easily accessible. Display areas should be neat and clean so that they are inviting to the customer. Retailers use displays for impulse-driven purchases, such as batteries and gift wrapping paper, to stimulate a quick sale. End-of-aisle displays often are used to give new products or specially promoted products better exposure.

Signs can be used to publicize promotions throughout the store. They may contain the store's logo or specific brand names and logos. Signs also help shoppers locate products.

© LuckyPhoto/Shutterstock.com

Why should retailers give careful thought to a store's interior?

Store Layout

Visual merchandising also involves the layout of the store. Music, product displays, lighting, and even climate control can affect the shopping experience. Stores should be clean and well lit. Stores that are brightly lit result in higher sales. Mood lighting and spotlights can be used to draw attention to certain products or product features. Merchandise should be organized in logical groupings by type, color, or some other characteristic.

Many stores go beyond the basics to create a pleasant shopping experience for customers. Nordstrom creates a special atmosphere with wide marble aisles, upholstered chairs and sofas around the dressing rooms, a pianist, and refreshments from its own restaurant. Busy shoppers want to spend less time shopping. They appreciate store layouts that are easy to navigate so they can find what they are looking for, get to a register, and check out quickly.

CHECKPOINT

Why is visual merchandising an important element of promotion?

6.4 Assessment

THINK ABOUT IT

1. Why are businesses willing to spend large sums of money to get celebrity endorsements for their products?
2. Why is word-of-mouth promotion so difficult for a business to control? How might a business have some influence over word-of-mouth promotion?
3. What are some examples of direct marketing techniques used by businesses?
4. What elements can be used in a display window to attract consumers' attention?

MAKE ACADEMIC CONNECTIONS

5. **PROBLEM SOLVING**   Select a product or service that you use frequently. Then choose a celebrity who you think would make a good endorser of the product or service. Explain what characteristics the endorser has that would make him or her a good fit for the product or service. Present your ideas about the celebrity endorser to the class.

6. **RESEARCH**   Conduct research to find a company that uses direct marketing as its primary form of promotion. Describe the history of the company and explain why direct marketing works well for the company's products or services.

7. **LANGUAGE ARTS**   Visit a store and look at its various displays and signage. Write a one-page report explaining how the store uses visual merchandising to promote its products.

Teamwork

Design a display window for a clothing store, hardware store, sporting goods store, or florist. Create a three-dimensional model or diorama using a box to represent the display window. Cut out photos or other images from magazines to represent the items on display. Present your model to the class and explain the reasoning behind your design.

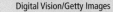

Digital Vision/Getty Images

PARTNERSHIP FOR
21ST CENTURY SKILLS

Making the Sale

Successful salespeople have skills that set them apart from the competition. They know their product, understand and respect the customers, listen carefully, and effectively read the body language of customers.

Salespeople should be the authority when it comes to the products and services they sell. They should learn everything about their company's products or services as well as competitors' products and services to be able to confidently communicate product features and benefits to consumers.

Salespeople should focus on customers. They should listen carefully to what the customer is saying and try to get to know them. Many salespeople do more talking than listening. They should avoid interrupting the customer. By letting the customer speak, the salesperson can learn more about the customer's wants and needs. Also, the more the customer talks, the more he or she becomes comfortable with the salesperson. This makes it easier to close the sale.

Learning body language can improve the communication process. By watching a customer's body language, salespeople can determine if the customer is showing an interest in the product. If a customer has his or her arms crossed, it could mean he or she is feeling uncomfortable and defensive. Salespeople should make sure to leave their arms at their sides to communicate openness. Leaning forward slightly and making eye contact indicates that the salesperson is interested in what the customer is saying. By nodding while the customer is talking, the salesperson indicates understanding and approval.

Salespeople need to have the right attitude and show enthusiasm. If the salesperson isn't enthusiastic about the product, the customer won't be either. Enthusiasm is contagious. When a salesperson conveys excitement about the product, customers are more likely to believe that there is something worthwhile about it. Another way to get customers excited about a product is to share customer success stories. Storytelling helps generate interest in the product.

Try It Out

Using the sales techniques described above, develop a sales presentation for a product or service that you will present to the class. Use the actual product or other visual aids in your presentation. At the end of the presentation, answer questions others may have about the product.

© Digital Vision/Getty Images

SUMMARY

6.1 Promotion

- The promotional mix is a combination of advertising, public relations, personal selling, and sales promotion.
- The AIDA concept represents the four stages of promotion—attention, interest, desire, and action. Marketers must determine which stage applies to the target market to develop an appropriate promotional mix.
- The promotional plan outlines how the elements in the promotional mix will work together to reach the target market. There are five steps in developing the promotional plan: (1) determine the target market, (2) identify promotional objectives, (3) set the promotional budget, (4) determine the promotional mix, (5) implement and evaluate the promotional plan.

6.2 Advertising and Public Relations

- Advertising is used more commonly than any other form of promotion to introduce new products to the market. For mature products, advertising is used to remind customers about them and to maintain market share.
- Public relations campaigns build goodwill and help the public develop a better understanding of a company, its products, and its philosophies.
- Publicity goes hand-in-hand with public relations. Businesses often receive publicity because of their public relations activities.

6.3 Personal Selling and Sales Promotion

- Steps in the sales process include (1) generating sales leads, (2) approaching the customer, (3) determining customer needs, (4) presenting the product, (5) overcoming objections, (6) closing the sale, and (7) following up with the customer.
- Typical kinds of sales promotions include price discounts, coupons, rebates, giveaways, contests, sweepstakes, product displays, samples, and loyalty programs.

6.4 Other Types of Promotion

- Endorsements are testimonials from a spokesperson who has used a product or service.
- Word-of-mouth promotion is one of the most effective ways of spreading the news about products and services.
- Direct marketing techniques include direct mail, catalogs, telemarketing, and e-mail.
- Visual merchandising should make the product easily accessible, interesting, and special to attract the most customers.

Read *Impact Advertising* on page 149 again to review how promotional products are used by businesses. Conduct online research to learn about some of the most unique or nontraditional promotional products. Describe them and explain how they could be used effectively.

Vocabulary Builder

Match each statement with the term that best defines it. Some terms may not be used.

1. The first contact that a salesperson makes with the customer
2. Any nonpaid form of communication designed to arouse public interest about a product, service, business, or event
3. Techniques used to get consumers to buy products or services from a non-retail setting
4. Activities and events that create goodwill for a business or other organization
5. The process that involves researching prospective customers before contacting them
6. A written statement to inform the media about a new product or special event

a.	approach
b.	close
c.	demonstration
d.	direct marketing
e.	endorsement
f.	follow-up
g.	personal selling
h.	preapproach
i.	press release
j.	promotion
k	promotional mix
l.	promotional plan
m.	public relations
n.	publicity
o.	sales promotion
p.	suggestion selling
q.	visual merchandising

7. Contact with a customer after the sale to ensure satisfaction
8. The process of displaying products in a way that makes them appealing and enticing to customers
9. Face-to-face communication between the buyer and seller that attempts to influence the buying decision
10. Marketing activities that provide extra value and buying incentives

Test Your Knowledge

11. The AIDA concept consists of all the following *except*
    a. attractiveness
    b. desire
    c. action
    d. interest
12. Which of the following is an advantage of advertising?
    a. it is free
    b. it works well for complex products that require an explanation
    c. it can be repeated many times to reinforce a message
    d. it results in short-term sales
13. The final step in the sales process is to
    a. close the sale
    b. follow up
    c. overcome objections
    d. present the product
14. Sales promotions
    a. increase consumer demand
    b. strengthen brand loyalty
    c. influence consumer behavior
    d. all of the above

15. Product endorsements
    a. do not require the endorser to actually use the product
    b. are usually not effective with teenagers
    c. must state factual information
    d. are an inexpensive form of promotion
16. Which of the following is *not* an example of a public relations activity?
    a. donating computer equipment to a high school
    b. advertising the opening of a new store
    c. sponsoring a community's summer fair
    d. volunteering to clean up the local park
17. The sales _____ should take place when the customer enters the store.
    a. approach   c. close
    b. preapproach   d. demonstration
18. Many new, small businesses rely on _____ because they do not have the funds available for other expensive forms of promotion.
    a. word-of-mouth promotion
    b. endorsements
    c. sales promotion
    d. advertising
19. Contacting the customer after the sale is referred to as _____.
    a. preapproach   c. suggestion selling
    b. follow-up   d. none of the above
20. All of the following activities will help improve sales performance *except*
    a. setting sales goals
    b. having sales staff meetings
    c. allowing salespeople to work freely with no monitoring
    d. informing sales staff about new merchandise

Apply What You Learned

21. You work at a bicycle shop. Write a plan of action that describes how you will approach each of the steps in the sales process to increase store sales.
22. A restaurant recently received negative publicity when some of its customers became ill after dining there. It discovered that the lettuce being served was contaminated with E coli bacteria. The restaurant's owner has asked you to develop a public relations campaign to fight the negative publicity and win back customers. Present your plan to the class.
23. Select a product or service that is heavily promoted to teenagers. Create a chart that lists all of the promotional mix elements (advertising, public relations, personal selling, and sales promotion). Next to each promotional mix element, describe how it is used to promote the product or service. If one or more of the elements are not used, provide an example of how they could be incorporated into the promotional mix.

24. **MANAGEMENT**   You are the marketing manager for an amusement park that has rides and water attractions. It wants to increase attendance by families. Develop a promotional plan for the park. Explain how you will accomplish each step in the promotional planning process. Prepare a PowerPoint presentation that outlines your plan.

25. **COMMUNICATION**   Create a sales promotion for a toy store that is trying to increase sales. Design a flyer describing the sales promotion that will be distributed to customers.

26. **SOCIAL STUDIES**   You are the marketer for a large consumer electronics retailer that has stores throughout the country. You have been asked to identify three special causes/charities to which the retailer could lend support. Research various social causes and charities to determine which three would be a good match for the retailer. Write a one- to two-page report that describes the causes/charities you chose and explains ways in which the retailer can contribute to or support them.

27. **TECHNOLOGY**   Conduct research to explain the impact of the Internet on promotional mix elements. How has the Internet changed the way products and services are promoted today? Do you think the use of the Internet has improved promotional efforts? Explain why or why not.

28. **PSYCHOLOGY**   The main objective of any promotion is to make a sale. The AIDA concept, which represents the four stages of promotion, often is used to accomplish this goal. Explain how psychology plays a role in the AIDA concept. In other words, how do the stages of promotion (specifically, attention, interest, and desire) influence consumer behavior?

29. **WRITING**   You own a car detailing service that is expanding its business. It will now offer additional services, including tune-ups, oil changes, fluid level checks, brake installation, and minor repairs to tires, air conditioners, engines, and exhausts. You have a database containing the e-mail addresses of all of your customers. Write an e-mail to inform your customers of the business's expansion. Include a description of a sales promotion that will encourage customers to try out the new services.

Your sporting goods company hired a popular athlete to endorse your athletic wear. Recently, the athlete has made headlines for his unruly conduct in public. In addition, he has made television appearances while wearing sports gear manufactured by one of your competitors. You are now concerned that his actions will have a negative impact on the sales of your products. You talk with the athlete, and he responds using the old adage, "there's no such thing as bad publicity."

As the owner of the company, how would you handle this crisis to ensure your sales are not affected? Do you agree that there's no such thing as bad publicity? Explain your answer. Would you continue to use celebrity endorsements as part of your promotion plan? Why or why not?

Reality ✓

Handling Bad Publicity on the Internet

The Internet has become a popular way of doing business. The number of prospective online customers and the speed at which they can be reached is virtually unlimited. However, negative publicity about a business can spread just as quickly online. With all of the blogs, chat rooms, and social networking sites, there are many places where consumers can post complaints. There are several strategies that can be used to fight back to ensure that a company's online presence won't be overcome with negative feedback.

Search engines are used by many Internet users to locate information about a business. Unfortunately, the results of this search may include links to negative feedback and comments. Businesses must stay on top of their SERP (search engine result pages) to be aware of any negative attention the business is generating. By seeking out negative feedback aimed at the company, it can confront it and respond to it in a respectful manner. The company can contact the customer who wrote the bad review to try to resolve the issue. This often is very effective. Once the issue is resolved, the business can request that the negative feedback be removed from the website. The business should avoid retaliating against the dissatisfied customer because that could lead to even more bad publicity.

Hiring an Internet marketing team to handle negative publicity and reduce the damage is another approach. The marketers can write positive articles about the business and its products and post them in response to the negative feedback. They can also write press releases and submit them to other websites that have a high search engine ranking, meaning the positive postings will move ahead of the negative postings when search engine results are displayed. When a company unfairly earns a bad reputation, it can reverse it by starting a positive public relations campaign.

Think Critically

1. Many companies depend on publicity to create public interest in their products and services. What role does the Internet play in publicity? Do you think the Internet has had a positive or negative effect on publicity?
2. Do you think it would be better for a company to address negative publicity that appears online or to ignore it? Explain your answer.
3. What kinds of information do you think should be included in articles written to overcome negative publicity?

You will use current desktop technologies and software to prepare and deliver an effective multimedia presentation. You will work on a team consisting of two to four members. Your team should design a computer-generated multimedia presentation on the assigned topic. The team is to make effective use of current multimedia technology in the presentation (examples: sound, movement, digital video, and so forth). Space, color, and text should also be used effectively in the presentation.

TOPIC   Sales promotions are constantly changing due to the economy, consumer trends, technology, and customer expectations. Your team has been asked to present at least five types of sales promotions that a bakery should consider to increase customer traffic, brand awareness, and sales. For each sales promotion, include a description of the target market, sales promotion objectives, budget, and methods for measuring and evaluating the effectiveness of the sales promotion. Also, prepare a schedule that shows when the promotions will be implemented throughout the year.

Teams will have from seven to ten minutes for oral presentations. Judges have an additional five minutes to ask questions.

Performance Indicators Evaluated

- Evaluate and delegate responsibilities needed to perform the required tasks.
- Demonstrate effective teamwork skills needed to function in a business setting.
- Demonstrate effective oral communication skills.
- Demonstrate knowledge of multimedia software and components.
- Apply technical skills to create a multimedia presentation that enhances the oral presentation.

Go to the BPA website for more detailed information.

Think Critically

1. Why must businesses constantly monitor and adjust their sales promotions?
2. How do you think the economy affects sales promotions?
3. Why should the Internet be considered part of the sales promotion strategy?

www.bpa.org

7

Advertising Media

IMPACT ADVERTISING

Chick-fil-A: Billboards That Work

Chick-fil-A® has created a very successful outdoor advertising campaign. Its billboards show three-dimensional cows that appear to be painting the signs with fun phrases, such as "Eat Mor Chikin" or "All Roads Leed to Chikin." The advertising campaign was created in 1995 and continues today. Since the start of the campaign, sales have increased from $500 million to $3 billion. There are five major reasons why Chick-fil-A's outdoor campaign is effective.

- **Clean and Simple**   Every billboard in the Chick-fil-A campaign is solid white with a short phrase in big, black letters. The Chick-fil-A logo is predominantly placed in the center of the billboard. Keeping the billboard simple is important since passersby only have a few seconds to read and digest the message.

- **Clever Theme**   What's funnier than two cows with poor grammar skills telling you to eat chicken instead of beef? The idea is to remind the viewer that there's something out there besides the same meal at the same burger joint. The core of Chick-fil-A's brand is its chicken, which is also the central theme of its billboard advertisements.

- **Change of Pace**   Phrases and short messages on Chick-fil-A billboards are changed frequently to maintain consumer interest. The cows are also changing. During football season, the cows wear helmets and jerseys. During the Christmas season, the cows might look like reindeer. Keeping the customer guessing makes the billboards more interactive. Billboards used bright swipes of yellow paint to represent the sunrise and to help promote Chick-fil-A's new breakfast menu.

- **Consistent Placement**   The Chick-fil-A campaign has been running for over 15 years. The consistent brand message and consistent location of billboards make it a fun campaign for consumers to follow. Although Chick-fil-A billboards are always changing their clever messages, they represent a consistent brand.

- **Call to Action**   Chick-fil-A's call for consumer action is to switch from beef to chicken. The clever outdoor advertising campaign has expanded to television commercials. Because Chick-fil-A sponsors college football and has its own bowl game, it created commercials showing cows parachuting into the stadium to knock down vendors selling hamburgers. Chick-fil-A also has a wide array of promotional items (key chains, shirts, visors, and more) that feature the cows.

1. Why do you think the Chick-fil-A campaign has been successful for so many years?

2. Why is a theme important in a long-term advertising strategy?

3. When using a billboard campaign, why should the message be changed frequently?

WHAT DO YOU KNOW?

7.1

Traditional Advertising Media

Goals
- Describe traditional types of advertising media.
- Identify advertising media selection criteria.

Terms
- media, p.182
- reach, p. 186
- frequency, p. 187
- lead time, p. 188

FOCUS ON ADVERTISING

Catchy Jingles

A jingle is a short tune used in advertising. It contains lyrics that promote a product or business. Advertising jingles are designed to infiltrate your memory and stay there. They are written in a way that makes them easy to remember. The shorter the better. The most common length for jingles is 30 seconds. Many of us remember the words to the Oscar Mayer®  Bologna song (Oscar Mayer has a way with b-o-l-o-g-n-a). Other well-known jingles have been written for Chili's® (I want my baby back, baby back, baby back ribs), Subway® (Five. Five dollar. Five dollar footlong), and Band-Aid® (I am stuck on Band-Aid brand cause Band-Aid's stuck on me). You can't get any simpler than the Meow Mix® jingle (meow, meow, meow, meow). Advertisers use jingles because they have a more memorable effect than the written or spoken word. As consumers roam the aisles of the grocery store, suddenly a jingle may enter their head, causing them to buy a certain product. Advertisers benefit from the instant recall that a radio or TV jingle provides.

Work as a Team Why do you think jingles are so popular among advertisers and consumers? Describe a current advertising jingle. Do you think it is effective? Why or why not?

© S1001/Shutterstock.com

Types of Advertising Media

A business cannot succeed without effective and targeted advertising. An important aspect of advertising involves choosing the appropriate **media**, which are the channels of communication used to send a message to the target market. Traditional types of media include television, radio, print, and outdoor media. The Internet is quickly gaining in popularity. Although television is still the dominant medium for advertising, the Internet has surpassed radio as the second most common medium, and print advertising ranks fourth.

Promotional objectives are an important consideration when selecting the advertising media. For example, if the objective is to demonstrate a product's ease of operation, a demonstration in a television commercial might work best. If the objective is to reach out to a selected group, such as runners, an advertisement in a fitness magazine could be the best choice. Advertisers must decide which type of media will be the most effective at conveying their message for the least amount of money.

Television Advertising

The average American encounters 61 minutes of television advertisements and promotions each day. Adults are exposed to television, cell phone, and GPS screens for about 8.5 hours each day according to a study released by the Council for Research Excellence. Since television was first introduced, businesses have had tremendous success using it as an advertising medium. Advertisements can be broadcast on network television, cable television, independent stations, and direct broadcasts on satellite television. Television advertising usually comes in the form of commercials and infomercials.

Advantages of Television Advertising
Television gives advertisers the ability to convey their message using sight, sound, and motion. It provides many creative opportunities for advertisers. Television advertising is more likely to have an emotional impact on consumers than any other type of advertising. It reaches a large number of people, making the cost per viewer low.

Advertisers can reach an audience on a national or local level with television advertising. Network television, including ABC, CBS, NBC, and FOX, reaches a large diverse audience. Advertisers carefully select the programming and time slots for their network commercials. *Primetime*—the middle of the evening—is when the greatest number of viewers are watching television. Automobile manufacturers, retailers, and soft drink companies may advertise during primetime shows such as *American Idol* to reach consumers between the ages of 18 and 49.

Insurance companies and senior care products are advertised on weekday mornings when a retired population is watching morning programs such as the *Price is Right*. Toys, fast food restaurants, cereals, and snack foods are advertised on Saturday mornings when children are watching cartoons. Cable television and direct broadcast satellite systems, such as DIRECTV and Dish Network, have channels devoted to specific audiences. Advertisers may air a commercial on the Hallmark Channel if their target market is women or on CNN if they are targeting young professionals.

© Monkey Business Images/Shutterstock.com

Why is television the most popular advertising medium?

Disadvantages of Television Advertising Although the cost per viewer is low, the overall cost of television advertising is quite high. Television advertisers have to pay to produce the commercial. In addition, they have to pay the networks to air the commercial, which can be very expensive depending on the time of day, the television show's ratings (number of viewers), and the length of the advertisement. The average length of commercials is 30 seconds, which limits the amount of information that can be communicated. Because of the lengthy creative and production processes, it could be months before a television advertisement is ever aired. When the commercial is finally aired, advertisers cannot be assured that consumers will watch it. Consumers may use the remote to channel surf during commercials. With the ad-skipping capabilities of DVR technology, consumers can fast-forward through commercials.

Radio Advertising

Radio can be an effective way to advertise. Radio station listeners can be segmented by demographics. For example, a pop rock station will attract younger listeners, while a classic rock station will attract older adults. Knowing the demographic profile of a radio station's listeners makes it easier for advertisers to reach their target markets. Radio commercials are effective at using sounds and catchy jingles to catch listeners' attention. Although businesses typically advertise on local radio stations, they now can get nationwide exposure on satellite radio and Internet radio broadcasts. Radio commercials can be created and produced in a relatively short period of time at a much lower cost than television commercials.

One of the biggest disadvantages of radio advertising is that it provides only an audio message because the product cannot be seen. Also, listeners can easily tune out commercials or change the station. Because listeners usually are doing something else while listening to the radio, it can be difficult to get their attention with an ad.

Print Advertising

Print advertising is one of the best ways to promote a business and its products. However, a print ad may have to work harder than a television ad to get the consumer's attention. Creative headlines and appealing visual images are necessary. Print advertising includes newspapers, magazines, direct mail, flyers, and brochures.

Why is radio a good medium to use when trying to target a specific audience?

Newspapers There are several advantages of newspaper advertising. Newspapers reach large numbers of people, and newspaper advertising is relatively inexpensive. Newspapers sell advertising space based on the advertisement's location, size, and color. Newspaper advertising allows businesses to target a specific geographic area. Retailers frequently advertise sales promotions in local newspapers.

Placing an ad in the newspaper is a fairly quick process, making it a good medium for time-sensitive material.

Newspaper advertising also has some disadvantages. Although newspapers reach a large audience, some of these people will be outside of the business's target market. Newspapers are not the best type of media when trying to reach a niche market. They are more effective for mass marketing. Since newspapers are published daily, the advertisement will have a short life span. High clutter from competing advertisements could mean some ads are overlooked. Finally, as more people turn to the Internet for news, newspaper readership is decreasing.

Magazines Another popular form of media is magazines. One of the biggest advantages of magazine advertising is the ability to target specific markets. While *Sports Illustrated* is popular with male sports enthusiasts, *Family Circle* is popular with women who are trying to juggle the responsibilities of home and work. Magazines also have a long life span. Many consumers save issues of magazines and look through them again, meaning ads are viewed more than once.

On the downside, magazine advertising can be expensive in comparison to newspaper advertising. Also, it takes much more time to produce and place an ad in a magazine. As with newspapers, magazines can be cluttered with ads. In many cases, over half of the pages in a magazine are devoted to advertising.

Direct Mail Direct mail can be a highly segmented advertising strategy when businesses use mailing lists that correlate with their target markets. Also, with the use of mailing lists, the advertising message can be personalized, which will elicit a more positive response. Direct mail campaigns are hidden from competitors, making it difficult for them to react quickly. It is easy to measure the effectiveness of direct mail advertising because the business can track the replies or orders received in response to the ad.

The biggest disadvantage of using direct mail advertising is that many consumers will treat it like junk mail without even reading it. Direct mail advertising can be expensive depending on the target market and the size of the campaign.

Flyers and Brochures Flyers may be mailed, distributed door to door, or placed on car windshields to advertise numerous things, such as community events, grand openings, and special sales. Businesses such as landscapers and painters use flyers to advertise their services. They are an inexpensive form of advertising. Brochures are used to describe a product or service in an easy-to-read, eye-catching format.

NETBookmark

Almost everyone is familiar with *National Geographic Magazine*. But did you know that the National Geographic Society publishes several other magazines, each targeted to a different audience? Access www.cengage.com/school/advertising and click on the link for Chapter 7. Read about the Society's publications. Then compare and contrast the characteristics of the target audience for *National Geographic Magazine* and *National Geographic Traveler*. What are some products or services that might be appropriate for each of the magazines listed?

www.cengage.com/school/advertising

Most brochures include color pictures to illustrate the product or service being advertised. Bi-fold and tri-fold brochures are common, and they are sized so that they can be mailed or displayed easily. Brochures can be an economical way to advertise. Businesses and other organizations use brochures to attract prospective customers.

When flyers are randomly mailed or placed on doorsteps and windshields, it is nearly impossible to measure their effectiveness. As with direct mail, flyers are often ignored. An increasing number of consumers are using the Internet to gather information about businesses and their products, making brochures less useful. Brochures often are handed out to people who have no interest in the business. Also, brochures tend to be easily misplaced.

Outdoor Advertising

Outdoor advertising can take a variety of forms, including billboards; posters; ads on the sides of buses and at bus stop shelters; signs in malls, sports arenas, and airports; and any other space designed specifically for ads outside the home. It is effective at reaching a broad market and provides wide exposure for local businesses. Local retailers, service businesses, entertainment venues, hotels, and restaurants are the leading outdoor advertisers. Billboards are attention-getting and provide around-the-clock exposure. Technological advances are making billboards more attractive to advertisers. Digital billboard displays let advertisers rotate their messages throughout the day. The biggest drawback to outdoor advertising is the limit on the length of the message. People must be able to view the ad quickly as they drive or walk by it. The location of outdoor advertising has an impact on its effectiveness. Advertisers must evaluate sites to find the most desirable ones.

CHECKPOINT

What are the traditional types of advertising media?

Media Selection Criteria

Media planning is required to ensure that a business's advertising message is carried out effectively. There are several key factors to consider when selecting the media for advertising, including the reach, frequency, lead time, and cost.

Reach

When choosing a media outlet, advertisers must consider the exposure it offers. The **reach** is the total number of people who will be exposed to an advertisement over a period of time. For a television ad, the reach is based on a show's ratings. If the first game of the MLB World Series is watched by 18 million people, that is the potential reach of an advertisement aired during that time slot. A show that has higher ratings will have a higher reach. The potential reach of a billboard can be measured by examining traffic statistics. The reach for newspapers and magazines is based upon their circulation, or the number of copies

Have you ever read a magazine while sitting in a waiting room? What does this indicate about the reach of a magazine advertisement?

distributed through subscriptions, newsstands, supermarkets, airports, and other locations. For newspapers and magazines, advertisers must also consider the *pass-along rate*, which is how many people read a single copy of the newspaper or magazine. A magazine that started out in a household may end up in the workplace or a medical office waiting room, where numerous other people can flip through the pages and be exposed to the ads. The pass-along rate increases the reach. Regardless of which advertising medium is used, the reach will be ineffective if the medium is not a good match with the target market. For example, since newspaper readership among teenagers is low, it might not be worthwhile to run an ad for a teen product in the local newspaper.

Frequency

Radio, television, and newspaper advertisements are repeated frequently to remind consumers about a product or service. **Frequency** is the number of times a person is exposed to an advertisement. Advertisers must consider the number of times the target market needs to be exposed to a message to meet its objectives. Although one exposure typically is not enough, too many exposures can cause the consumer to tune out. Higher frequency is more beneficial for new products or complex products than it is for well-known products.

Continuous advertising is a strategy in which advertisements are run steadily over an extended period of time to continuously remind consumers of a product or service. Because the insurance field is very competitive, insurance companies may use the continuous advertising strategy to remind consumers of their services. Think about how many times throughout the day you have seen commercials for Allstate, Progressive, or Geico insurance companies. With a *pulsing* strategy, advertising is heavier during certain times of the year, such as holidays. Although retailers may advertise year-round, they advertise more often during the Christmas holiday.

Advertisers also look at the relationship between reach and frequency by calculating the *gross impression*, which is the total number of people who have seen an advertisement (reach) multiplied by the number of times it has been run (frequency). Gross impressions offer one more way to measure the exposure received by an advertisement.

Lead Time

Lead time is the amount of time required to produce and place an advertisement. Generally, newspapers require the least amount of lead time, while television requires the most. A newspaper ad can be written and placed within days, meaning the advertiser can respond quickly to current events or competitor ads. Radio advertisements also require little lead time. A radio ad can be submitted within hours of airtime, and changes to the ad can be made quickly and easily. Magazines require advertisers to submit ads months in advance, and after ads are submitted, they cannot be changed. Television advertisements can take months to produce. The production process is long and often involves advertising agencies, producers, directors, equipment technicians, and actors, among others. The lead time for outdoor advertising can depend on the complexity of the ad and the availability of the desired location.

Cost

Cost could be the most important factor when it comes to selecting advertising media. The goal is to reach the most people at the lowest cost while staying within the advertising budget. A primetime 30-second television commercial can cost around $200,000, but it can cost over $700,000 for commercials aired on popular shows like *American Idol*. In addition, the costs of producing a television commercial could run between $300,000 and $400,000. Radio advertising costs vary by city and state. For example, New York City has some of the highest rates because it has a large population and, in turn, a large listening audience. Rates for a 30-second radio ad can run between $40 and $1,400. Radio commercials usually run several times a week for three to four weeks. The production costs for a radio advertisement are around $1,800.

Newspapers calculate prices based on the space required for the advertisement and the color of the ad (black and white vs. full color). Another factor that affects price is whether the newspaper is distributed nationally or locally. A full-page, black-and-white ad in the *Wall Street Journal* could cost over $160,000. In large cities with a large circulation, the same ad could cost around $70,000; in smaller cities, it could cost as little as $1,000. The same factors affect the costs of magazine advertising. For magazines with large circulations, a one-time, full-page, color ad could cost between $100,000 and $250,000. A similar ad in a local magazine with a lower circulation could cost less than $500. Billboards can cost between $1,000 to $3,000 a month, depending on location, reach, and projected impact. If a business has ten billboards, the cost could be as high as $30,000 a month.

Advertisers must consider whether the medium is cost efficient. A common way to measure cost efficiency is to determine the *cost-per-thousand (CPM)*, which is the dollar cost of reaching 1,000 members of an audience. (The "M" in CPM comes from the Roman numeral for 1,000.) The CPM formula is as follows:

$$CPM = \frac{\text{cost of media}}{\text{total audience}} \times 1,000$$

For example, if it costs $75,000 for an advertisement in a magazine with a circulation of 1.2 million people, the CPM would be $62.50. Advertisers can use this formula to compare the cost efficiency of two or more media choices.

CHECKPOINT

What criteria are used to help select advertising media?

7.1 Assessment

THINK ABOUT IT

1. Why are promotional objectives an important consideration when selecting advertising media?

2. Why is lead time an important consideration when choosing the type of advertising media to use?

3. How can an advertiser lower its newspaper advertising costs?

MAKE ACADEMIC CONNECTIONS

4. **COMMUNICATION**   Create a table that lists all of the traditional types of advertising media and the advantages and disadvantages of each type of media.

5. **MATH**   You have determined that a billboard advertisement along a busy freeway will be an effective means of communicating your company's message. Estimates show that 1 million people will drive past the billboard during a two-month period. If your company spends $3,000 each month to rent the billboard space for two months, what is the CPM (cost per thousand)? As an alternative, you could run a full-page ad costing $5,000 in a local magazine with a circulation of 800,000. Which alternative is more cost efficient?

6. **VISUAL ART**   Select a product and design a full-page, color advertisement to place in *Sports Illustrated* magazine. Make sure the product you are advertising is appropriate for the target market that reads *Sports Illustrated*. Research the cost of running this advertisement in one issue of the magazine's national edition.

Teamwork

Working with a partner, listen to the radio for one hour for two days. Keep track of the number of radio advertisements you hear during that time period. Describe the products and services being promoted. Were they local or national advertisements? Describe why the radio was the ideal medium for these advertisements.

The Internet and Advertising

Goals
- Describe various types of Internet advertising.
- Explain what factors businesses should consider when using Internet advertising.

Terms
- online advertising, p. 190
- spam, p. 191
- banner ad, p. 191
- pop-up ad, p. 191
- search engine ad, p. 192
- blog, p. 192
- social media, p. 193
- phishing, p. 194

myYearbook.com

Two high school students with help from their older brother created the social networking site myYearbook. Members can interact with friends by creating profiles, sending virtual gifts, and playing games. Since its launch in 2005, myYearbook has grown to be one of the top teen sites and one of the 25 most trafficked sites in the United States. The core audience for myYearbook is teens between the ages of 13–17, but the website's members also include young adults between the ages of 18–35. It has popular features such as myMag and Lunch Money that appeal to these age groups. MyMag is the largest online teen magazine in the world. Lunch Money allows members to earn virtual currency that can be used to buy virtual gifts or donated to various causes. The average user spends 26 minutes per visit and visits ten times a month. These statistics make myYearbook a popular advertising medium for businesses that are trying to reach the teen market and build long-term brand awareness. Advertising makes up two-thirds of the site's revenue.

Work as a Team   Why are social networking sites popular with advertisers? Which social networking sites have you visited? What kind of advertisements did you see?

The Internet's Role in Advertising

The Internet has had a major impact on the advertising industry. **Online advertising** is a form of promotion that uses the Internet and World Wide Web as the advertising medium to deliver marketing messages that attract customers. Online advertising is growing faster than any other type of advertising. Research group eMarketer estimates that online ad spending will increase to $46 billion in 2015, which will account for 24 percent of all ad spending. Newspaper and magazine subscriptions are very low among people in the 21- to 35-year-old market. As Internet access around the world continues to grow, companies large and small are advertising online. Although it is unlikely that online advertising will ever replace the other types of advertising, companies are realizing the benefits of using it as a key component in their marketing and advertising strategies.

Types of Online Advertising

Online advertising can be approached in many ways. Over the years, it has advanced from simple e-mail and banner advertisements to interactive social media advertising. Choosing the right approach depends on the product or service being advertised and the target market.

E-Mail Advertising E-mail is one of the quickest and easiest ways to reach customers. Many businesses collect e-mail addresses from customers and prospective customers, making it easy to send out information about promotions. Company websites often have an opt-in feature that allows customers to sign up for e-mails about the company and its products. Another approach is to hire a business that specializes in targeting, preparing, and sending e-mails to specific audiences. Because e-mail can be targeted and personalized easily, businesses can extend special offers of interest to specific individuals. E-mail advertisements sometimes get a bad reputation because of **spam**, which is an unwanted online communication that is sent out in mass.

Have you ever received an e-mail advertisement? Was the ad effective? Why or why not?

Banner and Pop-Up Advertising If you have spent any time surfing the Internet, you have most likely seen banner and pop-up ads. A **banner ad** is a small, rectangular advertisement that usually appears at the top or side of a web page and contains a link to the advertiser's site. Banner ads are also referred to as *display ads.* Early banner ads featured little more than text and an image. Today's banner ads are much more sophisticated and use flash animation, video, and audio to interact with website visitors. Banner ads can be placed on websites that attract the same target market. For example, if you visit a recipe website, you might see an ad for Kraft's Philly® Cream Cheese.

A **pop-up ad** is an online advertisement that opens on top of the current web page being viewed. The purpose of a pop-up ad is to increase traffic to a specific website. Pop-up ads can also be used to acquire e-mail addresses of individuals who are interested in receiving product information or other special offers for a product or service. Many consumers think pop-up ads are annoying and use pop-up blocking software to avoid them.

Why are many companies choosing to use search engine advertisements?

Search Engine Advertising A popular approach to online advertising is a search engine ad. A **search engine ad** is also known as a *paid search* because the advertiser pays the search engine to place ads near relevant search results based on keywords. Google is the most popular search engine, but others include Yahoo! Search and Microsoft's Bing. Search engine ads allow a business to target people who are searching for words or topics related to the business and its products. For example, if you enter the words "diamond earrings" into a search engine, links to several jewelers appear next to the search engine results. The main objective of search engine ads is to increase brand awareness.

Search engine advertising is a quick and effective way to promote a business online. It helps drive Internet visitors to the business's website. Advertisers pay a certain amount each time someone clicks on their link. Marketers must carefully evaluate website visits resulting from search engine advertising to determine which keywords are producing results.

Website Advertising Today, website advertising is especially critical for businesses—both Internet and traditional brick-and-mortar businesses. A *brick-and-mortar business* is one that has a physical presence, such as a building or store, not just an online presence. Large companies spend millions of dollars to develop, launch, and maintain their websites. However, there are some inexpensive ways for smaller businesses to set up websites. Website advertising may be a good choice for startup companies that have limited capital. It is also the fastest way to reach a global market.

Once a business sets up its website, it must draw targeted traffic to the site through effective website advertising strategies. Website addresses can be featured in traditional advertising media, such as print ads, or in press releases sent to Internet news sites. They can also be registered with search engines such as Google. Effective websites have attention-grabbing headlines, up-to-date articles, and customer testimonials. Companies encourage viewers to subscribe to their online newsletters or e-magazines. This allows the business to build a database of subscribers who are interested in the business and the products it offers.

Blogs A **blog** (web log) is a website maintained by an individual or business where entries (posts) that are intended for public access are made on a regular basis. Posts could include commentary on various topics, descriptions of events, reviews, and targeted advertising messages. Companies realize that some of their brands are featured on consumers' blogs, making them a powerful word-of-mouth promotional tool. Many blogs have a wide readership base that attracts thousands of visitors every month. Companies place paid advertisements on popular blogs about topics of interest to their target markets. Advertisers on top fashion blogs include Diet Pepsi and Nordstrom. Some companies have their own blogs. Whole Foods Market has a popular blog called the *Whole Story*. It consists of posts that provide exciting product ideas and how-to tips. Visitors can even search for posts by category.

Social Media Advertising Advertisers are realizing the value of social media and have begun to shift significant amounts of their advertising dollars into this technology. **Social media** are websites where users create and share information. Web-based and mobile technologies are used to turn communication into interactive dialogue. Early versions of social media included chat rooms, which provided a way for people around the world to communicate in real time about topics of interest. Although chat rooms still exist, they have largely been replaced with newer types of social media, including Facebook, YouTube, and Twitter. Research firm eMarketer estimates that Facebook's worldwide advertising revenue will grow to $7 billion in 2013, making Facebook the largest seller of online display advertisements.

Advertisers often use social media to create buzz about a product or brand. Once they have created interest, they rely on consumers to spread the word through their communications on social media sites. Customer satisfaction and company image can be tracked based on these communications. This information then can be used to improve advertising strategies. Procter & Gamble has found that social media is an efficient way to connect with its customers. During the 2010 Olympics, P&G coordinated its TV commercials with Facebook messages and tracked instant reactions to new commercials on Twitter.

Twitter Since its introduction in 2006, Twitter has grown by leaps and bounds. *Twitter* is a social networking and micro-blogging service that allows individuals to send short text messages of 140 characters in length, called "tweets," to friends and other followers. Registered users create a Twitter page on which they post tweets. Other users can choose to "follow" someone else's tweets. The average number of tweets a day has grown to 140 million.

Businesses are finding many uses for Twitter, including market research, advertising, public relations, and various other marketing activities. It is especially effective as a customer service tool. Businesses can respond quickly and inexpensively to customers' questions and complaints. Convenience and quick response times are why many customers prefer using Twitter instead of contacting a company's call center. Tweeting advertisements is becoming big business. Web-based companies like *Sponsored Tweets* and *MyLikes* recruit individuals to tweet advertisements for various companies. The tweeters, called "influencers," will tweet the advertisement to their list of followers. The tweeters are paid based upon their number of followers or the click-through rate (number of clicks on the advertiser's link) generated by the advertisements.

COOL FACT

Twitter has gained popularity worldwide. New tweeting records are set daily. Tweets generally spike during significant cultural events or disasters, such as after Japan's earthquake and tsunami on March 11, 2011, when Twitter users made over 177 million tweets in a single day.

Advantages and Disadvantages of Online Advertising

Online advertising has become an increasingly popular choice for many companies because it offers many advantages. One of the biggest advantages is flexibility. Companies can change the advertising message quickly so that it is always current. The Internet provides an interactive platform for communication between businesses and consumers. Consumers who have the opportunity to ask questions and provide feedback about companies and products are more likely to buy those products due to a higher level of consumer involvement. Online advertising has a broad reach, with the capability of reaching a global audience. Identifying and reaching target markets is also made easier with online advertising. For example, a hotel can target travelers and vacationers by placing an advertisement on a city's tourism website.

One of the biggest disadvantages of online advertising is the lack of control a company has over information that is posted by others. People can post negative feedback or inaccurate information on blogs or social networking sites. By the time these postings are addressed or removed, the company's reputation may be damaged already.

Other threats to online advertising include spamming and phishing. Spamming involves flooding the Internet with mass copies of the same message in an attempt to reach the largest audience possible. Although spam is associated with e-mail traditionally, there are now occurrences of text messaging spam and social media spam. Most spam involves advertising for get-rich-quick schemes or questionable legal and medical products and services. Spam lists are often created by scanning newsgroup postings, subscribing to Internet mailing lists, or searching the Web for addresses. Spam is an inexpensive way to send an advertisement to the mass market. Although most people find it annoying, spam has proven to be effective. It generates a bigger consumer response than do traditional direct marketing efforts, such as direct mail and telemarketing. That's why the volume of spam continues to grow.

Phishing is an Internet scam in which an e-mail falsely claims to be a legitimate business or other organization in an attempt to get personal information. The personal information is used to commit identity theft crimes. The e-mail asks recipients to update personal information, such as passwords, credit card numbers, social security numbers, and bank account numbers. The e-mail often contains an actual business's name and logo, making it look legitimate. Recipients of such e-mails should not respond to them. Instead, they should contact the company directly to verify the request is legitimate.

A phishing scam was carried out against eBay users in 2009 when they were notified that their accounts would be suspended unless they updated account information, including credit card information. The phishing scammer was arrested a year later in Romania after he and his partners in crime used the stolen data to withdraw over $400,000 from ATMs.

How can you avoid phishing scams?

Online Advertising Considerations

Before a business places an advertisement on the Internet, it should understand the costs involved. In addition, businesses should be familiar with the different ways to track the effectiveness of online advertising. Online advertising costs are rising because of the growth in the number of Internet users and the increased capabilities of tracking software.

Costs of Online Advertising

There is a variety of methods used to determine the cost of online advertising. With *cost-per-click (CPC) advertising*, advertisers pay for each click that their ad receives. Ten clicks at $1 a click would cost a company $10. Because this method can be quite costly, it gives advertisers an incentive to target their ads correctly. *Cost-per-thousand impressions (CPM) advertising* allows a company to pay for a certain number of impressions (on a per-thousand basis) instead of paying per click. An *impression* is a single instance of an ad appearing on a web page. In a CPM-based campaign, a company may pay $5 for 1,000 impressions. So for every 1,000 times a web page containing the company's ad is viewed, the company would pay $5. Visitors do not have to click on the ad. The downside to CPM-based advertising is that the minimum purchase of impressions could be more than a company requires. While $5 per thousand impressions is very appealing, a minimum purchase of one million impressions can add up quickly [($1,000,000/1,000) × $5 = $5,000].

How are mouse clicks used to calculate the costs of online advertising?

© Alexander Kalina/Shutterstock.com

A third method, *cost-per-action (CPA) advertising*, is growing in popularity. With CPA, the advertiser pays only when the website visitor takes a specifically defined action in response to an ad. For example, a website visitor may have to complete a survey, subscribe to a newsletter, or place an order. CPA-based advertising provides the flexibility to meet the objectives of various companies. It may be the best option for small companies with tight budgets. CPA advertising allows companies to run advertisements in more places for longer periods of time since the business only pays for specified actions. Companies may want to try several different methods of advertising simultaneously and track the results.

The Effectiveness of Online Advertising

Companies want to be able to measure the effectiveness of their online advertising. They may count hits, page views, visits, and unique visitors. Hits do not represent the number of people visiting a website. Instead, *hits* represent the number of elements (files) on a requested web page. For example, a web page containing four photos would be counted as five hits—four for the photos and one for the entire page. A *page view* is the web page in its entirety, including all images on the page. A page view could contain hundreds of hits, which would not provide an accurate measurement. So page views are counted, not hits. *Visits* track the number of times a specific user has visited a business's website. One user can make multiple visits to a website. Visits are tracked using *cookies*, which are data files that a business's website can store on a visitors hard drive for retrieval later. Data stored may include information such as the visitor's name, address, and pages viewed on the website previously. *Unique visitors* include the number of new people visiting the site.

SPOTLIGHT ON SUCCESS

© AP Photo/Bennet Group

PIERRE OMIDYAR

eBay

Pierre Omidyar, the founder of eBay, became fascinated with computers while in high school. After graduating from college in 1988 with a degree in Computer Science, he went on to work at various technology companies, which led to his interest in online commerce. In 1995, Pierre Omidyar created Auction Web, an online auction site, as a way to establish a venue for direct person-to-person auction of collectible items. The site quickly expanded from a sales channel for collectibles to a popular site for the sale of furniture, electronics, home appliances, cars, and other vehicles. The product categories have continued to grow over the years. Currently, the most expensive item ever to be sold on eBay was a yacht for $168 million. eBay earns revenue by collecting a small percentage of the final sale price.

Omidyar originally contained eBay's advertising program in-house by allowing eBay sellers to promote their products. The ads didn't link outside of the eBay website. In 2006 eBay signed deals to run ads from the Yahoo! and Google networks and canceled the in-house advertising program. Yahoo!'s and Google's ad-matching technology delivered banner (display) ads that were relevant and precisely targeted to eBay pages. Advertisers paid eBay each time their ads were clicked on. By using this advertising strategy, eBay could earn revenue even if a visitor did not buy something from the eBay site. eBay sellers criticized these ads. They felt the ads were competing with the products already on eBay and were driving shoppers away from the site. Apparently, the eBay sellers were right. In 2010 eBay began removing a large percentage of the advertisements from its site. Because most of the ads took the consumers off-site, the ads did little to drive sales. In 2011 Omidyar signed an agreement with Triad Retail Media, an online advertising services specialist. Triad and eBay will work together to create new display ads that will showcase items for sale on eBay. Omidyar's overall goal is to improve the customer experience for eBay buyers and sellers.

Think Critically

Why did eBay abandon its in-house advertising program in favor of working with Yahoo! and Google? What were the advantages and disadvantages of this deal? What did this experience reveal about the importance of customer relationships?

Many companies use web analytic software to track hits, page views, visits, and unique visitors. The software also tracks visitors' mouse movements while they are on the website to determine what information is viewed, when it is viewed, and how often it is viewed. Marketers can use this information to make adjustments that will make their websites more appealing.

▰▰▰▰▰ CHECKPOINT ◤◤◤◤◤

What factors should a business consider when advertising online?

7.2 Assessment

THINK ABOUT IT

1. What is online advertising?
2. What is an advantage and disadvantage of online advertising?
3. What is the difference between CPC advertising and CPA advertising?
4. What is spam and how does it negatively affect online advertising?

MAKE ACADEMIC CONNECTIONS

5. **TECHNOLOGY** Go online and visit several websites. Describe the types of online advertising you encounter. What businesses, products, or services are being advertised? Are the advertisements effective or annoying?

6. **MATH** A company sells computers for $2,000. It advertises them online, paying $5 CPM. The company has determined that it takes 5,000 impressions to sell one computer. What is the online advertising cost to sell one computer? What percent of the computer's selling price does the online advertising fee represent?

7. **COMMUNICATION** *Sponsored Tweets* has recruited you to develop a tweet advertisement about a new Italian restaurant. Since a tweet is limited to 140 characters, what will be the most effective message to send on Twitter?

8. **RESEARCH** Conduct research to learn more about Internet cookies. What types of online businesses use cookies? Why do they use them? How do cookies benefit online businesses? Do they benefit consumers in any way? Do you think a business should be required to get consent to use cookies? Are there any laws regarding them? Write a two-page report on your findings.

Teamwork
Prepare a PowerPoint presentation describing the different types of online advertising. Your presentation should explain the advantages and disadvantages associated with each type of advertisement. Show examples of the various types of online advertising.

Alternative Forms of Advertising Media

FOCUS ON ADVERTISING

Goals
- Recognize alternative forms of advertising media outlets.
- Describe the latest advertising media trends.

Terms
- transit advertising, p. 199
- aerial advertising, p. 199
- cinema advertising, p. 199
- product placement, p. 200
- mobile advertising, p. 201

The Advertising Industry Goes to School

School districts that are desperate to bring in revenue for budgetary reasons are turning their buses into billboards for local businesses. School buses offer high visibility as they make daily trips throughout communities. Advertisements have popped up on buses in New Jersey, Arizona, Texas, Colorado, New Mexico, and Tennessee. Many other states are also considering the idea. A sampling of the advertisers include insurance and real estate agencies, banks, a toy store, an ambulance company, and auto dealerships. In 2008, a school district in Colorado signed a four-year $500,000 contract with a bank to display ads on buses, the athletic complex, and the school district's website. Some consumer groups and parents are alarmed by ads on buses. They believe that U.S. children are already exposed to too many advertisements. But the need for additional revenue is too great for many schools. School districts try to avoid controversy by carefully selecting appropriate ads. Ads for alcohol, tobacco, politics, and churches are generally prohibited.

Work as a Team What are the pros and cons for placing advertisements on school buses? Do the pros outweigh the cons? Which local businesses do you think could advertise on your school buses?

© anyunov/Shutterstock.com

Other Advertising Outlets

While the newspaper, television, magazines, radio, and Internet are the most common methods of advertising, there is a wide variety of alternative media that can be used to reach the target market. Alternative forms of media can play an important role in the overall advertising strategy.

Transit Advertising

Transit advertising includes ads that appear on the interior or exterior of public transportation (buses, taxis, subways) and other vehicles. This form of advertising is closely related to billboard advertising. Transit advertising now uses digital signage, making it easy to customize and change messages. Although many transit ads are placed on signs in or on a vehicle, *vehicle wraps* are ads consisting of pictures and graphics that completely encase the vehicle.

Transit advertising is more effective when the target market consists of adults who live and work in metropolitan areas. Since people take public transportation to and from work each day, transit advertising is a good way to expose commuters to a message. Over 4 million people ride the New York subways each day, giving transit ads a large audience. Transit advertising is effective at building or maintaining brand awareness. Because transit ads can go unnoticed as people go about their daily routines, ads must be creative and eye-catching, but not lengthy.

Aerial Advertising

Advertising in the sky is known as **aerial advertising**. Banners with advertising messages are hooked onto planes that fly over stadiums, beaches, and entertainment venues to capture the interest of potential customers. Some of the airplanes use loud speakers, combining audio and visual elements. Skywriting delivers messages in the form of white cloud formations. Blimps are used to advertise at outdoor college and professional sporting events. Some have full-color LED screens. Small blimps are also available for rental. Hot air balloons imprinted with company names and logos can be seen flying over special events.

Cinema Advertising

Cinema advertising includes ads that run in movie theaters before the start of movies. Theaters offer 40-foot screens and great sound systems for viewing ads. Now ads can even be shown in 3D. Ads can be targeted based on the film's rating (G, PG, PG-13, and R). Both local and national companies can advertise. With all of these benefits, big screen advertising is becoming more popular. Over $600 million is invested each year in cinema advertising. Advertising is also included on popcorn boxes and cups that are sold at movie concession stands. Sometimes the concession stands offer product samples. Upcoming movies are advertised using *trailers* (previews) shown before the feature presentation.

Why might a business choose to advertise at a movie theater?

Product Placement Advertising

Consumers often skip over commercials and use the remote control to flip to other channels when commercials are playing. Thus, advertisers are finding other ways to get their brands noticed. **Product placement** is a form of advertising in which a business's product, service, or name is used in a television show, movie, video game, or other form of entertainment. Because specific brands are being promoted, this form of advertising is also known as *brand placement*. Coca-Cola cups sit on a table in front of the judges for *American Idol*. Charmin® bathroom tissue and Pringles® snacks have been included as part of the challenge prizes awarded to contestants on *Survivor*. The film *Iron Man 2* featured more than 64 brands. Companies pay for product placement on popular television shows and movies to increase brand awareness. TV shows and movies offer large audiences and a global reach. When viewers develop an emotional connection with the show or movie and its characters, they have a higher recall of the brands used.

Video game advertising, also called advergaming, is a way to promote brands using video games. Companies pay to have their brands featured in the games played by millions of consumers every day. Brand names can be found on billboards, storefronts, and racecars appearing in the game. Young adult males between the ages of 18 and 34 are the primary target market for video games. Various research organizations predict that spending on video game advertising will reach between $700 million and $1 billion in 2014.

Why are directory ads (in print or online) a good way to reach consumers?

Directory Advertising

Telephone directories like the *Yellow Pages* have been around for a long time. Specialized telephone directories have been designed for neighborhoods, ethnic groups, and other special interest groups. A telephone directory is an advertising medium that consumers use to seek out products or services. Larger ads that use color and higher-quality graphics attract more attention. Directory advertising is often used to supplement other advertising media. As people turn to the Internet to search for product and service information, they use telephone directories less often. As a result, many online versions of directories, such as YP.com (yellowpages.com), are now available, offering advertisers another way to reach consumers.

CHECKPOINT

What are some alternative forms of advertising media?

Latest Advertising Media Trends

The advertising industry is continuously searching for new, creative strategies to get the message to targeted customers. Advertising trends have changed dramatically as marketers look for new ways to keep pace with technology and media. By staying informed about the latest developments, marketers can identify related advertising opportunities.

Video Advertising

Video advertising is one of the fastest-growing forms of online advertising. While traditional advertising is on the decline, the number of video ads seen online is rising. By 2014, eMarketer estimates that video advertising will account for 15 percent of total online advertising spending. Videos can be embedded on company websites or exported to other websites, such as YouTube. Marketers have found that when a video is featured within an online article, website visitors tend to play the video before they start reading the article. Videos can run from 15 seconds to several minutes.

Webisodes are video ads that run as a series of episodes on a website. Bertolli®, a brand of Italian food, created six webisodes that followed three people to Italy to talk to leading chefs about the inspiration behind Bertolli's frozen meals. Some companies pay to sponsor a website or a portion of it. Website visitors may have to view a video ad from the sponsoring company when they click on one of the website links. The advertiser is able to capture the visitor's undivided attention for 15 seconds or less.

Companies are slipping advertisements under the radar by using viral videos. *Viral videos* become popular through Internet sharing. Marketers create videos and post them on video-sharing websites like YouTube. People that think the videos are funny, cool, or informative share them on social networking sites and through personal e-mails. When the video is circulated, it could get over a million views. In some instances, product users will create and post videos that go viral. Such was the case with the Diet Coke and Mentos® experiment, which drew more than 7.5 million viewers. It was so popular that Coke and Mentos sponsored the production of a second video, which drew over 4 million viewers.

Mobile Advertising

Another trend that is having a major impact on the advertising industry is mobile advertising. **Mobile advertising** directs messages to consumers' Internet-enabled mobile devices, such as smartphones, MP3 players, and digital tablets like the iPad. The growing number of mobile devices represents many opportunities for advertisers

Would you like advertisements sent to your cell phone? Why or why not?

to reach potential customers, especially younger consumers. Ads can be sent directly to mobile devices. Marketers believe mobile advertising can be very effective for local retailers, restaurants, entertainment businesses, and service providers if used to send promotional offers, such as coupons and price discounts. New GPS-based consumer-tracking technology will enable advertisers to send location-based messages to smartphones when the consumer is close to the point of sale, such as when he or she walks by a restaurant or into a mall. Major brands may sponsor video podcasts that allow mobile device users to download videos of their favorite TV shows. According to eMarketer, mobile advertising spending in a recent year was over $700 million.

CHECKPOINT
Describe one advertising media trend.

7.3 Assessment

THINK ABOUT IT

1. Why is transit advertising more effective in large cities?
2. What are some of the advantages of product placements in TV shows, movies, and video games?
3. Why is mobile advertising becoming more popular?

MAKE ACADEMIC CONNECTIONS

4. **VISUAL ART** You have been asked to design an advertising vehicle wrap for your favorite restaurant. The vehicle wrap will cover a city bus. Draw the advertisement that you will use to wrap the bus.

5. **RESEARCH** Conduct research to learn about video game advertising. Prepare a PowerPoint presentation that describes how advertising is incorporated into this type of media. Provide examples of product placement in various video games. Also, describe some of the various target markets advertisers are trying to reach.

6. **DECISION MAKING** Select a movie that is currently showing in the theaters. Make a list of five businesses, products, or services that could advertise before the start of the movie. Describe the target market for each item and explain why it is a good fit with the movie. Also, explain why you think cinema advertising would be a good advertising strategy for the five items you chose.

Teamwork
Select a product or service that you think could benefit from online video advertising. Develop three webisodes for the product or service. Describe the content of each webisode and explain how it promotes the product or service. Act out one of the webisodes and videotape it to share with the class.

Sharpen Your
21st CENTURY SKILLS

PARTNERSHIP FOR
21ST CENTURY SKILLS

Protecting Against Identity Theft

Identity theft is the act of stealing personal information to use for illegal purposes. Thieves can use stolen social security numbers to apply for credit. Stolen credit card numbers can be used to run up charges. The Federal Trade Commission (FTC) estimates that over 9 million Americans have their identity stolen each year. Since identity theft is on the rise, you should know how to protect yourself.

- *Keep your social security number confidential.* Only certain businesses have the right to your social security number, including motor vehicle departments, tax agencies, and businesses such as banks and employers that report income. If you are asked for your social security number, ask why it is needed.

- *Shred old receipts containing account information.* Bank deposit receipts, credit card statements, and any other old documents that contain sensitive personal information should be shredded. Identity thieves can learn a lot about you by rummaging through your trash. This is commonly known as *dumpster diving.*

- *Shop on secure websites only.* When you place an order online, the letters at the beginning of the address bar at the top of the page should change from "http" to "https." The "s" at the end indicates it is a secure site. Also, look for a lock icon or a VeriSign logo that certifies the site is secure.

- *Check statements carefully.* Check credit card statements and bank statements closely for suspicious activity. You should also check your credit reports regularly. You are entitled to a free copy of your credit report once a year. Check your reports for inaccurate information.

- *Protect online accounts with intricate passwords.* Use passwords for credit card and bank accounts. Combinations of letters, numbers, and special characters make the strongest password. Avoid using easily accessible information such as your birthday, phone number, social security number, or pet's name as passwords.

- *Verify the source before sharing personal information.* Do not give out information on the phone, through the mail, or online unless you are sure you are dealing with a legitimate organization. The person may be trying to obtain credit card or bank account numbers.

Try It Out

Learn more about identity theft. Search for more tips on how to prevent it. Find out what to do if your identity is stolen. Using all of the information you gather, create a brochure that can be distributed to other students. Use "Identity Theft Awareness" as the title.

SUMMARY

7.1 Traditional Advertising Media

- Traditional types of advertising media include television, radio, print, and outdoor. Each medium has advantages and disadvantages.
- When selecting the media to use, advertisers should consider the media's reach, frequency, lead time, and cost.
- A common way to measure a medium's cost efficiency is to determine its cost-per-thousand (CPM), which is the dollar cost of reaching 1,000 audience members.

7.2 The Internet and Advertising

- Online advertising is a form of promotion that uses the Internet and World Wide Web to deliver marketing messages that attract customers.
- Online advertising can take on many forms, including e-mails, banner and pop-up ads, search engine ads, website ads, blog messages, social media messages and ads, and Twitter messages.
- Although online advertising offers many benefits, such as flexibility, currency, and interactivity, spam and phishing scams can reduce the effectiveness of online advertising.
- There are several methods used to determine the cost of online advertising: cost-per-click (CPC) advertising, cost-per-thousand impressions (CPM) advertising, and cost-per-action (CPA) advertising.
- Common ways to measure the effectiveness of online advertising include hits, page views, visits, and unique visitors.

7.3 Alternative Forms of Advertising Media

- Alternative forms of media can play an important role in an advertising strategy. They include transit advertising, aerial advertising, cinema advertising, product placement advertising, and directory advertising.
- Video advertising is one of the fastest-growing forms of online advertising. Video ads can be embedded on company websites or exported to other sites. The video may become viral if it is circulated online via e-mails, video-sharing sites, and social networking sites.
- Mobile advertising is used to send messages to mobile devices, such as smartphones, MP3 players, and digital tablets.

WHAT DO YOU KNOW? Now

Read *Impact Advertising* on page 181 again to review Chick-fil-A's outdoor advertising campaign. Visit Chick-fil-A's website to see how the restaurant incorporates the same theme in its online advertising. Do you think the advertising campaign works well in both media outlets? Explain why or why not.

Vocabulary Builder

Match each statement with the term that best defines it. Some terms may not be used.

1. Internet scam in which an e-mail falsely claims to be a legitimate business or other organization
2. Small rectangular ad that appears at the top or side of a web page and contains a link to the advertiser's site
3. Website maintained by an individual or business where entries that are intended for public access are made on a regular basis
4. Total number of people who will be exposed to an advertisement over a period of time
5. Advertising that appears on the interior or exterior of public transportation and other vehicles
6. Using a business's product, service, or name in a television show, movie, or other form of entertainment
7. Websites where users create and share information
8. Channels of communication used to send a message to the target market
9. Number of times a person is exposed to an advertisement
10. Amount of time required to produce and place an advertisement

a. aerial advertising
b. banner ad
c. blog
d. cinema advertising
e. frequency
f. lead time
g. media
h. mobile advertising
i. online advertising
j. phishing
k. pop-up ad
l. product placement
m. reach
n. search engine ad
o. social media
p. spam
q. transit advertising

Test Your Knowledge

11. What is the most popular type of advertising media?
    a. print
    b. radio
    c. television
    d. Internet
12. All of the following are traditional types of advertising media *except*
    a. television
    b. social media
    c. radio
    d. newspaper
13. One of the biggest disadvantages associated with newspaper advertising is the
    a. high cost
    b. long lead time
    c. large circulation
    d. short life span
14. One of the biggest disadvantages associated with television advertising is the
    a. low cost per viewer
    b. large, diverse audience
    c. long lead time
    d. use of sight and sound

15. The number of times you see the McDonald's advertisement while watching a baseball game on television is called
    a. reach
    b. frequency
    c. lead time
    d. pulsing

16. If an online advertiser pays for an ad only when a website visitor clicks on the link and places an order, the _____ method of payment is used.
    a. CPC
    b. CPA
    c. CPM
    d. CPT

17. _____ is used to gather personal information from an individual illegally through the use of an e-mail.
    a. Phishing
    b. Spam
    c. Bait and switch
    d. Computer virus

18. Which of the following is *not* a characteristic of radio advertising?
    a. segmentation by demographics is easy
    b. both local and national companies can use this medium
    c. a short lead time is required
    d. it is the best medium for mass marketing

19. A TV show's ratings are an indication of its
    a. reach
    b. frequency
    c. lead time
    d. pulsing

20. All of the following are true about search engine ads *except*
    a. they are known as a *paid search* because the advertiser pays the search engine to place ads near relevant search results
    b. they are ineffective at increasing brand awareness
    c. they help drive Internet visitors to a business's website
    d. they can be used to target people based on keyword searches

21. Data files that a business's website stores on a visitor's hard drive for retrieval later are called
    a. spam
    b. cookies
    c. hits
    d. banners

22. If it costs $350,000 for an advertisement on a television show that has a reach of 5 million people, what is the CPM?
    a. $75
    b. $70
    c. $0.07
    d. $0.70

Apply What You Learned

23. You want to increase sales at your fast food restaurant that has several locations with drive-through windows that are open until 2 A.M. Your target market is young adults between the ages of 18–24. How could you use aerial advertising and mobile advertising to promote your restaurant?

24. Watch for product placements on one of your favorite TV shows. Which products or brands were shown or used on the program? Explain why the products/brands and TV show are a good match. Recommend other product placements that you think would work well on the show.

25. A local attorney has asked for your advice regarding the best media to use to advertise his new law practice. What recommendations will you make? Explain why.

Make Academic Connections

26. **COMMUNICATION**   You are the marketing manager for a major university bookstore. Your university wants to boost school spirit. You have developed a campaign where registered students can trade a t-shirt or sweatshirt from another university in exchange for a brand new t-shirt imprinted with your university's name and logo. Write a tweet to be sent to all university students that will encourage them to take part in the trade-in promotion.

27. **PROBLEM SOLVING**   You own a furniture store. Describe two different target markets for your products and services. Outline an advertising strategy that uses at least two different types of advertising media for each target market. Explain why the media you selected will be the most effective at reaching your target markets.

28. **CONSUMER LAW**   Fraudulent online advertising can take the form of spam and phishing scams. Conduct research to learn about federal and state laws and government and consumer protection agencies that help protect consumers from the dangers of such scams. Give a presentation describing the types of protection available.

29. **TECHNOLOGY**   Learn about advertising opportunities that are available on Facebook. Then describe how an outdoor skating park could use Facebook to advertise. Prepare an advertisement for the park to place on Facebook.

30. **DECISION MAKING**   Develop a continuous advertising strategy and a pulsing advertising strategy for one of the following businesses: automobile manufacturer, department store, restaurant, movie theater, or hardware store. (You can develop a continuous strategy for one business and a pulsing strategy for another business or develop both strategies for the same company.) Present both strategies to the class.

You overhear the conversation between two classmates who have successfully created a phishing scheme that makes e-mail recipients believe they are receiving an official message from the school's administration. The fraudulent e-mail has been sent out to community members asking them to support the school's effort in raising money for the beautification of a local park. An official-looking contribution form containing the school's logo is attached to the e-mail. Recipients are asked to enter their donation amount and credit card number. The students plan to use the credit card numbers illegally to make purchases for themselves.

What action would you take in this situation? How could you alert the community about the phishing scheme? How could this scheme harm community members and the school?

Reality ✓

Put a Stop to SPAM

Spam, consisting of unwanted e-mails, can be overwhelming. E-mails trying to sell you unwanted products or services or pitching get-rich-quick schemes can quickly overload your inbox. Also, sorting through spam to get to legitimate e-mails can be time consuming. In addition, spam can spread computer viruses. Once your e-mail address gets on a spammer's list, it is almost impossible to remove it. However, there are some steps you can take to avoid spam.

Use two e-mail accounts. Create an e-mail address for personal use and one for public use. Give out the public e-mail address when asked for this information anywhere on the Web or by businesses that are likely to send out unwanted advertisements. This will help keep your primary e-mail account free of spam.

Use a unique e-mail address that contains both letters and numbers. Your e-mail address may affect the amount of spam you receive. Some spammers use a "dictionary attack," which is a technique where the spammer sends out thousands or millions of e-mails using randomly generated e-mail addresses in the hopes of reaching a large percentage of actual e-mail addresses. Dictionary attacks are often successful because people tend to use easily predicted e-mail addresses. The e-mail address *jsmith@domain.com* is likely to get more spam than *js63fac!@domain.com*. An e-mail address should use a combination of letters, numbers, and special characters. Also, the longer it is, the better.

Check the privacy policy when you submit your e-mail address to a website. The privacy policy will indicate how the company plans to use the information you submitted. If there is any indication that the company will sell your address, opt-out or do not submit your e-mail address.

Watch out for checkboxes. When you complete a form or sign up for something online, there is often a checkbox that gives the company permission to send you information about products. Often, this checkbox is already checked. Avoid receiving unwanted offers by making sure the box is unchecked.

Use a spam filter. Many e-mail programs provide a tool to filter out potential spam. Spam programs are also available for purchase. These programs will help manage spam by moving it into a separate folder and blocking future e-mails from the spammer.

Think Critically

1. Why is it important to fight spam vigilantly?
2. What can you do to help avoid spam when using the Internet?
3. Why should you carefully select your e-mail address?

You will design a plan to start an Internet marketing business or enhance a component of an existing Internet marketing business. You must conduct market research and prepare a business plan based upon the research results.

This project consists of a written document and an oral presentation. The body of the written document should follow the outline below.

I. Executive Summary (one-page description of the project)
II. Introduction (type of business or enhanced component proposed)
III. Analysis of the Business Situation
    A. Products and/or services offered
    B. Research to support Internet opportunity
    C. Market segment analysis
    D. Competitors
IV. Proposed Business Outline
    A. Facility needs and/or enhancements
    B. Proposed ownership structure
    C. Business operations (including vendors, manufacturing, modes of transportation, shipping, personnel needs)
    D. Proposed budget
    E. Web presence and design
V. Conclusion (request for financing and summary of key points)
VI. Bibliography
VII. Appendix (optional)

You must demonstrate the following skills when completing this project:

- communications skills—the ability to exchange information and ideas with others through writing, speaking, reading, or listening
- analytical skills—the ability to derive facts from data, findings from facts, conclusions from findings, and recommendations from conclusions
- critical thinking/problem-solving skills
- production skills—the ability to take a concept from an idea and make it real
- teamwork—the ability to be an effective member of a productive group
- priorities/time management—the ability to determine priorities and manage time commitments and deadlines
- identification of competitive conditions within market areas

Go to the DECA website for more detailed information.

Think Critically

1. Why is research essential before starting a new Internet marketing business?
2. What questions should you ask about the competition?
3. What are some of the latest Internet advertising trends?

www.deca.org

8

Effective Advertising and Sales Promotion

Flo: Live from Progressive Insurance

Selling insurance is not an easy sale. So Progressive Insurance® knew it had to come up with a creative advertising campaign to capture and hold the public's attention. Flo, a fictional character who appears in commercials for Progressive Insurance, was introduced in 2008, and she has appeared in over 50 commercials since her debut. Flo is an extremely enthusiastic, upbeat sales clerk who wears a heavy dose of makeup and sports a retro hairstyle. She has become one of the most recognizable mascots on television today. The character, played by actress and comedian Stephanie Courtney, has been cited in news articles as having a sizable fan base on social networks like Facebook. Multiple websites are dedicated to Flo, and she is popular on Twitter and other Internet forums.

© David Adame/AP Images for Progressive Insurance

The Flo brand is flourishing. The *Boston Herald* once referred to Flo as "the commercial break's new sweetheart." The commercials use Flo to symbolize the helpful, friendly service customers will get when they choose Progressive. Flo sells insurance policies packaged in boxes on shelves in an insurance superstore, giving the impression that shopping for insurance is as simple as a trip to the store. The commercials also emphasize the importance of listening to customers. Flo closely listens to her customers and then provides a customized, cost-saving insurance solution from Progressive. Her character is so popular that the insurance company actually gets calls from people who want to buy insurance directly from Flo.

Throughout the advertising campaign, Progressive has introduced many other quirky characters posing as customers. The goal is to introduce characters that represent consumers who have different insurance needs. Customers at the insurance superstore have ranged from expectant parents to a retired couple to a motorcyclist. In all cases, Progressive emphasizes that customers can get customized policies to meet all their insurance needs and save money while doing so.

In an industry where the market is flooded with many large insurers—each with ad budgets totaling hundreds of millions of dollars a year, Flo has brought widespread brand recognition to Progressive Insurance. Progressive has created an advertising campaign that is humorous, entertaining, and most importantly, memorable.

WHAT DO YOU KNOW?

1. Why do you think mascots are commonly used in advertising? How does having a memorable mascot benefit a business?

2. Why is it important for advertisements to be entertaining, especially when used in industries such as insurance?

3. Progressive continually runs ads showing new customers shopping at the insurance superstore. Why is this important?

8.1

Developing an Effective Advertising Campaign

© gary718/Shutterstock.com

Goals
- Explain the need for creativity in advertising.
- Describe the desired results of an advertising campaign.

Terms
- creative brief, p. 214
- synergy, p. 214
- brainstorming, p. 214

FOCUS ON ADVERTISING

Advertising Themes

Major amusement and theme parks like Disney and Universal Studios create advertising campaigns that distinguish them from the competition. Disney's themes and rides are based on popular Disney characters, such as Mickey Mouse, Snow White, and Alice in Wonderland, that attract families with younger children between the ages of 6 and 12. As an extension of this theme, Disney launched an advertising campaign called, "Let the Memories Begin." The campaign emphasized family vacations and memories. Home videos and snapshots that captured Disney memories of regular families were featured in Disney advertisements. Universal Studios' themes and rides are based on Universal movie characters like Spiderman, the Incredible Hulk, and Harry Potter, which tend to attract an older audience.

While Disney emphasizes family and memories in its commercials, Universal Studios uses edgier advertising that emphasizes extreme roller coasters, in-your-face effects, and extreme stunts that appeal to teens and adults. By incorporating the parks' themes into the advertising campaigns, Disney and Universal are building brand recognition.

Work as a Team Why are themes commonly used in advertisements? How can themes be used by businesses to build an identity?

© Christopher Sykes/Shutterstock.com

The Need for Creativity in Advertising

Advertising agencies typically have creative departments where print ads, television commercials, and other marketing communications are produced. These departments are staffed by writers who choose the words in advertisements, graphic artists who plan and construct visual layouts, and other specialists who transform the strategy into actual advertisements.

Creativity can be defined in many ways. It could be described as a different way of looking at things or a new way of thinking. Creativity often is associated with fresh, new ideas. Creativity is a key element in effective advertising campaigns. It makes an advertisement stand out from the crowd, earning it more attention and making it more memorable. Creative ads make an emotional connection with the audience.

Although creativity is important, an advertisement cannot be judged on creativity alone. Creative advertising must have a purpose—to influence consumers' product and brand buying decisions.

Elements of Creativity in Advertising

There are many kinds of creative styles used in the advertising industry, but creative ads share common features. Creative ads that have one or more of these elements are more memorable and are more likely to influence the consumers' buying behavior.

- *Creative ads make a connection with the target audience.* They offer worthy content and enjoyment that draws prospective customers' attention to a company's products and services. The ads are relevant because they provide information consumers need when making a buying decision. They also reflect emotions that consumers are experiencing as they shop for a specific product or service. If the target market for a restaurant is families, then advertisements need to reflect a fun, family atmosphere.

- *Creative ads have an element of unexpectedness.* They differ from ads for other brands in the same product category. They use unusual techniques to capture the audience's attention. The use of a talking Chihuahua that uttered the phrase "Yo Quiero Taco Bell!" in TV commercials made a lasting impression.

- *Creative ads use mischief in the form of tricks, pranks, and playfully naughty behavior to keep the audience interested.* Troublemakers and rebels are often featured in ads. "Mayhem" is a character used by Allstate® Insurance Company to demonstrate pitfalls such as collisions and storm damage that drivers may encounter. The importance of insurance coverage is communicated through mayhem's antics and Allstate's slogan, "Nobody protects you from mayhem like Allstate."

- *Creative ads provide concrete images.* Advertising messages that use tangible words and visual demonstrations are more memorable. Ford Motor Company's tagline for its trucks is "Built Ford Tough." Because "tough" is an abstract term, the tagline would not be as effective without a demonstration. Commercials feature Ford trucks pulling heavy loads.

- *Creative ads use storytelling.* Advertisers tell stories to emphasize important brand features. One of the most well-known examples of storytelling is the Subway™ advertising campaign featuring Jared. Jared lost almost 250 pounds by exercising and eating an all-Subway diet. Subway used Jared's story to help promote its menu as a healthier alternative to other fast food restaurants.

- *Creative ads build momentum.* Momentum can be measured by the buzz generated by an advertising campaign. When an advertising

Why do you think teams can come up with better ideas than individuals working alone can?

campaign gets people talking, leads to news stories, results in a following among celebrities and everyday consumers, it is building brand momentum.

Synergy from Teams

Successful advertising campaigns are created by teams consisting of members who have different areas of expertise. Advertising teams get direction from the **creative brief**, which is a description of what the advertising campaign is to accomplish. It states the objective of the advertising effort, which is to be carried out by the team. The client (advertiser) and various members of the advertising agency must work together to define the advertising objective and develop a creative, unique advertising campaign to achieve the objective. **Synergy**, which is the sum of the results produced by a team, is important to creative advertising. The idea behind synergy is that the whole is greater than the individual parts. Under the direction of a team leader, each team member will have a specific assignment. But through coordination and collaboration, the team as a whole will produce and implement the advertising campaign.

It has been shown that teams come up with better ideas. Brainstorming is one way to generate creative ideas. **Brainstorming** is an organized approach of generating a large number of ideas in a group setting. During brainstorming sessions, team members generate a list of ideas to help achieve objectives. In the case of advertising, teams may brainstorm ideas about the best way to communicate a message to the target audience. Ideas should not be judged or criticized because this will discourage participation. Brainstorming sessions likely will involve some kind of conflict, which can be good or bad. A clash of ideas among members could result in a breakthrough of new ideas and solutions. On the other hand, a clash of personalities among group members often leads to a shutdown in communication. Good team leaders will guide the group through both kinds of conflict.

///////// CHECKPOINT \\\\\\\

Why is creativity an important element in advertising?

Determine the Desired Results of an Advertising Campaign

Advertising objectives identify the desired results of an advertising campaign. All advertising efforts are directed toward the achievement of the advertising objectives. Often the objectives depend on the target market's level of experience with the brand. Objectives are set to move consumers from brand awareness to brand loyalty.

- *Build brand awareness.* This is the initial objective for new brands of products and services. If consumers are not aware of the brand's existence, few sales will be made. To build brand awareness, advertisers may use many forms of promotion, including advertising, sales promotion, and publicity.

- *Communicate product benefits.* In addition to making consumers aware of a brand, companies need to communicate its benefits. To do this, advertisers must supply information that explains the benefits obtained from purchasing the product. A consumer wants to know, "What's in it for me?" Advertisers may promote benefits related to money, health, convenience, leisure time, family, the environment, or other issues.

- *Encourage trial purchases.* Companies must encourage consumers to try a specific brand for the first time. Advertisements and sales promotions work in conjunction to meet this objective. Advertisements draw attention to the product, and sales promotions (coupons, free samples, price discounts, and rebates) motivate consumers to try it. At this stage, it is important that the brand live up to expectations so consumers have a positive experience.

SPOTLIGHT ON SUCCESS

© Michael L. Abramson/Time Life Pictures/Getty Images

THOMAS J. BURRELL
Burrell Communications

Thomas J. Burrell is the founder of Burrell Communications, formerly Burrell Advertising. Burrell Communications is one of the nation's leading African-American owned full-service advertising agencies. Burrell's path in life began while in high school. After taking an aptitude test, Burrell was identified as artistic and persuasive. A teacher suggested that those skills were compatible with the advertising industry. The idea interested Burrell, so he set his sights on a career in advertising. Upon entering college, Burrell joined the college newspaper staff and an advertising fraternity. During his senior year of college in 1961, he became the first African-American to work at a Chicago advertising agency when he got a job in the mailroom. Within a year, he was promoted and began writing advertising copy for well-known accounts like Alka-Seltzer. He continued to move up the ladder and work at various other agencies until in 1971 he left to begin his own advertising agency.

Burrell decided to focus on a largely ignored market at that time—African-American consumers. Burrell was a pioneer of the movement from mass marketing to targeted marketing. He began creating advertising that accurately reflected African-American values, lifestyles, and aspirations. McDonald's and Coca-Cola were two of the agency's first major clients. The principle behind Burrell's ads was "positive realism." His ads showed people who had thoughtful and caring interactions with family, friends, and neighbors and who had dreams and aspirations. Before Burrell entered the market, there were very few people of color in television commercials. He set out to build brand awareness while breaking stereotypes. In many instances, his ads broke color barriers and proved to be just as popular with white audiences. His success earned him many more prominent clients, including Procter & Gamble, Toyota, General Mills, Verizon, and Marriott. Companies hired Burrell's agency to reach youth and urban markets. In 1999, Advertising Age designated him one of the "Top 100 Advertising People" who have shaped the course of advertising history. In 2005, he received the industry's highest award when he was inducted into the Advertising Hall of Fame by the American Advertising Federation. Although Burrell retired in 2004, he still serves as a consultant to the advertising agency that still bears his name.

Think Critically
What influence did Burrell have on the advertising industry? How did he help identify the need for targeted marketing? Why do advertisers need to consider race and ethnicity?

- *Create, change, or reinforce consumers' attitudes about a brand.* After consumers try a brand, they develop beliefs and attitudes about it. If the brand meets their needs, consumers' attitudes will be positive. Advertising is used to remind consumers about the product's benefits and encourage repeat purchases. Advertisers try to convince consumers that their brand is superior and persuade consumers to switch brands.
- *Attain brand loyalty.* This is the objective that every company strives to meet. When consumers develop a strong brand preference, they become loyal customers. A company must continue to provide a brand that provides more satisfaction than competitive brands, and the advertising campaign must continue to communicate the benefits of the brand.

CHECKPOINT

What are some of the desired results of an advertising campaign?

8.1 Assessment

THINK ABOUT IT

1. Review the various elements of creativity used in advertising on p. 213. Describe an advertisement that uses one of these elements.
2. Why is teamwork important to the creative advertising process?
3. Why do advertisers have to address the question, "What's in it for me?" How does this help advertisers achieve a desired result?

MAKE ACADEMIC CONNECTIONS

4. **WRITING**   Conduct online research to learn about an advertising agency that managed a successful advertising campaign. Write a two-page report that describes the campaign. What was the objective of the campaign? What role did creativity play in the campaign? Explain why it was effective.
5. **PROBLEM SOLVING**   You opened a new ice cream shop in your neighborhood. Your advertising objective is to encourage trial purchases. Outline some creative strategies for accomplishing your objective. Present them to the class.
6. **ETHICS**   Creative advertising can sometimes be controversial because of the unusual techniques used to capture an audience's attention. Describe a current ad or one in the past that created controversy. Explain why it was controversial and how the advertiser reacted.

Teamwork

Your team operates the school store, which sells school supplies, school sprit items such as t-shirts and stickers, and snacks. Brainstorm at least ten creative advertising strategies to increase sales at your store. Narrow the list down to the top five ideas. Present them to the class and have them vote on the best strategy.

8.2

Marketing Research for Advertising

Goals

- Explain the marketing research process.
- Describe the benefits and limitations of marketing research.

Terms

- sample, p. 218
- primary market research, p. 219
- survey, p. 219
- focus group, p. 219
- secondary market research, p. 220
- marketing-information system, p. 222

Spreading the Word Online

Word-of-mouth advertising has always been a powerful promotional tool. Ninety percent of consumers trust recommendations made by people they know. Today, through the power of the Internet, word-of-mouth advertising has taken on an even more expansive role. More than ever, people are going online to research products before they make a purchase. In fact, about 4 out of 5 individuals in America with Internet access do this on a regular basis. An increasing number of individuals are also using feedback forums and connecting with one another through social networking sites and blogs to learn more about products and e-tailers. Research indicates that 70 percent of individuals trust consumer opinions posted online. Almost 50 percent of Americans believe that online sites containing product reviews and comments have influenced their decisions to purchase particular brands or services to at least some extent. A business that allows consumers to post feedback and reviews on its website can benefit greatly if the process is handled properly.

Work as a Team How is word-of-mouth advertising related to consumer research? How can a business benefit from online word-of-mouth advertising?

What Is Marketing Research?

Every business needs information to make marketing decisions. Information can be obtained through marketing research. *Marketing research* is the process of planning, collecting, and analyzing the data needed to solve marketing problems. Marketing research provides information about consumers, products, services, brand awareness, advertising, prices, wants and needs, and much more. The information collected during the marketing research process can be used to create a new marketing plan or analyze the current one to determine if changes are needed. Marketing research also helps businesses understand what is happening in the marketplace. It identifies opportunities in new, untapped markets. Although marketing research can be a costly and time-consuming process, the benefits usually outweigh the costs.

Steps in Marketing Research

Marketing research involves a scientific approach to decision making. A step-by-step method is used to collect accurate and meaningful data that will improve the quality of the decision-making process.

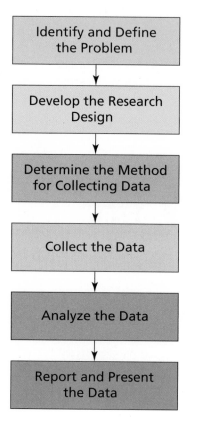

Identify and Define the Problem The introductory phase of the marketing research process involves a clear and precise understanding of the problem at hand. It is crucial that the research team clearly identifies, understands, and defines the problem because all the subsequent activities involved in the research process work toward solving the problem. Research teams make use of customer feedback, internal and external data reports, sales graphs, and purchasing patterns to define the problem accurately. The problem should be specific so that researchers know what to study. The problem may be presented in the form of research questions such as, "Should the existing marketing mix be changed? If so, how?"

Develop the Research Design After the problem is identified, researchers must determine how to solve it. The *research design* is the plan that specifies how the marketing research process will be implemented. It identifies which research questions must be answered, how and when the data will be gathered, and how the data will be analyzed. This process often involves joint discussions between the research team, industry experts, and management. The strength of the research design has a major impact on the success or failure of the research process.

Determine the Method for Collecting Data After researchers have decided what kinds of additional data are needed, they must determine the best way to collect them. Data may be collected through surveys or questionnaires. Company records, government reports, and other research studies may also provide the information needed.

Collect the Data When researchers gather information from consumers, they are not able to survey all members of a target market. Instead, they choose a **sample**, which is a smaller group that is representative of the target market. The target market must be clearly defined to avoid sampling errors. Larger samples provide more data, giving researchers a more complete picture of what they are studying.

Analyze the Data Once the information has been collected, it should be organized in a meaningful way so that it can be interpreted and analyzed by decision makers. When large amounts of information are collected, computers and statistical programs aid the analysis process. If numerical data are collected, researchers can calculate the percentage of responses or average responses to each question. Numerical data make comparisons much easier. Non-numerical data are collected through open-ended questions and are more difficult to analyze. Researchers may categorize non-numerical data based on similar responses. Researchers may also do a cross-tabulation, which lets researchers compare the responses to one question in relation to the responses of other questions. For example, researchers could look at the relationship between gender and favorite brand of a product.

Report and Present the Data All the effort that goes into the research process is wasted if the findings and the results are not presented properly. The entire marketing research project must be properly documented. Researchers should prepare a written and oral report to present conclusions and recommendations to management. The report likely will include tables, charts, and graphs to summarize the data collected. Based on the findings, researchers can propose a solution to the problem identified in the first step of the marketing research process. All of the data presented enable management to make an informed decision.

Primary Market Research

Researchers primarily use two different processes when collecting data—primary market research and secondary market research. **Primary market research** is the process of collecting data for the first time to use in solving a specific problem. Primary market research offers the benefit of direct contact with customers through a survey or interview. This type of research can be tailored to meet the needs of an organization and provide specific and detailed information. Primary data are collected directly by the organization that conducts the research. The results are available only to the researching organization, providing it with an edge against the competition.

Types of Primary Market Research Primary market research is conducted using several different methods. One of the most popular methods is the **survey**, which is a list of questions used to obtain facts, opinions, and attitudes. Surveys are also called *questionnaires*. Surveys may contain *closed-ended questions* that give respondents selections from which to choose. They may also contain *open-ended questions* that allow respondents to provide their own answers. Surveys may be conducted in person, through the mail, by telephone, or online. Another primary market research tool is the **focus group**, which consists of a small number of people recruited to discuss a topic being studied. Focus group members are carefully selected based on target market characteristics. A professional moderator guides the discussion using open-ended questions.

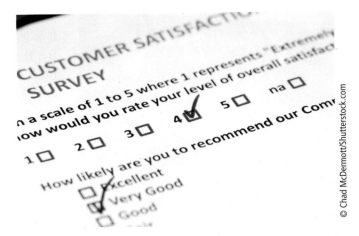

Why are surveys used as part of the marketing research process?

Some researchers use the observation method to collect primary data. Researchers watch and record people's behavior without interacting with them. Observations can be made in person or with video cameras. One-way mirrors allow researchers to observe the reactions of people as they test products. Researchers can also pose as mystery shoppers to evaluate the customer experience. Experiments are another way to collect primary data. In an experiment, all variable factors remain constant except the one being studied. For example, if researchers are trying to determine the best type of package to use for a product, they may conduct an experiment to see how consumers react to the product packaged in a box, in a can, or in a bottle.

Advertising and Primary Market Research In advertising, primary market research is used to measure the effectiveness of an advertising message. Research can be conducted both before and after the ad is released. Before the ad is released, focus groups can be used to get people's opinions and thoughts about a brand or an advertising concept. Observation can be used to gauge consumer reaction to proposed ads. Advertisers can even use home videos recorded by consumers to learn about product usage. By observing consumers in real settings, advertisers gain a better understanding of the target market, enabling them to develop messages that are more meaningful. After the ad is released, researchers use focus groups to perform recall tests. Consumers are given questionnaires to see what they remember about the ad. This helps measure advertising effectiveness.

Secondary Market Research

Most organizations rely on **secondary market research**, which is the process of collecting and analyzing data previously gathered for other purposes. Secondary market research can save time and money. It is useful in learning about industry or market trends, the competition, and consumers.

Advantages and Disadvantages There are several advantages of secondary market research. Large amounts of secondary data are available online, making them easy and convenient to access. This also makes secondary data less expensive to obtain. An abundance of data is available for free online. Secondary data collection is often used to help set the stage for primary market research. Researchers may find that the exact information they were looking for is available through secondary sources, eliminating the need and expense required to obtain primary data.

There are some disadvantages of secondary market research. Data collected through primary market research are highly controlled by the marketer. This is not the case with data collected by others. The quality of secondary data should be scrutinized closely to ensure it is reliable. In addition, the data may not be timely. Data can become

Why might a researcher choose to use secondary data instead of primary data?

outdated quickly in fast-changing markets. Secondary data often are not presented in a form that exactly meets the marketer's needs. For example, a report obtained through secondary market research may define age groups differently than the company's research plan does. Finally, because secondary data are made available to many companies, the use of such data provides no real competitive advantage.

Secondary Market Research Sources Vast amounts of data in already-published sources are available to researchers. Data on population, family size, household income, economic trends, industry forecasts, and much more are easily accessible. Data could come from internal sources, such as company reports, or external sources, such as government reports. Some of the best sources for secondary market research include the following:

- Internal company reports—Most businesses keep detailed records about customers, sales, costs, inventory, and business operations. Much of this information is useful for marketing decision making.

- Trade and professional associations—Membership-supported trade and professional associations represent the interests of those operating in a specific industry or profession. These associations can provide research information such as industry trends obtained from surveys given to the association's members. Information may also be reported in the association's magazines or newsletters. Accessing this information may be as simple as visiting an association's website. Some associations limit access to their research to members only, which involves paying membership dues.

- Nonprofit organizations—Societal causes are supported by many nonprofit groups. Nonprofit categories include the environment, education, and health care, among many others. Researchers will find that many of these groups actively conduct market research to support their agenda and provide their studies on their websites.

- Government reports—Many federal, state, and local governments offer a full range of helpful materials including information on consumers, domestic business, and international markets. The most well-known government data-collection agency is the U.S. Census Bureau (www.census.gov). The website FedStats.gov provides easy access to a variety of data and statistics published by government agencies.

- Business websites—To find information about a specific company, researchers can visit the company's website. Annual reports not only provide information about a company's financial standing but also state the company's mission and plans for the future. Information about competitors' products and services is available on their websites.

NETBookmark

The Sierra Club is the oldest environmental organization in the United States. Access www.cengage.com/school/advertising and click on the link for Chapter 8. Read through the Sierra Club media kit (particularly the demographics and circulation information). What three adjectives best describe the typical Sierra Club member? In which types of products or services do you think Sierra Club members would be interested? Would an online advertising campaign be an effective way to reach Sierra Club members? Why or why not?

www.cengage.com/school/advertising

- News and media sources—Possibly the most widely used types of secondary data are articles and other reports found through commercial news sources. Options include magazines, newspapers, television news, and other video/audio programming. Nearly all of these sources are also available online.

Marketing-Information Systems

Marketing information is the basis for marketing decisions involving product improvements, price and packaging changes, advertising, media buying, and distribution. To ensure that the marketing research process is carried out efficiently, businesses must have a marketing-information system in place. A **marketing-information system (MKIS)** is an organized method of collecting, storing, processing, and reporting information that is needed to make marketing decisions. Today, most businesses use a computerized system. Setting up an MKIS can be a time-consuming, labor-intensive, complex task. After it is up and running, continuous maintenance is required to ensure the data in the system are accurate and current.

The MKIS acts as a data warehouse that stores relevant internal company records as well as information collected through continuous marketing research efforts. The storage system must be well organized so that information is easy to locate. It is often password protected so that only authorized users have access to the data. Processing data is one of the most important functions of the MKIS. It involves analyzing, summarizing, merging, or comparing information so that decisions can be made. Specific computer programs that have formula, graphing, and sorting capabilities, such as database and spreadsheet programs, are available to assist with the processing function. After the data are processed, reports can be generated for use by decision makers. Information that is summarized in an easy-to-understand, well-organized format aids the decision-making process.

CHECKPOINT

What are the steps in the marketing research process?

Benefits and Limitations of Marketing Research

According to the Council of American Survey Research Organization, spending on marketing research in the United States has reached approximately $7 billion annually. Many businesses think it is money well spent because of the benefits it offers. However, businesses must also consider the challenges and limitations associated with marketing research.

Benefits of Marketing Research

Businesses need information to make marketing decisions. Marketing research often is the main source of data for decision makers. Marketing research can benefit a business in several ways.

- *Marketing research reduces the risk of doing business.* The results of some market research may indicate that a company should not pursue a planned course of action. For example, marketing research may indicate that few people would be willing to buy a new product or service.

- *Marketing research helps a company identify threats and opportunities.* Research helps businesses learn what consumers like and dislike. For example, when research indicated that fuel-efficiency was important to automobile owners, this was a threat to auto manufacturers that had largely ignored this factor in favor of producing gas-guzzling trucks and SUVs. However, this research also identified an opportunity—a market for hybrid automobiles.

- *Marketing research guides a company's communication with consumers.* Good research enables companies to create more effective and targeted marketing campaigns. Zip codes collected through market research can be used by retailers to plan suitable direct mail campaigns. Companies may advertise during a football game if market research indicates that the target market frequently watches televised sporting events.

- *Marketing research helps companies track their progress.* Ongoing marketing research allows a company to make comparisons against data previously collected. For example, if a company is trying to increase its market share among women, it can track customer demographics through a survey to determine if this market has grown. If not, the research could indicate that a new marketing strategy is needed.

How does marketing research help a company track its progress?

Limitations of Marketing Research

Accurate, up-to-date information obtained through marketing research can be of enormous value to a business. However, marketing research does have its limitations.

- *Marketing research is not an easy task.* With the large volumes of secondary data available and the complexities of obtaining primary data, marketing research is best left to the experts.

- *Gathering and processing data can be very expensive and time consuming.* As mentioned above, many organizations have to hire marketing research specialists to research and collect data or to conduct extensive surveys. The entire research process, including the planning, collecting, and analysis stages, can take several months.

- *The value of the research findings depends on the accuracy of the data collected.* Secondary data may be old and obsolete. Primary data could be misleading because of sampling errors or biases on the part of the consumer or interviewer.

- *Marketing research does not guarantee success.* Marketing research can identify opportunities and make predictions, but it is not an exact science. The ultimate decisions are made by management. Marketing research is not foolproof, but it does give a business a fighting chance to succeed in the marketplace.

• *Marketing research data must be protected.* Researchers must ensure that any personal information obtained from marketing research participants is kept confidential and used only for lawful purposes. The Market Research Society (MRS) has a code of conduct that encourages research organizations to conduct research in an ethical manner.

///////▲ CHECKPOINT ◣◣◣◣◣◣

What are some of the benefits and limitations of marketing research?

8.2 Assessment

THINK ABOUT IT

1. What is the difference between primary and secondary market research?
2. What are three good resources for secondary market research?
3. What role does the marketing-information system play in the overall marketing research process?
4. Do you think the benefits outweigh the limitations of marketing research? Explain why or why not?

MAKE ACADEMIC CONNECTIONS

5. **MATH**   Your company wants to expand by adding another location. You first decide to conduct research by sending out a survey to residents living near the location you are considering. The community has a population of 300,000 people, and you want to survey 5 percent of that population. To get a broad perspective, you decide to send 40 percent of the surveys to 28- to 38-year-olds; 30 percent to 39- to 48-year-olds; 20 percent to 49- to 60-year-olds; and 10 percent to those over 60. How many total people will you survey? How many people will you survey in each age group?

6. **PROBLEM SOLVING**   Think about a problem that you need to resolve. State it as a research question. Identify how you will use each of the steps in the marketing research process to answer the question.

7. **TECHNOLOGY**   Conduct research to learn more about spreadsheet and database programs. Describe the features or capabilities of these programs and explain why they are useful tools in the marketing research process. If possible, use an actual spreadsheet or database program to demonstrate one of the features in class.

 Teamwork

Create a ten-question survey about the school cafeteria to determine what students like and dislike about it. Questions can pertain to the food and the environment or atmosphere. Use 25 percent of your school's population as the sample. Analyze the survey results and prepare a report containing recommendations on how the cafeteria could be improved. Present the report to your principal.

8.3

Developing an Effective Sales Promotion Strategy

Goals

- Identify consumer sales promotions.
- Identify trade sales promotions.

Terms

- coupon, p. 226
- rebate, p. 227
- premium, p. 227
- sampling, p. 228
- push money, p. 229
- deal loader, p. 229
- trade allowance, p. 229

Government-Sponsored Promotions?

FOCUS ON ADVERTISING

Businesses commonly use sales promotions to create a short-term increase in sales by offering some form of incentive to buyers. Apparently, even the government uses sales promotions. During the summer of 2009, the U.S federal government implemented the "Cash for Clunkers" program in an attempt to stimulate a slow economy. The "Cash for Clunkers" program was a sales promotion that provided rebates of up to $4,500 to owners trading in older, gas-guzzling cars and trucks for new, more fuel-efficient vehicles. Proponents of the "Cash for Clunkers" program believed that it would jump-start the recovery of the auto industry, which was suffering because of the recession. The promotion was a success in creating short-term sales. Nationally, automobile dealers reported making more than 690,000 sales under the government's $3 billion "Cash for Clunkers" rebate program. By the program's close, dealers had claimed $2.88 billion in rebates.

Work as a Team Why do you think the federal government's "Cash for Clunkers" promotion was effective? What other types of sales promotions could the government use to improve economic conditions?

Consumer Sales Promotion

Sales promotion generally involves short-term, incentive-offering and interest-creating marketing activities, other than advertising, personal selling, and public relations. The purpose of sales promotion is to motivate and influence a purchase or other desired action from the

Lesson 8.3   Developing an Effective Sales Promotion Strategy   **225**

company's customers. Sales promotion offers a direct incentive to act by providing value that is over and above the product's value at its regular price. These temporary incentives can be offered at a time and place where the buying decision is made to increase the likelihood of an immediate sale. Sales promotions are increasing at a fast pace because of competitive market conditions and consumer demand for greater value.

Sales promotion is an important component of a business's overall marketing strategy. It often is used in conjunction with the other forms of promotion—advertising, public relations, and personal selling. A business's profitability is greatly enhanced with an effective sales promotion strategy.

Sales promotions are aimed at consumers for many reasons. They are used to encourage trial purchases when a new brand is introduced as well as repeat purchases during the later stages of a product's life cycle. Sales promotions also encourage consumers to buy larger quantities. Several sales promotion techniques are used to attract attention and create demand for a product or service.

Coupons

A **coupon** is a certificate that entitles the buyer to a price reduction on a product or service. Coupons are the most common form of sales promotion. Coupons appeal to price-sensitive consumers. They are an effective way to encourage new-product use through trial purchases, which could also lead to brand switching. When placed inside packages, coupons encourage repeat purchases. Coupons are distributed through newspapers, magazines, and direct mail. Online and in-store coupon distribution is increasing. In-store coupons are more likely to influence consumers' buying decisions and have a higher redemption rate.

Price Deals

Price deals can have an immediate impact on consumer demand. They are used frequently to encourage the trial use of a new product, to

Why do businesses sometimes use coupons to promote their products?

recruit new customers for a mature product, or to convince existing customers to purchase larger quantities. Price deals allow customers to save money instantly when the purchase is made. Price deals work effectively when price is the consumer's top priority or when brand loyalty is low.

The most common type of price deal is the discount. Buyers learn about price discounts in the store or through advertising. Signs advertising percentage markdowns are located near the merchandise or in the storefront windows. Many types of advertisements, including flyers, newspaper advertisements, and television commercials, are used to notify consumers of upcoming discounts. The bonus pack is another type of price deal. It offers a larger size of the product at the same price as the standard size. Bonus packs are also sold as banded packs, which include two or more units of a product (or similar products) banded together and sold at the regular single-unit price. For example, a toothbrush and toothpaste may be banded together.

Rebates

A **rebate** is a refund of money offered to consumers who purchase a specific product. Rebates are used to increase the quantity or frequency of a purchase. Although rebates are offered on a wide variety of products, they often are used as a value enhancement for higher-priced products, such as automobiles, computers, and major appliances. Rebates are a good way to encourage consumers to make purchases they have been postponing. Because customers often are required to fill out rebate forms with their names, addresses, and other data, companies can use rebate programs to collect information about customers.

Premiums

A **premium** is an item offered to consumers for free or at a reduced price with the purchase of another item. Premiums reinforce the consumer's buying decision and increase consumer demand. Examples of premiums include a free prize inside of a cereal box or a free garden tool for attending the grand opening of a hardware store. The use of premiums by McDonald's has popularized its Happy Meal™. Incentives that are given away for free at the time of purchase are called direct premiums. These offers provide instant gratification. Direct premiums are used to lure prospective buyers to a business. Mail premiums require the customer to perform some act in order to obtain a premium through the mail. For example, the consumer may have to save one or more box tops or proofs-of-purchase and mail them along with a small payment in return for a promotional item, such as a cooler or T-shirt.

Loyalty Marketing Programs

Companies use *loyalty marketing programs*, or *frequent-buyer programs*, to reward customers for making repeat purchases. Loyalty marketing programs require that consumers keep buying the same brand or shopping at the same store to get the reward. By offering ongoing incentives, companies are able to build long-term relationships with customers. Frequent-flyer clubs for airlines and hotels, frequent-buyer programs for retailers, and cash back bonus credit cards are popular loyalty marketing programs. Such programs sometimes prove to be a deciding factor when choosing among competitors offering comparable brands.

Sampling

An important goal of any promotional campaign is to get the product into the hands of the consumer. **Sampling** provides consumers with the opportunity to use a product on a risk-free trial basis. Sample products must have benefits or features that will be obvious while being tested by the consumer. Sampling is a useful technique for new products, but it also works well for brands that want to increase their market share. Samples may be distributed in many ways, such as by mail or door to door. For example, sample-size cereal boxes can be packaged with the daily or Sunday newspaper. These methods permit selective sampling in targeted geographic areas. In-store sampling is common for food products and cosmetics. Scratch-and-sniff samples are included on product packages or magazine advertising inserts. Samples often are handed out where consumers gather for organized events. Sometimes, consumers can request free samples by visiting a company's website.

Why are sweepstakes popular types of promotions among businesses and consumers?

Contests and Sweepstakes

Companies use contests and sweepstakes to gain publicity and to create interest in a product or brand. *Contests* allow consumers to compete for a prize based on their skills or abilities. For example, Doritos® and Pepsi MAX® sponsored a contest in which contestants had to create a Super Bowl commercial for a top prize of $1 million. *Sweepstakes* award prizes based purely on luck. Thus, more consumers enter sweepstakes than contests. The Ford Motor Company ran a "Mustang 5.0 Fever Sweepstakes" to award one lucky random winner a new car. Instant-winner scratch-off cards given out by retailers and fast food restaurants are popular among consumers. In order for contests and sweepstakes to be effective, the prizes must be worthwhile and the game must be interesting or entertaining.

Point-of-Purchase Displays

Retailers use *point-of-purchase (POP) displays* to promote a particular brand and encourage impulse buying. POP displays include special racks, display cartons, banners, signs, price cards, and mechanical product dispensers. They are commonly found at the end of aisles or near cash register checkout lanes. High product visibility is the goal of POP displays. POP displays provide or remind consumers about a brand and its benefits.

CHECKPOINT

Describe one type of consumer sales promotion.

Trade Sales Promotions

Trade promotions are incentives that manufacturers offer retailers to encourage them to stock their products and ensure they get the proper attention. Trade promotions help *push* a product through the distribution channels (from the manufacturer to the final consumer). Effective trade sales promotions create loyalty among retailers and increase their enthusiasm for marketing the product. Trade sales promotions include the following:

- **Push money** is a bonus given to salespeople for selling a specific brand. The manufacturer of refrigerators might pay a $30 bonus for each unit of a particular model sold between January 1 and April 1. Retailers must carefully manage push money programs to ensure salespeople do not ignore customers' needs in order to earn a bonus.

- A **deal loader** is a premium given by a manufacturer to a retailer for ordering a certain quantity of a product. There are two types of deal loaders. The *buying loader* is a gift given for making a specified order size. The *display loader* gives the contents of a display to the retailer after the promotional campaign. For example, Black & Decker, a tool manufacturer, may have a display of power tools at a hardware store as part of a special promotion. When the program is over, the hardware store receives all of the tools on the display if a specified order size was achieved.

- A **trade allowance**, or *trade deal*, is a reward offered by manufacturers to retailers in exchange for supporting the manufacturer's brand by performing various marketing activities. For example, a retailer that buys 15 cases of a product during a certain period might receive a *buying allowance* of $6.00 off each case. Retailers that feature a manufacturer's product in their advertisements or create their own in-store display for the product could receive an *advertising allowance. Slotting allowances* are fees paid to retailers for access to certain slots or shelf space. For example, food manufacturers may pay to have their products located on grocery shelves at eye level or at the end of aisles.

What is a slotting allowance? Why do manufacturers use them?

- Sometimes manufacturers will offer retailers free merchandise instead of a buying allowance (price deduction). For example, a pasta sauce manufacturer may throw in one free case of pasta sauce for every 20 cases the retailer orders.
- To ensure that its products are being described and demonstrated properly, some manufacturers will provide product and sales training for retail personnel. This commonly occurs for complex products such as computers, home theater systems, security systems, and exercise equipment. As an alternative, manufacturers may send their own representatives to perform in-store demonstrations for customers.

CHECKPOINT

Describe one type of trade sales promotion.

8.3 Assessment

THINK ABOUT IT

1. How do sales promotions motivate consumers to make a purchase?
2. How is a price deal different from a rebate?
3. Why do manufacturers use trade sales promotions?

MAKE ACADEMIC CONNECTIONS

4. **MATH**   A retailer who buys a minimum of 35 cases of cereal will receive a buying allowance of $5.00 off each case. A minimum purchase of 50 cases results in a buying allowance of $6.50 off each case. If cases sell for $60.00 each, what would be the price and cost savings for a purchase of 40 cases? What would be the price and cost savings for a purchase of 60 cases?

5. **DECISION MAKING**   Find an example of a sales promotion in any of the media outlets (print, radio, TV, or Internet). Describe the promotion and rate it as a good or poor promotion. Explain your rating. Then describe an alternative sales promotion that could be used for the same product or service.

6. **ETHICS**   In an attempt to reduce its inventory, a TV manufacturer offers push money to the salespeople working for a consumer electronics store. They will receive a $50 bonus for each of the manufacturer's TVs they sell over the next 30 days. What ethical issues could arise from this situation?

Teamwork

As part of the marketing team for a new ice cream manufacturer, develop a consumer sales promotion and trade sales promotion plan for your product. Use at least two consumer sales promotions and two trade sales promotions. Share your plan with the class in a PowerPoint presentation.

Sharpen Your
21st CENTURY SKILLS

Digital Vision/Getty Images

Creating Promotional Displays

PARTNERSHIP FOR
21st CENTURY SKILLS

Businesses often promote their products at *trade shows*, which are exhibitions where companies in the same industry can showcase and demonstrate their newest products and services. They may also set up booths to promote products at malls and organized events such as fundraisers and fairs. Promotional displays are a good way to draw people to the booths. A display should identify the product and generate interest among prospective customers. Because a display has only about three to five seconds to catch the attention of people passing by, considerable thought should go into the design. Tips for creating an effective display are listed below.

- *Use images and graphics to attract attention.* Bold colors and photos of the product can convince people to take a closer look. If the business sells sporting equipment, sports-related images will help attract the target market. Displays can use videos to show product demonstrations.

- *Make the company name prominent.* The company name should be easy for everyone to see. Display it along with the company logo.

- *Create a simple and easy to remember headline.* The headline should capture the attention of the company's target audience. A display promoting household cleaning products could carry the headline, "Leave the dirty work to us."

- *Feature the company website address.* Many people prefer to visit a company's website before visiting the business or talking to a salesperson.

- *List two or three product benefits, but keep them short.* For example, short phrases such as "save time and money," "look great," and "improve your health" can pique curiosity.

- *Promote a free giveaway to encourage people to visit the booth.* Companies can hand out free promotional items such as pens and calendars or free samples of the product being promoted. Many people find free refreshments irresistible.

- *Have the display staffed at all times.* Someone should be there to greet visitors. The greeters can engage visitors in conversation about the product and answer questions.

Try It Out

Your school is having an open house for parents and students. During this event, student clubs and groups are allowed to set up booths to promote their organizations. Select a student club or group and create a display to promote its role at the school, club-related activities, and upcoming events. The goal of the display is to increase the club's or group's membership.

© Scott Prokop/Shutterstock.com

SUMMARY

8.1 Developing an Effective Advertising Campaign

- Creativity is a key element in effective advertising campaigns. Creative advertising has many characteristics. It makes a connection with the target audience, has an element of unexpectedness, uses mischief to keep the audience interested, provides concrete images, uses storytelling, and builds momentum.
- Successful advertising campaigns are created by teams consisting of members with different areas of expertise. Team members coordinate and collaborate to produce and implement the advertising campaign.
- Objectives for the advertising campaign include building brand awareness; communicating product benefits; encouraging trial purchases; creating, changing, or reinforcing consumers' attitudes about a brand; and attaining brand loyalty.

8.2 Marketing Research for Advertising

- Marketing research helps businesses make decisions. Steps in the marketing research process include (1) identifying and defining the problem, (2) developing the research design, (3) determining a method for collecting data, (4) collecting the data, (5) analyzing the data, (6) reporting and presenting the data.
- Primary market research offers the benefit of direct contact with customers through a survey or interview. It can be tailored to meet the needs of an organization and provide specific and detailed information.
- Secondary market research offers the benefit of convenient access to data that have already been collected for other purposes. It can save time and money.
- A marketing-information system is an organized method of collecting, storing, processing, and reporting information that is needed to make marketing decisions.

8.3 Developing an Effective Sales Promotion Strategy

- Sales promotion generally involves short-term, incentive-offering and interest-creating marketing activities.
- Types of consumer sales promotion include coupons, price deals, rebates, premiums, loyalty marketing programs, sampling, contests and sweepstakes, and point-of-purchase displays.
- Trade promotions are incentives that manufacturers offer retailers and include push money, deal loaders, trade allowances, free merchandise, and training.

WHAT DO YOU KNOW? Now

Read *Impact Advertising* on page 211 again to review the advertising campaign used by Progressive Insurance. Conduct online research to learn about Progressive's latest advertisements. Has the advertising strategy changed? If so, how? What creative elements are used in the new ads?

Chapter 8 Assessment

Vocabulary Builder

Match each statement with the term that best defines it. Some terms may not be used.

1. A reward offered by manufacturers to retailers in exchange for supporting the manufacturer's brand
2. The process of collecting data for the first time to use in solving a specific problem
3. An organized approach of generating a large number of ideas in a group setting
4. A smaller group that is representative of the target market
5. Bonus given to salespeople for selling a specific brand
6. A description of what the advertising campaign is to accomplish
7. A small number of people who were recruited to discuss a topic being studied
8. A certificate that entitles the buyer to a price reduction on a product or service
9. The sum of the results produced by a team
10. An item offered for free or at a reduced price with the purchase of another item

a. brainstorming
b. coupon
c. creative brief
d. deal loader
e. focus group
f. marketing-information system
g. premium
h. primary market research
i. push money
j. rebate
k. sample
l. sampling
m. secondary market research
n. survey
o. synergy
p. trade allowance

Test Your Knowledge

11. Advertising creativity is associated with which of the following concepts?
    a. fresh, new ideas
    b. a new way of thinking
    c. attention-grabbing and memorable elements
    d. all of the above
12. When an ad is generating buzz by getting people to talk about it, it is building _____.
    a. sales
    b. momentum
    c. synergy
    d. concreteness
13. Generally, an advertising campaign objective could include all of the following *except*
    a. build brand awareness
    b. encourage trial purchases
    c. collect research data
    d. communicate product benefits

14. Marketing research is the process of ____ the data needed to solve marketing problems.
    a. collecting
    b. analyzing
    c. planning
    d. all of the above

15. The plan that specifies how the marketing research process will be implemented is known as the
    a. research approach
    b. data analysis
    c. annual report
    d. research design

16. The fourth step of the marketing research process is to
    a. develop the research design
    b. identify and define the problem
    c. collect data
    d. report and present the data

17. All of the following are limitations of marketing research *except*
    a. it is expensive
    b. it increases the risk of doing business
    c. it is not an easy task
    d. it depends on the accuracy of the data collected

18. Which of the following is an advantage of secondary market research?
    a. secondary data are less expensive to obtain than primary data
    b. observation can be used to view consumers' reactions
    c. the data are always current and never outdated
    d. the data provide a competitive advantage

19. A bonus pack is an example of a(n)
    a. sample
    b. rebate
    c. price deal
    d. POP display

20. A(n) ____ is a premium given by a manufacturer to a retailer for ordering a certain quantity of a product.
    a. trade allowance
    b. rebate
    c. refund
    d. deal loader

Apply What You Learned

21. Ads that show concrete images (visual demonstrations) are more memorable. List some ideas for concrete images that could be used in an advertisement for a new gum that promotes its "long-lasting flavor."

22. A manufacturer selling durable outdoor patio furniture at home improvement stores wants to increase sales. Explain how the company could use a deal loader (buying loader and/or display loader) to motivate the home improvement stores to sell more of its patio furniture.

23. Work in a group to practice the brainstorming process. Brainstorm ideas for promoting an upcoming school event. Your objectives are to increase awareness and encourage attendance.

24. **VISUAL ART** Select a product that is a common "back-to-school" purchase. Design a POP display for the product to remind customers to buy it before heading back to school. Show a diagram of the POP display. Explain what types of stores it will be displayed in and where it will be located within the stores.

25. **CREATIVE THINKING** In past years, Doritos, a major sponsor of the Super Bowl, has challenged individuals to submit creative advertisements for the Doritos brand to be aired during the Super Bowl. Form a team with two or three other students and develop a new Doritos' commercial for next year's Super Bowl. Remember to keep the Super Bowl's audience in mind when creating the commercial. Videotape the commercial and present it to the class.

26. **CAREER PLANNING** You have always dreamed of opening either a lawn care business or pet-walking service in your neighborhood. Before taking the plunge into business ownership, you decide to conduct some research. You need to answer the following questions: How many people live in your community and what is their average income? How many would be willing to hire a lawn/pet-walking service? How much would they be willing to pay for various lawn/pet-walking services? List any other questions you would like to have answered. Describe the research process you will use. Will you use primary or secondary market research to gather your information? What sources will you use? Write at least ten questions for a survey you could send to local residents.

27. **PROBLEM SOLVING** Your school's band needs to raise some money for a school trip. To raise awareness, the band decides to sponsor a contest for students. The winner will be allowed to accompany the band on its school trip. Design a contest that would appeal to all students and provide some publicity for the band. Explain how the winner will be determined.

28. **SOCIAL STUDIES** Working with a partner, conduct research to learn about a nonprofit group in your city. Help the group increase awareness of the cause it supports by developing a creative print advertisement that makes an emotional connection with the target audience. Present the advertisement to the class.

You are the marketer for a new insurance company that decides to get creative by adding a little mischief to its ad campaign. Its TV advertisement shows a rambunctious young boy performing dangerous stunts on bikes, skateboards, and rollerblades. The ad's tagline is, "We're there for you because accidents happen." Although the ad has been effective at raising brand awareness for the insurance company, consumers are complaining that the ads promote risky behavior on the part of young children.

What will you do? How can you keep the element of mischief in your ads without offending consumers?

Reality ✓

Is That Promotion Really a Deal?

Promotions are common in today's marketplace, but consumers are becoming more skeptical of them. Although some advertisements and sales promotions are honest and straightforward, others are deceptive or have fine print that defines limitations and exclusions. Department stores and office supply stores are notorious for sales promotions that contain several exclusions. If consumers read the fine print at the bottom of the coupon or advertisement, they will discover that many brand-name products are excluded from the discounts being offered. Oftentimes, the excluded items are the products that consumers want most. A 50-percent-off sale may apply to selected merchandise only. Signs that promote "up to 50 percent off" likely mean that smaller discounts apply to most of the merchandise.

Consumers must also watch for discounts that are based on inflated prices. For example, a retailer may advertise a product "on sale" for $61.99, which is a discount from the retailer's regular price of $69.99. However, the manufacturer's suggested retail price (MSRP) is only $59.99. By doing a quick search online using sites such as pricegrabber.com, consumers can track down the best deals on many products. Businesses having going-out-of-business and liquidation sales are also known to inflate prices, taking advantage of consumers who are expecting rock-bottom prices. By doing research before shopping, consumers can detect inflated prices.

Consumers also should beware of promotional contests and sweepstakes. Although many of them are run by reputable companies that are trying to promote a product or service, others are fraudulent. Some sweepstakes are simply a way to collect information that can be sold to advertisers, leading to unsolicited telemarketing calls or e-mails. Sweepstakes "winners" may find that the "free" cruise they have won can be claimed only after paying costly service and handling fees. Contests that require skill or knowledge can lure consumers in with easy initial tasks or questions. Then consumers must pay a fee to enter the next level of the contest, which contains progressively more difficult tasks and questions. Contestants rarely win.

Think Critically

1. How can consumers be assured that a promotion is really a good deal?
2. Why do retailers need to be concerned about consumer skepticism of promotions? How can they reduce their skepticism?
3. Give an example of a questionable advertisement, sales promotion, contest, or sweepstakes that you have encountered. Why wasn't it a "good deal"?

Marketing involves the distribution of products and services to the consumer. This event provides recognition for FBLA members who possess knowledge of the basic principles of marketing. In this event, you will be challenged to present a solution to an interactive case study involving sales promotion.

PROBLEM   You have been hired by a local jewelry store called Impressions. It carries high-priced, finer jewelry and offers customized designs. Sluggish economic conditions have drastically decreased the profits for Impressions, and the owner has called upon you to develop sales promotions that will bring customers back to the store and increase sales. The sales promotions must not discount the value of the jewelry sold at Impressions. You must explain four sales promotions to revive sales for Impressions while maintaining the integrity of the store's high-end image.

You have 20 minutes to create a solution to the marketing (sales promotion) challenge. You may use two 4" by 6" note cards during the preparation and performance of this event. Information may be written on both sides of the note cards. Note cards will be collected following the presentation. No reference materials, visual aids, or electronic devices may be brought or used during the preparation or performance.

You will have seven minutes to interact with the store's management team (judges) and present your sales promotion strategies.

Performance Indicators Evaluated
- Demonstrate critical thinking and problem solving.
- Describe the case study and explain your recommendations.
- Demonstrate good communication skills.
- Explain the strengths and weakness of your proposed solution.
- Effectively answer questions.
- Explain how effective sales promotions can revive sales.
- Explain the importance of maintaining the company's integrity and value.
- Organize ideas into a realistic sales promotion strategy.

Go to the FBLA website for more detailed information.

Think Critically
1. Why is it important to consider Impressions' high-end image when developing the sales promotion strategies?
2. What should be avoided when developing a special sales promotion to increase Impressions' customer traffic?
3. What kind of sales promotion could Impressions use that would help create loyal customers?

www.fbla.org

9

Communicating Effective Advertising and Promotional Messages

9.1 Role of Communication

9.2 Types of Communication

9.3 Effective Advertising and Promotional Messages

IMPACT ADVERTISING

The Message: "Just Do It"

In a 1988 meeting between Nike's ad agency and a group of Nike employees, the head of the ad agency spoke about the company's can-do attitude. This conversation resulted in Nike's highly recognizable "Just Do It" slogan, which is rated as one of the most memorable slogans in advertising history. Nike thought the slogan could be applied to competitive athletes as well as people interested only in fitness. Today, Nike is the world's largest sporting goods manufacturer.

Nike's rapid rise to fame in the 1990s can be attributed largely to the "Just Do It" slogan and Nike's association with successful sports figures. In the ten years between 1988 and 1998, Nike was able to increase its share of the domestic sport-shoe business from 18 percent to 43 percent. Nike spent $300 million on overseas advertising that centered around the "Just Do It" campaign. Worldwide sales grew from $877 million to $9.2 billion over the same ten-year period. The success of the campaign is remarkable considering that an estimated 80 percent of the sneakers sold in the United States are never used for their intended purpose. They more often are used as a fashion statement.

During the 1980s, Reebok was the leader in the sport shoe industry. It had captured the women's aerobics shoe market. Sales continued to rise as consumers began buying Reeboks as a casual, everyday shoe. Nike's marketing tactics and its campaign to overtake Reebok gambled on the idea that the public would accept sneakers as fashion statements. Nike also was able to tap into the fitness craze at the time with its "Just Do It" campaign. It expanded its target market beyond the reliable 18- to 40-year-old male consumer to include female and teenage consumers. Nike's marketing campaign created a strong association between Nike and the concept of fitness.

The "Just Do It" campaign reassured consumers that Nike was a quality brand. Early on, Bo Jackson, John McEnroe, and Michael Jordan proved to be credible spokespersons for Nike. If Michael Jordan could play an entire NBA season in a pair of Nikes, the average weekend warrior could trust the durability of its shoes. Nike continues to use celebrity endorsements from the likes of Maria Sharapova and LeBron James to increase brand awareness. Celebrity endorsements have appealed to the consumers' sense of belonging and hipness.

© PRNewsFoto/Nike/AP Photo

1. **What characteristics do consumers associate with the slogan, "Just Do It"?**

2. **Do you think Nike would have been as successful without the use of athletes as spokespersons? Why or why not?**

3. **How did Nike redefine the sport shoes market?**

239

Role of Communication

FOCUS ON ADVERTISING

Goals
- Explain the components of the communication process.
- Explain the purposes of advertising and promotional communication.

Terms
- communication, p. 240
- encoding, p. 241
- communication channel, p. 241
- decoding, p. 242
- noise, p. 242
- feedback, p. 243

Advertising Language Blunders

Advertising messages that are popular in one part of the world may have totally different meanings in another part of the world. One U.S. advertiser tried to market his folded-over pizza, called a calzone, to Spanish speakers. "Calzone" means "underwear" in Spanish. PepsiCo's tagline "Come Alive with Pepsi" was translated into Chinese as "Pepsi brings your ancestors back from the dead." Many more botched advertising and branding efforts were cited in a recent national survey of people who speak English as a second language. Of the 513 people surveyed, 57 percent said they had spotted advertising that was incorrectly translated from English into other languages. Even though the blunders are often humorous, they end up costing the advertiser sales. Close to 50 percent of respondents tune out the message if an advertisement is poorly translated, and about 65 percent interpret bad translations as evidence that the advertiser doesn't care about the consumer. To be effective, translated advertising copy must be crafted as if it were originally written in the target market's language.

Work as a Team How can a company that markets its product globally avoid advertising miscommunications? Conduct research to learn about other advertising language blunders and share them with the class.

The Communication Process

Communication is the exchange of meaningful information between two or more people. The effectiveness of communication is measured by how well the message is understood. Effective business communication commonly accounts for the difference between success and failure, or profit and loss. Marketing communication usually involves sending a sales message to potential customers. However, marketers can also be receivers when they receive feedback from customers.

The Communication Process

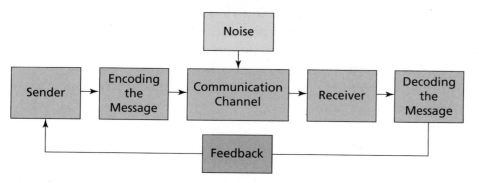

The Sender

The *sender* is the originator of the message. An individual, group, or company can initiate the communication. The sender of an advertisement or promotion is the company that created the ad. The source is initially responsible for the success of the message. All communication begins with the sender whose experiences, attitudes, knowledge, perceptions, and culture influence the message. Both verbal and nonverbal language will affect the receiver's understanding of the message.

Encoding the Message

The *message* is what is being communicated. **Encoding** is the conversion of ideas or thoughts into a message. Language, gestures, symbols, and imagery are used to encode messages. The encoding process is influenced by the sender's beliefs about the receiver's knowledge and perceptions and by the additional information the sender wants the receiver to have. The language and symbols used by the sender must be familiar to the intended receiver of the message. Companies use advertisements to communicate messages. For example, Hershey's advertisements for York Peppermint Pattie® convey the message to "Get the Sensation" by biting into the candy's cool, refreshing peppermint covered in dark chocolate. The message is encoded using spoken words, images, and body language.

The Communication Channel

To transmit the message, the sender uses a **communication channel**, or a medium, to distribute the message. Common communication channels for advertising and promotion include television, radio, newspapers, magazines, salespeople, direct mail, signage, and the Internet. Communication channels greatly affect the receiver's level of understanding. Factors to consider when choosing a communication channel include the target audience, the urgency of the message, the need for feedback, the content of the message, and the size of the audience receiving the message. For example, when immediate feedback is necessary, salespeople may be more effective at conveying the message. For mass communications, television and the Internet may be the most effective channels. Selecting the appropriate communication channel will help ensure the message reaches the intended receiver.

The Receiver

The *receiver* is the individual or individuals to whom the message is directed. For advertisements and promotions, the receiver usually is the target market, or prospective customers. The level of comprehension will depend on how much the receiver knows about the topic, his or her interest in the message, and the relationship and trust that exists between the sender and receiver.

Decoding the Message

Successful communication occurs when the receiver correctly interprets the sender's message. **Decoding** is the interpretation of the language and symbols to uncover the meaning of a message. The message is not always decoded properly. Just as the sender's message is influenced by his or her experiences, attitudes, knowledge, perceptions, and culture, the receiver's interpretation of the message is influenced by the same factors. The receiver may modify the meaning of the message to reflect his or her own knowledge or perceptions. When marketers target global markets or other cultures, translation problems could lead to miscommunication.

Noise

Communication barriers have a negative effect on the communication process. **Noise** includes any distraction or interference that acts as a barrier to a message. Noise can occur during any stage of the process. It can take many forms, including a radio playing in the background, another person interrupting your conversation, unfamiliar words used in an advertisement, verbal language that conflicts with body language, and any other distractions that slow down or prevent the transmission of the message.

What kinds of communication noise are evident in this photo?

There are three types of noise: external, internal, and semantic. *External noises* include sights, sounds, smells, textures, and other environmental factors that distract attention away from the message being communicated. *Internal noise* includes an individual's thoughts or feelings that interfere with communication. Daydreaming and feeling tired or ill are internal noises that will diminish the understanding of the message being communicated. *Semantic noise* occurs when there is no shared meaning in a communication. Words or symbols mean different things to different individuals or elicit different reactions. For example, abstract words such as "attractive," and "peaceful," can be interpreted differently. Other sources of semantic noise include poorly developed speech, discriminatory remarks, highly emotional words, and controversial symbols. Language barriers in international markets can also result in semantic noise.

NETBookmark

Body language is the nonverbal communication that occurs in every face-to-face encounter with another person. All of our nonverbal behaviors send strong messages. When we communicate with another person, more than half of our message is transmitted through our body language. How good are you at recognizing and interpreting body language? Access www.cengage.com/school/advertising and click on the link for Chapter 9. Take the Body Language Quiz, making a note of your score on each question. How did you do? If possible, compare your results with a classmate. Did any particular questions stump everyone?

www.cengage.com/school//advertising

Feedback

After receipt of a message, the receiver may respond in some way to the sender. The receiver's response to the message is **feedback**. Feedback may be in the form of a spoken comment, a written message, a smile, or some other action, such as redeeming a coupon or taking a survey. Even the lack of a response is a form of feedback. Without feedback, the sender cannot confirm whether the receiver understood the message. Feedback allows a company to measure the effectiveness of its advertising and promotional messages. It also gives the company an opportunity to take corrective action if miscommunication occurs. Today, many companies use the Internet to collect feedback through e-mails, blog postings, social networking sites, and website surveys.

CHECKPOINT

What are the components of the communication process?

Purposes of Advertising and Promotional Communication

The goals of advertising and promotional communication are to inform, persuade, and remind target audiences. Many times, marketers will attempt to achieve more than one of these goals in a single communication.

Inform

When a new product or service enters the market, advertising and promotional messages are used to inform consumers about it. These messages are designed to spark interest. Consumers usually will not buy a product or service until they understand the purpose of the product and the benefits it offers. Advertising may be used to communicate product benefits such as safety, nutritional value, fuel efficiency, superior quality, and others. Promotions may communicate other reasons for consumers to make a purchase, such as special prices or free giveaways. Individuals who are interested in purchasing a new automobile may be more likely to take action after hearing about a promotional offer requiring no down payment and no interest charges for 36 months. In this case, the roles of informing and persuading overlap.

Informative messages are very important for complex and technical products, such as financial services or computers. Consumers want to collect and compare information before making complicated buying decisions. Personal selling may be the best communication method for complex products. Marketers may also want to send informative messages about existing products with new or improved features that make them more appealing to consumers. The latest technique used by marketers to keep consumers informed is a QR code placed in advertisements. A *QR (quick response) code* is a square, black-and-white bar code that can be scanned by smartphone users to access videos, coupons, maps, and other information about a product or service.

How do advertisements that inform and advertisements that persuade differ?

Persuade

After the target market has a general awareness of the product, advertising and promotional communication is used to persuade consumers to take action and buy the product. Persuasive advertising is commonly used during the growth stage of a product's life cycle. A business will use advertisements and promotions to identify competitive advantages in an attempt to persuade consumers to buy its product or to switch brands. To be effective, marketers must know which product benefits are most appealing to their target market. Advertisements that emphasize relevant benefits are more persuasive. Persuasive messages often try to appeal to emotional needs, such as love and self-esteem.

Providing an immediate incentive persuades consumers to act soon. Consumers are motivated by promotional call-to-action statements such as, "Receive 10 percent off your oil change this weekend only," or "Redeem this coupon for a free drink with a food purchase." However, when a business advertises special sales and promotions every day of the week, the communication loses its effectiveness.

Remind

The third goal of communication is to remind consumers about existing products and services. This type of communication is used during the maturity stage of a product. Consumers are already aware of the brand and its benefits, but marketers want to remind them why they like it. Coca-Cola airs TV commercials that show people enjoying a Coke. The purpose of the advertisement simply is to remind consumers about Coca-Cola products. Sometimes a sign displaying the brand name is all that is needed. A sign containing only the McDonald's name and logo acts as a reminder to swing by the restaurant on the way home.

///// CHECKPOINT \\\\\

What are the three purposes of advertising and promotional communication?

9.1 Assessment

THINK ABOUT IT

1. What is the difference between encoding and decoding a message?
2. Why is feedback important in the communication process?
3. How is advertising and promotional communication used to persuade consumers?

MAKE ACADEMIC CONNECTIONS

4. **VISUAL ART**   Select an advertisement or promotion you have seen recently. Using the ad or promotion as the message, design a poster that illustrates how each of the elements in the communication process has been implemented.

5. **COMMUNICATION**   Using the Internet, find an advertisement or other promotion that resulted in miscommunication. Describe what caused the miscommunication and how the business handled it.

6. **RESEARCH**   Locate three different advertisements or promotions that meet the following purposes: to inform, to persuade, and to remind. Describe the advertisements or promotions and explain how they fulfill their intended purpose.

Teamwork

As a team, select a product or service with which team members are familiar. Acting as marketers for the product or service, determine what your communication objective(s) will be—to inform, to persuade, or to remind. Then create a print advertisement or promotion for the product or service that will help achieve the objective(s) you identified.

9.2

Types of Communication

Goals
- Explain why interpersonal communication is an important part of advertising and promotion.
- Describe other types of communication used by businesses.

Terms
- interpersonal communication, p. 246
- context, p. 247
- agenda, p. 250
- mass communication, p. 250

FOCUS ON ADVERTISING

Mass Communication That Works

Mass communication has been used by companies for over 100 years. Two well-known historical examples include Ford and Coca-Cola. When Henry Ford began producing the Model T automobile in 1908, he marketed it as the "universal car" that would meet the needs of all buyers. His mass communication approach helped propel the Model T to the top of the market. Asa Candler used the same approach to market his soft drink, Coca-Cola. He considered Coca-Cola to be the only soft drink consumers needed. He launched an extensive national advertising campaign to promote the soft drink. No product in history has generated more total sales than Coca-Cola. Today, many companies have shifted away from using mass communication in favor of delivering advertising messages targeted to specific segments of the population. However, companies will continue to use mass communication for products that have a broad appeal and few distinguishing characteristics. The popularity of the Internet and its effectiveness as a mass communication tool help strengthen this form of advertising.

Work as a Team Provide an example of a company that uses mass communication to deliver its advertising message. Why do you think the company chose to use mass communication?

© Rob Wilson/Shutterstock.com

Interpersonal Communication

Communicating "one on one" with another person is referred to as **interpersonal communication**. Skillful interpersonal communication requires effective speaking and listening skills. One of the benefits of interpersonal communication is the ability to have a two-way conversation. One person can ask questions, and the other person can give an immediate response. Although interpersonal communication generally applies to oral communication, it could also include written and nonverbal forms of communication.

Interpersonal communication skills are essential in today's business environment. They help build strong customer relationships. Certain forms of promotion are heavily dependent on interpersonal communication. A business may use telemarketers, e-mails, blogs, salespeople, or customer service representatives to communicate with customers. Interpersonal communication allows businesses to specifically target individual customers. By working one on one with the customer, the salesperson can promote a product or service in a way that other forms of advertising and promotion cannot.

The Context of Interpersonal Communication

Interpersonal communication is influenced by **context**, which is the situation in which communication occurs. People communicate differently in different contexts. *Psychological context*, or mental context, describes the emotions, moods, needs, desires, and personalities of the participants in the communication process. Being tired, happy, angry, or empathetic can have an effect on what the sender says and how the receiver interprets it. Thus, a salesperson may want to gauge a customer's emotions before making a sales pitch. *Relational context*, also called social context, involves the roles, responsibilities, and status of the participants. A salesperson may switch between formal and conversational communication styles depending on his or her relationship with the customer. *Historical context* is based on previous or similar experiences. If customers have reacted a certain way to a sales presentation in the past, the salesperson may assume other customers will react the same way.

© Deklofenak/Shutterstock.com

How can the relational context affect interpersonal communication?

Environmental context refers to the physical location in which the communication takes place. Factors to consider include the place, time of day, noise level, lighting, temperature, and season. *Situational context* involves the social aspects of where the communication takes place. The communication that occurs between a salesperson and a customer may be different if it takes place in an office setting versus a restaurant or other social setting. *Cultural context* includes learned behaviors and rules that affect interaction. Some cultures consider it rude to make long, direct eye contact and, thus, avoid eye contact out of politeness. If the other person in the communication process belongs to a culture where long, direct eye contact signals trustworthiness and respect, there may be a misunderstanding and communication breakdown.

When communicating, individuals must determine what is appropriate based on the specific situation. Salespeople may need to change their behavior and communication style to fit the context.

Why is it helpful to plan ahead when making a presentation?

Oral Presentations

Oral presentations involve communicating a message to an audience. They are very common in business situations. Business managers must present financial news and company goals to the owners and employees. Advertising agencies must present their strategies to potential clients. Salespeople must demonstrate products or services to customers. Most of these presentations involve advance notice, allowing time for preparation. Sometimes individuals are called upon to give an *extemporaneous presentation*, which is an impromptu or unplanned presentation.

Planning the Presentation Making a good oral presentation is a learned skill that involves careful planning. Speakers who learn about their audience give presentations that have a greater impact. The presentation will not be successful if the content is too difficult for the audience to understand or if the structure is too complicated. Some basic questions the speaker should ask about the audience are as follows:

- To whom will I be speaking? (Learn about the age range, culture, socioeconomic status, and educational background of the audience.)
- What do they know about my topic already?
- What will they want to know about my topic?
- What do I want them to know by the end of my presentation?

When planning the presentation, the speaker must identify the purpose of the presentation. The purpose may be to inform, to motivate, to persuade, or to entertain. Salespeople may want to accomplish several of these goals in a single presentation. The oral presentation should follow a simple and logical structure. Because there will be a time limit on the length of the presentation, the speaker should present only the topics that the audience needs to know. Preparing an outline will help the speaker organize his or her ideas to ensure important topics are covered adequately. Finally, the speaker should practice before delivering the presentation. Practicing in front of a mirror or a video camera can increase confidence.

Delivering the Presentation When making presentations, speakers need to be aware of their voice quality. Factors affecting voice quality include volume, speed, fluency, clarity, and pronunciation. A speaker can improve voice quality by practicing. Presentations are much more effective when the speaker communicates using a conversational style. Pleasant facial expressions and good eye contact will help the speaker develop a rapport with the audience. Finally, speakers should dress appropriately and avoid wearing distracting clothing or jewelry.

SPOTLIGHT ON SUCCESS

PAULA DEEN
Chef, Author, and TV Personality

Paula Deen was a homemaker and bank teller before becoming a professional cook. Paula considered herself a good Southern cook, so she started a small home-based catering company, The Bag Lady, where she made sandwiches and other meals that were delivered by her sons. The Bag Lady was very successful and soon outgrew Paula's kitchen. She then opened her own restaurant, The Lady, inside a Best Western Hotel in Savannah, Georgia, in 1990. Her success continued to grow and Paula moved out of the hotel five years later and opened a restaurant, renamed The Lady & Sons, in downtown Savannah. One of the restaurant's customers was a publishing representative and encouraged Paula to publish her first cookbook, *The Lady & Sons Savannah Country Cookbook*, in 1997. Her rise to fame began shortly thereafter.

What's even more remarkable about Paula's success is that at one time she had agoraphobia, which is the fear of open and public places. Her contact with restaurant guests over the years helped her overcome her fear. She gained national recognition when she promoted her cookbook on QVC, where it became one of the best selling cookbooks. She went on to write several more cookbooks over the years. In 1999 Food Network came calling. She appeared on several episodes of *Doorknock Dinners* filmed in Savannah as well as on *Ready, Set, Cook!* She finally landed her own show, *Paula's Home Cooking*, in 2002.

From her early days, Paula's restaurant customers appreciated her gracious hospitality and the way she made them feel like family. Over the years, her sincere, folksy communication style and Southern charm have helped her build a huge fan base. Her success has been made possible largely because of her communication style. Her pleasant personality seems to resonate with others.

Think Critically
Although Paula Deen is an excellent cook, that's not the only reason behind her success. What else helped her succeed? Why are strong communication skills essential to a businessperson's success?

Speakers should try to capture the audience's attention at the start of the presentation. This can be done by posing a question, reciting a famous quote, telling a humorous story, or discussing current events that will act as a springboard for the presentation. After getting the audience's attention, the speaker should outline the major points he or she intends to cover. A written **agenda**, which is a list of topics to be discussed at a meeting, may be handed out to the audience. An agenda acts as an outline and checklist for the presentation. Throughout the presentation, speakers can simplify difficult points by using plenty of examples. At the conclusion of the presentation, the speaker should summarize the major points communicated. Time should be allotted during and after the presentation for questions from the audience. Effective speakers anticipate questions and prepare answers in advance.

Professional speakers are able to make presentations with limited or no notes. However, less experienced speakers may feel more confident if they use notes. Using visual aids to highlight major points will reinforce the content of the message and make the presentation more interesting. Visual aids include charts, photographs, cartoons, posters, videos, and computer-generated slides. Multimedia presentation software, such as PowerPoint, helps speakers prepare professional-looking visuals.

CHECKPOINT
Why is interpersonal communication an important component of advertising and promotion?

Mass Communication and Internet Communication

Other types of communication used by marketers are mass communication and Internet communication. Mass communication is one of the most common ways to deliver advertising and promotional messages. However, the Internet is having a major impact on marketing communication. It can be used for mass communications as well as for more targeted communications.

Mass Communication

Mass communication involves communicating a message to a large, diversified audience using mass media. Typical forms of mass media include television, radio, magazines, newspapers, and the Internet. Mass media is used for marketing, advertising, and promotion. Companies launch new products, make important company announcements, highlight community service, and advertise sales and other special events through the use of mass communication.

One of the biggest advantages of mass communication is its wide reach. Businesses can target a global audience. It is also much more cost-efficient than using interpersonal communication to reach customers. One advertisement can reach more people in a shorter amount of time than one salesperson can.

Mass communication does have some disadvantages. Whereas interpersonal communication is a two-way flow of information, mass communication is only a one-way flow. It does not allow for immediate feedback because the message receiver cannot respond directly to the message sender. Marketers must wait to see whether the target audience's reaction to an advertisement or promotion is positive or negative. Because mass media is used to communicate with large audiences consisting of diverse groups of people, targeting specific audiences is more difficult. Marketers cannot be sure they are reaching their intended target audience. Also, clutter from competitors' messages or other distractions can reduce the effectiveness of mass communication.

Internet Communication

Social media are websites where users create and share information. The interactive component of social media has improved communication between businesses and consumers. By interacting with consumers, businesses can develop more effective advertisements and promotions. Types of social media and the ways businesses use them to communicate with consumers are described below.

- *Blogs*—Businesses write and post thought-provoking articles of interest to bloggers, respond to blogger queries, gather feedback and ideas shared by bloggers to enhance marketing activities, and recruit bloggers to be brand advocates.

- *Facebook*—Businesses start a fan page for a product or brand, share useful articles and links that would interest customers, market products by posting information about upcoming sales or promotions, and share research or survey data to gain credibility.

- *Twitter*—Businesses track what's being said about them and their products, post self-promotional tweets, direct Twitter followers to the business's Facebook page or YouTube videos, and post the latest breaking company news.

- *YouTube*—Businesses post business-related and product-related videos that inform, demonstrate, and entertain.

- *Online communities*—Businesses create an online website devoted to a specific brand and post information about the brand and brand-related events.

Today's businesses must have a social media presence. Social media may become the primary form of communication used by businesses in the future. The collaboration between businesses and

Why is it important for a business to have a social media presence?

consumers through social media produces innovative ideas. It also strengthens customer loyalty because consumers have a higher level of involvement in the development of products and services to meet their needs.

////////// CHECKPOINT \\\\\\\\\\

Why are mass communication and Internet communication popular ways for businesses to deliver messages?

9.2 Assessment

THINK ABOUT IT

1. How is interpersonal communication different from mass communication?
2. How does psychological context affect interpersonal communication?
3. How can a speaker capture the attention of an audience before giving a presentation? Provide a specific example.
4. How can Internet communication strengthen customer loyalty?

MAKE ACADEMIC CONNECTIONS

5. **COMMUNICATION**   Select a charitable organization or cause that you want to promote. Assume that you have to give a presentation about the organization or cause to inform others about it and persuade them to support it. Prepare a detailed outline of your presentation. The outline should contain three sections—the introduction, the feature presentation, and the conclusion. Describe topics that will be discussed in each section.

6. **SPEECH**   Critique a presentation you recently saw. Was the presentation effective? Why or why not? Was the speaker knowledgeable about the subject and did he or she provide relevant information? Did he or she use an appropriate communication style for the audience? Were visual aids used? Explain how the presentation could have been improved.

7. **TECHNOLOGY**   Conduct research to learn about online communities. Select one that is devoted to a brand. It may be a community that was created by users of the brand or by the company that manufactures the brand. Prepare a PowerPoint presentation that informs others about the online community. Explain how the website benefits the community members as well as the company and its brand.

Teamwork

Prepare a five-minute oral presentation about a product that you want audience members to buy. Follow the guidelines for giving an effective oral presentation. Prepare a PowerPoint presentation to enhance the information that you will share with the class. Additional visual aids can be used. All team members must participate in the presentation.

9.3

Effective Advertising and Promotional Messages

Goals

- Explain the four Cs of communication.
- Describe how to create effective advertising messages.

Terms

- 4Cs Model, p. 254
- voluntary attention, p. 256
- hedonic needs, p. 257
- involuntary attention, p. 257
- unique selling proposition, p. 257

FOCUS ON ADVERTISING

The Power of Advertising Slogans

Creating a successful slogan for a business is an important component in the overall marketing strategy. Successful slogans pack a few words into a strong, memorable message. Tony the Tiger growled his way to fame using the Kellogg's Frosted Flakes® "They're G-r-r-r-eat" slogan in the 1950s. "The Best Part of Waking Up Is Folgers in Your Cup" is the slogan that Folgers® has used in its commercials since the 1960s. The jingle has been rearranged and performed by many famous musicians. Taco Bell urged consumers to "Think Outside the Bun." Its slogan encouraged consumers to make the switch from regular fast food burgers served on buns to its Mexican food served in taco and tortilla shells. Capital One® credit card asked consumers, "What's in Your Wallet?" The simple slogan cut right to the point and made consumers ask themselves that very question, which was Capital One's goal. It helped raise consumer awareness of the brand by 98 percent. The right choice of words for an advertising slogan can mean instant brand recognition.

Work as a Team Brainstorm to create a list of five memorable advertising slogans. Explain what makes them so memorable and effective.

© Mike Flippo/Shutterstock.com

The Advertising and Promotional Message

What makes a television commercial memorable? Why do some brands have a loyal following? What makes a salesperson a top performer? Why do some promotional e-mails work better than others? It all comes down to the message. A piece of communication that is concise, relevant, worthwhile, and compelling is more likely to move the consumer to action.

The Four Cs of Communication

Effective communication is the key to successful advertising and promotional campaigns. It can be achieved by using the **4Cs Model**—comprehension, connection, credibility, and contagiousness. Messages that contain these four components make a bigger impact with the audience. Dunkin' Donuts used the 4Cs Model to develop an advertising campaign that built an emotional connection with customers. Its "America Runs on Dunkin'" advertisements communicated a simple message—Dunkin' is an expert in making coffee and donuts, not soy lattes, for "regular folks." Its commercials poked fun at other, more pretentious coffee shops that offered coffee drinks with hard-to-pronounce names.

Comprehension Communication should be simple enough for the target audience to understand. Messages should be short and concise. A lengthy message that uses technical jargon will not be well received by the audience. Repetition aids comprehension. Advertisers should repeat the most important elements of the communication, such as the brand name.

Connection Making a connection means that the message evokes some kind of reaction from the audience. The message will have meaning and significance for the audience and will usually trigger emotions, such as excitement, anger, empathy, guilt, happiness, or sadness. When the message makes a connection, audience members are more likely to make a change in their behavior or take some kind of action.

© Marty Ellis/Shutterstock.com

What makes someone a credible spokesperson for a business's product or service?

Credibility The audience must believe *who* is saying the message (the brand or communicator's voice) and *what* is being said. When this does not happen, the connection begins to break down. The message should come from a person of authority or a trustworthy source. When backed by data and research, the message is more credible. Even if the audience comprehends the message and connects with it on an emotional level, it will not have the intended effect on the audience if it isn't credible.

Contagiousness Have you ever noticed that when you see a television commercial that is clever or humorous, you share it with your friends, reenact it, or repeat the slogan or catch phrase in conversations? This is an example of a contagious message. Contagious messages are energetic, new, different, memorable, and relevant. The message should evoke an emotional response, make an impact, and motivate the target audience to do something.

Put the 4Cs in Action

As advertisers develop advertising and promotional messages, they should apply the 4Cs Model. Messages should be easy to comprehend, make a connection with the audience, have credibility, and be contagious. By showing the advertising or promotional message to a test group of consumers before releasing it to the general public, advertisers can determine if the 4Cs have been achieved. Questions to ask to help evaluate the effectiveness of the communication include the following:

- Does the audience understand the main idea or point of the message?
- What does the message instantly communicate to the audience?
- Can the audience recall the message?
- Does the message evoke an emotional response from the audience?
- Does the audience think the message or messenger is believable?
- Does the message motivate audience members to react in some way?
- Would audience members be likely to spread the message to others?

Based on the answers to these questions, advertisers can make modifications as needed to ensure their message has the maximum impact on the target audience.

CHECKPOINT

What are the four Cs of communication?

Advertising That Makes an Impact

The importance of advertising in today's business environment is immense. Advertising campaigns often determine the success of products and services. Advertisers continually face the challenge of breaking through ad clutter and capturing the attention of consumers who are uninterested in the advertiser's message. They must somehow motivate consumers to pay attention and process the message.

What Is Effective Advertising?

Effective advertising focuses on the needs of the consumer and convinces the consumer to buy a specific product or service to fulfill those needs. As businesses develop their advertising campaigns, they need to consider how to create effective advertising. Effective advertising has the following characteristics:

1. *It is created from the consumer's perspective.* Advertising must relate to the consumer's, not the business's, needs and wants. Effective advertising demonstrates a keen insight into what consumers are looking for when making buying decisions about products and services.

Revlon
ColorStay™
Mineral Lipglaze
Revlon's **first** longwearing lipgloss
that lasts for **up to 8 hours**
• Unique mineral complex conditions lips
• One step for hours of comfortable color
• Available in 12 gorgeous, glossy shades

UP TO **8** HOURS

NEW

REVLON®

What promise is being made in this advertisement? Why is it important that Revlon deliver on this promise?

2. *It finds a unique way to break through the clutter.* Advertisements can be found in every medium—newspapers, magazines, television, radio, and the Internet. Because consumers see a massive number of advertisements daily, advertisers find it difficult to stand out from the crowd. Advertisers must compete for the consumers' attention by using unique and memorable advertising techniques.

3. *It never overpromises and underdelivers.* Once consumers have been deceived by an advertiser that promised results or benefits that went undelivered, they will lose respect for the business. Effective advertising must be truthful. If an ad says that a car can go from 0 to 60 mph in 6 seconds, the product better be able to meet that promise.

4. *It does not allow creativity to overwhelm the marketing strategy.* Although creativity is important, it should not overshadow the purpose of advertising, which is to inform, persuade, or remind the audience about the product or service. An advertisement that doesn't meet its objectives is ineffective no matter how clever or humorous it might be.

5. *It works in conjunction with the other elements in the marketing strategy.* Using an integrated marketing communication strategy ensures all advertising and promotional messages about a product or service are compatible and deliver consistent messages.

Processing Advertising Messages

When creating advertising messages, advertisers should consider how to increase consumers' motivation, opportunity, and ability to process advertising messages. Because brands in most product categories are similar, advertisers must create advertising messages that generate enthusiasm and interest among consumers about a specific brand.

Motivation to Process Advertising Messages An advertising message is only effective if it captures a consumer's attention. Advertisers must find ways to motivate consumers to view or listen to an advertisement. There are two forms of attention. **Voluntary attention** is devoted to an advertising message that meets a consumer's current purchasing goals. For example, if a consumer is remodeling a kitchen, an advertisement that provides information about home appliances would likely attract his or her attention. In addition to informational messages, consumers are receptive to advertising messages related to **hedonic needs**, which are needs that focus on enjoyment and pleasure. A TV commercial for an amusement park that shows a family having a good time at the park would likely capture the attention of family-oriented consumers.

Involuntary attention is captured by the use of various attention-gaining techniques. Unusual, distinctive, unpredictable, or unexpected messages may be used to attract attention. For example, an advertiser may use a **unique selling proposition (USP)**, which is an advertisement that emphasizes a unique quality or significant consumer benefit. Domino's® Pizza increased sales with its USP, "Pizza delivered in 30 minutes or it's free." Colors, sounds, images, and videos make it difficult for consumers to ignore some advertisements. Although drivers may pass many billboards along the highway without looking at them, the Chick-fil-A billboards with the three-dimensional cows are hard not to notice.

Why are advertisements that appeal to hedonic needs more likely to capture consumers' attention?

© StockLite/Shutterstock.com

Opportunity to Process Advertising Messages Consumers must be given the opportunity to fully comprehend and process the meaning of advertising messages. The advertiser's goal is to get consumers to decode, or interpret, information by making it as simple as possible for them to do so. Repetition aids the decoding process. By repeating information about the brand and repeating the advertisement over an extended period of time, advertisers increase the chances of getting their point across.

Reducing the time needed to process an advertising message also increases its effectiveness. Lengthy or wordy advertisements distract from the message. By using an image to help convey the message, fewer words are needed.

Ability to Process Advertising Messages To ensure that consumers will fully understand an advertising message, advertisers need to determine the consumers' existing knowledge about the product or service. If consumers are already familiar with the product or service, advertisers can spend more time promoting the brand and less time explaining the product features. For example, an effective advertisement for Snickers® might consist of only the Snickers brand name and a picture of a person eating the candy bar. However, this advertising strategy would not work well for a new product that is unfamiliar to consumers. Without knowing about the product and its benefits, consumers would not fully comprehend such an advertisement.

If consumers are unfamiliar with a product or service, advertisers must communicate the message they want to convey about it. If advertisers are trying to communicate intangible concepts, they should clarify their meaning. Concepts such as fresh, strong, and healthy have different meanings to different people. Brawny® promotes its paper towels as having quality, strength, and durability. To bring these concepts to life, Brawny uses a lumberjack as its mascot. Lumberjacks are known for being strong, tough, and rugged.

///////// CHECKPOINT \\\\\\\\

What makes an advertising message effective?

9.3 Assessment

THINK ABOUT IT

1. Describe how to use the 4Cs Model to create advertising messages.
2. Who would be a credible spokesperson for a pain reliever such as Tylenol®? Why would this person add credibility to product advertisements?
3. What is a unique selling proposition? How is it used by advertisers?

MAKE ACADEMIC CONNECTIONS

4. **RESEARCH**   Find an advertisement that meets all of the qualifications of an effective advertisement listed on pp. 255–256. The advertisement may be a print, radio, TV, or Internet advertisement. Describe the advertisement and explain how it meets each of the qualifications.
5. **MARKETING**   Select a product or service that you think has a unique quality or significant consumer benefit. Create a print advertisement for it that promotes the unique selling proposition. Explain why the USP you identified would motivate consumers to buy the product or service.
6. **PSYCHOLOGY**   Your company manufactures a new diet soft drink. The advertising slogan is "Diet never tasted so refreshing." Describe how you could bring the meaning of "refreshing" to life in a TV advertisement. How would you make this concept more relevant to the audience?

Teamwork
Create a public service announcement that raises awareness of an issue that affects teenagers, such as underage drinking. Write the announcement using the 4Cs Model. Then read the announcement to the class and evaluate the effectiveness of your communication using the list of questions on p. 255.

Digital Vision/Getty Images

Using Presentation Technology

At some point in time, you most likely will have to give a presentation. Students make presentations as part of a project assignment. Business owners make presentations to sell their business ideas to potential investors. Salespeople make presentations to persuade customers to make a purchase. The use of technology can enhance presentations.

There are a number of multimedia presentation software programs available that can help you produce a professional-looking presentation. Two of the most popular are Microsoft® PowerPoint and Apple® Keynote. Through the use of such programs, you can create an electronic slide show containing text, graphics, hyperlinks, spreadsheets, digital photos, video or sound, and animation. When creating a multimedia presentation, there are a few tips to keep in mind.

- *Don't overload your slides with too much text or data*. Keep them simple. As a general rule of thumb, use no more than six words per line and six lines per slide. When using bullet points, use no more than three or four per slide.

- *Font size should be large enough to read easily*. Fancy fonts and all capital letters can be difficult to read.

- *Use contrasting colors for backgrounds and text*. Backgrounds that are light colored with dark text, or vice versa, provide the best visibility.

- *Use pictures and graphics to help make a concept clearer*. Place your graphics in a similar location on each slide so the audience knows what to expect.

- *Number the slides and give them a title that helps introduce the topics on the slides*. Titles help tie the concepts together.

- *Limit the number of slides*. If you have too many slides, you may end up rushing to get through all of them. On average, one slide per minute works well.

- *Give the audience a handout of the slides to help them follow the presentation*. By having a handout, audience members won't have to take as many notes and can focus their attention on your presentation.

Try It Out

The school guidance counselor has asked you to prepare a presentation about the college admission process. Create a five-minute multimedia presentation that describes what students should do (or should not do) to improve their chances of gaining admission to a college.

PARTNERSHIP FOR
21ST CENTURY SKILLS

© Stephen Coburn/Shutterstock.com

SUMMARY

9.1 Role of Communication

- Communication is the exchange of meaningful information between two or more people. The effectiveness of communication is measured by how well the message is understood.
- The sender in the communication process encodes ideas and thoughts into a message, which is sent through a communication channel. In advertising, the communication channel could include television, radio, newspapers, magazines, salespeople, direct mail, signage, and the Internet.
- The receiver in the communication process decodes the message by interpreting the language and symbols used and responds to it by giving feedback. Noise may distract the receiver and act as a barrier to the message.
- Advertising and promotional communications are used to inform, persuade, and remind target audiences.

9.2 Types of Communication

- Interpersonal communication between people involves a two-way flow of information. It may include oral, written, and nonverbal forms of communication.
- Interpersonal communication is affected by psychological, relational, historical, environmental, situational, and cultural contexts.
- Mass communication is a one-way flow of information from the sender to a large audience.
- Internet communication provides an interactive component and occurs through social media websites such as blogs, Facebook, Twitter, YouTube, and online communities.

9.3 Effective Advertising and Promotional Messages

- Effective advertising communication applies the 4Cs Model—comprehension, connection, credibility, and contagiousness.
- Effective advertising takes the consumer's view, finds unique ways to break through the clutter, never overpromises, does not allow creativity to overwhelm the marketing strategy, and works in conjunction with the other marketing elements.
- Advertisers should create advertising messages in a way that increases consumers' motivation, opportunity, and ability to process them.
- Consumers give ads their voluntary attention if the message meets their current needs. Otherwise, advertisers must use techniques to get consumers' involuntary attention.

Read *Impact Advertising* on page 239 again to review the launch of Nike's "Just Do It" advertising campaign. Conduct online research to learn about Nike's current advertising strategy. Do its latest advertisements follow the 4Cs Model? Are they effective as defined in the chapter?

Vocabulary Builder

Match each statement with the term that best defines it. Some terms may not be used.

1. The situation in which communication occurs
2. An advertisement that emphasizes a unique quality or significant consumer benefit
3. Needs that focus on enjoyment and pleasure
4. The receiver's response to the message
5. Communicating one on one with another person
6. The conversion of ideas or thoughts into a message
7. The interpretation of the language and symbols to uncover the meaning of a message
8. A list of topics to be discussed at a meeting
9. Any distraction or interference that acts as a barrier to a message
10. Communicating a message to a large, diversified audience

a. agenda
b. communication
c. communication channel
d. context
e. decoding
f. encoding
g. feedback
h. 4Cs Model
i. hedonic needs
j. interpersonal communication
k. involuntary attention
l. mass communication
m. noise
n. unique selling proposition
o. voluntary attention

Test Your Knowledge

11. _____ context describes the emotions, moods, needs, desires, and personalities of the participants in the communication process.
    a. Relational
    b. Psychological
    c. Historical
    d. Cultural

12. _____ context is based on previous or similar experiences.
    a. Relational
    b. Psychological
    c. Historical
    d. Cultural

13. _____ may include a spoken comment, a written message, a smile, or some other action, such as taking a survey, in response to a message.
    a. Feedback
    b. Context
    c. Decoding
    d. Encoding

14. Promotional and advertising messages should not be used to _____ the audience.
    a. inform
    b. persuade
    c. remind
    d. manipulate

15. Communication involves
    a. words
    b. body language
    c. symbols
    d. all of the above
16. ____ is *not* part of the 4Cs Model of communication.
    a. Compassion
    b. Connection
    c. Credibility
    d. Comprehension
17. Tips to follow when delivering an oral presentation include all of the following *except*
    a. use a conversational style when communicating
    b. avoid making eye contact
    c. use examples to simplify difficult points
    d. use visual aids
18. Which of the following is an advantage of mass communication?
    a. it is a one-way flow of communication
    b. it allows for immediate feedback
    c. it is a good way to target a specific audience
    d. it makes it easier to target a global audience
19. Effective advertising
    a. focuses on the business's needs and wants
    b. makes creativity the top priority
    c. delivers a message that is different from the company's other marketing communications about the product or service
    d. none of the above
20. Which of the following techniques will help consumers process advertising messages better?
    a. using intangible concepts
    b. using lengthy and wordy messages
    c. repeating the advertisement several times
    d. avoiding the use of images to eliminate distractions

Apply What You Learned

21. You are the marketer for a local water park. Attendance has been down because of a slow economy. Create a print or radio advertisement to convince consumers that the water park offers good entertainment value and dollar value during current economic conditions.
22. Watch five television commercials and evaluate each one using the 4Cs Model. (You can use the questions on p. 255 to evaluate the commercials.) Was each of the four Cs present? If not, which ones were missing?
23. Locate examples of advertisements (print, TV, radio, or Internet) that demonstrate an effort to increase consumers' motivation, opportunity, and ability to process the message. (You may select one advertisement that demonstrates all three concepts or different advertisements for each concept.) Explain how the advertisements you chose illustrate these concepts.
24. Select a product or service and explain how all three types of communication (interpersonal, mass, and Internet) could be used to deliver an advertising message for it.

25. **CIVICS** You are running for student body president of your class. You must prepare a speech to announce your candidacy and communicate your platform (the issues you will tackle if elected president). Use the tips for planning and delivering oral presentations given on pp. 248–250. Apply the 4C Model when preparing your speech. Give the speech in class.

26. **COMMUNICATION** List five types of communication noises that distract from or interfere with high school students' attention while at school. Describe each type of distraction and explain what can be done in schools to eliminate it so that students can focus more of their attention on learning. Write a one-page report on this topic.

27. **PSYCHOLOGY** Effective advertisements find a way to break through the clutter and stand out from the numerous other advertisements. Identify two television commercials that you consider memorable. Explain why they are memorable. Do you think they are effective at delivering the advertising message? Why or why not?

28. **MATH** The four sports magazines listed below have similar target audiences and are used by advertisers to deliver advertising messages about their sports products. Also listed below is the number of ad pages sold for each of these magazines over a three-year period. Calculate the following: (a) total number of pages sold each year; (b) percentage share each magazine has each year (rounded to the nearest whole percentage). Create a bar graph comparing Year 1, Year 2, and Year 3 for all four magazines based on total pages sold.

Magazine	Year 1 Ad Pages	Year 2 Ad Pages	Year 3 Ad Pages
ESPN	555.25	480.50	499.75
Golf Digest	325.00	285.25	268.75
Sporting News	375.25	301.00	368.50
Sports Illustrated	889.25	906.75	835.50

Your company manufactures popular designer blue jeans that are sold for $100. A recent news report indicated your jeans are manufactured at sweatshops in another country where workers earn only $0.75 per hour. Your company has now moved production of the jeans to another facility that pays fair wages. However, your brand is still suffering from a bad reputation.

As the owner of the company, what would you do? What would be the best way to inform consumers that your company has corrected the problem? How would you persuade consumers to buy your jeans?

Reality ✓

Multicultural Promotions

In today's multicultural world, businesses must find ways to communicate with other cultures and ethnicities. The African-American population comprises approximately 13 percent of the U.S. population. The buying power of African-Americans has risen steadily over the years and is projected to grow to more than $1.2 trillion by 2013. African-Americans are known to have strong bonds with family and their communities.

To reach out to the African-American market, Burger King (BK) decided to emphasize the value of family and community. FamFest was a six-city festival created by BK that traveled to public parks in top African-American markets, including Atlanta, Chicago, Houston, Miami, New Orleans, and New York City. The exciting event offered a free day of family-reunion style fun that included entertainment, local DJs, family-friendly activities, and BK product sampling.

Families had the opportunity to participate in BK Fresh Apple Fry relays, Build-a-Whopper contests, the King's Obstacle Course, a Royal Dance competition, and other challenges that used BK product tie-ins. BK-branded tents surrounded the family activities, and BK brand ambassadors distributed gift cards called "Crown Cards." The large BK stage served as a backdrop for performances and live entertainment. Entertainers and actors from shows popular with the African-American market participated in the events. BK donated $2,500 to a local community-based organization in every city where FamFest was held. Community-based organizations receiving the donations were determined by online voting by consumers.

FamFest was a major success in African-American communities. BK strengthened consumer brand perception in key markets by tapping into family lifestyles. Of the 4,531 BK Crown Cards distributed at FamFest, 91 percent were redeemed at restaurants. Eighty percent of attendees indicated that BK would be their next fast food visit, compared to 61 percent of the general population.

Think Critically

1. Explain the value of a cultural marketing event like FamFest. Do you think FamFest could be used to successfully target other cultures? Why or why not?
2. Do you think the communication process used by BK to deliver its promotional message was effective? Why or why not?
3. After the initial surge in sales from FamFest, how can BK maintain sales? What can BK do to remind customers to eat at one of its restaurants?

Startup (new) companies are faced with the challenge of competing against national corporations that have strong name recognition. Consumers are hesitant to hire the services of a company that has little or no name recognition. Startup companies are challenged to determine their target market, develop a message that resonates with the target market, and maintain an advertising campaign that reinforces their brand. In in this event, you will use strategic planning and problem-solving skills to provide a solution for a startup business.

PROBLEM   Three college graduates decided to start a transportation company (Reliable Transportation) that will cater to the needs of an aging population. Marketing research indicates that many senior citizens who no longer drive need reliable transportation to take them to medical appointments, grocery stores, and other activity-related events.

Your team has been asked to create an advertising message that will inform and persuade the target market to use the services of Reliable Transportation. Senior citizens are on a limited budget, and they are highly concerned about prices charged for goods and services. The advertisement should emphasize reliable service for an affordable price. Your team must write the copy for the Reliable Transportation advertisement.

Performance Indicators Evaluated
- Evaluate and delegate responsibilities needed to perform required tasks.
- Demonstrate teamwork skills needed to function in a business setting.
- Demonstrate self-esteem, self- and team-management, and integrity.
- Demonstrate a working knowledge of business management concepts.
- Demonstrate critical-thinking skills needed to make decisions and solve problems.
- Demonstrate a working knowledge of entrepreneurial concepts.

Go to the BPA website for more detailed information.

Think Critically
1. When creating the advertisement, why is it important to focus on the concerns of senior citizens?
2. What are the major concepts that will be emphasized in your advertising campaign for Reliable Transportation?
3. What communication channels would be good choices for distributing the advertising message for Reliable Transportation?

www.bpa.org

10°

Management of Effective Advertising

© gary718/Shutterstock.com

Guerilla Advertising

While walking along a city sidewalk, it's not uncommon to encounter unique examples of guerrilla art (street art or graffiti). Tags (the street artist's name or message) left by individuals who climbed into precarious positions, impromptu murals on the sides of buildings, and bizarre urban art are all a part of city life that is admired by some while despised by others. In the past, advertisements were clearly recognized as being different and separate from guerrilla art. They were easily recognizable as advertisements, and no one expected them to be anything else. Although today's urban environment still includes separate instances of art and advertisements, some advertisements now look surprisingly like art.

Guerilla advertising involves the display of an unusual or unexpected advertisement in a common, everyday place to create buzz about a product or service. For example, amongst the white stripes in a city street crosswalk, one of the stripes is clearly brighter and whiter than the other stripes. That stripe contains a picture of Mr. Clean®, the mascot for Mr. Clean household products. On another city street, a 3D rendering of a pool of sharks along with the message, "Don't step into danger," was painted on the sidewalk as part of a public service campaign to warn people about pedestrian accidents. A giant, 6-foot-tall cup of coffee is tipped over on a sidewalk, revealing a coffee spill. The paper towel maker Bounty® placed a sign next to the coffee spill to let passersby know that Bounty "makes small work of BIG spills." On a subway, the overhead handrails have been turned into barbells. An advertisement for a fitness company is placed above the barbells.

What's the difference between guerrilla art and guerrilla advertising? You might think that the distinction between the two would be obvious, but the lines are highly blurred. Art often is thought of as beautiful. But what about advertisements that are truly beautiful? What about the street artists who are paid to use their art to advertise a product? Is that still advertising, or can it also be art? The line is blurred even further when you see the invasion of corporate logos and slogans in public places. At what point do advertisements become graffiti? Although guerilla advertising may not be admired by all, it accomplishes two important goals. It gets noticed and is memorable.

© Rob Ahrens/Shutterstock.com

WHAT DO YOU KNOW?

1. **Why do you think an increasing number of companies are using guerilla advertising?**

2. **Have you seen guerilla advertising in your city or in another city? If so, describe it.**

3. **Although guerilla advertising gets noticed and is memorable, do you think it's effective? Explain why or why not.**

The Advertising Plan

Goals
- Identify the steps in creating an advertising plan.
- Recognize the various types of analyses that should be performed when creating an advertising plan.

Terms
- advertising plan, p. 268
- situational analysis, p. 269
- SWOT analysis, p. 269
- creative strategy, p. 270
- return on investment (ROI), p. 271

FOCUS ON ADVERTISING

Breaking through the Ad Clutter

When creating an advertising plan, advertisers must determine a way to break through all of the ad clutter, or the nonstop blitz of advertisements. Consumers have gone from being exposed to about 500 ads a day in the 1970s to over 3,000 ads a day today. Television commercial breaks

have grown longer since the early days of television. In addition, the number of commercial breaks has gone from four per hour to five or six per hour. The commercial spots have actually grown shorter, which means more commercials can air during the longer commercial breaks. Broadcast radio sometimes seems to have more commercials than music or entertainment. In magazines, readers often have to flip through numerous pages of ads before getting to any real magazine articles. Many advertisers believe the solution is to develop more creative advertising campaigns that will get noticed. However, there is an opposing viewpoint. Some believe that less ad clutter is the answer. They argue that by reducing the number of advertising messages, each message would then have a greater impact.

Work as a Team What do you think about all of the ad clutter in today's marketplace? Do you agree that fewer ads may have more impact on consumers? Why or why not?

What Is the Advertising Plan?

The **advertising plan** describes the goals of an advertising campaign, methods to use to accomplish those goals, and ways to evaluate whether those goals are achieved. Developing the advertising plan requires research about the audience, product, and type of media to use to deliver the most effective message. Although the content of an advertising plan will vary based on the product or service and market, the general outline of an advertising plan will be similar. Steps for creating the advertising plan are described below.

Perform a Situational Analysis

A **situational analysis** describes the environment in which a business is operating. Before planning an advertising campaign, a business needs to review its history and take a look at where things stand currently. It needs to review its current products, target market, competitors, and financial condition. Industry and market trends and the state of the economy should also be considered. An analysis of all of these factors will help advertising planners determine the best type of message, timing of the message, and the most effective forms of media for a successful advertising campaign.

A **SWOT analysis**, which is an examination of a business's strengths, weaknesses, opportunities, and threats, is often conducted as part

Why is it important to perform a situational analysis when creating an advertising plan?

of a situational analysis. Strengths and weaknesses are internal factors. Strengths could include the business's marketing expertise or its new, innovative product. Weaknesses may be related to the business's bad reputation or its poor location. Opportunities and threats are external factors. An opportunity could include a new international market. A threat may involve a new competitor or rising material costs. The key issues that are identified in the SWOT analysis must be considered as the advertising plan is developed.

Set Advertising Objectives

Advertising plans are based on objectives that describe the desired results of the advertising campaign. In many cases, a business has more than one advertising objective for a campaign. Common advertising objectives include the following:

- Build consumer awareness of a product or brand
- Communicate product or brand benefits
- Generate interest in a product or brand
- Create, change, or reinforce consumers' attitudes about a brand
- Persuade consumers to switch brands
- Attain brand loyalty
- Increase sales

The objective must be clearly stated and include criteria for success that can be measured. Measurable objectives are often stated in quantitative terms and specify a time frame. For example, if a fitness center wants to increase interest among senior citizens, its advertising objective might be to attract 200 new members over the age of 60 within three months.

Determine the Budget

After the advertising objectives have been identified, it is time to create the budget. There are several methods businesses can use to determine the budget. Unfortunately, some businesses base the budget on what they can afford. In other words, the advertising budget depends on how much money is left over after all of the business's expenses are covered. This is not the best method because it doesn't always meet the business's advertising needs.

Other businesses use the historical method to determine how much to spend on advertising. They use the amount spent on advertising in the previous year and make adjustments for inflation to arrive at the new budget. Again, this may not be the best method. The historical method does not take into account other factors, such as changes in the market or competition. Other methods used to determine the budget involve allocating a percentage of sales, matching competitors' budgets, and calculating the cost of the tasks necessary to achieve the advertising objectives. These methods will be discussed in more detail in Chapter 12.

Develop the Creative Strategy

The **creative strategy** describes who the target market is, what the advertising message should be, and how the message will be communicated. Before an ad can be created, the business must determine the purpose of the advertising message, such as to inform, to compare, to persuade, to remind, or to defend. It must also determine the best medium for communicating the message to the target audience. For example, the strategy used to introduce a new brand of sports apparel might include developing a television commercial to air during sporting events, a print ad to run in sports-related magazines, and/or a radio ad to air on stations that attract young professionals between the ages of 18–34. The creative strategy should be highly focused and precise. It will guide and direct the advertising team, including the copywriters and art directors, as they create the ad.

Execute the Plan

Once the strategy is in place, the creative development process begins. The business often works with copywriters and art directors to create the advertising concept. Ad copy, slogans, headlines, designs, illustrations, photos, and scripts are important elements of the creative development process.

What is the purpose of the creative strategy?

Marketers frequently test their advertising campaigns in focus groups consisting of members of the target audience. Feedback may suggest that changes are needed. Once the business approves the creative concept, the actual advertisement(s) will be produced. Producers and directors help create television commercials.

A media planner identifies when and where the ads will be placed. Will the ad be in the format of a 30-second commercial aired during primetime on network TV or will it be aired on a cable network, such as ESPN, that appeals to a specific target market? Or perhaps it will be a print ad that will be placed in the newspaper during the holiday season? The timing of the ad will be planned to achieve the highest reach.

Evaluate the Plan

The advertising campaign must be evaluated to determine if the objectives outlined in the advertising plan were met. The criteria stated in the objectives can be used to measure the effectiveness of the advertising campaign. For example, if the advertising objective of a fitness center is to attract 200 new members over the age of 60, this can be measured easily by counting the number of new memberships that meet these criteria. Businesses need to be able to quantify the results.

When it comes to advertising, businesses are highly interested in their **return on investment (ROI)**, which is the amount earned as a result of money invested, expressed as a percentage. The equation for ROI is as follows:

$$\frac{\text{Gain from investment} - \text{Cost of investment}}{\text{Cost of investment}} \times 100$$

In the case of advertising, "gain from investment" refers to the profit earned as a result of the advertising campaign. If the advertising campaign for the fitness center cost \$25,000 and generated \$100,000 in additional sales, the ROI is 300 percent [(100,000 − 25,000/\$25,000) × 100].

▰▰▰▰ CHECKPOINT ◤◤◤◤◤

What are the steps in creating an advertising plan?

Advertising Plan Analyses

Performing a situational analysis is the most time-consuming task in the advertising planning process. Businesses must consider many internal and external factors that could affect the advertising plan. Specifically, businesses need to take a close look at the industry, the market, competitors, and globalization.

Industry Analysis

An industry analysis focuses on the developments and trends within an entire industry. It helps a business understand its position relative to other businesses producing similar products and services. It also identifies opportunities and threats that can be addressed in the planning process. Questions to ask when performing an industry analysis include the following:

- What is the estimated size of the industry (in total sales or number of products/services sold)?
- What is the expected outlook of the industry? (Is it on the rise or decline?)
- What are the sales trends in the industry over recent years?
- What are the product/service trends in the industry?
- Who are the leading businesses (top brands) in the industry?
- What types of marketing strategies are commonly used in this industry?
- Is the industry sensitive to economic conditions?

Market Analysis

A market analysis is performed to learn more about current and potential users of a product or service. It helps clearly define the target market and its needs. Questions to ask about the market include the following:

- Who is the target customer?
- What is the size of the overall target market?
- What features and benefits are most important to the target customer?
- What would motivate the target customer to buy our company's product or service instead of the competitors'?
- What is the best way to reach the target customer?
- How is the market changing?

What information should businesses gather about their target market?

Competitor Analysis

After studying the industry and the market, it is important to take a look at the competitors. A competitive analysis will help a business determine its competitive advantages or disadvantages relative to other businesses. Businesses can use this information to develop strategies to overcome the competition. Questions to ask about competitors include the following:

- Who are the competitors?
- What threats do they pose?
- What are the strengths and weaknesses of the competitors?
- What marketing strategies do the competitors use and how successful are those strategies?
- How are the competitors likely to respond to changes in our marketing strategies?

Global Analysis

Many businesses are expanding into international markets. Even if a business's advertising strategy has been successful in its own country, the same advertising may not work well in different countries or cultures. Target markets differ from country to country in terms of how they perceive or interpret the advertising message. Businesses must decide when they can standardize advertising campaigns throughout the world and when they must customize advertisements for different cultures.

Standardize for Greater Efficiency Some businesses believe that advertising travels from country to country. Proponents of this viewpoint argue that many cultures, especially those of industrialized countries, have become so similar that the same advertising will work throughout the world. By developing one approach for multiple markets, an advertiser saves a substantial amount of time and expense by not developing a separate campaign for each culture. The 2006 World Cup was broadcast in 189 countries to one of the largest global television audiences. MasterCard implemented a standardized approach that appeared in 39 countries. The advertising agency developed a spot called "Fever," in which more than 100 cheering fans from 30 countries appeared. Since the ad had no dialogue, it worked for any language. The tagline, "Football fever. Priceless," appeared under the MasterCard logo at the end of the advertisement.

Why is culture an important factor when deciding upon an advertising campaign?

Standardized advertising is likely to be more effective among consumers who live in countries that have similar economic, technological, legal, social, and cultural environments. There are two types of consumers who are good candidates for the standardized advertising approach: (1) affluent people who are "global citizens" and who come into contact with ideas from around the world through their travels, business contacts, and media experiences; and (2) young people whose tastes in music and fashion are strongly influenced by MTV and other media that broadcast many of the same images to multiple countries.

Even when similarities exist, the standardization approach does not always work well. Consumers in different countries have varying customs, so they simply do not use products the same way. Kellogg's, for example, discovered that people in Brazil typically do not eat a big breakfast—they're more likely to eat cereal as a dry snack. Some large corporations like Coca-Cola have been fairly successful at using a standardized approach, but even the soft drink giant must make minor modifications for each culture, such as showing close-ups of local faces in their product advertisements.

Customize to Appeal to Local Tastes Many businesses recognize the huge variations across cultures. They feel that each culture is unique, with its own value system and customs. When this is the case, businesses should tailor the advertising to each specific culture. There are many reasons to customize advertising. Consumers in other countries speak different languages, and intended meanings in one language are very different in other languages. Cultural sensitivities vary widely, and advertisers who try to export their own symbolism to another country are taking a great risk. In China, an advertisement for Nippon Paint (a Japanese brand) caused an uproar. It showed a sculptured dragon unable to keep its grip on a pillar coated in smooth wood-coating paint. Dragons are potent symbols in China, and seeing one easily defeated by a Japanese product proved too much for the Chinese culture.

CHECKPOINT

What types of analyses should a business perform when creating an advertising plan?

10.1 Assessment

THINK ABOUT IT

1. What is the purpose of the advertising plan?
2. Why is the creative strategy an important component of the advertising plan?
3. How can a competitor analysis be used to create effective advertising?
4. Although the world is linked through social media, why does standardized advertising not always work?

MAKE ACADEMIC CONNECTIONS

5. **PROBLEM SOLVING**   Setting measurable objectives is an important step in developing the advertising plan. Measurable objectives should be quantifiable and have a time frame. Set two measurable advertising objectives for a new Italian restaurant in your neighborhood.

6. **MATH**   A bookstore sets an advertising goal to increase its book club memberships by 15 percent over last year's memberships. If last year's memberships totaled 540, how many memberships will the bookstore have if it achieves its goal? If the bookstore spent $12,000 on the advertising campaign and made $18,500 in sales from new members, what is the store's ROI?

7. **INTERNATIONAL**   Name a company that you believe could successfully use standardized advertising for its product in other countries. Create a standardized ad for the product. Describe any minor adjustments that would be needed when the ad is shown in other countries.

Teamwork

As the advertising agency for a local or national company of your choice, you have been asked to perform a SWOT analysis. Identify the company's strengths, weaknesses, opportunities, and threats. Based on the SWOT analysis make a recommendation about the advertising message the company should communicate to its target market. Present the analysis and advertising message to the class.

Creation of the Advertisement

Goals

- Describe different advertising creative formats.
- Identify processes involved in the copywriting, art, and production stages of advertising.

Terms

- image advertising, p. 276
- comparison advertising, p. 277
- copywriting, p. 279
- slogan, p. 279
- illustration, p. 279
- storyboard, p. 280
- layout, p. 280

Using Multiple Creative Strategies

Most companies use one mascot in their advertising campaigns, such as the Energizer Bunny® for Energizer batteries. Geico probably uses more company mascots at one time than any other company in the history of marketing. When watching a Geico ad, you might see the Gecko, the Cavemen, the googly-eyed pile of money named Kash, or all three. Each mascot is memorable and will forever be linked to the brand. Currently Geico has no fewer than six different ad campaigns running, each with its own unique tone, style, flavor, and message. Most brand builders believe that using multiple creative strategies is the wrong way to create a cohesive, focused brand image. In most cases, consistency is the key to making messages memorable. Geico breaks these widely accepted branding rules. It does so by keeping its advertising messages simple. The concept of cost savings runs throughout all of the ads, and Geico's famous tagline, "15 minutes could save you 15 percent or more on car insurance," opens or closes most of its advertisements.

Work as a Team Why is consistency usually an important element of an advertising campaign? How has Geico been able to successfully maintain several different creative strategies?

© Julien Tromeur/Shutterstock.com

Select a Creative Format

The information outlined in the creative strategy portion of the advertising plan is used by the creative team to develop the advertisement. Numerous creative formats can be used to convey the advertising message to the target customers. The advertiser must select the format that will be the most effective at meeting the advertising objectives. The format used must make an *advertising appeal*, which serves to capture the audience's attention and identify a reason for the consumer to buy the product.

Slice-of-Life Advertising

Slice-of-life advertising portrays a scene from everyday life. Advertisements depict people in normal social settings, such as at the dinner table, at a park, or in their car. The audience feels like it is watching or listening to a real event. The goal of slice-of-life advertising is to socially embed the brand in the consumer's everyday life. Subaru's "Baby Driver" commercial in which a father hands the car keys over to his 16-year-old daughter for the first time depicts a life experience with which many parents can identify.

Lifestyle Advertising

When using lifestyle advertising, advertisers have to understand the psychographic characteristics—interests, attitudes, and opinions—of their target audience. This form of advertising attempts to develop an image or identity for the brand. It not only promotes the product, but it also promotes a way of living. Lifestyle advertising is depicted in Mountain Dew® commercials. The brand presents itself as the choice for consumers who have a young attitude and active lifestyle.

Testimonial Advertising

When a spokesperson endorses a product in an advertisement, it is known as a testimonial. The endorser may be a well-known celebrity or athlete, a knowledgeable professional such as a doctor, or a satisfied customer who uses the product. The idea behind testimonial advertising is that prospective customers are more likely to trust a recommendation coming from a third party than from the business itself. Microsoft used this strategy very effectively by featuring its customers talking about Microsoft products in its "I'm a PC" advertising campaign. Consumers often want to emulate popular celebrities and athletes, so using them as product endorsers can favorably influence buying decisions.

Humorous Advertising

Humor is used in advertising as a way to make an emotional connection with the audience. When humor is used appropriately, consumers develop a positive and memorable association with the brand. People actually enjoy humorous ads and talk about them with others. However, humorous ads have to do more than just entertain. There must be a direct link between the humor and the brand; otherwise, people will remember the joke but not the brand. Advertising humor works best for established and commonly purchased products. Unknown, risky, expensive, or sensitive products are not normally suitable for advertising humor.

Image Advertising

Image advertising promotes the general perception of a product or service rather than its function or purpose. It is effective at building brand awareness, creating familiarity, and contributing to the development of a mental picture of the brand or product in the minds of consumers. Celebrities often are used to help promote the desired image. Image advertising attempts to generate positive attitudes about a brand, company, or concept through the use of visual images. Few words appear in visual ads. Instead, visual images are used to depict a brand's attributes or to evoke feelings about the brand. Visual ads are commonly used for fashion, fragrance, and luxury products. But they can also be used for well-known brands such as Nike, McDonald's, and Coca-Cola. McDonald's golden arches may immediately produce mental images of its golden fries.

Scientific Advertising

Scientific advertising uses research or scientific evidence to promote a brand. This type of advertising is effective when showing the results of pain relievers, hair growth products, weight loss remedies, and skin creams. The Federal Trade Commission (FTC) carefully monitors scientific advertising to make sure that it is accurate and not misleading.

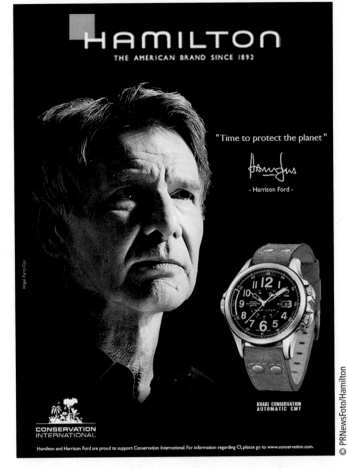

What image do you think this ad is trying to project for Hamilton watches? How does the use of a celebrity reinforce this image?

Product Demonstration Advertising

Product demonstration ads show how to use the product, identify the benefits of using the product, and emphasize the value of owning the product. Product demonstrations are based on the motto, "seeing is believing." Truck manufacturers produce commercials that show their trucks pulling heavy loads to demonstrate their towing capacity. Infomercials frequently demonstrate the latest cooking and cleaning devices.

Musical Advertising

Advertisers often choose to convey their message through the use of music. Music functions as a bridge between the target audience and the advertisement. The audience becomes more engaged when a familiar tune or catchy jingle is used. In addition, music can trigger an instant emotional response from the target audience. Using music in advertising increases brand awareness and recall of a product and its brand name. Apple effectively used music in its TV commercials for the iPod. Commercials featuring dark silhouetted characters listening to their iPods and dancing to upbeat music were a hit with consumers.

Comparison Advertising

Comparison advertising is used to promote the superiority of a brand by comparing its features to those of a competitive brand.

Advertisers may use a direct comparison by naming the competitor's brand or use an indirect comparison by referring to it only as "the leading brand." Comparison advertising generally is used by businesses that are trying to compete with the market leader. Comparative advertising can be convincing, but it also can be risky. The business making superiority claims must be able to support them. For example, the National Advertising Division (NAD) of the Counsel of Better Business Bureaus investigated Campbell Soup Company's claim that consumers preferred its soups to Progresso's. Although market research supported the claim, NAD still required Campbell's to modify the ad to reduce consumer confusion. NAD works closely with the FTC to monitor advertising.

▨▨▨▨▨ CHECKPOINT ◣◣◣◣◣

What creative formats can be used to deliver an advertising message?

SPOTLIGHT ON SUCCESS

Photo copyright of Charlie McQuilkin

CHARLIE McQUILKIN
Young & Rubicam

Over 15 years ago, Chevron, an oil and gas company, launched the now-famous advertising campaign featuring the lovable, clay-animated Chevron cars. The inspiration for the advertising campaign featuring the animated cars came from Charlie McQuilkin, an associate creative director at the advertising agency Young & Rubicam. After watching the clay animation movie *Creature Comforts,* Charlie thought the technique would be a good fit for a new Chevron campaign. McQuilkin set out to answer, "How do you talk to folks about gasoline?" His answer: "Who better to talk about gasoline than the thing that consumes it, the car?"

Under Charlie's direction, Young & Rubicam collaborated with Aardman Animations, the creators of the *Creature Comforts* film, to produce a number of highly successful television commercials. The most challenging element about bringing the car characters to life was finding the right voice to match each car's personality. To find the best voices for the car characters, Americans from across the country were interviewed about what it would be like to be a car and why an engine would prefer using Chevron gasoline with Techron®, a fuel treatment additive that keeps engines cleaner. Once the voices were recorded, the artists at Aardman created car characters and produced the commercials. Chevron's animated cars encouraged consumers to use Chevron with Techron gasoline for a cleaner, happier car.

The Chevron cars advertising campaign is still going strong today. The cars have become animated spokesmodels for Chevron and have turned into an unusual moneymaker for the nation's third-largest oil company. Chevron extended its successful advertising campaign by introducing a line of toy cars based on the animated clay figures used in the commercials. The Chevron cars are so popular that they receive fan mail. Adults and children love the cars that originated from a creative concept developed by Charlie McQuilkin, who went on to become the Senior Vice President, Group Creative Director at Young & Rubicam.

Think Critically
How did Charlie McQuilkin and Chevron put a unique spin on testimonial advertising in the Chevron car ads? Which other creative formats were used? Why has this advertising campaign had long-term success?

Determine Copywriting, Art, and Production Strategies

The creative team plays the biggest role in the execution stage of the advertising plan. The creative team consists of copywriters and art directors, who work together closely to create ad copy and visuals. The creative brief is the starting point for the creative team. The *creative brief*, which is developed as part of the creative strategy process, is a description of what the advertising campaign is to accomplish. It describes the advertising message objective, key product features and benefits to be emphasized, the suggested mood or tone of the advertisement, and the media mix. It guides copywriters and art directors through the creative process. The production team steps in to complete the execution of the advertising plan.

Copywriting and Art Directing

Copywriting is the process of using words to express creative ideas and concepts. In advertising, copywriters must effectively communicate the benefits and value of a brand in a new or unique way. The copywriting process varies depending on the media used. However, one element of copywriting is common across all media formats. Copywriters must create a slogan, or tagline, that will appear in all of a company's advertisements. A **slogan** is a short, memorable phrase that establishes an identity for a brand.

Print Advertising Components of print advertising include the headline, subhead, and body copy. A *headline* is used to capture the reader's attention. It may provide information about the brand, emphasize a brand claim, or arouse the reader's curiosity. The *subhead*, which usually appears below the headline, provides brand information not included in the headline. *Body copy* describes the brand in more detail. Copywriters are challenged to use familiar words and phrases in an interesting and exciting way.

Art directors are responsible for the visual elements of print advertising. One of the most important visual elements is the **illustration**, which is the actual drawing, photography, or other type of art used in the advertisement. The illustration should work with the ad copy to attract the attention of the target audience and communicate brand features or benefits. By creating interest, illustrations entice people to read the ad copy. Illustrations also help create the desired image for the brand. If a clothing manufacturer is targeting teenagers, its print ads may contain pictures of teens having fun while wearing the manufacturer's clothing. The pictures set the tone for the ad.

Radio Advertising Because radio advertising is restricted to an audio-only format, copywriting can be challenging. Copywriters may decide to use a music format, such as a jingle, or a dialogue format, which often involves a conversation between two people. Another option is to write the advertisement in the form of an announcement to be read by the disc jockey (DJ), news commentator, or even a celebrity. Because most radio ads are limited to 30 or 60 seconds, the copywriter must capture the listener's attention early. Short words and sentences should be used so they can be processed easily. The ad should create images in the minds of listeners. Finally, because there are no visuals, the brand name should be repeated several times to make an impression.

Television Advertising Television provides a highly creative opportunity for copywriters. Television commercials can evoke emotions and communicate brand values in ways that other advertising formats cannot. Copywriting for television advertising must sell the brand while entertaining the audience. Copywriters are challenged to coordinate the words with the visual images. The ad copy should not be too wordy so it doesn't interfere with the visual impact.

Copywriters work with art directors to create the **storyboard**, which is a sketch that provides the play-by-play sequence of visual scenes and ad copy used in the television advertisement. The storyboard is the roadmap for coordinating these elements. The copywriters and art directors also work with the producers and directors of the television commercial to make sure the copy supports and enhances the video.

Digital Advertising Copywriting for digital/interactive media is very challenging. It is a cross between print advertising and television advertising. Even though the message is in print format, it often has a video or audio element. Copywriters have to appeal to vastly different audiences on company websites, blogs, social media sites, and mobile devices. Audiences for digital advertising often seek out the ads, meaning they have more incentive to read or watch the ads. Consumers prefer interactive ads that allow them to customize the content of the web page by entering personal information. Digital advertising is effective at raising brand awareness.

The Production Process

After the creative concept developed by the copywriters and art directors has been finalized and approved, the production stage will begin. For print advertising, this may involve selecting the proper font (style and size) for the ad copy, hiring a photographer, selecting models for the ad, and finalizing the design and layout. The **layout** is a drawing of the print advertisement showing where all the elements in the ad are positioned. For radio advertising, the production process involves hiring an announcer or actors to read the ad. If music or a jingle is used, musicians and singers are hired. The ad is then recorded at a sound studio. These steps may not be necessary if the DJ is going to read the ad live on air.

TV production is a much more complex process. There are three stages—preproduction, production, and postproduction. During the preproduction stage, the creative team and the producer create a production schedule, hire a director,

Who are the various people that may be involved in the advertising production process?

assemble a production crew, select a location, cast the actors, and hire music suppliers. In the production stage, the commercial is filmed. A well-laid plan and highly trained technicians help ensure this process goes smoothly, but unexpected events such as bad weather and intrusive noises can cause disruptions. After the commercial is filmed, it enters the postproduction stage. Editors, sound engineers, voice-over specialists, special effect artists, and others finish the commercial. It may go through several rounds of editing and assembly before the master copy is completed. Copies of the master are made and distributed to every TV station that is part of the media plan.

///////// CHECKPOINT \\\\\\\\\

What are some of the important processes in the copywriting and art directing stages of creating an advertisement?

10.2 Assessment

THINK ABOUT IT

1. What is the purpose of comparison advertising? Provide an actual example of this type of advertising.

2. What is image advertising? Provide an example of image advertising that uses a celebrity or athlete. How does the celebrity or athlete contribute to the image of the advertised product?

3. Why do copywriters and art directors have to work together closely throughout the creative development process?

MAKE ACADEMIC CONNECTIONS

4. **COMMUNICATION**   Find an advertising example that uses two of the creative formats described in the lesson. For example, an ad might present scientific research or evidence about a product and compare it to a competitor's product. Describe the ad and explain whether the creative formats used are effective.

5. **VISUAL ART**   You are the art director for a clothing manufacturer that has a teen clothing line. Prepare an illustration for an advertisement that will appear in popular teen magazines. The theme of the advertisement is "Fashion That Lets You Go to the Head of the Class." You can use drawings, photos, or pictures from magazines in your illustration.

6. **LANGUAGE ARTS**   You are working on a lifestyle print advertisement for a nutrition bar that is low-calorie and fortified with vitamin supplements. The target market is active adults between the ages of 18–35. Write the headline, subhead, and body copy for the ad.

Teamwork

Your advertising agency has been hired to create a 60-second radio advertisement for the local shopping mall. Develop a concept for the ad, select a creative format for it, and write a script. Present the radio ad to your classmates, who will be acting as the owners of the shopping mall.

Analysis and Evaluation of Advertising Messages

Goals
- Describe various methods used to evaluate advertising effectiveness.
- Identify simple approaches to use in determining advertising effectiveness.

Terms
- recognition test, p. 283
- recall test, p. 283
- attitude study, p. 283
- resonance test, p. 284

FOCUS ON ADVERTISING

Advertising Ineffectiveness

Successful advertising campaigns increase brand awareness and company profits. However, not all advertising strategies are effective. There are a number of signs that point to ineffective advertising. When the advertising focuses on how great the company is instead of explaining why consumers should use its product or service, consumers are likely to tune out. The target customer should be the main focus of the advertising campaign. Another sign that the advertising is ineffective is if consumers are confused by the message. If the advertisement doesn't clearly communicate the purpose of the product or service, consumers will be confused. Ineffective ads do not include a call to action. Consumers should be told what to do—"buy now to get special financing," "stop in today for a free sample," "visit our website to register." Sales can also be an indicator of ineffective advertising. If a company's sales decrease or do not change, then the advertising isn't doing its job. Testing advertising campaigns before and after they go public can provide advertisers with valuable feedback that can be used to create effective advertising.

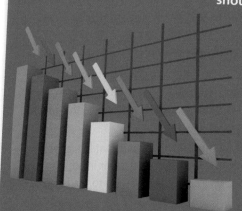

Work as a Team Select an advertisement that you think is ineffective and discuss why. How can it be improved?

Evaluate Advertising Effectiveness

The final step in the advertising plan is to evaluate the effectiveness of the advertising campaign. There are many reasons to measure the effectiveness of advertising. It determines whether the advertising message made an impact on the target audience. It identifies which

How well would you perform on a recognition or recall test for advertisements? What makes some more memorable than others?

strategies worked and which didn't. It also provides useful information that advertisers can use to make future advertising messages more effective. Finally, it is used to justify the investment in advertising.

In most cases, measuring the results of an advertising campaign is directly related to the advertising objectives. It is important to determine if the advertising objectives were met. To do this, businesses use direct and indirect measures. A direct measure looks at the relationship between advertising and sales. Companies compare advertising expenditures and sales to determine the impact of advertising campaigns. An indirect measure looks at the target audience's reaction to the advertising. There are several indirect measures that advertisers can use as described below.

Recognition and Recall Measures

After target audiences are exposed to ads, advertisers often measure what the audience members remember about them. Recognition and recall tests help measure whether the ads were effective at increasing brand awareness. A **recognition test** measures a lower level of brand awareness by determining whether audience members remember seeing the ad. Audiences are asked if they recognize the ad and if they can name the company sponsoring the ad or the brand name of the product in the ad. Recall requires more actual memory of an ad. A **recall test** measures how much the audience remembers about the advertising message. If audiences indicate they recognize the ad, they are then asked more specific questions relating to brand attributes. Results are tabulated from both tests to determine the recognition and recall scores.

Attitude Measures

A common advertising objective is to create, change, or reinforce consumers' attitudes about a brand. An **attitude study** measures consumer attitudes before and after exposure to an ad. Target audience members

COOL FACT

A University of Iowa research study indicated that TV viewers who use DVR devices to fast-forward through commercials at a slow speed can recall the ad even better than one seen at normal speed. This is likely because viewers pay more attention to the screen so they can stop right at the start of the television show. Results are not the same when the viewer fast-forwards at a high speed.

are recruited and surveyed about their attitude toward the advertised brand and competitors' brands before being shown the ad. Then audience members are shown the ad, and their attitudes are measured again to see if they have changed. The goal of the advertising message is to produce a positive attitude about the brand and build brand preference.

Emotional Measures

One way to generate interest in a brand and attain brand loyalty is to make an emotional connection with consumers. Ads that appeal to consumers' emotions have a stronger and longer-lasting effect. To make an emotional connection, advertising messages must be relevant and meaningful. A **resonance test** measures the extent to which an advertising message resonates or strikes a chord with the target audience. This type of test usually is given in a group setting. The ad is shown to the group and then discussed. Advertisers question group members to see if the advertisement matches their own experiences.

Behavioral Measures

The main purpose of an advertising campaign often is to influence consumers' behavior. Advertisers want consumers to take some kind of action, such as visit a website or make a purchase. There are several behavioral-based measures that advertisers can use, many of which are related to sales. Businesses can measure the effectiveness of their advertising campaign by comparing sales before, during, and after the ad campaign. Since most advertising has a delayed effect, ad-driven sales may not materialize immediately. Coupons that customers redeem for a discount are frequently included in print ads. The code included on the redeemed coupons can help a business track which ad generated

How can a business use behavioral measures to evaluate the effectiveness of an advertising campaign?

the best results. Businesses sometimes offer an incentive for customers who state that they are responding to an advertisement. "Mention this ad and get a 10 percent discount on your first order." This provides an easy way to measure the effectiveness of the ad.

Technology has improved the way consumers' behavior can be tracked. Research companies can supply selected households with handheld scanners and electronic meters that are attached to TV sets. This equipment tracks brand purchases, coupon use, and television advertising exposure. This data helps advertisers measure the impact of advertising and promotions on consumers' buying behavior.

///////// CHECKPOINT \\\\\\\\

How can advertisers evaluate the effectiveness of advertising campaigns?

Other Strategies to Determine Advertising Effectiveness

In addition to the methods previously discussed, there are some other simple methods of determining the effectiveness of advertising. Companies can track the number of new customers, requests for information, phone inquiries, retail store traffic, website traffic, and other data that can be classified into meaningful numerical data.

- *Track retail traffic.* Count the number of people who enter the store after the advertising campaign has been implemented. Compare this to the average store traffic before the campaign.

- *Use a website stat counter to determine the number of visitors to the company's website.* Businesses that advertise on the Web should compare pre- and post-advertising traffic on the website. The web host has the capability to provide businesses with daily, weekly, or monthly reports.

- *Ask people how they found out about the company.* When a company receives a call or visit from a new customer, it can ask how the customer learned about it. Did a sign in another customer's yard, a newspaper ad, its website, or Craigslist bring the customer to the business?

- *Discontinue advertisements and measure any changes in business.* Companies that have regularly advertised in the newspaper every week for years should stop advertising for a few weeks to see if there is any change in business. If there is no noticeable difference, the business may be able to cut that form of advertising. This strategy can also be used for other forms of advertising.

- *Use different telephone numbers.* The performance for an advertisement can be tracked

NETBookmark

E-retailers use *promotional codes* (also called *key codes* or *coupon codes*) in online ads as well as print ads and direct mail. For example, an online clothing retailer might add the following message to a magazine ad: "Get 10% off when you enter the code *10off* at checkout." Access www.cengage.com/school/advertising and click on the link for Chapter 10. Examine the many promotional codes available on the site. How can a company use promotional codes to measure the effectiveness of its advertising? Why might a company use a different promotional code for the same promotional offer on another website?

www.cengage.com/school/advertising

by using different contact phone numbers or a toll-free number. When a company receives calls to a phone number that is listed only in an advertisement, it is easier to track the results.

- *Use direct-response advertisements.* Give consumers the opportunity to respond directly through a website or reply card. Postcards that offer a simple prepaid "drop in the mail for more information" type of response can help a company gauge the effectiveness of a direct mail campaign.

Measuring advertising effectiveness is one of the key components for a successful marketing campaign. Knowing how to track and measure the performance of advertising activities will not only make an organization more efficient but also stretch its advertising dollars as far as possible.

CHECKPOINT

What are some simple ways to measure advertising effectiveness?

10.3 Assessment

THINK ABOUT IT

1. How do recognition and recall tests differ?

2. What is a resonance test? Why are emotional measures an important way to measure advertising effectiveness?

3. Give an example of a direct-response advertisement you or your family received recently. Did you or someone else respond to it? Why or why not?

MAKE ACADEMIC CONNECTIONS

4. **COMMUNICATION** Design a prepaid postcard that consumers can fill out to request additional information about courses and programs offered by an online learning institute, such as the University of Phoenix. The postcard will be included in various entertainment magazines commonly read by young adults.

5. **MARKETING** Your fast food restaurant is one of the sponsors of a local college's football games. As a sponsor, you can advertise on the back of the football game tickets. Design an ad that will allow you to track its effectiveness. Show the ad to the class and explain how its built-in tracking capabilities will work.

6. **MANAGEMENT** You are the general manager for a new luxury hotel that has been built in a popular convention city with a population of 2 million people. You are working on an advertising campaign that will increase consumer awareness and, ultimately, the occupancy rate and profit. Write five advertising objectives for your new hotel and explain how the success/failure of each objective can be measured.

 Teamwork

Working in a team, choose a product and design an attitude study that measures consumer attitudes before and after exposure to an ad. The pre-test and post-test should each contain ten survey questions that can be answered easily by consumers.

Sharpen Your
21st CENTURY SKILLS

Designing a Storyboard

Once a concept or script is written for a television commercial, the next step is to make a storyboard. A storyboard visually tells the story of an animation, panel by panel, similar to a comic book. Basically, storyboards should answer the 5Ws: who, what, when, where, and why. The storyboard should show the following elements:

- the characters in each frame
- the placement and location of the characters in each frame
- the script (dialogue) for the characters
- the time lapse between each frame, indicating the total duration of the commercial
- camera angles—close up shots or far away shots

Storyboards help creators of advertisements plan their animation out shot by shot. For example, when designing a storyboard for a fire safety commercial, the first frame may show a young child trapped in a burning building. The second frame might show a fire fighter knocking down the door of the building. Additional frames would play out the story until the final frame shows the fire fighter carrying the child out of the building to safety.

Storyboards are a valuable design tool. They provide a simple way to organize the story and point out holes in it. Storyboards also allow the creative team to discuss the animation with other people to get feedback on their ideas. It is easier to make changes to the storyboard than it is to make changes during the production of the commercial. Storyboards also help identify the appropriate props and other equipment needed to create the set when the commercial is filmed.

Most commonly, storyboards are drawn in pen or pencil. However, photos, pictures from magazines, or computer art can be used to make storyboards. The drawings don't have to be fancy. The use of basic shapes, stick figures, and simple backgrounds can bring the story to life. Storyboard frames can be drawn on index cards, which can be rearranged to illustrate the parts of the story.

Try It Out

Your advertising agency has been hired to create a 30-second television commercial for a local Mexican restaurant. Develop a concept for the advertisement and create a storyboard that provides a play-by-play sequence of the visual images and ad copy for the television commercial. Present the storyboard to the class, who will be acting as the owners of the Mexican restaurant.

PARTNERSHIP FOR
21ST CENTURY SKILLS

© Betul Kilic/Shutterstock.com

SUMMARY

10.1 The Advertising Plan

- The advertising plan describes the goals of an advertising campaign, methods to use to accomplish those goals, and ways to evaluate whether those goals are achieved.
- Steps in creating an advertising plan are (1) perform a situational analysis, (2) set advertising objectives, (3) determine the budget, (4) develop the creative strategy, (5) execute the plan, and (6) evaluate the plan.
- When performing a situational analysis, businesses must consider several factors, including the industry, the market, competitors, and international markets.

10.2 Creation of the Advertisement

- Advertisers have many creative formats from which to choose when developing the advertising campaign. Creative formats include slice-of-life, lifestyle, testimonial, humorous, image, scientific, product demonstration, musical, and comparison advertising.
- Copywriters, art directors, and producers work together closely to execute the advertising plan.
- Copywriters create slogans for the brand. Art directors create the illustration to depict the visual image of the ad. Copywriters and art directors work together to create the storyboard, which provides a play-by-play sequence of visual scenes and ad copy for a television advertisement. Producers hire directors and assemble the rest of the production crew.

10.3 Analysis and Evaluation of Advertising Messages

- The final step in an advertising campaign is to evaluate its effectiveness. It is important to determine whether the advertising message made an impact on the target audience.
- There are several methods of measuring advertising effectiveness, including recognition and recall tests, attitude studies, resonance tests, and behavioral measures.
- Simple ways to evaluate advertising effectiveness include tracking retail traffic, using a website stat counter to track visitors, asking people how they found out about a company, discontinuing advertisements to measure changes in business, using different telephone numbers in advertising campaigns, and using direct-response advertisements.

WHAT DO YOU KNOW?

Read *Impact Advertising* on page 267 again to review the examples of guerilla advertising. Conduct research to find another example of a company that has used this advertising tactic. Do you think this is a good way for the company to reach out to its target audience? Why or why not?

Vocabulary Builder

Match each statement with the term that best defines it. Some terms may not be used.

1. Describes the environment in which a business is operating
2. Advertising that is used to promote the superiority of a brand by comparing its features to those of competitors'
3. Advertising that promotes the general perception of a product or service rather than its function or purpose
4. Measures how much an audience remembers about an advertising message
5. The actual drawing, photography, or other type of art used in an advertisement
6. A short, memorable phrase that establishes an identity for a brand
7. The process of using words to express creative ideas and concepts
8. The amount earned as a result of money invested
9. Measures the extent to which an advertising message strikes a chord with the target audience
10. A drawing showing where all the elements in a print ad will be placed

a. advertising plan
b. attitude study
c. comparison advertising
d. copywriting
e. creative strategy
f. illustration
g. image advertising
h. layout
i. recall test
j. recognition test
k. resonance test
l. return on investment (ROI)
m. situational analysis
n. slogan
o. storyboard
p. SWOT analysis

Test Your Knowledge

11. All of the following are examined in a SWOT analysis *except*
    a. weaknesses
    b. threats
    c. strengths
    d. objectives
12. If the advertising campaign for a national company cost $100,000 and it generated $250,000 in additional sales, what is the ROI?
    a. 1.5%
    b. 150%
    c. 15%
    d. 250%
13. Which of the following questions is *not* addressed in the creative strategy?
    a. Who is the target market?
    b. What is the advertising message?
    c. How should the advertising message be communicated?
    d. How can sales be increased?

14. A(n) _____ analysis studies the target customer.
    a. industry
    c. market
    b. competitor
    d. SWOT
15. _____ advertising shows people in normal, everyday social settings.
    a. Slice-of-life
    c. Image
    b. Lifestyle
    d. Comparison
16. _____ advertising is very visual and is commonly used for fashion, fragrance, and luxury products.
    a. Slice-of-life
    c. Image
    b. Lifestyle
    d. Comparison
17. In a print ad, the _____ is used to capture the reader's attention.
    a. subhead
    c. body copy
    b. headline
    d. none of the above
18. Which of the following activities occurs during the postproduction stage of a television commercial?
    a. the commercial is edited and assembled
    b. the production schedule is created
    c. the production crew is hired
    d. all of the above
19. A(n) _____ test measures a lower level of brand awareness by determining whether audience members remember seeing an ad.
    a. recall
    c. resonance
    b. attitude
    d. recognition
20. Which of the following is *not* a common method used to measure advertising effectiveness?
    a. tracking retail traffic
    b. using different telephone numbers in advertisements
    c. comparing advertisements to competitors' advertisements
    d. using direct-response advertisements

Apply What You Learned

21. Describe a testimonial advertisement that you have seen recently. Outline the product features emphasized by the spokesperson. Do you think the spokesperson was a good choice? Why or why not? Rate the effectiveness of the advertisement and the spokesperson and explain your ratings.
22. Select a popular TV commercial from the past or present. Based on the advertising message, what do you think the advertising objective might be? Write the advertising objective using measurable criteria. Describe the creative format used. Do you think the creative format helped make the commercial popular? Why or why not?
23. Carry a notebook with you throughout the week. Make a note of any brand images with which you come into contact throughout the week. For example, you may pass a picture of Colonel Sanders on a KFC building on your way to school. Next to each image, record how the images make you feel or any associations you might have with them.

24. **SOCIAL STUDIES**   Find an example of lifestyle advertising that you believe is trying to appeal to teenagers. Describe the product or service and the lifestyle depicted in the advertisement. Do you think the ad accurately portrays a teenager's lifestyle? Does the ad help develop an identity for the brand? How do you think the ad could be improved to make it more appealing to teens? Answer these questions in a one-page report.

25. **VISUAL ART**   Select a product or service that you think would benefit from image advertising. Create a print ad that uses visual images to promote the product or service. Include ad copy, but don't be too wordy. The images chosen should do most of the "talking" for the product or service.

26. **RESEARCH**   Conduct research and prepare an industry analysis for a new home interior design company. When conducting the analysis, answer the questions shown on p. 272. Prepare a report that presents your analysis. Conclude the report with a description of how the analysis could affect the advertising plan.

27. **SCIENCE**   Your company sells various kinds of teas. You want to promote the health benefits of tea in your advertising. Conduct research to learn about scientific studies and evidence that support this claim. Then prepare an advertisement based on your research.

28. **MARKETING**   Because the U.S. population is growing older, many companies are targeting the senior citizen market. Select an advertisement for a product or service that targets senior citizens. Based on the ad, create a resonance test that could be given to a focus group to determine the ad's effectiveness.

29. **WRITING**   Write a radio commercial to promote a new outdoor activities park that offers camping, canoeing, fishing, hiking, biking, and swimming. Identify the advertising objective and determine the creative format to use. The radio commercial should be 60 seconds long.

You have been hired to create an advertisement for a local ice cream manufacturer, Tasty's Frozen Treats. There are three major ice cream manufacturers serving the area, making the local ice cream industry very competitive. Tasty's wants you to develop an advertising campaign that will build brand preference among local consumers. The company's owner strongly suggests that comparison advertising be used with the tagline, "I scream, you scream, we all scream for the best ice cream in the city—Tasty's." However, Tasty's does not have any evidence to back up this claim.

How would you respond to the owner's request? What would Tasty's have to do in order to make this claim in its advertisements? What other ways might you suggest that Tasty's use comparison advertising?

Reality ✓

When Image Advertising Goes Bad

Ford Motor Company had a long running theme, "Quality Is Job One." Its image as a manufacturer of quality automobiles and trucks was enhanced with testimonials from Ford employees pledging their commitment to vehicle quality. Commitment carries a promise of truthfulness; Ford's quality statement promised safe vehicles. Consumers who trusted Ford's image as a supplier of quality automobiles became skeptical when some Ford automobiles unexpectedly caught on fire, causing trauma for owners. Not only did Ford have to investigate the cause of the fires, but it also had to do damage control and reduce financial losses by reassuring the public that the problem would be resolved. In other words, Ford had to reinforce its image as a company that was committed to quality. Ford quickly recalled the faulty vehicles and worked to polish its tarnished image. Today Ford remains one of the best-selling auto manufacturers in the U.S. market.

Martha Stewart Living Omnimedia is another company that suffered a tarnished image when Martha Stewart was found guilty of illegal insider stock trading. Martha Stewart Living produces magazines, television shows, and a collection of kitchen and home décor products. Stewart earned a reputation as a wholesome, domestic homemaker. This image resonated with her fans. The value of the company's stock dropped drastically after news of her indictment. Stewart spent five months in jail, while her image was attacked by the media. This business crisis illustrated the vital link between a company's image and its success. Some networks stopped airing Stewart's shows, and the number of advertisers in her magazines declined. After her release from jail, Stewart launched a highly publicized comeback. She was able to overcome the negative publicity and is more popular than ever today.

These two case studies illustrate an important point. If a company is going to build an image, it must be able to live up to it.

Think Critically

1. Why should a company take its image seriously when doing business?
2. Do you think a company has to change its advertising strategy when confronted with negative publicity that could tarnish its image? Why or why not?
3. How could companies like Ford and Martha Stewart Living use advertising to rebuild their images?

The Advertising Campaign Event provides an opportunity for you to demonstrate promotional skills necessary for advertising management personnel. (You may work with two partners to complete this event.) You should prepare an image advertising campaign of any length for a luxury automobile manufacturer and present the campaign to a prospective client/advertiser. You should also present an appropriate budget and select media. Follow the outline below in preparing the written document.

I. Executive Summary (one-page description of the campaign)
II. Descriptions
   A. Description of the product, service, company, or business selected
   B. Description of the client/advertiser
III. Objective(s) of the Campaign
IV. Identification of the Target Market
   A. Primary markets
   B. Secondary markets
V. List of Advertising Media Selection Necessary for the Campaign
VI. Budget (detailed projections of actual cost)
VII. Schedules of All Advertising Planned
VIII. Schedules of All Sales Promotion Activity(ies) Planned
IX. Statement of Benefits to the Client/Advertiser
X. Bibliography
XI. Appendix (optional)

Visual aids that are appropriate for an actual advertising campaign presentation may be used. You have 15 minutes to set up and present the advertising campaign to the judge (client). The judge has five minutes to ask questions about the presentation.

Performance Indicators Evaluated

- Clearly and accurately analyze the target market and consider the secondary target markets for the product(s) and/or service(s) selected.
- Stress product/service benefits that appeal to the target markets.
- Define the media selections in terms of reach, frequency, and continuity.
- Create a realistic budget that considers all costs that would be incurred for the campaign.

Go to the DECA website for more detailed information.

Think Critically

1. Why would a luxury automobile manufacturer use image advertising?
2. Are there specific times of the year when you think the advertising campaigns would be more effective? Explain your answer.
3. What are four advertising themes you will promote throughout the year for the automobile manufacturer? How will these themes resonate with the target market(s)?

www.deca.org

11

Consumer-Oriented Advertising and Sales Promotion

© gary718/Shutterstock.com

The Snapple Challenge

Snapple is a manufacturer of a wide variety of premium beverages. Even successful companies like Snapple look for ways to raise brand awareness. What better way to do that than to team up with one of the most popular network television shows—*The Celebrity Apprentice*. *The Celebrity Apprentice* is known for its challenges in which celebrities are given a marketing task related to a well-known brand. Snapple sponsored the largest and most extensive brand task in *Apprentice* history. Finalists Bret Michaels, lead singer for the rock band Poison, and Holly Robinson Peete, an actress, worked alongside the Snapple research and development team to develop a new Snapple tea, design the label, and name the product. In addition, they were asked to create a marketing plan that included a 30-second television commercial and a print advertisement promoting their new tea.

Bret, a lifelong Type 1 diabetic, developed Diet Snapple Trop-a-Rocka Tea to help raise money for the American Diabetes Association and its mission to prevent and cure diabetes. In honor of the HollyRod Foundation, Holly created Snapple Compassionberry Tea. The HollyRod Foundation helps families who have autistic children access affordable treatment and compassionate care.

© PRNewsFoto/Dr Pepper Snapple Group, Inc./AP Photo

Instead of choosing one winner, Snapple said, "You're hired," to both Bret and Holly. Both of their handcrafted, *Celebrity Apprentice*–inspired teas, which contained labels identifying the celebrity's chosen charity, were made available nationwide. In addition, Snapple supported both causes by giving the American Diabetes Association and the HollyRod Foundation $250,000 each.

Snapple's sponsorship of *The Celebrity Apprentice* challenge was an effective way to show its commitment to delivering unique flavors to Snapple customers. It resulted in two great-tasting new teas for consumers and garnered support for two very important causes, helping it build goodwill among consumers. Snapple and both of the charities could be declared "winners" because of the increased exposure they gained.

1. Why did Snapple sponsor *The Celebrity Apprentice*, considering it cost them $500,000 in donations?

2. How did Snapple benefit from its newly found relationship with the American Diabetes Association and the HollyRod Foundation?

3. How did celebrities enhance the Snapple brand in this case?

4. What should a company consider before choosing to be a sponsor?

WHAT DO YOU KNOW?

Consumer-Oriented Advertising

Goals
- Define consumer-oriented advertising and explain how it is used.
- Describe how sponsorships can be used to make a connection with consumers.

Terms
- consumer-oriented advertising, p. 296
- stereotype, p. 299
- sponsorship, p. 300

Chrysler Ads Help It Make a Comeback

When creating ads for products, companies must know the social backgrounds and values of their target markets to make a connection with them. Chrysler did just that in its "Imported from Detroit" ad campaign. The ads paid tribute to the country's industrial roots and the working-class Americans who helped build the U.S. auto industry. The commercials were set in Detroit, Michigan, which was once known as the world's car capital because of the many car manufacturers located there.

When the U.S. car industry fell on hard times, so did Detroit. Foreign car manufacturers made large gains in the U.S. market. Chrysler's "Imported from Detroit" commercials were a reminder of Detroit's (and Chrysler's) rise and fall and its determination to make a comeback. Chrysler pitched its brand as luxury for those who've earned it through hard work and determination. Chrysler's profits increased substantially shortly after the ad campaign was launched.

Work as a Team Why were Chrysler's advertisements so effective at making a connection with consumers? Why are consumers' values an important consideration when creating an ad campaign?

Advertising That Speaks to Consumers

Businesses that focus on consumer needs are rewarded with higher sales. The best strategy to gain a consumer's business is to show interest in their needs, design products based upon those needs, and develop promotional campaigns that are relevant to them. **Consumer-oriented advertising** is created from the customer's perspective to make the message more appropriate and significant for customers. When advertisements are designed with specific consumer needs in mind, consumers will feel connected with the brand and purchase more of the product. For example, the top priorities for teenagers are very different from the priorities of their parents and grandparents. Consumer-oriented advertising makes the necessary adjustments to meet the needs of its target market. The extra time spent on research to determine consumer needs is well worth the effort.

Consumer-Oriented Advertising Approaches

Consumer-oriented advertising uses many approaches to deliver a message, as described below. Oftentimes, these approaches include emotional or rational appeals because they are effective at making a connection with customers.

The Human Element Many of today's advertisements are based on emotional connections. Advertisers hope to trigger emotional feelings so that consumers become emotionally attached to a product or identify with the brand. These advertisements typically focus on human relationships, such as the bond between a father and son as they share Oreo® cookies. However, there is a growing trend to use emotionally based advertisements when promoting business relationships. Bank advertisements focus on relationships with consumers by showing how the bank cares about and nurtures its customers.

How is your baby's skin different?

It loses moisture nearly 2X faster than yours. Use JOHNSON'S® Baby Lotion 2X a day to replenish the moisture she needs. Dermatologist-tested and the #1 choice of hospitals, it's gentle enough to use both morning and night.

The Voice of the Youth The voice of the youth is increasingly being portrayed in advertisements. The ads focus attention on such things as the environment, anti-drug campaigns, and youth leadership roles. TruGreen, a lawn and landscape services company, chose a tween spokesman, Bobby Sinclair, who represents a young entrepreneur with a successful lawn business. Verizon Wireless used Susie, a young girl with a lemonade stand, to show how its high-tech services could help all business owners take their company to the next level. Both commercials represent the youthfulness of entrepreneurship and resonate well with adults. Brands such as these look upon youths as the next generation of consumers and hope to build brand awareness and loyalty among them now.

What advertising approach is Johnson & Johnson using in this advertisement?

Health Awareness Health has become a primary focus for today's consumer. Current lifestyles and schedules leave little time for exercise or participation in sports. Instead, today's consumers are turning to health food products, diets, and supplements for healthier lifestyles. Product advertisements are focusing on health benefits to attract customers. Food products promote "whole-grain goodness." Celebrities like Jennifer Hudson are featured in advertisements showing the amazing results of weight loss programs like Weight Watchers. Advertisements for prescription medications promise many health benefits. As a result of these ads, consumers now request the advertised medications by name when they visit their doctor.

© NicolasMcComber/Shutterstock.com

Why are advertisers using "common" consumers to sell their products?

The Common Consumer Consumers are slowly becoming disillusioned with the perfect consumer who is the perfect size and has the perfect face as well as the perfect family living in the perfect house. Consumer-oriented ads are now featuring the "common" consumer, or someone who is easier to identify with and more believable. Dove launched the successful "Campaign for Real Beauty," which featured real women, not models, promoting Dove's beauty products. By challenging the stereotypical view of beauty, Dove's ads made a big impact on consumers. The common consumer is also frequently featured in ads for household products, such as laundry detergents.

Social Media Today, harnessing the interactive nature of the Internet allows advertisers to create advertising that motivates the consumer to take some kind of action. Using social media sites allows the advertiser to involve the consumer in the marketing process. Doing so often leads to a sale. For example, Frito-Lay® used its website to advertise its chips made with all natural ingredients. To entice website visitors, Frito-Lay asked them to vote in the "Ruffles Next Flavor Fever" promotion to choose from among 16 new flavors. Those consumers who voted are more likely to try the new flavor.

High-Involvement Purchases When consumers make purchases involving large amounts of money, they do not take the decision lightly. They have a higher level of involvement in the purchase, meaning they spend more time and effort before making a buying decision. When buying a television, car, or vacation, consumers actively seek out information, talk with friends, and find out all they can about the prospective purchase. Advertising is a relatively weak influence for high-involvement purchases. Word-of-mouth advertising, consumers' previous experience, and expert recommendations have a bigger influence.

Although advertising in and of itself is not the deciding factor in a high-involvement purchase, it helps consumers decide upon the product characteristics they will consider when comparing competing products. For example, there are hundreds of makes and models of cars, but we consider only those that make our short list. Advertising helps determine which cars make the consumer's short list. To ensure they are on this short list, businesses must know which product features are most important to their target markets and promote those in their advertising. Consumer-oriented advertising that emphasizes relevant benefits will be more meaningful and make a bigger impression on consumers.

Challenges for Consumer-Oriented Advertising

Constantly changing consumer values and attitudes present a major challenge for consumer-oriented advertising. Economic, political, and social factors affect consumer attitudes and their buying behaviors. Uncertain economic conditions make many consumers evaluate the necessity of a purchase. Advertisers may promote a luxury car's performance and low lease price of $499 a month because these attributes were identified as being important to the target market. However, these attributes are not attractive when consumers are concerned about losing their job during a recession.

The political climate can make consumers more skeptical about spending. Increased taxes leave consumers with less income to spend on products and services. Social causes that are important to consumers can also influence their spending. A company's affiliations with certain organizations or support for certain causes may motivate a consumer to buy (or not buy) from that company. Even when advertisers carefully analyze target market needs to develop relevant advertising, they cannot always control factors such as these.

Stereotyping is another risk related to consumer-oriented advertising. A **stereotype** is a generalization about the "typical" characteristics of a specific group of individuals. Stereotyping could occur when advertisers try to categorize the target market. Not all middle-class consumers are part of a family of four, and not all wealthy consumers are college graduates. To categorize a group of people solely based on their level of income or education, gender, geographic location, or some other characteristic is a risky strategy. Consumers living in the same small community have different values and attitudes. Consumer-oriented advertising does not have a one-size-fits-all strategy for target markets.

CHECKPOINT

What is consumer-oriented advertising?

Public Relations and Sponsorships

Public relations is another effective way to reach out to consumers. The main goal of a public relations campaign is to enhance a company's reputation. However, more companies are using it as a way to work their brand into the everyday conversations of target consumers. Today's business world is extremely competitive. Companies need to have an edge that makes them stand out from the crowd, something that makes them more appealing and interesting to the public. A sponsorship can be a powerful promotional device that enables companies to make a connection with consumers. A **sponsorship** is a company's support of an issue, cause, or event that is consistent with company objectives. Sponsorships may involve supporting community events, national events, or nonprofit organizations and charities. Well-planned sponsorships can demonstrate brand values, increase visibility, and boost goodwill. On the other hand, poorly thought-out sponsorships can alienate customers, so companies must approach sponsorships cautiously.

What are the benefits to a company, such as Allstate, that sponsors a local baseball team?

There are many factors that a company should consider before becoming a sponsor. Different forms of sponsorship say different things about an organization. Companies must determine if they want their sponsorship to have an international, national, regional, and/or local impact. Sponsorship of charities demonstrates humanity and responsibility. Sponsorship of sports will boost the company's profile. Cultural sponsorship may help the company reach a niche market. Sponsorship of education or research shows the company is a forward-thinking organization. To ensure a successful sponsorship, certain steps should be taken.

1. *Define short-term and long-term objectives for the sponsorship.* A short-term objective might include sponsoring a single event to reinforce the company's image and generate interest among potential customers. A long-term objective could be to build a positive association through a continuous sponsorship that would result in brand loyalty.

2. *Align the sponsorship with the company's and target market's values.* Companies want to choose a sponsorship that is consistent with other corporate, consumer, and community communications.

Mixed messages can be damaging. Companies should also conduct research to find out what matters to its customers (outside the company) and look for opportunities to get involved.

3. *Budget the company's time and money effectively.* Work out a realistic financial agreement between the company and the organization being sponsored. The costs of entertaining, promotional products, and publicity should be considered. If company funds are limited, sharing the company's expertise or donating its products and services can be just as valuable as cash.

4. *Promote the sponsorship.* Companies should advertise their involvement with the event or cause. They should take advantage of opportunities to associate their brand with the sponsored activities in all promotions.

▚▚▚▚ CHECKPOINT ▚▚▚▚

How can sponsorships be used by businesses to make a connection with their target markets?

11.1 Assessment

THINK ABOUT IT

1. Why do advertisers often apply a human element to their advertising?
2. Why is social media an effective outlet for consumer-oriented advertising?
3. What factors should be addressed to help ensure a sponsorship is successful?

MAKE ACADEMIC CONNECTIONS

4. **MARKETING**   Describe an advertisement that attempts to reach consumers using one of the approaches discussed on pp. 297–299. Do you think the advertising approach worked well for the advertised product or service? Explain why or why not.

5. **PROBLEM SOLVING**   Working with a partner, develop a TV advertisement presented from a youth's perspective for one of the following products/services: automobile, hotel, or laundry detergent. Write the script for the ad and present it in class. If possible, use props to add interest to the presentation.

 ### Teamwork

Choose a local company and develop a sponsorship plan for it. Decide if the sponsorship will be for a community event, issue, or cause. Will the sponsorship be short-term or long-term? How does the sponsorship align with the company's target market? Will the company provide financial support or other kinds of support? How will the sponsorship be promoted? Prepare a PowerPoint presentation that addresses all of these issues and describes the sponsorship plan.

FOCUS ON ADVERTISING

Goals

- Explain the purpose of consumer-oriented sales promotions.
- Describe how direct marketing is used to reach consumers.

Terms

- consumer-oriented sales promotions, p. 302
- tie-in promotion, p. 304
- marketing database, p. 306
- RFM analysis, p. 306
- cross-selling, p. 307
- direct retailing, p. 307

Online Sweepstakes Attract New Customers

Sweepstakes are a popular form of promotion because they generate enthusiasm and have great publicity potential. The rise in the use of the Internet has made online sweepstakes especially popular. The positive

impact of a well-executed online sweepstakes can extend far beyond temporary publicity if the sponsoring company has long-term customer relationships in mind. Through the registration process, companies can gain valuable customer information that can be used for future communications and promotions. By choosing the sweepstakes prizes carefully, the sponsoring company can attract new customers. In "The Costco 12 Days of Giveaways Sweepstakes," prizes were chosen to showcase popular holiday gift items that people could purchase at Costco. After entering the sweepstakes, registrants were directed to a sales page featuring discount deals on those same items as well as many other products. This gave customers who were thinking about buying these specific products a reason to buy them from Costco.

Work as a Team What types of information might a company collect about customers during the sweepstakes registration process? How could this information be used for future promotions?

Sales Promotions and the Customer

Consumer-oriented sales promotions include a variety of incentives designed to encourage customers to buy a specific brand. The most popular consumer sales promotions are directly associated with product purchasing. These promotions enhance the value of a product purchase by either reducing the overall cost of the product or by adding more benefit or quantity for the regular purchase price. Tying a promotion to an immediate purchase is a popular form of sales promotion. Common consumer-oriented sales promotions include the following:

- Coupons – certificates that entitle the buyer to a price reduction on a product or service
- Rebates – refunds of money offered to consumers who purchase specific products
- Price deals – discounts, consisting of percentage markdowns, and bonus packs, consisting of larger-size products offered at the same price as standard-size products
- Loyalty marketing programs – frequent-buyer programs that reward repeat customers with special deals and prices
- Sampling and free trial offers – products that are given to consumers on a risk-free trial basis
- Premiums – items offered to consumers for free or at a reduced price with the purchase of another item
- Contests and sweepstakes – competitive games that give consumers the opportunity to win prizes
- Point-of-purchase (POP) displays – special racks, display cartons, banners, signs, and product dispensers set up at retailers to promote a particular brand and encourage impulse buying

Why are POP displays commonly used to promote products?

Consumer-Oriented Sales Promotion Objectives

Sales promotions are often used to produce a short-term increase in sales. However, sales promotions can also be used to achieve other objectives such as creating brand awareness or building brand loyalty.

Purchase-Building Sales Promotions Incentives such as coupons, rebates, price discounts, and premiums create an immediate demand for a product or service. *Purchase-building sales promotions* are designed to create short-term increases in sales. These types of promotions have three common characteristics.

- They generally involve price.
- They require minimal effort on the part of consumers.
- They are offered for a limited time only.

Purchase-building sales promotions are used to influence and speed up the consumer's buying decision. Consumers may make a purchase based solely on a sales promotion offer. For example, a

© Lisa F. Young/Shutterstock.com

consumer who is thinking about purchasing a laptop computer sometime in the future may expedite the purchase because of a discount or rebate being offered. Another consumer may decide to purchase one manufacturer's laptop instead of another's because of a special promotion. A contest or sweepstakes sponsored by the laptop manufacturer may also entice consumers to make a purchase.

Brand-Building Sales Promotions In order to survive a highly competitive marketplace, companies must create a brand preference among consumers that leads to long-lasting relationships. *Brand-building sales promotions* help build long-term brand loyalty and brand value among consumers. These types of promotions help strengthen the bond between the brand and the consumer. Common characteristics of brand-building sales promotions include the following:

- They are less frequently related to price.
- They offer promotional rewards for repeat purchases.
- They are valid for an extended period of time.

Companies use brand-building sales promotions to gain new customers and retain current ones. Sampling and free trial offers help attract new customers who may eventually become repeat customers. Loyalty marketing programs help retain customers by rewarding those who make repeat purchases of certain products. Premiums imprinted with the brand's name and logo act as a reminder and, thus, a brand builder. Carefully selected premiums that reinforce the image of a brand are also effective. For example, a hair salon that offers a free manicure with the purchase of a haircut is reinforcing the salon's image of self-indulgence. Contests and sweepstakes that have a close tie-in to the brand's image can also have the same reinforcing effect. The Pillsbury Bake-Off® contest requires contestants to create a new recipe using Pillsbury ingredients for a chance to win $1 million. This contest, which has been sponsored by Pillsbury for over 60 years, has created strong brand awareness and loyalty.

Tie-In Promotions

A growing number of companies are developing tie-in promotions. A **tie-in promotion** is a joint promotion of two or more products or services. The intention of this type of promotion is to increase brand awareness and sales of both products. The tie-in may involve brands from the same company or from different companies. Tie-in promotions are more effective when there is a logical connection between the brands. In a tie-in promotion offered by Apple and PepsiCo, customers with winning Pepsi bottle caps could redeem them for free songs from the iTunes Store. Pepsi has a long history of incorporating music into its marketing campaigns to promote its youthful image, making the Pepsi iTunes promotion a logical one. Tie-in promotions are cost-effective because the cost is shared among multiple brands. They also give companies a broader market presence, enabling them to reach out to new customers.

Consumer Benefits

Consumer-oriented sales promotions are popular with consumers because of the many benefits and rewards they provide. Sales promotions allow consumers to

- save money through the use of coupons, rebates, and price deals
- reduce the time spent making buying decisions by stopping the search process to take advantage of a promotional offer
- buy higher-quality products for lower prices
- try a product they otherwise would not have tried
- be entertained by contests and sweepstakes

The rewards received from sales promotions can be immediate or delayed. An immediate reward delivers a benefit as soon as the consumer takes the desired action. For example, saving money by using a coupon offers an immediate reward. A delayed reward may occur days, weeks, or even longer after the consumer takes action. Consumers may have to wait six to eight weeks for a mail-in rebate. Consumers respond better to immediate rewards.

CHECKPOINT

Why do businesses use consumer-oriented sales promotions?

© Monkey Business Images/Shutterstock.com

What are some ways consumers can benefit from an auto manufacturer's sales promotion?

Direct Marketing

Direct marketing involves techniques used to get consumers to make a purchase in a nonretail setting, such as the consumer's home or office. It is frequently used for consumer-oriented promotions. Promotional messages may be delivered through direct mail, catalogs, telemarketing, e-mails, and infomercials. Frequently, companies will obtain mailing lists or create marketing databases with names and addresses of target customers. Direct marketing campaigns can be personalized for each recipient. For example, a heating and air conditioning company may make a direct appeal to a consumer by sending out a promotional letter containing the recipient's name. This personal appeal raises the consumer's level of interest. Direct marketing can help a company achieve the following promotional objectives:

- Generate new business leads and sales
- Increase sales from existing customers
- Re-establish relationships with former customers
- Increase customer loyalty

Direct marketing often works best with a niche market. By focusing on a niche market, or a market with specific interests, it is easier to develop a promotional message that appeals to them.

Marketing Databases

A **marketing database** is a collection of names, addresses, and behavioral information gathered from individual customers. Behavioral information could include customer characteristics, past purchases, and brand preferences. Companies may build their own database or use database services provided by marketing research companies. A marketing database is a valuable tool for direct marketing. It allows companies to connect with customers using personalized offers that are timely and relevant. For example, a customer's date of birth is commonly collected and stored in marketing databases. Using this information, a company can send out personalized birthday cards containing special offers to its customers.

A marketing database enables companies to perform various analyses. The **RFM analysis** calculates the value of each customer based on *r*ecency, *f*requency, and *m*onetary factors. It measures how recently and how often a specific customer is buying from a business and how much money the customer

© Kasiutek/Shutterstock.com

How can a marketing database be used by a company to build customer loyalty?

is spending each time. The best customers can be identified and rewarded with special offers to help build customer loyalty. Another use for marketing databases is **cross-selling**, which is a direct marketing program aimed at customers who already purchase other products from the company. For example, a food manufacturer may identify customers that already purchase its cereal and send them special offers to entice them to try its breakfast bars.

Other Types of Direct Marketing

Direct retailing is the process of selling products through representatives who work door-to-door or at home sales parties. Companies that use this approach include Avon, The Pampered Chef, and Longaberger Baskets. Sales representatives may demonstrate products and explain special promotions in person at after-work parties. They may also deliver product catalogs so that customers can place orders by phone. Many sales representatives are now setting up websites where customers can view products and special promotions online as well as place orders.

SPOTLIGHT ON SUCCESS

© Horst Ossinger/epa/Corbis

GEORGE FOREMAN

Lean, Mean, Fat-Reducing Grilling Machine

Once the heavyweight-boxing champion of the world, George Foreman is now the champion of infomercial endorsements. After hanging up his gloves, he became a spokesperson in 1994 for an indoor grill made by Salton. The company had promoted the grill at industry trade shows with little interest, but when Foreman signed on to do infomercials, worldwide sales skyrocketed to $375 million. Foreman was signed to a five-year deal worth $137.5 million, one of the biggest endorsement deals in history for an athlete.

The link between the boxer and the grill came about soon after George Foreman's remarkable comeback in boxing when in 1994 at the age of 45 he regained the heavyweight world championship title. Foreman attributed his success at the time to his healthy lifestyle and his healthy eating habits, which made him a perfect spokesperson for the grill. The grill simultaneously cooks both the top and bottom surfaces of food on an indented, angled surface that allows fat and grease to drain.

The "Lean, Mean, Fat-Reducing Grilling Machine," as it became known, was promoted heavily in infomercials by George Foreman as a way to "knock out the fat." The combination of Foreman's likable personality and the unique features of the grill made it a big success. Building on this success, George Foreman and Salton designed a string of other Foreman-endorsed products. In 2007, Applica Consumer Products, Inc., acquired Salton and with it, the George Foreman® brand.

The success of the George Foreman Grill spawned a variety of similar celebrity-endorsed products like the Evander Holyfield Real Deal Grill, the Carl Lewis Health Grill, and the Jackie Chan Grill, which targets Asians. However, none of the competitors were able to replicate the success of the original George Foreman Grill. The George Foreman Grill is a quality product that lives up to advertised claims, but this is not the sole reason for its success. It can be contributed largely to George Foreman himself, who consumers find greatly appealing.

Think Critically

Initially, a heavyweight boxer may seem like an odd choice as an endorser for a grill. Why do you think Foreman's endorsement has proven to be so valuable? Choose a product and select a famous celebrity who you think would make a good spokesperson for it. What makes the product and celebrity a good match?

Television shopping networks are another way to reach customers at home. Well-known shopping channels such as the Home Shopping Network (HSN) and QVC show products to home viewers, who can place orders directly on a toll-free line. Customers tune in to watch shopping segments targeted to audiences with specific interests, such as cooking, fashion, electronics, and many others.

CHECKPOINT

Why is direct marketing an effective strategy for consumer-oriented promotions?

11.2 Assessment

THINK ABOUT IT

1. How can a promotion be tied to the immediate purchase of a product? Provide two examples.
2. What is the difference between purchase-building sales promotions and brand-building sales promotions?
3. Why is a marketing database a valuable tool for a business that uses direct marketing?

MAKE ACADEMIC CONNECTIONS

4. **MARKETING**   You own Wash-n-Go, a successful car wash business that offers top-notch services. You want to begin a customer loyalty program to reward your best customers. Develop a customer loyalty program and create a flyer that describes the details of the program to your customers.
5. **PROBLEM SOLVING**   As the marketer for Sweets and Treats Bakery, you've been asked to create a sales promotion that will increase sales and create brand preference among customers. Describe one purchase-building sales promotion and one brand-building sales promotion for the bakery.
6. **TECHNOLOGY**   Use a spreadsheet to create a marketing database for either the car wash business or bakery described above. Create the fields for each type of data you believe the business should collect about its customers. Then explain how one or more types of data collected could be used in a sales promotion for the business.

Teamwork

As the marketers for Kellogg's cereal, your team has been asked to create a tie-in promotion involving a brand produced by another company. Select the other company to partner with and explain why it is a good match-up for Kellogg's. Present the tie-in promotion to the class and explain how each company/brand will benefit.

Branding and Positioning

Goals

- Explain why branding is important to the success of a business.
- Describe product positioning strategies.

Terms

- branding, p. 309
- brand equity, p. 310
- brand awareness, p. 310
- brand loyalty, p. 311
- brand image, p. 311
- generic brand, p. 311
- positioning, p. 312

FOCUS ON ADVERTISING

Genericizing Brand Names

Some product brands have become so popular that consumers use the brand name when referring to every product of that type regardless of who manufactures it. When this happens, the brand name becomes generic. Although a brand name may be trademarked, it doesn't stop consumers from referencing a brand name when talking about a product in general. Although this type of brand recognition is desirable, the trademark could be at risk if it becomes generic. Examples of brand names that have become generic include the following:

- Kleenex® – Many people refer to a basic facial tissue as a Kleenex.
- Xerox® – The terms "copy" and "Xerox" are used interchangeably.
- Rollerblade® – All inline skates are commonly referred to as Rollerblades.
- Band-Aid® – An adhesive bandage came to be known as a Band-Aid.
- ChapStick® – Many people ask for ChapStick instead of lip balm.

Work as a Team Brainstorm to identify other brand names that have become generic for a common product or service. What are the advantages and disadvantages for a brand that achieves this status?

© Diana Rich/Shutterstock.com

The Branding Process

A *brand* is the combination of unique qualities of a company, product, or product line. **Branding** is a marketing strategy used to build brand recognition. Successful branding makes a brand easily identifiable with a product or service. For example, when you hear the brand name

How does branding affect the consumer decision-making process?

Nike, you probably think of gym shoes. The mere mention of Ben & Jerry's likely creates images of unique premium ice cream flavors. There are several benefits of branding for companies.

- It builds name recognition, which helps a consumer distinguish between competing brands.
- It makes purchasing decisions easier because consumers are able to identify products with which they are satisfied and want to buy again, leading to repeat sales.
- It communicates a strong, consistent message about the product.
- It creates trust and an emotional attachment to the brand, which helps overcome the competition.
- It increases the sales of new products introduced under the already popular brand name (brand extensions).
- It allows companies with strong brands to charge higher prices.

Brand Equity

An important objective of any branding strategy is to build and enhance brand equity. **Brand equity** is the value that a company realizes from having a product with a recognizable name. It is built on brand recognition, perceived quality and reliability, longevity, brand loyalty, and often, memorable advertising campaigns. Brand equity can be positive or negative. The Applebee's® neighborhood brand is known for being a family-friendly restaurant that offers good food at reasonable prices. These attributes have a positive impact on Applebee's business. A negative brand equity occurs when a company's brand earns a bad reputation. After the Gulf Oil Spill in 2011, BP had a negative brand equity, which affected its business. Consumers temporarily boycotted BP stations.

Building brand equity requires a significant effort. To ensure that consumers are familiar with a brand and have positive associations with it, companies must focus on creating brand awareness and a brand image. This can be done with advertising, sales promotions, sponsorships, and other forms of promotion. A continuous promotional campaign is needed to enhance brand equity.

Brand Awareness The extent to which a brand is recognized and associated with a specific product or service is known as **brand awareness**. It does not mean that people prefer the brand—only that they can identify it. Reaching high levels of brand awareness is the goal of every company. A high level of brand awareness occurs when

The Progression of Brand Awareness

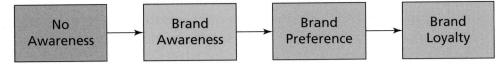

a consumer not only recognizes the brand but also understands the distinct qualities that make the brand different or better than the competition. Companies strive to move customers from brand awareness to brand preference and, finally, to brand loyalty. **Brand loyalty** is the consumer's commitment to purchase one brand over all other brands.

Today, in addition to advertising and other promotional techniques, many companies use viral branding as a way to increase brand awareness. *Viral branding* attempts to reach target customers by creating a "buzz" about a brand through online word-of-mouth advertising. Social media sites are used by consumers to spread the word about a product or service. Consumers often are more responsive to a brand suggested by other consumers.

Brand Image Consumers' buying decisions are often influenced by brand image. **Brand image** is the consumer's impression of a brand. It consists of the thoughts and feelings associated with a brand. These associations are created through the consumer's experience and observations. The product's quality, ease of use, functionality, price, prestige, and overall value affect brand image. However, a brand image is also based on emotional connections. For example, a consumer may have a positive image of the Starbucks' brand because of its reputation for great-tasting coffee but more importantly because of the "coffee experience" provided by the atmosphere and environment at the Starbucks' stores. Linking a product's image to emotions is known as *emotional branding*. The idea behind a brand image is that the consumer is purchasing not only the product but also the image associated with that product.

Some companies try to create a personality for their brand. They may present their brands as being wholesome and down-to-earth (Nature Valley) or daring and exciting (Harley-Davidson). Many jewelers and luxury automobile manufacturers, such as Rolex and Cadillac, try to make their products seem sophisticated. Brands like Lands End are thought of as rugged and outdoorsy. A brand's personality is conveyed in the company's advertising.

Generic Brands

A **generic brand** is a no-name product that competes with brand-name products. Generic brands are also called *private brands* or *store brands*. They are manufactured by less-prominent companies and sold by a store as its own brand. Consumers frequently choose generic pharmaceutical brands over the highly recognized, heavily advertised brand-name pharmaceuticals. There are also a number of generic

or store-brand supermarket goods, such as cereal and snack foods. The generic and store brands usually contain the same ingredients as brand-name products. Even retailers offer private brands or store brands as part of their clothing lines. Generic brands can be sold at a lower price because less money is spent on advertising and packaging. Many shoppers feel that generic brands are as good as brand-name products. Consumers' high acceptance of generic brands makes it even more important for companies with brand-name products to build brand loyalty among consumers.

▰▰▰▰▰ CHECKPOINT ◣◣◣◣◣

Why is branding an important process for a business?

Product Positioning Strategies

What happens when every company in the same industry says the same thing about its products? Customers don't know how to tell the difference between one product and another, so they are likely to make their decision based on price. When this occurs, the customer may not get the product that best fits his or her needs, and companies fail to maximize sales. While there is a segment of the market that is best served by low prices, this is not always the most effective way to attract customers.

Positioning is the process of creating a unique image or identity for a brand to distinguish it from competing brands. Successful companies communicate clearly, specifically, and thoroughly how they are different and how that difference makes an impact on the customer's life. Positioning is closely related to market segmentation because it focuses on the relevant wants and needs of the brand's target market(s). The ultimate goal of positioning for any company is to encourage consumers to choose its brand over competing brands. To accomplish this goal, companies use advertising and other promotional techniques to communicate the brand's image. There are various product positioning strategies used by companies.

Benefit Positioning

The most common positioning strategy is benefit positioning, which involves selecting one or more attributes (features) or benefits that are important to consumers and are the basis for making purchasing decisions. Coca-Cola Zero® uses benefit positioning to emphasize its full flavor with zero calories—two attributes that appeal to health-conscious consumers. Attributes and benefits are closely related to consumer needs. Positioning attempts to show consumers how a brand's attributes or benefits are capable of solving the consumers' problems. Benefit positioning may also tap into how a product makes consumers feel. For example, although Campbell soups may taste good, another benefit is promoted in its advertisements—the caring, nurturing relationship between a mother and her children, who are eating the soup.

A unique use of benefit positioning occurs when two companies bundle complementary products to create an "irresistible" package when compared to competitors' offerings. For example, McDonald's advertising may promote the Coca-Cola drinks it serves in its restaurants. This is appealing to those who eat at fast food restaurants and prefer Coca-Cola products.

Usage or Application Positioning

A brand may be positioned based on how it is used. Advertising attempts to communicate unique uses or applications for a product. For example, Tide to Go® is promoted as a portable stain remover that instantly removes food and drink stains from clothing. The fact that Tide to Go is portable and can be used when the stain occurs makes it unique and provides value to consumers.

User Positioning

User positioning associates a product with a group of consumers and their lifestyle. Advertising is used to present an image of the typical user of the brand. Stouffer's® promotes its frozen meals as a quick way for a busy family to enjoy a delicious meal. Jif® promotes its peanut butter as the one "choosy moms choose." User positioning often involves celebrity or athlete endorsements that project a desired image of those who use the product.

Price and Quality Positioning

Companies may use price or quality characteristics to position their brands. Price positioning emphasizes low or competitive prices. Advertising messages indicate that consumers are getting more value for their money. Retailers like Walmart and Family Dollar use price positioning. On the other hand, some companies promote a high-quality image that emphasizes the importance of quality over price. Advertising for the renowned jeweler Tiffany & Co. promotes the quality and craftsmanship of its diamonds and jewelry designs.

© dwphotos/Shutterstock.com

What is the advantage of using price positioning?

Competitor Positioning

Competitor positioning focuses on the differences between a company's product and well-known competing products. Auto manufacturers often compare their automobiles to competing automobiles that hold a strong market share. Ford's "Swap My Ride" advertising campaign gave Honda and Toyota car owners the opportunity to exchange their foreign-made car and drive a new Ford for one week. The ad campaign was very effective at changing consumers' perception about Ford's quality, safety, and innovation. As a result of the ad campaign, 30 percent of consumers polled indicated they intended to visit a Ford dealer before buying a car.

Repositioning

Products that were once successful may need to be repositioned due to changes in the marketplace. *Repositioning* involves changing consumers' perceptions about a brand. New competitors may enter the market and consumers' preferences and attitudes may change. Repositioning helps breathe new life into an old brand, making it more appealing to more consumers. BMW repositioned its brand by targeting the consumers' emotions. Advertisements that previously promoted BMW's engineering and performance began focusing on the driving experience. The advertising tagline changed from "The Ultimate Driving Machine" to "Sheer Driving Pleasure." BMW repositioned itself as a company that not only makes cars but also creates joy.

///////// CHECKPOINT \\\\\\\\\\

Why is product positioning important to the success of a company?

11.3 Assessment

THINK ABOUT IT

1. What is brand equity and why is it so valuable to a company?
2. How are a consumer's buying decisions influenced by brand image?
3. What is the most common positioning strategy and how is it used?

MAKE ACADEMIC CONNECTIONS

4. **HISTORY** Conduct research to learn about two companies throughout history that have had negative brand equity at some point in time. Prepare a PowerPoint presentation that explains what caused the negative brand equity and how the companies responded to it. Were they able to rebuild their brand equity?

5. **TECHNOLOGY** Describe an online viral branding campaign designed to increase the buzz about a product or service. Explain how it got started. Was it started by the company or by consumers? Was the campaign effective? Explain why or why not.

6. **RESEARCH** Conduct research to find an example of a company that uses benefit positioning by bundling its product with a complementary product from another company. Prepare a one-page report that describes the complementary relationship and explain why it is beneficial to both of the companies as well as consumers.

Teamwork

You and your team members work for an advertising agency. Select a positioning strategy for one of the following products: pizza, smartphone, bank, skateboards, or laundry detergent. Create a print advertisement that clearly communicates the product's position in the marketplace. Present the advertisement in class and explain how the positioning strategy chosen will promote the product's image.

Sharpen Your
21st CENTURY SKILLS

PARTNERSHIP FOR
21ST CENTURY SKILLS

Creating Your Personal Brand

In today's competitive workplace, it is important that you stand out from the crowd. One way to do this is to build your personal brand. Much like your favorite brands, such as Nike or Apple, your personal brand is the product you offer, which is composed of your expertise, personal style, personality, and public actions.

Nike brands itself as an expert in creating quality, fashionable sportswear. Imagination, design, and innovation are Apple's areas of expertise. Your personal brand must communicate your expertise. Maybe you want your brand to reflect your strong communication skills, leadership skills, or other quality. If you don't have much experience at something, then your personal brand may be defined by your passion, or an area in which you want to become an expert. To create your personal brand, identify the qualities that make you unique and that might be valued by an employer. Ask yourself the following questions:

- What are my strengths?
- What am I passionate about?
- What would I really like to accomplish in life?
- What contributions can I make?
- What does success mean to me?
- How would I like to be remembered?

Your style is also part of your personal brand. Your style is not so much about what you communicate about yourself, but how you do it. Style has a lot to do with your personality. You must determine if you are kind, witty, enthusiastic, positive, cutting edge, or a combination of characteristics. Get input from family members, friends, and others close to you. It's always a good idea to check with someone you know to make sure your idea of yourself matches what others think. Your personal brand is built from the thoughts, words, and reactions of other people. It's shaped by how you present yourself publicly. You can decide how you would like people to see you, and then work on publicly being that image.

After you have defined your personal brand, it is helpful to put it in writing by creating a personal brand statement. It should be one or two sentences that describe what you are best at (what value you provide) and how you do it uniquely. An example statement could be as follows: "I am a passionate, people-oriented leader who directs and motivates others to achieve goals."

Try It Out

Create your personal brand by answering the questions above. Then write a personal brand statement. Share your personal brand statement with others and get their reactions. Do they have the same image of you?

SUMMARY

11.1 Consumer-Oriented Advertising

- Consumer-oriented advertising is created from the customer's perspective to make the message more appropriate and significant for customers.
- Consumer-oriented advertising uses many approaches, including adding a human element, using the voice of youth, focusing on health awareness, featuring the "common" consumer, and providing product information for high-involvement purchases. Social media is often used to deliver these messages.
- Many companies are sponsoring issues, causes, or events as a way to make a connection with consumers. Sponsorships can demonstrate brand values, increase visibility, and boost goodwill.

11.2 Consumer-Oriented Sales Promotions

- Consumer-oriented sales promotions include a variety of incentives designed to encourage customers to buy a specific brand. They include coupons, rebates, price deals, loyalty marketing programs, sampling, premiums, contests and sweepstakes, and POP displays.
- There are two basic types of consumer-oriented sales promotions. Purchase-building sales promotions are designed to create short-term increases in sales. Brand-building sales promotions help build long-term brand loyalty and brand value among consumers.
- Consumer-oriented direct marketing campaigns use mailing lists or marketing databases to offer personalized promotions to consumers.

11.3 Branding and Positioning

- Branding builds name recognition; makes purchasing decisions easier; communicates a strong, consistent message about a product; creates trust and an emotional attachment to the brand; increases sales of new products introduced under an already existing brand name; and allows companies with strong brands to charge higher prices.
- Brand equity is the value that a company realizes from having a product with a recognizable name. Brand equity is built on brand awareness and brand image.
- Positioning enables companies to communicate how they are different from competitors. Positioning may be based on product benefits, product usage, product users, price and quality, and competitor differences.

WHAT DO YOU KNOW? *Now*

Read *Impact Advertising* on page 295 again to review an example of a sponsorship. Conduct research to learn about companies other than Snapple that have sponsored *The Celebrity Apprentice* challenges. Describe how the companies' brands benefited from these sponsorships.

Vocabulary Builder

Match each statement with the term that best defines it. Some terms may not be used.

1. The process of creating a unique image or identity for a brand
2. The consumer's commitment to purchase one brand over all other brands
3. A direct marketing program aimed at customers who already purchase other products from the company
4. A collection of names, addresses, and behavioral information gathered from individual consumers
5. A joint promotion of two or more products or services
6. A marketing strategy used to build brand recognition
7. A company's support of an issue, cause, or event that is consistent with company objectives
8. The consumers' impression of a brand
9. A generalization about the "typical" characteristics of a specific group of individuals
10. The extent to which a brand is recognized and associated with a specific product or service

a. brand awareness
b. brand equity
c. brand image
d. brand loyalty
e. branding
f. consumer-oriented advertising
g. consumer-oriented sales promotions
h. cross-selling
i. direct retailing
j. generic brand
k. marketing database
l. positioning
m. RFM analysis
n. sponsorship
o. stereotype
p. tie-in promotion

Test Your Knowledge

11. Social media websites are a popular way to deliver consumer-oriented advertising messages because
    a. they are interactive
    b. advertisers can involve consumers in the advertising process
    c. consumers who interact with advertisers online are more likely to try a product
    d. all of the above
12. Which of the following is *not* true about sponsorships?
    a. sponsorships may involve local events or national events
    b. any type of sponsorship will be looked on favorably by consumers
    c. sponsorships can help companies stand out from competitors
    d. companies should align sponsorships with the target market's values

13. A _____ is a sales promotion that refunds money to consumers.
    a. rebate
    b. coupon
    c. premium
    d. contest
14. Challenges for consumer-oriented advertising include all of the following *except*
    a. consumers' values and attitudes are ever-changing
    b. social media makes the advertising process more difficult
    c. economic, political, and social factors influence buying behaviors
    d. advertisers risk stereotyping when categorizing a target market
15. Brand-building sales promotions
    a. are frequently related to price
    b. are offered for a limited time only
    c. offer promotional rewards for repeat purchases
    d. require minimal effort on the part of consumers
16. Consumer-oriented sales promotions enable consumers to
    a. buy higher-quality products for lower prices
    b. save money through the use of coupons, rebates, and price deals
    c. try a product they otherwise would not have tried
    d. all of the above
17. The RFM analysis measures all of the following consumer buying behavior patterns *except*
    a. reaction
    b. frequency
    c. recency
    d. monetary
18. _____ branding is used to raise brand awareness by creating a buzz about a product through online word-of-mouth advertising.
    a. Emotional
    b. Benefit
    c. Viral
    d. none of the above
19. When consumers not only recognize a brand but also understand its distinct qualities, this is an indication of a high level of _____.
    a. brand equity
    b. brand awareness
    c. brand image
    d. brand positioning
20. Starbucks' image is largely based on providing a coffee experience and lifestyle for its consumers. Based on this, which positioning strategy should it use?
    a. competitor positioning
    b. usage positioning
    c. benefit positioning
    d. user positioning

Apply What You Learned

21. Describe how advertisers could use the human element approach in an advertisement for the following products and services: soup, boat, landscaping service.
22. Choose a product category, such as shoes, and identify at least three different brands. Describe their positioning strategies. How is each position communicated to the target audience?
23. Based on your recent shopping excursions, describe one purchase-building sales promotion and one brand-building sales promotion in which you participated or encountered. Then, describe a tie-in promotion you encountered.

24. Visit a supermarket and make a list of ten brand-name products and their corresponding generic brands from as many different product categories as possible. List the price for each product. Calculate the amount a consumer would save by buying only the generic brands.

Make Academic Connections

25. **PROBLEM SOLVING**   The newest location of your large, national supermarket has residents concerned that it will damage the small-town atmosphere of the community. What types of sponsorship activities could your company participate in to change local residents' attitudes about your business?

26. **MATH**   Your large, national supermarket recently located in a community of 25,000 people. The total market potential for supermarkets in this community is $22.5 million. Based on your successful positioning strategy, you obtained 78 percent of the total market. The other 22 percent is shared by two small grocery stores. What is the total market share in dollars for the large supermarket? For the two smaller grocery stores? If your market share grows to 82 percent, what is the total market share in dollars for your store? For the two grocery stores?

27. **RESEARCH**   Survey ten family members, friends, teachers, or other students to determine their favorite brands in the following three product categories: soft drinks, toothpaste, and restaurants. Next to each brand, have respondents describe the brand's image in their minds. Create a table or chart that summarizes the results. Present the results in class and discuss any similarities in the responses.

28. **VISUAL ART**   Design a print advertisement for one of your favorite brands that defines the personality of the product. Your advertisement should include images and text.

29. **MARKETING**   Cross-selling is used by companies to encourage customers who already buy one of their products to try their other products. Select a local or national company that sells more than one type of product or service. Design a cross-selling sales promotion for two of these products or services.

You are the marketer for a company that makes nutrition bars. The company's primary target market has been young, active adults, but sales have been low. To combat this, the company decides to reposition its product in the marketplace by building a brand image that targets teenagers. It wants you to develop an advertising campaign that shows images of nice-looking, fashionable teens eating the nutrition bar while having fun with friends. As a contrast, the company suggests showing images of overweight teens eating candy bars while doing homework. The company also suggests using a popular teen star as the product endorser.

What would you do? Do you agree with the company's positioning strategy for its new target market? Why might it be controversial? What other positioning strategy would you recommend?

Reality ✓

Ralph Lauren vs. U.S. Polo Association

Branding is a crucial process for businesses. It helps distinguish one company's product from others. A brand's logo is an important component of the branding process. A logo can be described as a shorthand way of identifying a brand. The Nike swoosh logo is as famous as the company name itself. When consumers see certain logos, they easily recognize the brand. Because of the importance of a brand logo, companies will take legal action to prevent others from using the same or a similar logo.

The U.S. Polo Assn. (USPA) brand products are authentic and officially sanctioned by the United States Polo Association, which has been the governing body for the sport of polo in the United States since 1890. Today USPA products are manufactured by Jordache and sold through the organization's licensing program in over 100 countries at independent retail stores, department stores, and U.S. Polo Assn. brand stores. The USPA brand carries clothing for men, women, and children, as well as accessories, luggage, watches, shoes, home furnishings, and more.

The USPA's trademark logo of a polo player riding a horse has a striking resemblance to the Polo Ralph Lauren trademark logo. Ralph Lauren sued the United States Polo Association and Jordache arguing that the USPA logo would likely be confused with Polo's logo. When referring to its logo, Ralph Lauren stated, "In the world of fashion, there are fewer trademarks of greater and significant value." Polo's iconic polo-player-on-horseback logo has graced the casual wear of preppies for decades.

At trial, USPA's lawyer argued that it made sense for USPA to use the horse logo because it is a common depiction of the sport of polo. A jury agreed and found that only one of four logos used by USPA infringed on the rights of the Ralph Lauren Corporation. The jury did not believe the USPA logo would confuse the public.

Think Critically

1. Go online and find images of both the Polo Ralph Lauren logo and the USPA logo. How are they similar? How are they different?
2. After viewing the logos, do you agree with the jury's verdict? Why or why not?
3. Why do you think Ralph Lauren is concerned about the similar logo? Can USPA benefit from having a similar logo?
4. If the jury had ruled in Ralph Lauren's favor, what changes would you suggest USPA make to its logo?

Applying for a job involves selling your personal brand. As part of the Job Interview Event, you will do this by preparing a letter of application and a resume. The letter of application introduces you to a potential employer and gives you the chance to briefly "sell" your qualifications. The resume describes your "brand" attributes that would be attractive to prospective employers.

PROBLEM You are applying for a marketing position with University Events, a company that organizes and manages concerts and other entertainment events at major universities throughout the country. The job description requires someone who has solid organizational, networking, interpersonal, and communication skills. In addition, candidates should have experience working as part of a team. The company also needs someone who is proficient in PowerPoint because he or she will be responsible for preparing presentation materials. The person hired will have to be available to work some evenings and weekends.

Send your letter of application and resume to the following address: Jennifer Smith, Director of Human Resources, University Events, 7500 Westin Oaks, Houston, TX 77046.

Performance Indicators Evaluated

- Demonstrate the ability to present your brand effectively on a resume.
- Communicate career knowledge and plans.
- Exhibit professional business writing skills.
- Highlight important personal attributes on a resume.
- Match your personal brand to the job requirements.
- Understand the needs of the prospective employer.

Go to the FBLA website for more detailed information.

Think Critically

1. What personal brand characteristics should be included on your resume to make an impact with the employer?
2. Why is it important to read the job description before writing your letter of application and resume?
3. Why do you think networking and teamwork skills are so important for this marketing position?
4. What other skills do you think would be valuable in this position?
5. If you have little or no job experience, what other types of experiences could you list on your resume that would relate to the job requirements?

www.fbla.org

12

The Economics of Advertising

12.1 Advertising and the Economy

12.2 Financial Planning for Advertising

12.3 Factors Affecting the Advertising Budget

© gary718/Shutterstock.com

Advertising in a Slow Economy

When slowdowns in the economy occur, advertising campaigns must be adjusted to address the needs and concerns of consumers who are feeling the economic crunch. Instead of focusing on product attributes, ads should focus on issues confronting consumers. For example, ads that emphasize "saving money" attract attention during periods of growing unemployment rates. Geico has a series of ads that emphasize the amount of money consumers could save by choosing its brand of insurance. The ads do not explain the insurance coverage or customer service provided by the company. Instead, the message conveyed to consumers is plain and simple: If you choose Geico, you will save money.

© Jamdesign/Shutterstock.com

Another advertising tactic used by companies during recessions is to emphasize value over luxury. Manufacturers of luxury autos often promote prestige and status with little regard for cost. In an economic downturn, luxury brands are challenged to create ads that convince consumers to buy expensive autos. Recessionary ads emphasize all of the value consumers get for their money, such as no maintenance fees during the lifetime of the vehicle, low monthly lease payments, and fuel economy.

Bundling products to increase their perceived value is an advertising strategy commonly used by cable, telephone, and Internet providers. Companies like Comcast and AT&T bundle all three services for one monthly fee, which is lower than if the services were purchased separately. Wireless phone services promote "family plan" packages as a way to provide phone service for the entire family at one low price. Consumers view the bundled products as a better value.

Some companies make the recession the primary focus of their ads. They promote "recession specials" or make the economy the theme of their ads. By doing so, companies are acknowledging the struggles consumers face. Offering special deals is their way of "lending a helping hand." Retailers, restaurants, and other businesses that sell nonessential items may use this advertising technique.

Because price is a major factor during a recession, companies may develop an advertising campaign that depicts their competitor as being "too expensive." In a Microsoft Windows ad, a shopper attempted to buy a laptop for under $1,000. After visiting a Mac store and other retailers, she discovered many more affordable options among Windows-operated laptops than among Mac laptops.

1. Why would a business adjust its advertising strategy during a recession?

2. How can a business promote its products or services favorably during a recession?

3. Which of the advertising strategies described above would have the most impact on your purchasing decisions? Explain why.

WHAT DO YOU KNOW?

Advertising and the Economy

Goals

- Identify economic factors that affect advertising.
- Describe how advertising stimulates the economy.

Terms

- purchasing power, p. 325
- cost of living, p. 325
- discretionary income, p. 326
- inflation, p. 326
- recession, p. 326
- gross domestic product (GDP), p. 327
- value, p. 327

FOCUS ON ADVERTISING

Fighting the Recession by Going Global

Because Americans were spending less money during the 2008–2010 recession, luxury automakers turned to the international market to boost their sales. BMW, Mercedes-Benz, and Audi all experienced significant growth worldwide. Luxury auto sales were strong in European markets, particularly in China. China is now the world's largest auto market. Previously, consumers in China did not have the financial means to purchase these highly desirable autos, but now China's newly affluent citizens can't seem to get enough of them. In a recent year, BMW's and Mercedes' sales in China doubled, and Audi sold nearly two-thirds more cars. It is evident that the status and high-end image of these luxury autos appeal to people in China, especially the younger consumers. The average age of a Mercedes' top-of-the-line S-class car owner in China is 26 years old compared to 55 years old elsewhere. With such a strong demand in China, luxury auto manufacturers are turning their attention to the needs of the Chinese market as a way to come out on top during the recession.

Work as a Team What are the advantages to a business of selling its product or service in many different markets, including global markets? Why is demand for luxury products high in China?

The Economic Environment

Many people believe that effective advertising depends solely on creativity. They think that businesses can increase their sales by attracting consumers' attention with a memorable advertisement. However, advertising and marketing in general are greatly affected by the condition of the economy. Marketing managers must understand and react to the economic environment. Economic factors to consider include consumers' incomes and purchasing power, inflation, and recession.

Consumers' Incomes

One of the most influential factors in consumers' buying behavior is their income. A significant shift in consumers' *disposable income*, which is the income left after income taxes are paid, can affect buying decisions. When income increases, important deciding factors in a purchase are the quality of the product and the satisfaction the consumer gains from the product. When income decreases, price may be the most important deciding factor. Thus, marketers must consider the income level of target customers.

A marketer who knows where the money is knows where the markets are. For example, according to the most recent census by the U.S. Census Bureau, states in the Northeast (Connecticut, New Hampshire, New Jersey, and Maryland) had the highest annual median household incomes at around $64,000, and the lowest poverty rates at around 9 percent. States in the South and Midwest (Mississippi, Alabama, Tennessee, South Carolina, West Virginia, and Kentucky) had the lowest median household incomes, ranging from approximately $35,000 to $41,000, and the highest poverty rates, ranging from 17 to 22 percent. Based on this data, companies promoting luxury items, such as jewelry and boats, may advertise more heavily in the Northeast, while discount stores may advertise more frequently in the South and Midwest.

Purchasing Power

Consumers' income is closely related to their purchasing power. **Purchasing power** is the value of a dollar (or other unit of currency) as measured by the amount of products and services it can buy. The more products and services that a consumer can buy with one dollar, the higher his or her purchasing power. Purchasing power is measured against the **cost of living**, which is the average cost of the basic necessities of life such as housing, food, clothing, utilities, transportation, health care, and other miscellaneous expenses. The cost of living varies among countries and even among cities within the United States. According to a recent study by Kiplinger's, a publisher of personal finance advice, New York City has one of the highest cost-of-living rankings, while Pueblo, Colorado, has one of the lowest. A worker in New York City would have to earn an annual income of nearly $127,000 to achieve the same standard (quality) of living as someone earning $50,000 in Pueblo. Groceries would cost 53 percent more; housing, 441 percent more; utilities, 112 percent more; transportation, 28 percent more; and health care, 38 percent more.

NET Bookmark

With a cost-of-living calculator, you can find out how your purchasing power would be affected if you move to another city. Access www.cengage.com/school/advertising and click on the link for Chapter 12. In the calculator, enter a current salary of $40,000, the name of your current location, and the name of a destination of your choice. What comparable salary would be required if you made the move? Enter three other destinations. Which city has the lowest cost of living?

www.cengage.com/school/advertising

When income is high compared to the cost of living, consumers have more **discretionary income**, which is the amount of money remaining for spending and saving after taxes and other essential expenses are paid. Consumers who have high discretionary income can consider buying products and services that meet their wants (nonessentials) rather than their needs (essentials). Marketers should track the purchasing power of their target customers. Those who have higher purchasing power can afford to spend more money and buy higher-priced items. Consumers who have low purchasing power will try to stretch their dollars by buying products that are on sale.

Inflation

Purchasing power is greatly affected by inflation. **Inflation** is an increase in the general level of prices for products and services and a decrease in purchasing power. When prices are rising faster than income is growing, consumers lose purchasing power. The U.S. government measures inflation using the *Consumer Price Index (CPI)*. The CPI is based on a list of products and services commonly bought by consumers. The index measures changes in price over time. For example, if the price of one of the commonly purchased products was $1.00 in a previous year and it is now $1.04, that is a 4 percent increase, or a 4 percent inflation rate. That means you need 4 percent more money to buy the same product. If income is not increasing by the same rate, consumers will not be able to buy as many products and services as they had in the past.

During times of inflation, companies must study the effect of price increases on demand for their products or services. Inflation forces consumers to make economical choices when shopping. Brand loyalty may decrease because many consumers will make purchases based on price.

Why is the value of a dollar cut during periods of inflation?

Recession

A **recession** is a period of time when the economy experiences a downturn. During a recession, sales are down, which forces businesses to cut back on inventories, lay off workers, eliminate pay raises, and reduce wages. Workers who have lost their jobs or who have their wages reduced cannot buy as many products and services. They are spending less and looking for ways to save money. Consumers often shift from brand-name products to generic or store brands because they are less expensive. Coupon use is on the rise during recessions. Product brands that help consumers save money can benefit from a recession. During the 2008–2010 recession, Arm & Hammer laundry detergent experienced an upswing in sales because it offers value and dependability at a lower price. Coleman, a camping gear manufacturer, experienced increased revenues because consumers began camping and fishing when they could no longer afford lavish vacations. Hyundai benefited because it offered a more affordable lineup of automobiles than its competitors. Because consumers tend to hold onto their possessions longer during a recession, there is an increased demand for repair services and remodeling services.

During a recession, many companies reduce their advertising budgets. They invest in other nontraditional forms of advertising that are more cost-efficient, such as product placement, social media, and mobile device advertising. Methods that allow consumers to interact with companies help build brand loyalty—an important company asset during a recession.

///// CHECKPOINT \\\\\

What economic factors have an influence on advertising?

- -

Advertising Stimulates the Economy

America has the largest consumer market in the world. It also happens to be the largest advertising market in the world. Every successful business spends money on advertising, ranging from public relations to television and Internet advertising. Advertising plays an important role in businesses. It helps generate revenue and profit by stimulating sales. However, the impact of advertising has a far greater reach. Advertising entices people to shop, and in turn, shopping stimulates the economy. Advertising works in many ways to spur economic growth.

- *Advertising helps grow the gross domestic product.*
  Gross domestic product (GDP) is the total dollar value of all products and services produced by a country within a certain time period. It is one of the primary indicators of the health of a country's economy. Advertising increases demand for products and services. As demand grows, more products and services are produced.

- *Advertising increases competition.* Competition motivates companies to produce better products and other competitive advantages that benefit the economy as a whole.

- *Advertising adds value to products and services.* **Value** is the consumer's perception of how much satisfaction a product provides beyond the price paid for the product. Advertising influences consumer perception by promoting brand images that are stylish, prestigious, exciting, and so on. By adding value, advertising generates more sales for a company.

- *Advertising plays a role in the recovery from a recession.* A resurgence in consumer spending is necessary for a country to overcome an economic slump. Some consumers cannot spend money because they have lost their jobs. The much larger group of consumers that holds the key to economic recovery includes individuals who have the money and job security to

© Alina Vasilescu/Shutterstock.com

How can advertising have an effect on the production of products?

spend, but choose not to. These consumers can be enticed through effective advertising.

- *Advertising generates jobs that have a positive effect on economic growth.* Advertising in the United States generates 18.2 million of the 153.7 million jobs. Employment in the advertising and public relations industries is projected to grow 8 percent through 2018.

- *Advertising funds a diverse, media landscape.* Without advertising, many of the world's media would not exist. To replace advertising revenues, newspapers would have to double their price. The variety of sports, drama, news, and children's programs that we have come to expect on radio and television would be unthinkable without advertising. Advertising funds new forms of communication, which break down borders and barriers across the world by giving a voice to many on the Internet.

- *Advertising and sponsorship play an essential role in funding sporting events.* The costs of running the 2012 Olympics in London will be entirely funded through sponsorships and related revenues. Sponsorships also support community sports teams, grassroots cultural events, and aspiring artists.

CHECKPOINT

What are some ways in which advertising spurs economic growth?

12.1 Assessment

THINK ABOUT IT

1. How do consumers' incomes and their purchasing power affect advertisers?
2. How might consumers' buying behavior change during periods of inflation and recession?
3. How can advertising help the economy rebound from a recession?

MAKE ACADEMIC CONNECTIONS

4. **STATISTICS** Visit the U.S. Census Bureau and search for the latest statistics available for people and households. In a one-page report, explain what types of data are available and how advertisers could use this data to create an advertising campaign.

5. **VISUAL ART** Design an advertisement that communicates the value of a product or service. Decide how you want the product or service to be perceived by the consumer and create an ad that will help shape consumers' perception.

Teamwork

During times of recession, many companies cut back on traditional advertising and look for nontraditional ways to reach customers. Your favorite pizza restaurant is one of these companies. Develop a social media advertising campaign for the pizza restaurant that allows it to connect with customers in a more cost-efficient manner. Use PowerPoint to present the ad campaign.

Financial Planning for Advertising

Goals

- Explain strategies used for setting the advertising budget.
- Describe the financial reports a business can use for planning and operating the company.

Terms

- percentage-of-sales method, p. 330
- competition-matching method, p. 330
- share of voice, p. 331
- objective-and-task method, p. 331
- market response model, p. 331
- income statement, p. 332
- balance sheet, p. 333

FOCUS ON ADVERTISING

Macy's Attempts to Gain Market Share

Macy's department stores launched a splashy advertising and marketing campaign costing over $100 million to gain market share. Macy's "Find Your Magic" campaign used celebrities to promote its brands on TV and online. Online videos featured a team of celebrity designers giving fashion makeovers to "everyday people." Macy's also introduced an in-store digital experience through the use of the Magic Fitting Room Mirror. Customers could see how they would look in outfits and use the web-connected, touch-screen mirror to share what they tried on via Facebook or e-mail. As another way to grow its market share, Macy's implemented a localization strategy called "My Macy's." The products and promotions at each Macy's store were tailored to local markets and local tastes. By using tracking technology, Macy's determined which products were popular at specific stores and then stocked those items. Macy's strategies have proven to be successful and have given them a competitive advantage.

Work as a Team Why have Macy's advertising and promotional strategies succeeded in increasing its market share? Do you think this justifies the high advertising costs?

© plumdesign/Shutterstock.com

Setting the Budget

While business costs such as electricity, rent, and insurance are fairly straightforward, determining the amount to spend on advertising is more complicated. Advertising costs are typically very expensive. Businesses must find a balance between spending too little and spending

too much. If too little is invested in advertising, sales goals may not be met. If too much is spent, unnecessary expenses will reduce profits. Marketers use various methods for setting an advertising budget.

Percentage of Sales

Many businesses use a percentage of sales as their guide for how much to spend on advertising. The **percentage-of-sales method** sets the advertising budget as a fixed percentage of past or projected sales. If a company allocates 4 percent of its projected sales of $50 million, the advertising budget would be $2 million. Rather than arbitrarily assign a percentage, it is better if businesses use their industry's average percentage as a guide. For example, the advertising-to-sales ratio for the home appliances industry is 1.9 percent, but it is 19.2 percent for the perfume and cosmetics industry. The average ratio for most industries is less than 5 percent.

Two advantages of this method are its relative simplicity and the direct relationship between expenditures and available funds. However, it has some disadvantages. Under this method, the advertising budget will increase when sales increase, and the budget will decrease when sales decrease. However, when sales decrease, more advertising, not less, may be needed to increase sales. Also, past sales are not always a good predictor of future sales. Changes in the economy, increased competition, market trends, or new technology can affect sales. Thus, using future sales projections or an average of last year's sales and future sales projections may result in a more accurate budget.

Why would a business monitor its competitors' advertisements?

© prodakszyn/Shutterstock.com

Competition Matching (Market Share)

Companies in highly competitive product markets, such as the soft drink industry, require higher advertising budgets to maintain their market share. Coca-Cola and Ford spend millions of dollars on advertising in order to be key players in their respective industries. The **competition-matching method** bases an advertising budget on the amount of money spent by competitors on advertising. Once a company estimates how much competitors are spending, it may decide to match or exceed that amount. By outspending its competitors, a company hopes to increase its market share.

Matching or exceeding competitors' spending also helps a company establish a significant **share of voice**, which is the company's portion (percentage) of overall advertising in a specific product category. For example, the share-of-voice ratio for Ford would be determined by calculating the total number of Ford ads as a percentage of the total number of all auto manufacturer ads. Companies introducing new products will often spend more on advertising to increase their share of voice. A higher share of voice will help a new brand stand out from existing, well-known brands. A brand's share of voice is partially responsible for its share of the market.

Although being aware of competitors' spending is smart, it is not always easy. This financial information may not be readily available, meaning a company would have to estimate competitors' spending by monitoring their ad campaigns. In addition, competitors may not be spending their advertising dollars wisely. Finally, not all competitors have the same company objectives and resources; so what works for one company may not work for another.

Objective and Task

The **objective-and-task method** of advertising budgeting estimates the cost of achieving advertising objectives. It is the most accurate strategy for creating an advertising budget because it relates spending to the objectives to be achieved. When creating the overall advertising plan, the company determines the objectives for its advertising campaign. The advertising team then identifies all tasks related to accomplishing those objectives. Once the necessary advertising tasks are determined, the cost of completing each task is calculated and a budget is established. If the budget is more than the company can afford, modifications may be needed. However, drastic cuts should be avoided to ensure advertising objectives are met. Otherwise, the advertising campaign may not have the desired impact.

Response Model

A **market response model** examines the number of sales generated in relation to the dollar amount spent on advertising. The purpose of this model is to help businesses understand how advertising affects sales. Response models are used to analyze how much sales will increase for every additional dollar spent on advertising. The general idea is that as long as sales exceed advertising expenditures, the business will continue spending on advertising. If sales decline, the business would have to determine if additional spending on advertising

How do market response models help businesses analyze the effect of advertising on sales?

could be justified. Prior years' sales and advertising expenditures data are used to create response models. Response models provide a basis for improved decisions regarding the amount spent on advertising.

///// CHECKPOINT \\\\\

What strategies can be used to set the advertising budget?

The Accounting of It All

Financial planning is an important aspect of all businesses. Advertising and related marketing activities cost money. Managing these costs along with other operating costs is important to the profitability of a business. When costs are controlled, money is available for important company activities, such as product development, market research, promotions, and customer services.

There are various financial reports a business can use for planning and operating the company. Two of the most important include the income statement and balance sheet.

Income Statement

The **income statement** reports a company's revenues, expenses, and net loss or profit for a specific period of time. It is also called a *profit and loss statement*. A sample income statement is shown below. *Revenue* is income received from the sale of products and services. *Operating expenses* are the costs of the day-to-day activities of a business. When expenses are subtracted from revenue, the result is a profit (net income) or loss (net loss).

$$\text{Revenue} - \text{Expenses} = \text{Profit or Loss}$$

The income statement provides financial information that shows the ability of a company to generate profit by increasing revenue and reducing expenses. Companies can see how profits are affected when advertising expenses are increased or decreased. They can also examine the relationship between advertising expenses and revenue.

Several variations of the income statement can be created. It may report the financial performance of the entire company or of a specific store in a specific region for a company doing business in several locations. For marketing

Parker Outdoor Services Income Statement For the Year Ended December 31, 20—		
Revenue		$125,000
Operating expenses:		
Salaries	$ 27,315	
Rent	10,800	
Utilities	1,260	
Advertising	3,125	
Insurance	900	
Supplies	615	
Other	615	
Total operating expenses		$ 44,630
Net income		$ 80,370

Torrez Products Balance Sheet December 31, 20—			
Assets		**Liabilities**	
Cash	$29,000	Accounts payable	$ 17,000
Accounts receivable	11,500	Loans payable	32,500
Supplies	5,075	Sales tax payable	5,300
Inventory	94,340		
Equipment	18,975	**Total liabilities**	$ 54,800
Building	33,000		
Land	12,975		
Furniture	6,225	**Owner's Equity**	
Vehicle	18,000	Felicia Torrez, capital	$229,290
Patent	55,000		
		Total liabilities and	
Total assets	**$284,090**	**owner's equity**	**$284,090**

purposes, an income statement can be developed to report the profitability of a specific market or for a specific product.

Balance Sheet

The **balance sheet** summarizes a company's assets, liabilities, and owner's equity (net worth) as of a specific date. A sample balance sheet is shown above. The relationship among assets, liabilities, and owner's equity can be expressed as an equation.

$$\text{Assets} = \text{Liabilities} + \text{Owner's Equity}$$

An *asset* is something of value owned by a business. Common types of assets include cash, accounts receivable, inventory, and supplies. *Accounts receivable* are the amounts owed to a business by its credit customers. Some assets are tangible while others are intangible. *Tangible assets* exist physically, such as equipment, furniture, buildings, and vehicles. *Intangible assets* are nonphysical resources and rights that are of value to the business because they provide some kind of advantage in the marketplace. Examples of intangible assets include intellectual property, such as copyrights, trademarks, and patents.

A *liability* is a financial obligation, or an amount owed by a business. The most common type of liability is accounts payable. *Accounts payable* are amounts owed to suppliers or vendors for merchandise or services purchased on credit by a business. Advertising-related accounts payable may involve charges for buying ad space in a magazine or newspaper, producing a television ad, renting a facility to film an ad, and hiring a spokesperson for an ad.

Owner's equity is the amount remaining after the value of the liabilities is subtracted from the value of the assets. It is called "owner's equity" because the owner of the business has the financial rights to the assets of the business after the liabilities are deducted. For corporations, it is referred to as *shareholders' equity*. Basically, the balance sheet calculates a company's wealth, or *capital*. The larger the capital, the more financially healthy the business is.

Marketers use the information obtained from a balance sheet for several purposes. The amount of inventory of products for sale may be an indicator of the effectiveness of the advertising campaign. The balance sheet also indicates whether there is money available to spend on the tasks that need to be completed to meet advertising objectives.

CHECKPOINT

How do financial reports contribute to the successful operation of a business?

12.2 Assessment

THINK ABOUT IT

1. How is the competition-matching method used to set an advertising budget?
2. Why is the objective-and-task method the most accurate strategy for creating an advertising budget?
3. What kinds of financial information do income statements and balance sheets contain?
4. How are tangible assets different from intangible assets?

MAKE ACADEMIC CONNECTIONS

5. **MATH** Your advertising agency has revenue of $50,000, a building worth $265,000, accounts receivable of $15,000, trademarks valued at $30,000, and liabilities totaling $84,000. What is the net worth of your company?

6. **FINANCE** Search the Internet for a public corporation's annual report. Find the income statement and compare its sales revenues, expenses, and net income or loss for two or more years. Calculate the percentage increase or decrease for each of these three items. Review the annual report for any references to the company's advertising costs. Are these listed on the income statement? If so, where?

7. **ACCOUNTING** Your company projects sales of $5 million for the upcoming year. Last year's expenditures for the company were as follows: salaries, $1,164,500; rent, $100,000; utilities, $30,000; advertising, $1,730,500; insurance, $125,000; and supplies, $250,000. You expect expenditures to increase 20 percent next year. Using the example on page 332, prepare an income statement for the company for next year.

Teamwork

As the advertising agency for a pet daycare business, specify the advertising objective for the company. For example, is the objective to inform, persuade, or remind consumers? Write a clearly stated, measurable objective. Then identify the tasks that would need to be completed to achieve the objective. After doing so, estimate the costs of carrying out each task and present it as the advertising budget.

Goals
- Describe factors that affect the advertising budget.
- Determine whether advertising spending generates brand awareness.

Terms
- commission system, p. 338
- fee system, p. 338
- incentive-based system, p. 338

FOCUS ON ADVERTISING

Low Prices, Every Day

Walmart realized it was losing customer confidence in its ability to deliver the lowest prices when it experienced a nearly two-year slide in revenue. Sales were suffering due to mistakes the retailer made on price and selection. It also faced increasing price competition from dollar stores and Amazon.com. In an attempt to bring back customers who no longer trusted the company to save them money, Walmart conveyed its low-price message in a new ad campaign that used the slogan, "Low Prices. Every Day. On Everything." The campaign emphasized that shoppers could find everything they needed at rock-bottom prices. It also promoted Walmart's price-matching strategy to combat any competitors that offered a lower price. In addition, Walmart restocked thousands of items it had stopped carrying in its effort to clean up its stores. These items were flagged using "It's Back" signs. All of the changes Walmart implemented communicated a return to its "Everyday Low Prices" roots in an effort to win back its target customers.

Work as a Team How did Walmart's ad campaign attempt to reconnect with its target market? How did this demonstrate the importance of the target market when planning an ad campaign?

Budgeting Considerations

Advertising budgets are important for small and large businesses. The advertising plan provides the outline for how you will inform, persuade, or remind customers about your business and the products and services

PIAGET

alone can guarantee that their watches are made exclusively in gold or platinum, created and manufactured in their own workshops.

PIAGET

The specialists in ultra thin watches, available at leading jewellers throughout the world.

Who do you think the target market is for this advertisement? What may be the best way to reach this target market?

it offers. The budget is an essential part of the advertising plan. There are several factors that can have an effect on the advertising budget.

Target Market

The target market for an advertising campaign has an impact on the advertising budget. While one business is targeting customers whose annual household income is around $500,000, another business may be targeting recent college graduates who make approximately $33,000 a year. Once a business defines its target customers, it must determine the best way to reach them. In addition to knowing the wants and needs of the target customers, businesses must find out what they read (newspapers, magazines), what television shows they watch, what websites or social networking sites they visit, where they shop, who they get shopping advice from, and what motivates them to buy. Selecting the best way to reach target customers and to motivate them to buy is based on target market characteristics. Because target market characteristics will vary, so will the advertising costs.

Media

The type of media selected for the advertising campaign also affects the advertising budget. A business may choose to promote its products or services using newspapers, magazines, the radio, TV, the Internet, billboards, or direct marketing. The cost can vary greatly depending on the media used. A print advertisement in a local newspaper may cost less than running an online advertisement on a popular website.

Advertising media prices may change during different times of the year, such as at the start of a new season or during popular holidays. While some media outlets may offer discounts, others will increase their prices if they feel their readership or viewership may peak during specific times or events. Businesses that want to place a print ad in a magazine's most popular issue of the year or air a television commercial during a highly televised event like the Super Bowl can expect to pay premium rates due to the timing of their ad. The location or placement of the advertisement will also affect the cost. An ad placed on the front page of the business section of the newspaper or during the first quarter of the Super Bowl will cost more than a less popular location or time slot.

Geography

Location affects the price of advertising in several ways. Newspapers, billboards, magazines, and other forms of advertising will cost more in larger cities where the advertising reach will be higher. If a business is trying to reach consumers in another country, it most likely will have to make some modifications to its advertising campaign to appeal to the culture and customs in the other country. The advertising budget should account for the extra time and effort needed to develop an international campaign. The costs of buying media around the globe should also be considered.

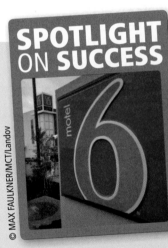

SPOTLIGHT ON SUCCESS

© MAX FAULKNER/MCT/Landov

TOM BODETT,
Motel 6

Motel 6 developed a unique concept in 1962 by offering travelers consistent quality, economy lodging at the lowest price of any national brand. The price of the original Motel 6 rooms was $6 (as reflected in the brand's name), emphasizing the low-price concept. Today, Motel 6 has over 1,000 properties with over 100,000 rooms, making it the largest economy motel chain in the United States.

Motel 6 is a household name, synonymous with quality and value. It enjoys the highest brand recognition of any economy lodging brand. This is largely due to Motel 6's advertising campaign, featuring on-air personality Tom Bodett who uses the tagline, "We'll leave the light on for you." The campaign began in 1986 and proved to be an instant success. It has won more advertising awards than any other brand in the lodging industry.

Motel 6 was acknowledged by *Ad Age* magazine as having one of the top 100 advertising campaigns in the last 100 years. Motel 6 was the only lodging company to earn this distinction.

Motel 6 has become synonymous with Tom Bodett. Bodett is the first and only spokesperson Motel 6 has ever had. Bodett was recruited by The Richards Group advertising agency after one of its agents heard him as a commentator on a public radio station. The Richards Group felt that Bodett's warm and friendly commentary style would be the right personality for the Motel 6 brand, which targets the budget traveler. Today, Bodett's voice can still be heard on the radio and television as he speaks about his life as a road warrior and the value of Motel 6. He works closely with the Motel 6 marketing team to keep the ad campaign fresh and to convey a message that meets the ever-changing needs of the target market.

Think Critically

How can a spokesperson help a company reach its target market? Why do you think Motel 6 has continued to use Tom Bodett as its spokesperson for so many years?

Product Life Cycle

The advertising needs of a product vary as it moves through the stages of the product life cycle. When new products are introduced, they require heavy advertising to make customers aware of their existence and to communicate their benefits. During the growth stage, advertising costs increase as businesses try to build brand preference, often by promoting differences among brands. Product differentiation is often necessary in highly competitive markets, such as the laundry detergent market. In the maturity stage, advertising costs continue to grow as businesses advertise to remind consumers about their brand in order to maintain market share. Advertising costs are reduced during the decline stage of a product and are eventually eliminated.

How are advertising agencies compensated?

Advertising Agency Compensation

If an advertising agency is used, businesses need to account for this in their advertising budgets. Agencies are paid in different ways. The **commission system** of payment is based on the amount of money a business (advertiser) spends on advertising media. Agencies are paid a percentage, such as 15 percent, of the total amount billed by a media organization. With a **fee system**, agencies are paid an hourly rate for different services provided. In recent years, the **incentive-based system**, which bases the agency's fee on the achievement of agreed-upon performance objectives, has become more popular. Objectives could include increasing brand awareness or increasing sales. The shift to incentive-based systems is partly because more companies are moving away from traditional forms of media, such as TV and radio, in favor of social media. Businesses believe incentive-based systems encourage agencies to look beyond traditional mass-media advertising and develop other unique ways of reaching customers.

CHECKPOINT

What factors influence the amount spent on an advertising budget?

The Advertising Costs of Brand Awareness

Because the costs of advertising are so high, businesses must be able to justify their spending. Often, the main purpose and desired result of advertising is to make consumers aware of a business's brand. Various methods can be used to measure brand awareness.

The Sales Method

By using the sales method, businesses measure brand awareness based on the volume of sales. Tracking increases in sales revenue throughout the duration of and after an ad campaign can indicate how effective the ads are at creating brand awareness.

The Trial-and-Error Method

As a follow up to the sales method, businesses may use the trial-and-error method. If sales don't increase, businesses may test out other promotional methods to increase consumer awareness. For example, instead of just running a television ad, a business may also post an ad on a blog that is frequently visited by members of its target market. The trial-and-error method works well for online advertising because a business can change advertising techniques quickly and easily. The business can then measure the effectiveness of the various forms of advertising used.

The Awareness/Preference Method

In a competitive environment, advertising is used to promote the benefits of one brand over another to help establish consumer preference. Brand awareness and preference cannot always be measured by sales. Instead, consumer research must be conducted. Feedback cards, product surveys, and product testing are good ways to measure brand awareness and preference.

Show-of-Interest Method

Rather than measuring sales, businesses can measure the advertising's effectiveness by the show of interest it generates. For retailers, increased customer traffic is an indicator. It can also be measured by product inquiries (via phone, e-mail, website, or trade shows).

The Readership/Viewership Method

Businesses devote lots of time and money to determine if anyone is watching, listening to, or reading their advertisements. The best readership/viewership studies determine not only if the target customers are exposed to the message but also if they are responding to it. For example, after reading or viewing an ad, do consumers make a purchase at a store or place an order online?

How can customer inquiries be used to measure brand awareness?

The Anecdotal Method

Periodically business must measure the effectiveness of advertising campaigns with their gut and heart, and not so much with their head. The anecdotal method involves advertisers keeping their eyes and ears open for feedback about the advertising campaign.

A customer may post a comment on a blog or on the business's website. Or a customer may share feedback with a customer service representative or salesperson. These types of comments and feedback help measure whether the advertising message is getting through to the target market.

**////// CHECKPOINT **

How can businesses determine if advertising spending succeeded in creating brand awareness?

- -

12.3 Assessment

THINK ABOUT IT

1. How can the target market affect the advertising budget?
2. Why do you think businesses prefer to use the incentive-based system of compensation for advertising agencies?
3. How can consumer feedback help a business measure the effectiveness of advertising spending?

MAKE ACADEMIC CONNECTIONS

4. **MATH**   The cost for renting a billboard on a busy freeway is $2,500 per month. The freeway is traveled by 2,700,000 people each week. Another billboard located on a state highway traveled by 870,000 people each week costs $1,200 per month. What is the cost per person per month for each billboard?

5. **RESEARCH**   Conduct research to determine the cost to air a 30-second commercial on your favorite radio station. Find out if the cost is higher during the holiday season. Also, learn about the different pricing options offered by the radio station. What would be the most cost-efficient way for a new gift shop in your area to advertise on the radio?

6. **PROBLEM SOLVING**   The gift shop described in the problem above has determined that its radio ad is not increasing sales as much as expected. You suggest using the trial-and-error method to test out other types of promotion. Recommend other types of promotion the gift shop can use in coordination with the radio ad.

Teamwork

Your marketing team has been asked to use focus groups to measure how well advertisements create brand awareness and brand preference. Select three television commercials for three different brands of the same type of product, such as a smartphone. Create a survey containing ten questions that will help determine the effectiveness of the ads. Show the focus group (your class) the commercials and have them complete the survey. Compile the results and present the commercial that was deemed the most effective.

Sharpen Your 21st CENTURY SKILLS

Digital Vision/Getty Images

Creating Your Personal Budget

Just as a business sets a budget to help it meet its financial goals, you can create a budget to help you achieve your personal goals. A budget gives you an opportunity to evaluate your current financial situation and tailor your plan in a way that will help you reach your goals. Follow the steps below to prepare a personal budget.

1. *Estimate your income.* Include all the money you expect to receive from your job, allowance, gifts, or other sources. You may receive income weekly or monthly, but it helps to look at the big picture by determining how much income you earn during an entire year.

2. *Estimate your expenses.* Expenses include amounts you pay for clothes, lunches, bus fares, and other living and entertainment expenses. You may also have a car payment, insurance payment, or other type of loan payment. If you live on your own, you would have rent and utility expenses.

3. *Plan your savings.* Decide how much of your income you want to set aside for future needs. Savings help you pay for expected and unexpected expenses. Savings are also an important factor in achieving your personal goals. For example, if your goal is to buy a car or go on vacation, you will need to save for it.

4. *Balance the budget.* If your expenses plus savings exceed your income, you must adjust your budget to make them balance. To do this, you will have to lower your expenses, save less, or increase your income.

A sample budget is shown below. Spreadsheet software is very useful when preparing a budget. It performs all of the calculations and allows you to make adjustments easily so you can see how the budget would be affected by changes to the income, expenses, or savings amounts.

After you have prepared your budget, you can see if it will accommodate your personal goals. Will you have enough savings to buy a car or go on vacation? If not, what changes can you make to your budget? Your budget should be a tool you use in your personal life to help you make good decisions.

Try It Out

Prepare a personal budget based on your own income and expenses. If you have no income, assume you earn $85 weekly from a part-time job.

PARTNERSHIP FOR 21ST CENTURY SKILLS

ANGELA CHIN BUDGET FOR 20—			
Income	**Weekly**	**Monthly**	**Yearly**
Work (part-time)	$70.50	$282.00	$3,384.00
Allowance	15.00	60.00	720.00
Savings account interest	.50	2.00	24.00
Total income	$86.00	$344.00	$4,128.00
Expenses			
Clothes and shoes	$20.00	$ 80.00	$ 960.00
Loan payment to parents	15.00	60.00	720.00
Lunches	20.00	80.00	960.00
Entertainment/miscellaneous	16.00	64.00	768.00
Total expenses	$71.00	$284.00	$3,408.00
Savings			
Deposit to savings account	$15.00	$ 60.00	$ 720.00
Total expenses and savings	$86.00	$344.00	$4,128.00

SUMMARY

12.1 Advertising and the Economy

- Consumers' income affects their buying decisions. When income increases, consumers focus on the quality of a product and the satisfaction it provides. When income decreases, consumers focus on price.
- The more products and services that a consumer can buy with one dollar, the higher his or her purchasing power. Purchasing power is measured against the cost of living, which is the average cost of the basic necessities of life.
- During periods of inflation, prices rise, meaning consumers cannot buy as many products and services as they had in the past. During a recession, the economy experiences a downturn, and consumers spend less.
- Advertising helps generate a company's revenue and profit by enticing people to shop, which stimulates the economy.

12.2 Financial Planning for Advertising

- There are several methods to use when setting the advertising budget, including the percentage-of-sales method, competition-matching method, objective-and-task method, and the response model.
- The income statement summarizes a company's revenues, expenses, and net loss or profit for a period of time. It allows a business to look at the relationship between advertising expenses and profit.
- The balance sheet summarizes a company's assets, liabilities, and owner's equity (net worth). It indicates how much money is available to spend on advertising.

12.3 Factors Affecting the Advertising Budget

- Factors that could affect the advertising budget include the target market, media selections, geography, product life cycle, and advertising agency compensation.
- Advertising spending should result in brand awareness. Brand awareness can be measured using the sales method (by tracking the volume of sales), trial-and-error method (by testing other promotions), awareness/preference method (by using surveys), show-of-interest method (by tracking the interest generated from an ad), readership/viewership method (by determining response rate to an ad), and the anecdotal method (by monitoring customer feedback).

WHAT DO YOU KNOW? Now

Read *Impact Advertising* on page 323 again to review how the economy affects advertising strategies. Find an ad that uses one of the advertising strategies described in *Impact Advertising*. Describe the ad and evaluate how effective it is at addressing the concerns of consumers in the midst of a recession.

Chapter 12 Assessment

Vocabulary Builder

Match each statement with the term that best defines it. Some terms may not be used.

1. The value of a dollar as measured by the amount of products and services it can buy
2. Advertising agency payment based on an hourly rate for services provided
3. Examines the number of sales generated in relation to the dollar amount spent on advertising
4. Total dollar value of all products and services produced by a country within a certain time period
5. Advertising agency payment based on the amount of money a business spends on advertising media
6. A company's portion (percentage) of overall advertising in a specific product category
7. An increase in the general level of prices for products and services and a decrease in purchasing power
8. The consumer's perception of how much satisfaction a product provides beyond the price paid for it
9. The amount of money remaining for spending and saving after taxes and other essential expenses are paid
10. Advertising budgeting method that uses a fixed percentage of past or projected sales

a. balance sheet
b. commission system
c. competition-matching method
d. cost of living
e. discretionary income
f. fee system
g. gross domestic product (GDP)
h. incentive-based system
i. income statement
j. inflation
k. market response model
l. objective-and-task method
m. percentage-of-sales method
n. purchasing power
o. recession
p. share of voice
q. value

Test Your Knowledge

11. A _____ is *not* an example of an intangible asset.
    a. patent
    b. building
    c. trademark
    d. copyright
12. A(n) _____ is a financial obligation, or an amount owed.
    a. liability
    b. asset
    c. accounts receivable
    d. tangible asset
13. The formula for determining profit is
    a. Liabilities + Owner's equity
    b. Assets + Owner's equity
    c. Revenue – Expenses
    d. Expenses – Revenue
14. Often, the *main* purpose of advertising spending is to
    a. create a brand image
    b. create brand awareness
    c. differentiate products
    d. introduce a new product

15. Consumers who have high discretionary income
    a. have low purchasing power
    b. should only buy products and services that meet their needs
    c. can consider buying products and services that meet their wants rather than their needs
    d. none of the above
16. Which of the following methods of setting an advertising budget is the most accurate?
    a. competition matching
    b. percentage of sales
    c. response model
    d. objective and task
17. The financial statement that shows a company's net worth on a given date is the ____.
    a. income statement
    b. profit and loss statement
    c. balance sheet
    d. owner's equity statement
18. Advertising stimulates sales and the economy in all of the following ways *except* by
    a. decreasing competition
    b. growing the gross domestic product
    c. adding value to products and services
    d. generating jobs
19. Which of the following factors has an effect on the advertising budget?
    a. product life cycle
    b. target market
    c. media selections
    d. all of the above
20. The ____ is used to analyze how much sales will increase for every additional dollar spent on advertising.
    a. percentage-of-sales method
    b. market response model
    c. objective-and-task method
    d. competition-matching method

Apply What You Learned

21. During a recession, consumers spend less. Describe how a consumer may try to stretch his or her dollars when shopping. What advertising strategies could a business use during a recession to motivate consumers to buy its products or services?
22. When the economy experiences inflation, prices for products and services increase. Brand loyalty may decrease as a result of rising prices. How can a company maintain brand loyalty during periods of inflation?
23. Describe three characteristics of the target market for luxury cars. Explain how these characteristics could affect the advertising budget.
24. Advertising that adds value to products and services can entice consumers to make a purchase. Select an advertisement that you believe adds value to the advertised product or service. Describe the advertisement and explain how it influences the consumer's perception.

25. **RESEARCH** Select an upcoming national or international sports or entertainment event. Conduct research to determine which companies will sponsor the event. Why do you think these companies chose to sponsor the event? In a one-page report, describe all the ways in which these sponsorships are stimulating the economy.

26. **VISUAL ART** The cost of advertising media can increase tremendously during holiday seasons. Select a product that typically is advertised heavily during the holidays. Create a holiday print advertisement for the product. Then create another print ad for the product that could be used during the summer season.

27. **INTERNATIONAL** A TV manufacturer wants to sell its new, high-priced 3D TV internationally. It knows that purchasing power and cost of living greatly affect consumers' buying habits. Conduct research to find the cost of living in other countries. Taking into consideration the country's culture and cost of living, recommend three international markets for the TV manufacturer. Justify your recommendations.

28. **MANAGEMENT** You are the head of the advertising department for a company that sells several popular products and that is getting ready to launch a new product. The CEO for the company does not want to budget much money for advertising this year because the company has been in existence for 80 years and already has name recognition. You must explain the importance of advertising throughout the various stages of a product's life cycle. Create a list of ten solid reasons that the company should spend money on advertising.

29. **MATH** If a restaurant uses the percentage-of-sales method to create its advertising budget based on 2.2 percent of projected sales of $2.5 million, what is the advertising budget? If the restaurant decides to use the competition-matching method and wants to exceed the competition's advertising budget of $45,000 by 5 percent, what is its budget? Which method results in the highest advertising budget?

You are the accountant for a popular regional department store. Recently, two well-known national department stores have located in the same community. Since their arrival, sales at the regional department store have dropped by 14 percent. To compete with the national department stores, the owner has decided to do a complete renovation to make the facility more appealing to customers. To do so, the owner must obtain a loan from the bank. The bank has asked to see the store's financial statements, including the income statement and balance sheet. Because of the drop in sales, the owner is concerned that he will not be granted a loan. He asks you, the accountant, to change the revenue and operating expense amounts to make the store appear more profitable than it is.

What would you do? What might the consequences be if you change the financial statements?

Reality ✓

Bargains from Groupon

Groupon (group coupons) is an online service that offers its members deep discounts on products and services. Groupon targets local communities by advertising and reaching out to people in specified areas. It has over 80 million members in more than 400 markets and thousands of cities around the world. It has sold more than 22 million Groupons in North America, saving consumers more than a billion dollars and generating millions of dollars in revenue for participating businesses.

Each day there is one fabulous deal per city. Deal seekers can sign up for free at Groupon to receive daily alerts about offers. Special prices are offered for everything from spa treatments to sky diving lessons, limo rides, and even teeth whitening. In order for the discount to be extended to Groupon members, collective buying must occur. In other words, a certain number of people (usually around 20) have to purchase the coupon. Once the minimum collective buying is reached, the merchant will accept the coupons, and the consumer's credit card will be charged. Most of the deals last only a day, so consumers must act fast before the deals expire.

Although Groupon sounds like a great deal for consumers, what's in it for participating businesses? Simply put, businesses gain exposure. Even though they have to share the revenue with Groupon, often 50/50, they can increase the size of their customer base by using Groupon to generate consumer traffic. They attract customers who might never have shopped at the business otherwise. Groupon is changing the way businesses, especially small businesses, promote their products and services and get sales.

Before participating in Groupon, businesses must consider several factors. Does the business have the excess capacity and staff to handle a surge in customers? One pizza restaurant experienced a large volume of customers when it sold more than 9,258 Groupons offering a $10 pizza for $5. Does the business risk damaging its brand image by giving out large discounts? Most importantly, businesses need to do the math to determine if the revenue earned will offset the deep discounts given. In many cases, Groupon is a win-win for both consumers and local businesses.

Think Critically

1. Why do you think Groupon has experienced such a high success rate?
2. Do you think Groupon is an effective advertising strategy to use during slow economic times? Why or why not?
3. Are there any disadvantages of Groupon for consumers and businesses? Explain your answer.

Prepared Speech Event

Effective speaking skills are essential to the success of those working in the advertising field. As an advertising agent, you must be able to explain the benefits of advertising and the need to budget an appropriate amount of money for this important task. The Prepared Speech event lets you demonstrate your communication skills, which involve securing, arranging, organizing, and presenting information orally.

PROBLEM You are the advertising agent for a new supermarket located in a city with a population of 200,000 that already has five competing supermarket chains with a total of 20 stores located throughout the city. The new supermarket is opening six stores in the community. You must prepare a speech to give to the owners of the supermarket that explains the importance of advertising, the best types of advertising to use to launch the new supermarket brand within the community, and recommended strategies for differentiating the supermarket from the competition. You must also explain how much the advertising campaign will cost and the benefits reaped from the expenditure.

You should consider the purpose of the speech, such as to inform, to educate, to motivate, or to persuade. Keep in mind the three basic elements of an effective speech and presentation, which include the introduction, the body, and the conclusion. During the speech, it is important to be enthusiastic and to use proper grammar.

The speech will be given in front of a panel of judges (in this case, your classmates) and a timekeeper. You will be given one minute to set up for your speech. Your speech should be at least five minutes and no more than seven minutes. A flip chart, posters, and/or props may be used during the speech.

Performance Indicators Evaluated

- Demonstrate effective communication skills.
- Demonstrate skills in developing a speech using the three basic elements of an effective speech—the introduction, body, and conclusion.
- Utilize nonverbal gestures as needed.
- Apply speaking techniques using appropriate tempo and pitch.
- Secure facts and data from multiple sources, emphasizing research skills.

Go to the BPA website for more detailed information.

Think Critically

1. How can good speaking skills benefit an advertising career?
2. Why is research important when preparing a speech?
3. How do the three elements of a speech—introduction, body, and conclusion—contribute to its effectiveness?

www.bpa.org

13

Legal and Ethical Issues Affecting Advertising

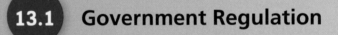

13.1 **Government Regulation**

13.2 **Self-Regulation**

13.3 **Ethics in Advertising**

© gary718/Shutterstock.com

You're a Winner!

Nationally recognized companies use sweepstakes to heighten the interest of consumers. A sweepstakes is an effective way to draw attention to a brand. Sweepstakes come in many forms and offer a variety of prizes, including large sums of money.

The letter arrives in the mail, proclaiming, "You're a Winner!" It states that you are among two people vying for a prize of $11 million. All you have to do is send in the attached form, and the money is as good as yours. You may have to subscribe to a few unwanted magazines as a prerequisite to collecting the winnings and becoming a millionaire. The aforementioned letter arrives in the mailboxes of millions of households every year. Most people know offers like this are too good to be true, but there are always those who believe otherwise.

Publishers Clearing House (PCH) is a direct marketing company that offers a magazine subscription service. It has held a sweepstakes since 1967. Over the years, many people, often senior citizens, have received a notice in the mail from PCH declaring them the winner of millions of dollars. Some of these naive customers were so elated with the news that, rather than trust the post office to return the "winning" ticket, they flew it to the PCH headquarters themselves. Unfortunately, upon their arrival at the offices, they were not greeted with a check. It was pointed out that they had not read the fine print of the ticket, which stated that the ticket holder was a winner only if his or her number was the one drawn from millions of other numbers.

Numerous lawsuits have been filed against PCH on behalf of consumers who felt they were duped by false advertising. As a result, PCH has paid out millions of dollars in settlements. In addition, it was ordered to reform its business practices. PCH was banned from using false statements, such as "you're a winner" or "you're guaranteed to win." It must also provide consumers with a sweepstakes fact sheet, which clearly states the odds of winning and explains that purchases do not increase the consumer's chances of winning. PCH also was banned from targeting specific consumer groups, such as senior citizens.

© iQoncept/Shutterstock.com

WHAT DO YOU KNOW?

1. Why do you think PCH was found guilty of using deceptive advertising?

2. Why does deceptive advertising frequently target senior citizens?

3. What advice would you give someone who plans to enter a sweepstakes?

FOCUS ON ADVERTISING

Goals

- Explain the need for government regulation of advertising and the role of the Federal Trade Commission.
- Describe the purpose of other government regulatory agencies.

Terms

- Federal Trade Commission (FTC), p. 351
- Federal Communications Commission (FCC), p. 354
- Food and Drug Administration (FDA), p. 354
- Alcohol and Tobacco Tax and Trade Bureau (TTB), p. 354

A Wristband with Special Powers?

Does a wristband really have the power to improve your balance, flexibility, strength, and coordination? That's what the company Power Balance has led many consumers to believe. It is one of many companies now selling "performance-enhancing" accessories, including wristbands and necklaces. Power Balance claims its wristband, featuring a holographic disk, interacts with the energy frequencies of the body to help people feel their best. Their claims are backed by endorsements of professional athletes, who are often seen wearing the wristbands. However, doctors and scientists are accusing Power Balance of using scientific-sounding claims to scam customers. A study by the *Journal of Sports and Science Medicine* found the holographic bands were no better at improving performance than an inexpensive band that could be purchased at a discount store. Since then, Power Balance has admitted that there is no credible scientific evidence behind its technology. A class-action lawsuit was filed against Power Balance for purposely misleading the public and making false advertising claims.

Work as a Team Do you think the claims made by Power Balance were misleading? Do you think it was necessary to take legal steps against Power Balance? Justify your answers.

Legal Factors Affecting Advertising

In the early days of advertising, businesses could get away with saying pretty much anything in their advertisements. Little or no legal restrictions existed regarding how a company promoted its products.

Misrepresentations, exaggerations, and outright lies were common in advertisements. Today's advertising is regulated at many levels, ranging from federal, state, and city laws. The laws and regulations seem endless, making it necessary for businesses to understand the restrictions that apply to advertising to avoid fines or a loss of business.

Federal Legislation

The federal government has passed many laws that affect marketing and advertising. These laws are designed to protect consumers from unfair or deceptive business practices. The primary laws are listed below.

- *Federal Trade Commission Act of 1914* – This law created the **Federal Trade Commission (FTC)** to regulate unfair methods of competition and unfair or deceptive acts that may affect competition.

- *Food and Drug Act of 1906* – This law regulated the content and labeling of food and drug products and led to the creation of the Food and Drug Administration (FDA). It was replaced by the *Food, Drug, and Cosmetic Act* of 1938, which required extensive product research, testing, and proof of effectiveness and safety.

- *Wheeler-Lea Act of 1938* – This law, which is an amendment to the FTC Act, is commonly known as the Advertising Act. It outlawed false and deceptive advertising practices. It granted the FTC special powers to regulate advertising on food, drugs, cosmetics, and medical devices.

- *Lanham Act of 1946* – This law is also known as the Trademark Act because it regulates the use of trademarks and established penalties for trademark infringement.

- *Cigarette Labeling and Advertising Act of 1965* – This law required cigarette packages to carry warning labels identifying the health

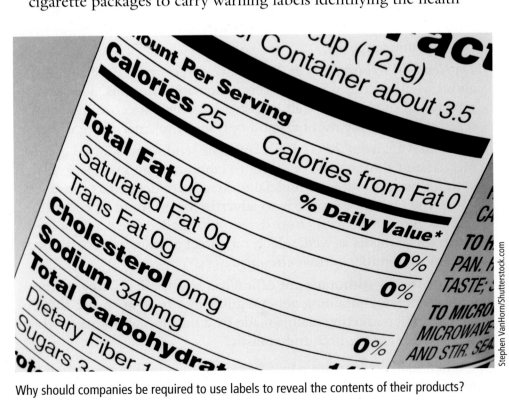

Why should companies be required to use labels to reveal the contents of their products?

hazards of smoking. The act was amended in 1969, mandating that all print advertising also carry warning labels. Cigarette advertisements were banned on radio and television in 1970.

- *Fair Packaging and Labeling Act of 1966* – As a result of this law, consumer product labels must disclose basic information such as ingredients, contents, quantities, weights, and the manufacturer of the product to allow consumers to make product comparisons more easily. This law applies to all types of products, such as groceries, cosmetics, and household cleaners and chemicals. The *Nutrition Labeling and Education Act* of 1990 went further by requiring that labels disclose the amount of specified nutrients in foods, including calories, fat, salt, and other nutrients.

- *Children's Television Act of 1990* – This law regulates the number of minutes of advertising permitted during children's television shows. Commercials are limited to 12 minutes an hour on weekdays and 10.5 minutes an hour on weekends.

- *Telemarketing and Consumer Fraud and Abuse Prevention Act of 1994* – Deceptive and coercive telemarketing practices were prohibited by this law, and restrictions were placed on the time of day when telemarketing calls could be made.

- *Children's Online Privacy Protection Act of 1998* – Commercial websites directed to children or websites that attract a general audience must obtain parental permission before collecting information from children under age 13.

- *Do Not Call Registry Act of 2003* – Consumers now have a choice about whether they want to receive telemarketing calls. This act established the Do Not Call Registry, which allows consumers to register their phone numbers and opt out of telemarketing calls.

- *CAN-SPAM Act of 2003* – This law bans sending unwanted commercial e-mail messages, or spam, to computers and wireless devices without permission. Commercial messages are defined as those for which the primary purpose is to advertise or promote a product or service. A recent federal court decision expanded the reach of the act to social media as well, which can affect a business's social media ad campaign under certain circumstances.

- *Green Guides* – Although not officially a law, the FTC created the Green Guides, containing general guidelines to help ensure that environmental marketing claims made by a business about its products and services are credible and realistic.

When marketers create advertisements, they must know whether they are in compliance with these laws. It may be necessary for a business to consult with an attorney who specializes in advertising before launching an advertising campaign.

The Federal Trade Commission

The FTC is the nation's consumer protection agency. The work of the FTC touches the lives of consumers every day. It enforces many of the laws described previously. It is the government regulatory agency most directly involved in overseeing the advertising industry. The FTC is headed by five commissioners, who are nominated by the President and approved by the Senate. The commissioners oversee the *Bureau of Consumer Protection*, which performs much of the FTC's work. The Bureau of Consumer Protection strives to protect consumers against unfair, deceptive, or fraudulent practices in the marketplace by

- conducting investigations of possible violations of the law
- pursuing legal action against companies and people who violate the law
- developing rules to protect consumers
- educating consumers and businesses about their rights and responsibilities
- collecting complaints about consumer fraud and identity theft and making them available to law enforcement agencies across the country

The Bureau of Consumer Protection has several divisions that focus on different areas of expertise. The Advertising Practices Division takes action against unfair or deceptive advertising and marketing practices, specifically those that raise health and safety concerns or that cause financial harm. It closely monitors claims made about food, over-the-counter drugs, dietary supplements, alcohol, and tobacco. In recent years, monitoring and developing effective enforcement strategies for new advertising techniques and media have become priorities.

The Marketing Practices Division specializes in monitoring and regulating Internet, telecommunications, and direct mail fraud; deceptive spam; fraudulent business, investment, and work-at-home schemes; and violations of the Do Not Call and CAN-SPAM laws. It has developed new strategies and techniques to fight the latest high-tech scams used to defraud consumers.

CHECKPOINT

What is the FTC's role in regulating advertising?

Other Government Regulatory Agencies

Although the FTC is responsible for monitoring unfair and deceptive business practices and enforcing consumer protection laws, other government agencies also have a role in protecting consumers. Advertisers should know the purpose of these regulatory agencies and understand how they impact the advertising industry.

Federal Communications Commission

The **Federal Communications Commission (FCC)** monitors and regulates interstate and international communications by radio, television, wire, satellite, and cable. To broadcast radio, TV, or wireless communications in the United States, the owner or operator must obtain a license from the FCC. The broadcast license can be revoked if the owner or operator is in violation of any laws.

The FCC handles consumer complaints about advertising. Complaints may involve the nature of the products being advertised; the timing of certain ads (for example, during mealtime); commercials that are considered indecent or in poor taste; copyright, libel/slander, patents, and trademark violations; and unwanted text messages and e-mails. The FCC also receives complaints regarding false and misleading advertisements. Complaints can be filed on the FCC's website. The FCC works closely with the FTC to enforce consumer protection laws.

Food and Drug Administration

The **Food and Drug Administration (FDA)** ensures that food, cosmetics, drugs, and medical devices are safe and effective. It also ensures that these products are honestly, accurately, and informatively represented to the public with proper labeling. Advertisers can be prosecuted for false labeling. Special labeling is required for products that are considered dangerous or hazardous, such as household cleaners and medications. Many food, drug, and cosmetic advertisements make claims about all natural ingredients, rapid weight loss, hair growth, or younger-looking skin. If these claims cannot be substantiated, the FDA will work with the FTC to put a stop to these violations. In addition, the FDA has the authority to regulate the ingredients in tobacco products and the way they are distributed, sold, and marketed. For example, the FDA has banned tobacco companies from sponsoring sporting and entertainment events and has outlawed free cigarette samples. Currently, the FDA is closely monitoring the fast food industry.

© iofoto/Shutterstock.com

Why does the FDA closely monitor advertising claims about cosmetics?

Alcohol and Tobacco Tax and Trade Bureau

At one time, all federal regulations involving alcohol were issued by the Bureau of Alcohol, Tobacco, and Firearms (ATF). In 2003, the ATF was split into two divisions, one of which is the Bureau of Alcohol, Tobacco, Firearms, and Explosives. The other is the **Alcohol and Tobacco Tax and Trade Bureau (TTB)**, which implements and enforces a broad range of provisions to ensure that alcohol products are created, labeled, and advertised in accordance with federal laws and regulations. Federal law mandates that alcoholic beverages carry a warning label that informs and reminds consumers about the health hazards that may result from the consumption of alcoholic beverages. The TTB established the Alcohol Beverage Advertising Program to help monitor advertising of alcoholic beverages. Instead of increasing total alcohol consumption, the objectives of most alcoholic beverage advertisers are to encourage consumers to switch to their brand and to create brand loyalty.

United States Postal Service

The U.S. Postal Service (USPS) regulates direct mail advertising. It investigates mail fraud scams, such as foreign lotteries, free-prize schemes, pyramid schemes, investment fraud schemes, and work-at-home schemes. It prosecutes individuals and companies that commit such scams. The Postal Inspection Service receives inquiries and investigates complaints from consumers who feel they have been defrauded by offers received via the mail.

SPOTLIGHT ON SUCCESS

© AP Photo/Harry Cabluck

GREG ABBOTT

Attorney General of Texas

Attorney General Greg Abbott is the 50th Attorney General of Texas. After graduating from The University of Texas with a BBA in Finance, he received his law degree from Vanderbilt University. Shortly after graduating from law school, he was partially paralyzed by a falling tree while jogging. Navigating in a wheelchair does not keep Attorney General Greg Abbott from fulfilling his responsibility of protecting the citizens of Texas. Abbott and his team of more than 700 attorneys who represent the State of Texas enforce the state's laws.

As the state's chief law enforcement official, Attorney General Abbott has made protecting children and families the focus of his administration. He files numerous lawsuits against companies that use unfair business practices. In a recent lawsuit, he accused an auto warranty company that conducted business in Texas of repeatedly violating telemarketing laws by contacting people on the state and federal "do not call" lists. The company also failed to disclose that the costly warranties were loaded with limitations and required out-of-pocket payments for repairs to be completed. In another lawsuit, Abbott charged a Texas company with orchestrating an unlawful marketing scheme that exaggerated the health benefits of its products in order to increase sales. The company's marketing materials falsely claimed that its dietary supplements could cure and treat Down Syndrome, cystic fibrosis, cancer, and other serious illnesses. On a larger scale, Abbott is investigating Google after receiving complaints that the company is manipulating its paid search results in a way that suppresses competition. Abbott and his team of attorneys are conducting a review of Google's business practices.

On a more personal level, Abbott reaches out to Texas citizens by writing and posting weekly articles on the Attorney General of Texas website. The articles offer general consumer advice on topics such as the latest consumer scams, mail-in rebate laws, consumer recalls, telephone fraud, and the Texas Deceptive Trade Practices Act. Although Abbott has many responsibilities as the Attorney General of Texas, one of his biggest roles is to serve and protect the rights of all Texas citizens by enforcing health, safety, and consumer regulations.

Think Critically

If federal regulatory agencies serve to protect consumers, why do state attorneys general also need to play a role in consumer protection? How do Gregg Abbott and other state attorneys general serve their citizens?

States and Cities

Advertisers are also subject to state and local laws. Different states have different regulations governing what can be advertised. For example, some states prohibit advertising for certain types of alcoholic beverages, and most states restrict the use of federal and state flags in advertising. Keeping up with the different state laws can be difficult for national advertisers. The state's attorney general is responsible for protecting the public interests of the state and its residents. Consumer complaints about advertisements can be filed with the state's attorney general office. Further advertising restrictions are imposed by cities and municipalities. For example, laws regarding the placement and content of billboards will vary among different municipalities. The city or county district attorney's office handles numerous complaints about false or misleading advertising.

///////// CHECKPOINT \\\\\\\\\

What is the FCC's involvement in the advertising industry?

13.1 Assessment

THINK ABOUT IT

1. Select two of the federal laws described in this lesson and explain the effect they have on advertisers.

2. How does the FTC help protect consumers?

3. Describe a circumstance under which the USPS might investigate an advertiser.

MAKE ACADEMIC CONNECTIONS

4. **RESEARCH** Conduct research to learn about an advertiser that violated one of the federal laws described in this lesson. Write a one-page report describing the violation. Also, name the government agency that enforced the law and explain the penalty that was applied.

5. **COMMUNICATION** You purchased a nationally advertised product from Weight-B-Gone, which claimed you would lose a minimum of ten pounds in one week by taking the company's weight loss supplement. You followed the instructions closely and actually gained two pounds in one week. Write a letter to the appropriate government agency about your experience and the fraudulent claim.

Teamwork

The FTC and other government agencies enforce many laws that regulate the marketing and advertising industries. Conduct research to learn about the arguments for and against government regulation. Then form two teams to debate this issue.

13.2

Self-Regulation

Goals

- Explain the concept of self-regulation and identify how it is applied in the advertising industry.
- Recognize how consumers can regulate business practices.

Terms

- self-regulation, p. 357
- consumerism, p. 360
- boycott, p. 360
- change agents, p. 361

FOCUS ON ADVERTISING

Toyota Pulls Its Ads

In 2009 ABC News began reporting on the problem of "runaway Toyotas" that were experiencing sudden acceleration problems. The reports preceded the large recalls issued by Toyota. Less than a year later, 173 Toyota dealers in five southeast states pulled their commercials from local ABC TV stations due to "excessive stories on the Toyota issues." The dealers shifted their commercials to non-ABC stations in the same markets "as punishment for the reporting," according to an ABC station manager. The Southeast Toyota dealers are located in Florida, Georgia, Alabama, South Carolina, and North Carolina and sell 20 percent of all Toyotas sold in the United States. ABC stations lost advertising revenue by pulling the commercials. However, ABC executives made no apologies for its investigative reports in which details were released and questions were asked about Toyota's safety problems. Shortly thereafter, Toyota began airing new commercials that discussed recall-related issues and stressed its commitment to safety and quality.

Work as a Team What effect did the media have on Toyota and its advertising? Do you think the actions of both organizations were justified? Why or why not?

Advertising Industry Accountability

In addition to government regulation, the advertising industry itself has developed procedures and standards to deal with unfair and deceptive advertising practices. **Self-regulation** is the advertising industry's attempt to regulate and control its actions. Several members in the advertising industry have established voluntary rules of behavior to help maintain the general integrity of advertising.

National Advertising Review Board

The National Advertising Review Board (NARB) is one of the most important self-regulation organizations in the advertising industry. It was formed in partnership with the Council of Better Business Bureau's National Advertising Division (NAD). The NAD and NARB were established to uphold standards of truth and accuracy in national advertising. The NARB is made up of 70 professionals from three different categories: national advertisers, advertising agencies, and public members consisting of academics and former members of the public sector.

Complaints about the truthfulness or accuracy of advertisements from consumers, competitors, or local branches of the Better Business Bureau (BBB) are referred to the NAD. When the NAD can't resolve a complaint, it is forwarded to the NARB, where a panel evaluates the complaint. If the issue still cannot be resolved, it is forwarded to the FTC or another government regulatory agency. The NAD and the NARB cannot impose penalties on advertisers, but they are influential enough to deter questionable advertising practices. The NAD and the NARB investigate only national advertisements, not local ones.

Better Business Bureau

In addition to the national BBB, local and state BBBs handle consumer complaints and dispute resolutions. Among those complaints fielded are misleading or false advertising claims. Because the NAD and the NARB only investigate national advertisements, local BBBs often review complaints about local advertisements that appear only in the cities and towns served by the advertiser. The BBB can ask a business to stop using ads that appear to be deceptive, but it cannot legally force the business to do so. If fraud is suspected, the local BBB will alert local, state, and federal law enforcement agencies. Deceptive advertising and other questionable business practice complaints that go unresolved will be reported on the local BBB's website. In an attempt to avoid these kinds of problems, the BBB provides information to businesses about responsible advertising practices.

Advertising Agencies

Advertising agencies work with clients to develop effective advertising campaigns. Because an advertising agency is legally responsible for the advertising it creates, the advertisements must be truthful, accurate, and trustworthy. Advertising agencies should know and obey all local, state, and federal regulations regarding advertising. The American Association of Advertising Agencies (AAAA), also called the 4As, helps regulate the advertising industry by monitoring industrywide advertising practices. Agencies must apply for membership, and any agency judged to be unethical is denied membership. AAAA developed a

COOL FACT

According to an annual report released by the BBB, consumers filed 1.1 million complaints against North American businesses in 2010, reflecting a ten percent increase over the previous year.

Creative Code that members are expected to follow. It states that members will not create advertising that contains the following:

- False or misleading statements or exaggerations
- Testimonials that do not reflect the real opinion of the person giving the testimonial
- Misleading price claims
- Claims insufficiently supported by scientific or professional evidence
- Material that is considered offensive, indecent, or obscene to the general public or minority groups, including racial and ethnic groups, religious groups, age groups, and the disabled population

Media Organizations

Self-regulation among media organizations helps ensure that misleading, deceptive, or offensive advertising does not reach consumers. The National Association of Broadcasters Code Authority monitors radio and television advertising. Television commercials also must be screened and approved by the individual television networks before being aired. Networks may reject an advertisement for inaccuracies or poor taste. Certain products, such as toys and those with health-related claims, must be approved by both the Code Authority and the television network. The Code Authority can reject an advertisement even if it was approved previously by the network.

Print publications have their own policies and standards regarding the acceptance and rejection of ads. They have in-house departments set up to review advertisements. Businesses that use direct mail or other direct marketing campaigns may become members of the Direct Marketing Association (DMA). The DMA promotes strong business ethics through its programs and guidelines.

Why is it important for television networks to carefully screen commercials aimed at children?

Competition

Competing companies often monitor each other's advertisements, especially those making direct comparisons. When a company believes that one of its competitors has made false advertising claims, it will report the questionable advertising to the appropriate regulatory agencies. The company may even file a lawsuit against its competitor. The pizza chain Papa John's slogan is "Better Ingredients. Better Pizza." In an advertising campaign, Papa John's alleged that its sauce and dough were better than Pizza Hut's because they were made with fresh tomatoes and filtered water. Pizza Hut filed a false advertising lawsuit. Originally, a jury sided with Pizza Hut, agreeing that Papa John's claims were false or misleading, and Papa John's was ordered to stop using its famous slogan. The decision was overturned by an appeals court who decided consumers did not rely on Papa John's "better ingredients" claims when deciding which pizza to buy.

Consumer Awareness

Today, businesses are finding that consumers want to play a bigger role in the marketing process. Although there are many government and independent regulatory agencies that monitor advertising, consumers also act as regulatory agents. Consumers are very active in ensuring their rights are protected. Individuals can report deceptive or misleading advertising practices to the appropriate regulatory agencies. Individual consumers have less influence over businesses than do groups of consumers working together on the same cause. **Consumerism** involves the organized effort of consumers to influence business practices. Consumer groups speak their opinions and recommend changes. To express disapproval or to pressure a company to make changes, consumers may stage a **boycott**, which is an organized effort to avoid purchasing goods and services from a particular company. National advertisers have responded to threats of boycotts by pulling their advertisements from television programs that consumers found offensive.

How can boycotts affect business practices?

There are a number of consumer protection agencies that assist in the regulation process. These agencies provide helpful consumer information, assist in resolving consumer problems, and field consumer complaints.

- *National Consumers League (NCL)* – As the nation's oldest consumer organization, NCL's mission is to protect and promote social and economic justice for consumers. It represents consumers on marketplace issues. It operates the Fraud Center, which tracks the latest telemarketing and Internet scams.

- *Consumer Federation of America (CFA)* – This association of non-profit consumer organizations strives to protect consumers through research, advocacy, and education. The CFA investigates consumer issues, behavior, and attitudes through surveys, focus groups, and investigative reports. It also distributes information on consumer issues to the public and news media.

- *Federal Citizen Information Center (FCIC)* – The FCIC assists federal agencies in the development, promotion, and distribution of helpful consumer publications. It publishes the *Consumer Action Handbook* offering helpful consumer tips, which is available for free in print or online.

- *Consumers Union* – This organization has the largest consumer product testing facility in the world. It publishes *Consumer Reports* magazine, which provides test results and product ratings. To remain unbiased, Consumers Union buys all of the products it tests and accepts no advertising.

These four consumer protection agencies are just a few of the many consumer organizations that help consumers battle unfair business practices. With the backing of a consumer agency, consumers can become **change agents**, or people who bring about meaningful changes that add value to their lives and other's.

///// CHECKPOINT \\\\\
How can consumers act as a regulatory agent for business practices?

13.2 Assessment

THINK ABOUT IT

1. How does the National Advertising Review Board help regulate the advertising industry?
2. Why do competitors monitor and police the advertising industry?
3. What is consumerism and how does it affect marketing and advertising?

MAKE ACADEMIC CONNECTIONS

4. **MATH** A luxury automobile manufacturer advertises the lease price for one of its most popular models at $359 per month for 24 months. The mileage allowance for the lease is 15,000 miles a year. If the consumer exceeds the mileage allowance at the end of the lease, he or she will be charged $0.15 for every mile over the limit. The fine print in the advertisement states that the consumer must also make a down payment of $2,700. What is the REAL cost of leasing the luxury vehicle for 24 months if the vehicle's mileage is 33,500 at the end of the 24-month lease?

5. **COMMUNICATION** Learn more about the services provided by the Better Business Bureau by conducting online research. Design a three-fold brochure describing the BBB's services that could be handed out at a consumer awareness event.

6. **HISTORY** Conduct research to learn about successful boycotts throughout American history. Write a two-page report describing one or more of the boycotts and the changes made by businesses in response to the boycotts.

Teamwork
Select a product or service of your choice and create a print advertisement that makes exaggerated or misleading claims. Then revise the advertisement so that the claims are accurate and truthful. Present the two advertisements to the class and explain why one is acceptable while the other is not.

13.3
Ethics in Advertising

Goals
- Identify the ethical aspects of advertising.
- Explain how the FTC assures truth in advertising.

Terms
- ethics, p. 362
- deception, p. 363
- puffery, p. 363
- defamation, p. 363
- subliminal message, p. 364
- cease-and-desist order, p. 367
- corrective ad, p. 367
- affirmative disclosure, p. 368
- disclaimer, p. 368

FOCUS ON ADVERTISING

Promoting Products with a Social Mission

Companies are under great pressure to conduct business fairly and ethically and to contribute to society in a positive way. TOMS Shoes, a company that sells clothing, shoes, and accessories, meets all of these criteria. While traveling in Argentina, Blake Mycoskie discovered that many children were shoeless, which can lead to soil-transmitted diseases and other injuries. In an effort to help, Blake founded TOMS and pledged to give a pair of shoes to a child in need for every pair of TOMS' shoes purchased. TOMS launched a digital advertising campaign that described its social mission and encouraged consumers to help TOMS make an impact on the world. To help raise more awareness of the cause, TOMS sponsored an event in which consumers were asked to go barefoot for one day. Studies have shown that U.S. consumers are increasingly motivated to buy products that have a connection to a particular social cause, even if they have to pay more for the product. TOMS' unique advertising campaign was a hit and helped provide more than 1 million pairs of shoes to kids in need since 2006.

Work as a Team Why do you think TOMS' advertising campaign was so successful with consumers? How does it illustrate an ethical approach of marketing a product?

The Ethical Aspects of Advertising

In advertising, ethics are an important consideration. **Ethics** are moral principles that guide the actions and behaviors of a person or group. Ethics involve conduct that is right or wrong. Ethical advertising can be defined in many ways. Characteristics of ethical advertising may include honesty, fairness, accuracy, integrity, and sensitivity. However, ethical advertising can be difficult to determine because it often comes down to an individual's personal judgment. Generally, ethical criticisms of advertising involve the issues described below.

Advertising Can Be Deceptive

Deception involves making false or misleading statements in an advertisement. Deceptive advertising harms consumers and competitors, so it is closely regulated by government agencies such as the FTC. In some cases, deception is easy to detect. If a diet product fails to deliver on its guarantee of a 10-pound weight loss in one week, the advertising is deceptive, and the advertiser faces legal consequences. A sales advertisement containing "small print" that excludes certain items is often considered deceptive.

On the other hand, advertising that uses **puffery**, which is an exaggeration or a subjective opinion used to sell products, is legal because it cannot be proven true or false. For example, a restaurant that claims to serve the "best burger in the world" is using puffery because consumers are likely to interpret this claim as an exaggeration commonly made in advertisements. Another form of deception in advertising is **defamation**, which involves making a false or derogatory statement that gives a negative impression about a competing business or product. If the allegation made cannot be proven, a defamation lawsuit may be filed.

Although some advertising can be deceptive, most of it is not. Governmental regulation and self-regulation within the advertising industry help prevent this.

Advertising Can Create Needs and Promote Materialism

Many people question the ethics of selling consumers things they don't need. We don't need many of the things found in our homes. For example, advertising has convinced consumers that they should drink bottled water, even though many of the bottled water manufacturers

Has an advertisement ever motivated you to buy something you didn't need? Did you regret your purchase?

use water that comes from the same source as tap water. Advertising also is frequently criticized for encouraging *materialism*, which places an importance on money and possessions. Ads often portray products as symbols of status, prestige, happiness, and beauty. Clever advertising makes individuals feel as if they are entitled to the good things in life. In doing so, some people believe advertisers are encouraging self-indulgent behavior.

Although advertising does encourage consumers to make purchases, is this unethical? It is clearly unethical if the advertising is deceptive or misleading. In all other cases, consumers must act responsibly to avoid making purchases they don't need.

Advertising Can Be Manipulative

Some people criticize advertising for its powers of persuasion. They suggest that advertising compels consumers to take actions they would not otherwise take. Oftentimes, these actions are not in the consumers' best interests, such as buying something they cannot afford or will later regret. But most people are mentally capable of resisting these types of persuasive efforts.

Others claim that advertisers use subliminal messages to manipulate consumers. A **subliminal message** is information that your subconscious, or unconscious mind, receives without you fully realizing that you're receiving it. Because your conscious mind does not have time to analyze this type of message, the information is automatically accepted as being true, making it a persuasive force. Subliminal messages may take the form of words, images, or sounds. When you watch a professional sporting event, there are usually banners around the field that promote various businesses. Unknowingly, your subconscious may make a mental note about these advertised brands, leading you to buy the product or service. For example, you may develop a craving for McDonald's after seeing a sign for it in the outfield. Product placements are considered another form of subliminal advertising. While your conscious mind is taking in the movie, your unconscious mind might notice brands placed throughout the movie. However, whether or not these types of subliminal advertising methods influence your buying decisions is unclear.

Advertising Can Be Controversial

Advertising of products and services such as tobacco, alcoholic beverages, and gambling and lotteries is considered controversial by many consumers. They believe that advertisements make these products appealing and increase consumption. However, studies have shown that family, friends, and peers have more influence over cigarette and alcohol use than do advertisers. Recently, with obesity on the rise, advertising that promotes fast food companies has become controversial. Many argue that it is the consumers themselves, not the advertisers, who are responsible for overeating.

Controversy also occurs when consumers think advertising is offensive or in poor taste. To make their advertisements stand out from

What makes some weight loss advertisements controversial?

the ad clutter, some advertisers resort to tactics that are considered crude or lewd by some consumers. The topic of the advertisement or the way it is presented may be viewed as inappropriate. Because consumers have different tastes, their personal opinions on what they find offensive will differ. Advertisers should carefully consider the tastefulness of their ads and decide if they are willing to take a risk to capture the attention of their target market.

Advertising Can Play on People's Fears and Guilt

Advertising critics claim that some advertisements use fear or guilt to sell products and services to consumers. By highlighting the negative consequences or risks of not using an advertised product, advertisers try to influence consumer buying behavior. This tactic is often used to promote home security systems, insurance products, weight loss products, prescription medications, and charitable organizations. Often, vulnerable consumers, such as senior citizens or those with health-related issues, are targeted. Research has shown that advertisements using fear or guilt appeals are very effective. However, many critics feel that consumers already have enough to feel anxious about without advertisers giving them more reasons.

Advertising Often Targets Children

Children are especially susceptible to the persuasion tactics used in advertising. Advertising increases children's demands for toys, video games, snack foods, fast foods, and other products. Critics claim that advertising of certain movies and video games promotes violence and advertising of snack foods and fast foods leads to childhood obesity. The Children's Advertising Review Unit (CARU), which is part of the Council of Better Business Bureaus, closely monitors advertising

How have advertisers, such as McDonald's, changed the way they advertise food and beverages to children?

directed at children in all media to ensure it is not deceptive, unfair, or inappropriate for the intended audience. It also receives complaints about advertising practices and determines whether the practices violate CARU's standards as outlined in its *Self-Regulatory Guidelines for Children's Advertising*.

Because of pressure from critics, several of the largest U.S. food and beverage companies, including Campbell Soup, General Mills, Kellogg, Kraft, McDonald's, and PepsiCo, voluntarily adopted the Children's Food and Beverage Advertising Initiative. The Initiative is designed to cut back on advertising unhealthy foods to children under 12. It allows companies to advertise food and beverage products to children if the products meet certain nutritional criteria. The same advertising standards apply to all participating companies. These standards could force some brands to change recipes to include less sodium, fat, sugars, and calories.

In addition to monitoring the products being advertised to children, other aspects of advertising are also scrutinized. For example, a commercial that showed children by the poolside was criticized because there was no parental supervision at the pool. Another commercial that showed a girl at the museum going to the bathroom to brush her teeth was removed from the air when teachers complained that they'd never let a child leave the group unattended. When it comes to advertising directed at children, advertisers need to address a wide range of concerns.

CHECKPOINT

What are some of the ethical criticisms about advertising?

Truth in Advertising

Ethics in advertising is closely related to truth in advertising. To assure truth in advertising, the FTC and other governmental agencies enforce federal advertising laws (described earlier in the chapter) that prohibit deceptive or misleading statements in advertisements. Collectively, these laws are commonly referred to as *truth-in-advertising laws*. The FTC uses the following guidelines to determine if an ad is deceptive.

- The FTC looks at an ad from the point of view of the "reasonable" consumer (typical person looking at the ad). The FTC looks at the ad's words, phrases, and images to determine what it conveys to consumers.

- The FTC looks at the claims made in the ad. An *express claim* is literal and straightforward. "Our toothpaste fights cavities" is an express claim that the product will prevent cavities. An *implied claim* is one made indirectly or by inference. "Our toothpaste fights plaque that causes cavities" is an implied claim that the product will prevent cavities. Although the ad doesn't literally say it prevents cavities, it would be reasonable for a consumer to conclude that from the statement. Under the law, advertisers must have proof to back up express and implied claims that consumers take from an ad.

- The FTC looks at what the ad does *not* say to determine if the failure to include information gives consumers a misimpression of the product. For example, if a company advertised a bundled package containing shampoo and conditioner but failed to disclose that the package contained trial sizes instead of standard sizes of the products, the ad may be viewed as deceptive.

A toothpaste ad may imply that it fights cavities without expressly claiming it does. Do you think implied claims are ethical? Why or why not?

- The FTC looks at whether a claim would be "material." A material statement is one that is likely to influence a consumer's decision to buy or use the product. Material claims generally pertain to a product's characteristics, such as its performance, features, size, and price. If a company falsely claims that its nutrition bar is made from all natural ingredients, this would be a material misrepresentation to consumers who make purchases based on this factor.

- The FTC looks at whether the advertiser has sufficient, documented evidence to support the claims in the ad. Evidence could include tests, surveys, or scientific data.

If the FTC determines that a company's advertising is deceptive, it may take one of several actions. It may issue a **cease-and-desist order**, which is a legal order to discontinue a deceptive ad. The FTC may also force a company to run a **corrective ad**, which will rectify any false impressions created by deceptive advertising. If an ad does not disclose important material facts about a product, the FTC may require **affirmative disclosure**, whereby future ads must include the material facts that were not disclosed in a previous ad. The FTC may also impose a *fine*, or a monetary penalty, on a company that violates truth-in-advertising laws.

Many advertisers are including disclaimers on their ads to protect themselves from legal liability. A **disclaimer** is a statement that outlines the limitations of a product. Ads for weight-loss drugs often promote excessive weight loss. Disclaimer statements inform consumers that the weight loss results shown in the ads are not typical or are in conjunction with diet and regular exercise.

▰▰▰▰ CHECKPOINT ◼◼◼◼

How is truth in advertising monitored by the FTC?

13.3 Assessment

THINK ABOUT IT

1. What is the difference between deception and puffery in advertising?
2. How does advertising play on people's fears and guilt? Provide examples.
3. What actions can the FTC take against deceptive advertising?

MAKE ACADEMIC CONNECTIONS

4. **INTERNATIONAL** Conduct research to learn about regulations on advertising directed at children in other countries. Prepare a PowerPoint presentation describing some of the restrictions. How do the child-related advertising laws and regulations compare to those in the United States?

5. **ETHICS** Find a disclaimer in an advertisement. It can be a print, radio, television, or online ad. What is the disclaimer? Do you think the advertiser has an ethical obligation to include the disclaimer? Does the disclaimer alter your view of the advertised product? Explain your answers.

6. **CONSUMER ECONOMICS** Advertising has been accused of causing consumers to buy products they don't need. Look around your house to find products that your family doesn't need or use. Calculate the approximate cost of the unneeded items to determine how much money could have been saved. Assume this amount represents a yearly average over the past five years. How much wasteful spending occurred over those five years?

 ## Teamwork
Find an advertisement that illustrates each of the following concepts—puffery, materialism, manipulation, controversy, and appeals based on fear or guilt. Present the advertisements to the class and explain the ethical concerns related to each one.

PARTNERSHIP FOR
21ST CENTURY SKILLS

Understanding Contracts

A *contract* is a legally binding agreement between two or more parties that creates an obligation of some type. As a consumer, you are likely to enter into a contract at some point in time. If you get a credit card or open up a credit account, get a loan to buy a house or car, rent an apartment, or finance the purchase of furniture, appliances, or other consumer goods, you will have to sign a contract. When you sign a contract, you are agreeing to certain conditions, such as making a monthly payment on a specified date throughout the duration of the loan.

For a contract to be considered legally binding, certain elements must exist, as described below.

- *Agreement* – A contract has legal agreement when there is an offer and acceptance. In other words, one party must offer to do something, and a second party accepts or agrees to the offer. If the second party makes a counteroffer, there is no agreement. A *counteroffer* is a change to the original offer.

- *Consideration* – Something of value exchanged for something else of value is known as consideration. Consideration may be an item of value, money, a promise, or a performed service. If one party gives something but receives nothing in return from the second party, the contract may not be enforceable.

- *Capacity* – Parties to a contract must have contractual capacity, or be competent, to enter into a legal agreement. In other words, they must have the basic ability to properly evaluate and understand the consequences of a contract. Minors, intoxicated people, and mentally ill people cannot enter into a binding contract.

- *Legality* – A contract cannot have anything in it that is illegal or that would result in illegal activities.

- *Genuine assent* – A contract cannot be based on deceit or the use of unfair pressure or influence on the part of either party. It also is not binding if the contract is based on certain mistakes of fact.

Although oral contracts may be enforceable, some contracts must be in writing to be fully enforceable. Because oral contracts may be more difficult to enforce, many businesses and consumers prefer written contracts.

Try It Out

Working with a partner, create two scenarios. The first scenario should describe a contract for which all of the requirements listed above have been met, making the contract legally binding. The second scenario should describe a contract for which one or more of the requirements listed above have not been met, making the contract unenforceable.

© April Cat/Shutterstock.com

SUMMARY

13.1 Government Regulation

- There are numerous federal laws designed to protect consumers from unfair or deceptive business practices, such as false advertising. When marketers create advertisements, they must know whether they are in compliance with these laws.
- The Federal Trade Commission Act of 1914 established the Federal Trade Commission (FTC), which is the government regulatory agency most directly involved in overseeing the advertising industry.
- Other government regulatory agencies that work with the FTC to monitor and regulate advertising include the Federal Communications Commission (FCC), Food and Drug Administration (FDA), Alcohol and Tobacco Tax and Trade Bureau (TTB), U.S. Postal Service (USPS), and state and local government agencies.

13.2 Self-Regulation

- In addition to government regulation, the advertising industry practices self-regulation. It has developed voluntary rules of behavior to help maintain the integrity of advertising.
- Self-regulatory groups that monitor advertising to protect against unfair advertising practices include the National Advertising Review Board, Better Business Bureau, advertising agencies, media organizations, and competitors.
- Consumers themselves act as regulatory agents. They report deceptive or misleading advertising practices to the appropriate regulatory agencies. Numerous consumer protection agencies are available to assist in the regulation process.

13.3 Ethics in Advertising

- Ethics are the moral principles that guide the actions and behaviors of a person or group. Characteristics of ethical advertising include honesty, fairness, accuracy, integrity, and sensitivity.
- Advertising has been criticized for being unethical because it can be deceptive, manipulative, and controversial; create needs for unnecessary products; promote materialism; play on people's fears and guilt; and target children.
- The FTC enforces truth in advertising using specific guidelines to determine whether an ad is deceptive.
- Several actions can be taken against advertisers that violate truth-in-advertising laws. These actions include cease-and-desist orders, corrective ads, affirmative disclosures, and disclaimers.

Read *Impact Advertising* on page 349 again to review the deceptive strategies used by companies sponsoring sweepstakes. Conduct research to learn more about regulations put in place to stop these deceptive acts. Describe some of the regulations.

Vocabulary Builder

Match each statement with the term that best defines it. Some terms may not be used.

1. Government agency that regulates unfair methods of competition and unfair or deceptive acts that may affect competition
2. A legal order to discontinue a deceptive ad
3. The organized effort of consumers to influence business practices
4. The act of making false or misleading statements in an advertisement
5. A statement that outlines the limitations of a product
6. The act of making a false or derogatory statement that gives a negative impression
7. An organized effort to avoid purchasing goods and services from a particular company
8. Government agency that monitors and regulates interstate and international communications
9. An exaggeration or a subjective opinion used to sell products
10. Information that your subconscious receives without you fully realizing that you're receiving it

a. affirmative disclosure
b. boycott
c. cease-and-desist order
d. change agents
e. consumerism
f. corrective ad
g. deception
h. defamation
i. disclaimer
j. ethics
k. FCC
l. FDA
m. FTC
n. puffery
o. self-regulation
p. subliminal message
q. TTB

Test Your Knowledge

11. The _____ ensures that food, cosmetics, drugs, and medical devices are safe and effective and labeled properly.
    a. FTC
    b. FDA
    c. FCC
    d. SEC

12. Which of the following acts regulates the use of trademarks?
    a. Lanham Act
    b. Wheeler-Lea Act
    c. Federal Trade Commission Act
    d. Fair Packaging and Labeling Act

13. Which of the following restrictions is *not* part of the Cigarette Labeling and Advertising Act?
    a. cigarette packages must carry warning labels
    b. print advertisements for cigarettes must carry warnings
    c. smoking inside public buildings is banned
    d. cigarette advertisements on radio and television are banned

14. Which of the following advertising practices is legal?
    a. puffery
    b. deception
    c. defamation
    d. none of the above
15. The FTC protects consumers by
    a. conducting investigations of possible violations of law
    b. developing rules to protect consumers
    c. collecting complaints about consumer fraud
    d. all of the above
16. Which of the following statements about the National Advertising Review Board is *not* true?
    a. It works in partnership with the BBB's National Advertising Division.
    b. It investigates fraudulent claims made against local and national advertisements.
    c. The board is comprised of national advertisers, advertising agencies, and public sector members.
    d. It cannot impose penalties on advertisers.
17. Advertising that plays on people's fears and guilt has all of the following characteristics *except*
    a. it highlights the negative consequences of not using a product
    b. it targets vulnerable consumers
    c. it is ineffective
    d. it is often used for security systems and insurance products
18. An advertiser that has been identified by the FTC as having a deceptive ad may be required to
    a. cease and desist the ad
    b. run a corrective ad
    c. pay a fine
    d. all of the above
19. The _____ investigates mail fraud scams, such as foreign lotteries and free-prize, pyramid, and investment fraud schemes.
    a. USPS
    b. FCC
    c. FDA
    d. TTB
20. A(n) _____ claim in an advertisement is made indirectly or by inference.
    a. express
    b. implied
    c. material
    d. corrective

Apply What You Learned

21. Businesses often monitor advertisements in which a competitor makes a direct comparison to them. Describe an ad you have seen recently that compares one business or product to another. Do you think the comparison is fair or unfair? Explain your answer.
22. Major television networks air cartoons on Saturday mornings. List five types of businesses or products that are likely to be advertised during this time period. How do the ads try to appeal to the target market?

23. Obtain advertising that promotes a contest or sweepstakes. Carefully read the advertisement, including the "small print" (disclaimers). Do you think the contest or sweepstakes is deceptive in any way? If so, explain how.

24. Create a table that lists various consumer protection agencies and their purposes. Include the agencies listed in the chapter as well as others you research online.

Make Academic Connections

25. **RESEARCH** Because of the strong demand for environmentally friendly products, more businesses are producing and advertising products to meet this demand. Learn more about the FTC Green Guides that provide environmental marketing guidelines. Write a one-page report on your findings.

26. **MATH** Laws specify that TV commercials aired during children's television shows be limited to 12 minutes an hour on weekdays and 10.5 minutes an hour on weekends. Calculate how many minutes of commercials can be shown during 12 hours of children's television during the week and 8 hours of children's television during the weekend.

27. **COMMUNICATION** Your city council is considering a new local ordinance that will ban billboard advertising along the busy highway leading into your community. You own a hotel that frequently advertises on billboards. A large percentage of your customers visit the hotel because of the billboards. You plan to attend the next city council meeting to speak out against this ordinance. Prepare a speech that explains the benefits of billboard advertising for your community. Also, prepare a billboard ad for your hotel to present at the meeting.

28. **GOVERNMENT** Select one of the governmental regulatory agencies discussed in this chapter. Prepare a PowerPoint presentation that describes the purpose of the agency and its responsibilities. Also, explain how the agency affects the advertising industry.

29. **VISUAL ART** Select a product of your choice and create an advertisement for it that would be considered deceptive. Then revise the advertisement in a way that would be considered puffery. Present the advertisements to the class and explain why one advertisement is illegal while the other is not.

Easy In and Out is a national chain of fast food restaurants. In its advertisements, the restaurant claims that its burgers are made with 100 percent pure beef. You often eat at Easy In and Out because you believe its burgers are better since they are made with higher-quality ingredients. Recently, one of your friends started working for Easy In and Out. He told you that, in fact, the burgers are not 100 percent pure beef and contain other types of fillers. You feel as if you've been deceived.

What would you do? Do you think the restaurant's advertisements are illegal? Why or why not?

Reality ✓

Subliminal Messages in Advertising

When some people hear the term "subliminal advertising," they think about hidden messages embedded in ads. Legend has it that a man named James Vicary first attempted subliminal advertising over 50 years ago in a movie theater. Throughout the movie, he flashed a couple of different messages on the screen every five seconds lasting 1/3000th of a second. Messages included "Drink Coca-Cola" and "Hungry? Eat Popcorn." According to Vicary, Coca-Cola and popcorn sales increased dramatically. He concluded that the power of subliminal advertising had coerced unwitting buyers into making purchases they otherwise would not have considered. However, whether or not the data was falsified or even whether or not the experiment actually took place has always been a mystery.

The type of subliminal advertising described above is considered a deceptive business practice by the FTC. However, a legal kind of subliminal advertising can still be found in ads today. Advertisers appeal to consumers' senses and unconscious assumptions to persuade them to make purchases.

The five senses—touch, smell, sight, hearing, and taste—are often targeted in marketing campaigns. Images, symbols, colors, words, aromas, and body language can send out hidden messages. A store may use fragranced candles or music to draw in customers. However, if asked why they visited the store, shoppers are unlikely to mention the candles or music because those are subconscious factors. Marketers also know that consumers unconsciously stick to familiar, comforting rituals. In recent years, many companies such as Pepsi, Cheerios, and Doritos have started using retro styling on packaging, and sales have increased. Consumers may subconsciously purchase more of these products because images from their past are comforting and cheery. By tapping into consumers' subconscious minds, companies influence buying behaviors in unexpected ways.

Think Critically

1. Why do you think the type of subliminal advertising described by James Vicary is discouraged by the FTC?
2. Why are the five senses an important element of subliminal advertising?
3. How can consumers' customs, traditions, or rituals be used in subliminal advertising?

Ethical decisions are essential in the business world and the workplace. Working on a team consisting of two to three members, you will be challenged to present solutions to ethical situations encountered in the business world and the workplace. Your team will present and defend its positions related to an ethical dilemma.

TOPIC The United States is home to more obese people than anywhere else in the world. According to the CDC (Centers for Disease Control and Prevention), obesity in adults has increased by 60 percent within the past 20 years, while obesity in children has tripled in the past 30 years. A staggering 33 percent of U.S. adults are obese, and obesity-related deaths have climbed to more than 300,000 a year, second only to tobacco-related deaths. Fast food restaurants like McDonald's are being blamed for obesity in children. Critics claim that McDonald's advertising and menu items, such as the Happy Meal, are largely responsible for the overconsumption of McDonald's food. As a representative for McDonald's, you have been asked to explain the responsible actions it is taking to provide and promote healthier menu choices.

Your team has 20 minutes to review the ethical dilemma and work on a solution. Each participant can use two 4" by 6" note cards during the preparation and presentation. No reference materials, visual aids, or electronic devices may be used during the preparation or presentation. You have seven minutes to present the ethical dilemma and the recommended solution. Following the presentation, McDonald's executives (judges) have three minutes to ask questions.

Performance Indicators Evaluated
- Make ethical business decisions in the business world and workplace.
- Provide a rationale for ethical decisions presented.
- Demonstrate critical thinking and problem solving.
- Demonstrate good verbal communication skills.
- Effectively answer questions.

Go to the FBLA website for more detailed information.

Think Critically
1. Why do you think McDonald's Happy Meals are being blamed for causing obesity in children? Do you agree or disagree? Why?
2. What type of advertising campaign should McDonald's develop to change the public's perception of its menu?
3. Do you think McDonald's has an ethical obligation to promote healthier eating habits? Why or why not?

www.fbla.org

14

Advertising in a Multicultural Market

14.1 A Global Vision

14.2 Diversity and Advertising

14.3 Cross-Cultural Communication

Barbie Goes Global

In 1959, the Barbie doll was introduced at the American toy fair, and over 50 years later, she's still around. Since then, Mattel, the maker of Barbie, has sold over one billion Barbies. Barbie was one of the first toys to have a marketing strategy based extensively on television advertising. It was also one of the first times a company had focused on children as consumers.

Mattel originally promoted Barbie as a fashionable teenager who loved clothes and accessories, which were sold separately. The original Barbie was available as a blond or brunette. In 1961, a red-haired Barbie was added. The Barbie collection soon grew, and she became the girl who had everything—flashy clothes, the perfect boyfriend, a Corvette, a dream house, and an exciting career. (Barbie has had over 125 different careers.) As Barbie's popularity grew, Mattel expanded the line to reach other cultures. In 1980, the first African-American Barbie and Hispanic Barbie were introduced.

Barbie eventually entered international markets and is now sold in over 150 countries. However, it wasn't always a smooth transition. Barbie's bright blond hair, big blue eyes, white toothy smile, and statuesque pose were not well received in some cultures. So Mattel adapted Barbie based on the fashion and cultural trends of the various global markets. For example, the Japanese version of Barbie has a closed mouth because Japanese women rarely expose their teeth when they laugh. The Indian Barbie is dressed in a Sari and has a Bindi mark on her forehead.

Mattel has recently launched a major marketing campaign throughout Asia. To increase brand awareness, Mattel is taking Barbie on a "Pink Bus Tour" across China. Barbie also has her own website, and visitors can choose to view the site in over 20 different languages. In addition, Mattel has promoted Barbie through the sales of over 15 Barbie movies, which introduce new Barbie characters that are sold as dolls. The movies have been translated into many other languages, opening up new global markets for Barbie.

Mattel continues to expand the Barbie product line and move into new global markets using innovative marketing strategies. Barbie is truly a multicultural icon.

© AP Photo/Mark Lennihan

WHAT DO YOU KNOW?

1. Why do you think Barbie has succeeded in the toy market after all of these years?

2. Why do you think Barbie has found success in global markets? What makes her appealing across cultures?

3. Do you think the Internet is an important component in increasing global brand awareness of Barbie? Why or why not?

Goals
- Recognize factors that have an impact on global marketing.
- Describe global marketing challenges facing marketers.

Terms
- globalization, p. 378
- international trade, p. 378
- infrastructure, p. 380
- dumping, p. 383
- picturing, p. 383

FOCUS ON ADVERTISING

A Global or Localized Advertising Strategy?

When advertisers enter the global market, they must decide whether to use a global advertising strategy or a localized one. A global advertising strategy assumes that the markets throughout the world are becoming more alike. Companies that use this strategy believe products can be sold the same way all over the world. Ads contain the same theme, content, and slogan worldwide. A localized advertising strategy assumes that global markets have distinct characteristics and require unique advertising campaigns. Companies are finding that the product category should be the key factor in deciding which strategy to use. A global advertising strategy seems to work well for technology and apparel brands. It does not work well for foods and consumer packaged goods because of cultural differences. Consumer behavior and product usage influence advertising of these types of products. For example, in the Italian market, consumers want household cleaning products that are strong and tough, not convenient and timesaving as favored by U.S. consumers. Thus, U.S. manufacturers of household cleaners had to change their advertising focus from convenience to cleaning ability. A localized strategy accommodated different cultural behaviors.

Work as a Team Describe a product or brand for which a global advertising strategy would work. Describe a product or brand that you think would require a localized strategy. Justify your choices.

Global Marketing

Globalization is the integration of different societies, cultures, and economies from around the world. Globalization expands economic choices for consumers, sparks intense competition, and raises productivity and the standard of living for countries that participate in the international marketplace. As globalization continues to grow, so does **international trade**, or the sale of products and services to people in other countries. Businesses that want to move into international markets must develop an effective promotional plan that reaches across national and cultural boundaries. When creating a promotional plan, marketers must consider certain factors, such as a country's culture, demographics, economic conditions, and political environment.

Culture

Conducting business successfully in another country requires understanding and respect of that country's culture. *Culture* is the shared attitudes and behaviors of a specific social group. Key elements that make up a group's culture include its history, beliefs, values, customs, and language. Advertisers must understand other cultures to avoid blunders that lead to misunderstandings or mistrust. Dutch researcher Geert Hofstede determined that cultural differences could be studied by researching the following four factors:

- *Power Distance*—The extent of separation between social classes is known as power distance. In cultures with a high score in this category, an individual's standing in society, as measured by his or her power and social status, is important. Countries with a high power distance score include China, India, and the Arab countries. In countries with a low power distance score, equality is expected. Countries with low power distance scores include the United States, United Kingdom, Germany, and the Netherlands.

- *Individualism vs. Collectivism*—Cultures can be studied from an "I" (individualism) versus "we" (collectivism) standpoint. Individualistic cultures are more self-centered and emphasize individual goals. Individualistic cultures include the United States, United Kingdom, and France. Collectivist cultures view themselves as members of a strong cohesive group and consider the needs of the group more important than the needs of an individual. Collectivist countries include West Africa, South America, and China.

- *Uncertainty Avoidance*—A culture's tolerance level for unstructured or new experiences will determine how open its members are to new ideas and change. Cultures with high uncertainty avoidance prefer not to deviate from customs and traditions, while cultures with low uncertainty avoidance are more willing to take risks. Japan has a high uncertainty avoidance score, while the United States, United Kingdom, and China have low scores.

- *Masculinity*—In many cultures, men and women have different values. Men's values relate to assertiveness, competitiveness, and material success, while women's values relate to nurturing and caring for others. Masculine cultures encompass men's values. Japan is one of the more masculine countries, while the Netherlands ranks low on the masculine scale. The United States, United Kingdom, Germany, and China fall somewhere in the middle of the scale.

Once marketers have categorized a country based on these factors, they can determine the best promotional strategies to use to reach their target market. For example, China has high power distance, high collectivism, low uncertainty avoidance, and medium masculinity scores. So in China, advertisements may want to emphasize prestige, family relationships, or cutting-edge technology.

Demographics

Before promoting a product in another country, advertisers must be aware of the demographic makeup of the country. Demographics include consumer characteristics such as age, gender, social status, income level, education level, occupation, and household size. Marketers must answer several questions about prospective customers. Where are they located in the country—in urban or rural areas? What is the average income level of the country's citizens? Does the country have an older population, or does it have a younger, healthier population? Are the country's citizens highly educated? These factors greatly affect the types of products and services sold and the promotional campaigns used in a country.

Economic Conditions

Another major factor in global marketing is the level of economic development in a country. Knowledge of a country's economic development gives the marketer a basic understanding of the average consumer's wants, needs, and financial resources. Generally, countries are grouped into three development categories. *Highly industrialized countries,* also called developed countries, have strong business activity, highly educated populations, high levels of wealth, high standards of living, and good infrastructure. **Infrastructure** refers to a country's transportation, communication, and utility systems. Citizens in these countries have higher purchasing power and greater demand for products and services.

Newly industrialized countries are evolving from less developed to industrialized. They are characterized by improved educational systems, increasing technology, and expanding industries. Because the income levels are growing, marketers see these countries as an opportunity to reach new markets. *Developing countries* have little economic wealth and lack the resources necessary for development. They have low levels of industrialization and focus on agriculture or mining. Products sold in these countries are generally agricultural equipment, heavy construction equipment, or business products used for building infrastructure.

What are the characteristics of a developing country?

A country's economic development is a long-term picture of its economy. The short-term condition of a country's economy is also important. A country that has a strong and growing economy will have lower unemployment, meaning its citizens will have more money to spend. Businesses will be prospering, and the government will have more resources to allocate to roads, schools, and other services.

Political Environment

The political climate of a country has an effect on global marketing. Political systems throughout the world range from democratic, in which the citizens of the country control the decisions of the government and have many personal freedoms, to autocratic, where power is in the hands of one official or a small group of officials and the citizens have minimal personal freedoms. It is more difficult to conduct business in countries that have heavy government regulation. Some countries are politically unstable. Citizens in these countries are demanding economic and social reforms and may be trying to

SPOTLIGHT ON SUCCESS

© Courtesy of David Crawley

DAVID CRAWLEY
PepsiCo/Frito Lay

How does a young man who grew up in a small town in Kansas with limited financial resources end up conducting business in Russia? Determination, attention to detail, and a strong desire resulted in a successful international career for David Crawley. Crawley graduated from the University of Kansas with a degree in Psychology. He began his advertising career with Pepsi as an advertising agency field account executive at a Pepsi bottler in Tulsa, Oklahoma. Eventually, he worked for Pepsi in Houston, Texas. Crawley created many successful promotions for Pepsi products. His promotion ideas, creative design execution, and management style impressed Pepsi executives. He was soon put in charge of sports celebrity marketing and cross-merchandising promotions with Universal Studios, Pizza Hut, and Frito-Lay.

Crawley was introduced to international Pepsi executives who came to Houston to tour the local market. By that time, he was highly recognized for his successful accomplishments at Pepsi. He was chosen to lead the development and launching programs for Pepsi in Northern Mexico, which included the manufacture of Mirinda soft drinks (Pepsi's second-largest soft

drink in the world at the time). He was also involved in marketing activities for a fruit juice in Cyprus, an island in the Mediterranean Sea, and for Frito-Lay in Italy. Crawley helped develop the business plan to introduce Frito-Lay chips in Austria.

One of Crawley's biggest career achievements came after receiving a phone call from the European Business Development Manager of Snack Ventures Europe (a joint venture between PepsiCo and General Mills) asking him to help launch the Frito-Lay brand in Russia. David had two days to move to Moscow. Crawley quickly became indoctrinated to the new culture. While in Russia, he left PepsiCo and joined the advertising agency Young & Rubicom/Moscow as Deputy CEO. He helped manage the office reengineering and strategic brand development for Western and Russian companies seeking to create markets in Russia. After working and residing in Russia for three years, he returned to the United States. Upon his return, he started a consulting business to help other companies create emerging markets and brands. Crawley used his 25 years of international marketing communications experience to help many companies throughout his career.

Think Critically

How did working for a multinational company like PepsiCo lead to an international career for David Crawley? Why do you think international work experience is a valuable asset in today's business environment?

overthrow the government. Conducting business in these countries is risky, and marketers often avoid them.

What factors should a business consider when creating a global marketing plan?

Global Marketing Challenges

Even after marketers have thoroughly researched and developed an understanding of their target market in another country, they still must overcome other challenges to succeed in the foreign marketplace. They must develop a marketing mix to meet the unique needs of the international market. They also need to determine the media availability and advertising regulations in the other country.

Global Marketing Mix

Selling goods and services throughout the world requires a global marketing mix. A global marketing mix contains the same four elements—product, distribution, price, and promotion. However, adjustments to each of these elements may be needed because of different market conditions in other countries.

Product When selling a product in another country, a business must decide whether it can market the same product or whether the product has to be altered. Consumers in other countries use products differently, so products may need to be modified to meet local market conditions. Changes to flavors, sizes, colors, or even the electrical voltage may be required. In some cases, only the name of a product may need to be changed to avoid confusion when translated into a new language.

What marketing mix adjustments do you think Pizza Hut had to make to operate in Tel Aviv, Israel?

Distribution Getting the products to customers around the world can be a challenge. Timely air transportation is needed for perishable goods. Large quantities and large products commonly are transported across the ocean by ship. The channels of distribution are inadequate in many developing countries. A country may have only simple two-lane roads that are not well maintained. Mobile stores are used to reach rural areas in less-developed countries. Door-to-door sales are used to sell cosmetics, toothpastes, and detergents in India. For fast food restaurants in countries with congested roads, food delivery on motor scooters is more common than drive-through window service.

Price Global markets may have different standards of living. In some markets, the price of a product may have to be lowered. In other markets, there may be an opportunity to raise the price of a product. Citizens in developing countries lack purchasing power. Thus, a product may have to be simplified so the price can be lowered. On the other hand, high-priced luxury items sell well in oil-rich countries like Saudi Arabia.

A controversial pricing practice used by some companies is known as dumping. **Dumping** occurs when a company sells an exported product for a much lower price than the price charged for the same or similar product in the home market of the exporter. Companies may dump products to increase an overseas market share or to offset the lack of demand for the products at home.

Promotion A country's culture, customs, and language play a major role in the promotion element of the marketing mix. Consumers in different countries may use the same product for alternate purposes. For example, while the bicycle is used predominantly for leisure in the United States, it serves as the main mode of transportation in many other countries. Thus, when promoting a bicycle in another country, the advertising message should focus on the qualities that are important to the foreign consumer. Promotional mistakes occur when words used in advertisements are not translated properly. The language used in global promotions must be analyzed for cultural suitability. To avoid such mistakes, **picturing**, or the use of pictures to communicate a message, is being used by more advertisers. The belief is that pictures can speak to many cultures at once, so fewer words and more visuals are used in ads.

Media Options

The availability of media in other countries varies widely. Although the Internet has made global marketing easier, Internet access is still limited in many countries. Some countries have very few media options. A country may have several subcultures and language dialects within its borders. Each subculture may have its own newspapers and radio stations. In many cases, the newspapers represent a certain political philosophy. Advertisers need to be aware of this to ensure their brand's position is not in conflict with the political philosophies. Even in markets that have a wide range of media options, governments may place restrictions on the type of advertising permitted. Global television networks that are broadcast through cable and satellite are the best way to reach certain target markets. MTV has the capability to reach more than 300 million households worldwide, allowing advertisers to more easily reach the youth and young adult markets.

Advertising Regulations

There are many restrictions on international advertising, and they vary by country. The restrictions often reflect cultural values. Many countries have bans or special restrictions on advertising for specific types of products or services, such as medications, tobacco, alcohol, gambling, and religion. Most countries also have some form of legislation that places various restrictions on advertising to children. Advertisers must be familiar with the advertising regulations in the international market they are targeting. Generally, advertisers should have knowledge of the following:

- Types of products that can be advertised
- Types of message appeals that can be used
- Times during which ads for certain products can be aired on television
- Restrictions on the use of national symbols, such as flags and government seals, in ads
- Kinds of data that can be collected from consumers through promotional campaigns

///////// CHECKPOINT \\\\\\\\\

What are some of the challenges faced by global marketers?

14.1 Assessment

THINK ABOUT IT

1. What four factors can be used to help define a country's culture?
2. Why is economic development an important consideration in global marketing?
3. How might the marketing mix need to be adjusted for an international market?

MAKE ACADEMIC CONNECTIONS

4. **SOCIAL STUDIES**   Learn more about a culture in another country. Describe important demographic characteristics of the culture that you believe would have an impact on an advertising campaign targeting that country.

5. **RESEARCH**   Conduct research on a U.S. product that is sold in another country. Prepare a PowerPoint presentation that describes how the marketing mix was adjusted for the foreign market.

6. **POLITICAL SCIENCE**   Select another country and conduct research to learn more about its political environment. Does it have a democracy or autocratic form of government? How much control does the government exert over its citizens? What would be some of the challenges for a company that wants to sell its product there?

 ## Teamwork

You are part of a marketing team for a company that sells an educational video game that targets children under the age of 12. The company wants to market its video game globally. Select another country and research its culture, demographics, economic conditions, political environment, media options, and advertising regulations. Then present your recommendations for a global marketing plan for the video game.

14.2

Diversity and Advertising

Goals
- Describe the impact of diversity on advertising.
- Identify characteristics of growing ethnic markets.

Terms
- ethnocentrism, p. 385
- cultural diversity, p. 386
- visual diversity, p. 386
- acculturation, p. 389

FOCUS ON ADVERTISING

Targeting Smaller Ethnic Groups

Numerous immigrant communities can be found within the United States. Advertisers are learning that immigrants are a potential source of significant revenue and are finding ways to reach out to them. To reach Hispanic and Asian markets, advertisers often promote products during widespread cultural events such as Cinco de Mayo and the Chinese New Year. But marketers are also reaching out to smaller immigrant communities. Lufthansa®, a German airline that operates out of the United States, hangs banners at Iranian holiday festivals that wish the crowd a happy Norooz—the Persian New Year. Immigrants frequently fly to their home countries but tend to book flights with travel agents speaking their language. Knowing this, Lufthansa began sponsoring events around the Norooz holiday to promote its online booking service, weflyhome .com, which was specifically created for immigrants. During these events, Lufthansa raffled airline tickets to Iran and brought in singers and musicians to help Iranians celebrate their New Year. Becoming a part of the Iranian community paid off. Lufthansa began seeing spikes in airline and travel bookings following these events.

© Steve Snowden/Shutterstock.com

Work as a Team Why are companies focusing on smaller ethnic groups? What do advertisers need to do to reach these groups?

Cultural Diversity

Marketers must avoid **ethnocentrism**, which is the tendency to view and value things based on one's own cultural beliefs. Ethnocentrism is an obstacle to cross-cultural advertising. It prevents marketers from seeing important cultural differences among markets. Instead, marketers must be aware of **cultural diversity**, which is the coexistence of different ethnic, gender, racial, and socioeconomic groups. Diversity encompasses acceptance and respect of cultural differences.

The Changing Nature of the United States

Although there is diversity throughout the world, diversity can also be found within a country. The United States has been referred to as the "melting pot" because of its immigrant history and the growth of a diverse population. According to the 2010 U.S. Census, the Hispanic and Asian populations in the United States have experienced the fastest growth over the past decade. The rise in the Hispanic population accounted for more than half of the increase in the total U.S. population. But more than any other ethnic group, the Asian population grew the fastest. In addition, the purchasing power of Hispanics and Asians is growing at a faster rate than for other races and ethnicities.

The enormous growth of an ethnic population is creating huge marketing opportunities. However, the many subcultures within the United States make marketing and advertising more complex, requiring thorough cultural analysis. Marketers must be able to target subcultures by using effective cross-cultural or culture-specific advertising campaigns. Successful advertising campaigns begin with a thorough understanding of cross-cultural differences in values, attitudes, and behaviors. Planning multicultural advertising is similar to planning global marketing campaigns. Advertisers must decide how to adjust advertising campaigns to address cultural differences in local markets just as they would in global markets.

Handling Diversity in Advertising

Diversity in advertising is approached in different ways. Many advertisements use **visual diversity**, which shows Americans of different races and ethnicities interacting in schools, workplaces, homes, and other venues while consuming the advertised product. This enables advertisers to connect to a more diverse audience. However, ethnic audiences respond more favorably to culturally targeted advertisements.

People in the same ethnic groups share language, customs, values, and social views. These shared values influence beliefs, affect emotions, and affect purchase and consumption behaviors. If cultural values and beliefs are implanted in advertisements in a way in which consumers can "see themselves" and

How does the growth of ethnic populations in the United States represent marketing opportunities for businesses?

identify with the characters in the advertisements, ethnic groups are more likely to bond with the advertised brands. Studies have shown that Hispanics will choose brands that reflect their native values and culture. Thus, to be successful, advertising campaigns that target Hispanics should emphasize values and customs that are significant to their culture. Many advertisers, such as retailers, are trying to attract Hispanic customers by printing their ads in English and Spanish or by featuring Hispanic celebrities in the ads.

▰▰▰▰▰ CHECKPOINT ◣◣◣◣◣

Why is diversity an increasingly important factor in advertising?

Understanding Ethnic Markets

Diversity in the world of marketing means that one size does not fit all. Different cultures and ethnicities have different priorities. They also have culturally related consumption preferences. Family, religion, language, culture, and beliefs all play an important part in the buying decisions made by consumers from different cultures. Embracing a culturally diverse society can open up many opportunities for U.S. businesses. However, they must be willing to make an effort to understand the different cultures and their buying behaviors. Specifically, U.S. companies are reaching out to three growing ethnic markets—African Americans, Asian Americans, and Hispanic Americans.

African-American Market

African Americans currently represent 13 percent of the U.S. population. The purchasing power of African Americans has increased 60 percent over the past decade and is expected to grow to $1.2 trillion by 2015. The potential of the African-American market has advertisers spending large sums to reach them. Some of the most prominent companies in the United States are among the top ten advertisers in the African-American market, including Procter & Gamble, General Motors, L'Oreal, Dell Inc., Time Warner, and PepsiCo. There are several media outlets that specifically target African-American consumers, including BET (cable TV network), *Essence* and *Jet* magazines, and numerous radio stations. Marketing research has revealed the following about African-American consumers.

- They spend more hours watching TV than other ethnic groups.
- Internet usage among African Americans in a recent year was approximately 65 percent and is estimated to grow to 72 percent by 2014.
- They use more voice minutes on their mobile phones than other groups and are more likely to access the Internet through their mobile phones.
- They shop more frequently than other ethnicities but spend less on each trip.

What can marketers learn from African-American shopping habits?

- They shop less frequently at grocery stores and supercenters but more frequently at smaller retailers like drug stores, dollar stores, and convenience stores.
- They tend to spend more on food consumed at home.
- They less frequently take advantage of coupons, deals, or promotions while shopping.
- Their spending on personal and beauty care products exceeds the U.S. average spending in this category.

Asian-American Market

Asian Americans currently represent 5 percent of the U.S. population. The purchasing power of Asian Americans has increased 98 percent over the past decade and is expected to grow to $775 billion by 2015. The term *Asian* represents many subcultures, including the Chinese, Japanese, Filipinos, Vietnamese, Koreans, and Asian Indians. Asian-American households have the highest average family income of all groups in the country. Because of this, marketers are committed to understanding the Asian-American consumer's buying behavior and preferences. Characteristics of the Asian-American market include the following:

- They are much better educated than the average American and hold many top-level jobs in management, professional, and scientific fields.
- They place a strong emphasis on family and education.
- They are the most active computer and Internet users and are more likely to have newer technology.
- They watch TV less frequently than other groups, but they stream the most online video.

- They more frequently take advantage of special deals and promotions while shopping.
- They buy far more fresh produce, nuts, dried fruit, pasta, yogurt, soup, juice, and other drinks than the average U.S. consumer.
- They frequently shop at department stores, with nearly one-third visiting department stores at least one to three times a week.

Hispanic-American Market

Hispanic Americans currently represent over 16 percent of the U.S. population, but they are projected to account for more than 30 percent of the population by 2050. The term *Hispanic* represents people of many different backgrounds, including Mexicans, Puerto Ricans, Central Americans, Dominicans, South Americans, and Cubans. The purchasing power of Hispanics has increased 108 percent over the past decade and is expected to grow to $1.5 trillion by 2015. The rate of growth in Hispanic purchasing power tops all other ethnic groups in the United States.

Why is the Asian-American market appealing to U.S. advertisers?

Image courtesy of The Advertising Archives

There is a belief among many that once Hispanics learn to speak English, they become acculturated. **Acculturation** is the process by which members of one cultural group adopt the beliefs and behaviors of another group. However, studies have shown that while Hispanics may adopt some American customs, they still hold onto their own culture, heritage, and traditions. Approximately 61 percent of bilingual Hispanics prefer to speak Spanish in their homes, meaning that Spanish-language media is the key to connecting with the greatest number of Hispanic consumers. Marketing research also has revealed the following about Hispanic consumers.

- They use their smartphones for a wide range of mobile activities, including texting, mobile banking, and Internet access.
- Internet usage among Hispanics in a recent year was approximately 65 percent.
- They shop less frequently than other ethnicities but spend more on each trip.

- They tend to spend more on baby-related products than the average U.S. consumer.
- They spend more in supercenters, mass merchandisers, and warehouse clubs.
- They spend more than the average U.S. consumer on ingredients used to cook from scratch.
- The top ten TV shows for Hispanics are all Spanish-language programs. Telenovelas (Spanish soap operas) have a strong following.

///////// CHECKPOINT \\\\\\\\

Why do businesses need to have an understanding of ethnic markets?

14.2 Assessment

THINK ABOUT IT

1. What effect might ethnocentrism have on an advertising campaign?
2. How does the changing U.S. population impact advertisers?
3. Why are many companies using visual diversity in their ads?

MAKE ACADEMIC CONNECTIONS

4. **MATH** If the total U.S. population is 311 million, what is the population for each of the following ethnic groups: African Americans (13 percent of the population), Asian Americans (5 percent), and Hispanic Americans (16 percent)? Assume the estimated population growth rate over the next ten years for each of the ethnic groups is as follows: African Americans, 12.3 percent; Asian Americans, 43.3 percent; Hispanic Americans, 43 percent. What will be the population of each ethnicity in ten years?

5. **RESEARCH** Learn more about the acculturation of Hispanic Americans. Write a two-page report that describes ways in which Hispanics have adopted the American lifestyle, including its customs and traditions. Also, describe ways in which they still cling to their heritage.

6. **MARKETING** Your company sells organic spices and herbs. Choose one of the ethnic markets described in the lesson (African American, Asian American, or Hispanic American). Based on the consumer characteristics of the ethnic group chosen, create a print ad for your product.

Teamwork

The tourism center in your city has hired your team to create an *Ethnic Dining Guide* that can be given to out-of-town visitors. Identify ethnic dining categories to include in your guide. List the restaurants for each category. Include restaurant names, addresses, phone numbers, and a brief description of the types of food served.

Goals

- Recognize how verbal and nonverbal communication differ in other cultures.
- Explain the importance of the translation process in global marketing.

Terms

- explicit communicators, p.392
- implicit communicators, p. 392
- nonverbal communication, p. 392
- translator, p. 395
- back translation, p. 395

FOCUS ON ADVERTISING

Bilingual Advertising

Because of the multicultural environment in the United States, more and more advertisers are beginning to develop bilingual ads. Bilingual ads targeting Hispanics are very common. Spanish is spoken officially in 21 countries. For the most part, this one language can be used to reach many Hispanic subcultures, such as Mexicans, Puerto Ricans, Dominicans, and Cubans. However, reaching the Asian market through bilingual ads is not as easy. The Asian market consists of many subcultures, such as the Japanese, Chinese, Cantonese, Korean, Vietnamese, Thai, and Cambodian—each with their own language. That's why ad campaigns typically focus on the Asian Americans with the largest U.S. populations, or the Chinese, Koreans, and Vietnamese. The advertising industry refers to this as the CKV strategy. These three ethnic groups are also desirable because they have plenty of newspapers, magazines, and local radio and TV stations in their native languages. Because these three ethnic groups share common cultural values, marketers are able to design ads that have the same theme but use different languages. This makes advertising more cost-efficient.

Work as a Team If bilingual advertising is so challenging, why is it becoming more popular among advertisers? What types of media that target other cultures do you have in your community?

© Jin Young Lee/Shutterstock.com

Communicating Globally

Communication plays a major role in global marketing. When trying to sell products in another country, marketers must convey their advertising message in a way that consumers will understand. To do this successfully, U.S. marketers should understand the communication styles used in the countries where they are doing business. Both verbal and nonverbal communication styles should be studied.

Verbal Communication

Whether a marketer is creating an international advertisement or a salesperson is working abroad, they should understand the proper etiquette involved when communicating verbally in another country. To avoid communication misunderstandings, marketers should learn the answers to the following questions.

- *How are conversations opened and closed?* Different cultures have different customs regarding who addresses whom when and how. Certain ways of starting or concluding a conversation are considered rude or disrespectful. Marketers should research acceptable types of greetings to use; the importance of age, gender, or social position when speaking to others; and proper ways to end discussions.

- *What is the conversational style?* In some cultures, conversations are carried out in an interactive way, where one person speaks and then another person provides an immediate response. In other cultures, it is more appropriate to listen to the speaker without responding or interrupting him or her until the speaker is done. Some cultures find interruptions offensive because they believe the person is challenging the speaker's statements.

- *Is the use of silence ok?* In the United States, long bouts of silence in a conversation make people feel uncomfortable. In some other cultures, however, silence is a sign of thoughtfulness toward the speaker and is expected before a response is given.

- *Is it ok to use humor?* Although humor is used as a way to initially bond with others in the United States, not all cultures view it this way. Some consider it a sign of disrespect. Humor can also lead to misunderstandings when the speaker doesn't fully understand the culture.

- *Is explicit or implicit communication preferred?* **Explicit communicators** convey information in a concise, direct, and structured manner. They base decisions on logic and facts. This communication style is common in the United States. **Implicit communicators** convey information that is vague or has an implied meaning. They base decisions on intuition and feelings more so than logic and facts and strive for group harmony. Japan, China, and Mexico prefer this communication style. With implicit communicators, how something is said, which might involve the speaker's tone of voice, facial expression, gestures, or posture, matters more than what is actually said. By contrast, the actual words matter more than the intended meaning for explicit communicators. Implicit communicators tend to interpret directness in communication as uncivil and rude; explicit communicators tend to view directness as honest and inoffensive.

Nonverbal Communication

Nonverbal communication is any method of conveying information without using words. It could include body language, facial expressions, gestures, or postures. Understanding nonverbal communication can be as important to an international marketer as understanding verbal communication. Nonverbal communication between people helps them interpret feelings and intentions. It also indicates when a message is unclear. Some nonverbal signals are the same across cultures, but others have cultural meanings. If a marketer is not familiar with the local body language, misunderstandings can occur. So before conducting business in another country, marketers should learn as much as possible about nonverbal communication signals in that country.

Why is it important to know the proper way to greet people in other countries?

Personal Greetings The handshake is the standard form of greeting in many countries. A soft handshake in some cultures indicates respect while it represents a lack of confidence in other cultures. Individuals from some Asian countries believe handshaking violates personal space. Bowing is their preferred form of greeting, and the depth of the bow indicates the level of respect. While many individuals from Asian countries use the handshake when doing business in Western cultures, they still appreciate someone who respects their culture and personal space by bowing.

Eye Contact In the United States and other Western cultures, eye contact is considered important. Looking away or avoiding eye contact can be viewed as devious. In Japan and other Asian cultures, eye contact is considered disrespectful, especially with authority figures. Eye contact may be viewed as rude and arrogant.

Facial Expressions A smile sends a positive message and breaks the ice in many cultures. However, Chinese tend to smile easily when they feel difficulty or embarrassment. A smile because of embarrassment by a Chinese businessperson might be interpreted as being friendly by a Westerner, but really he or she is embarrassed. In Thailand, a smile is often used when giving an apology.

Personal Space Different cultures have different personal space requirements. People from parts of Latin America or the Middle East feel comfortable standing closer to each other. If you back away from them, they may be offended. In North America and Europe, people prefer greater interpersonal distances. If the person you are speaking to keeps backing away from you, give him or her more personal space.

Gestures There are many kinds of gestures that have different meanings in different cultures. What may be a friendly gesture in one culture can be an insult in another. While Americans do not think twice about using the pointer finger to direct someone's attention, most Asians consider this rude. Instead, they point with the entire hand. The okay or thumbs-up gesture is considered vulgar in some parts

NETBookmark

The cultural basis for color symbolism can be very powerful. Marketers who are communicating with a culture different than their own need to be aware of how different audiences view colors. Access www.cengage.com/school/advertising and click on the link for Chapter 14. Examine the international cultural meanings of various colors. Suppose you are marketing a new snack food to Latin America. What colors would be appropriate for the product packaging? What colors should be avoided? Would the colors you chose for the Latin American market also work well in India? Explain your answers.

www.cengage.com/school/advertising

of Latin America and other countries. Standing with your hands on your hips signifies anger in some countries. You should keep your hands out of your pockets and resist the tendency to put them under the table or behind your back. In some cultures, it is rude to sit with your ankle crossed over a knee because showing the soles of your shoes is offensive.

Personal Appearance You only get one chance to make a first impression. Your appearance tells the other person a lot about you. Business attire in the United States has become increasingly casual, but not all cultures respect this idea. Professional business attire shows respect and seriousness. There is less likelihood for distraction when individuals wear business attire. The best conservative business colors in the United States (black, grey, navy blue) are not necessarily acceptable in other cultures. In other cultures, clothing and accessories can suggest status.

Colors, Numbers, and Symbols Colors, numbers, symbols, and images are translated differently from one culture to the next. Color may have a special significance. If marketers don't understand what they're saying with colors, they can make big mistakes. For example, in China, red is associated with good luck, but in South Africa, red is the color of mourning. Many cultures consider certain numbers lucky or unlucky. In the United States, many hotels do not have a 13th floor. Asian cultures consider the numbers 4 and 9 to be unlucky. Nippon Airways in Japan does not have seat numbers 4 or 9. Symbols and images are also culturally sensitive. Every culture has its own set of symbols associated with different experiences and perceptions. In Chinese culture, dogs symbolize devotion and faithfulness, but in Islamic cultures, they symbolize impurity. Colors, numbers, and symbols with negative connotations abroad should not be used in advertising directed at those markets.

CHECKPOINT

How do verbal and nonverbal communication differ in other cultures?

Advertising in Another Language

The Internet, international sporting events like the Olympics, and global television networks like MTV have made consumers throughout the world aware of products, ranging from Coca-Cola to Buick. Globalized, or standardized, advertising campaigns are used to deliver the same message across all international markets. In other cases, advertisers use localized, or customized, advertising campaigns in which a unique message is conveyed to a specific market. Despite the type of advertising campaign used, the language in the ads must be adjusted for the market.

It's All in the Translation

Language is the key to effective cross-cultural advertising. Companies that fail to properly translate product names and slogans and check their meanings in the other language could be in for a rude awakening. The Coca-Cola name in China was first translated by the Chinese Coke employees as "Kekoukela," which meant, "bite the wax tadpole." Coke then researched 40,000 Chinese characters to find the phonetic equivalent "kokoukole," which roughly translates into "happiness in the mouth." Language also must be analyzed for cultural suitability. Video game manufacturer EA Sports' slogan, "Challenge Everything," was met with disapproval in religious and hierarchical societies that promote harmonious relationships and non-confrontation.

Nonverbal language must also be considered when developing cross-cultural advertising. Burger King developed a successful ad campaign in Europe for its new Texican Whopper. The ads featured a lanky American cowboy, a short, round Mexican wrestler wearing a cape resembling Mexico's flag, and the tagline, "the taste of Texas with a little spicy Mexican." Mexico protested against the ads due to their stereotypical portrayal of Mexicans and offensive use of the Mexican flag. The tagline along with the images used to symbolize the spicy flavor of the burger caused so much controversy that Burger King pulled the ads.

The Translation Process

Communication is effective abroad only after the message has been translated. Without translation, the message has no impact on the foreign consumer. A **translator** is an interpreter who converts a message from one language to another. Translators are involved in almost every aspect of intercultural communication, including advertising. Advertising includes all forms of communication and promotion, from a pamphlet to an international television campaign. Although translation of words

WELCOME VELKOMMEN
BIENVENUE WELKOM
VITAJTE VÄLKOMMEN
DOBRO DOŠLI WITAJCIE
WILICOM WILKOMMEN
ΚΑΛΩΣ ΗΡΘΑΤΕ VELKOMEN

© StockCube/Shutterstock.com

Do you know how to welcome someone or say hello in another language?

is important, there is a lot of meaning behind the words that must be understood to transfer advertising from one culture to another. Grammar, sentence structure, tone of voice, pronunciation, and body language are all factors that influence translations of advertising messages.

Companies often use a back translation process. **Back translation** is the process of translating a message that has already been translated into a foreign language back to the original language. In other words, a native speaker translates the message to his or her own language.

Then this translation is translated by another native speaker back to the original language. This process helps ensure that words and meanings are translated correctly.

Advertising translation can make or break a campaign and, more importantly, the perception of a brand. Ideally, the translation will have a positive effect that results in increased brand awareness and increased demand from the global target market. Poor translations can result in a negative effect, which occurs when the translation diminishes the strengths of the brand in the international market and becomes a disadvantage for international producers and distributors.

CHECKPOINT

Why is the translation process an important function of global marketing?

14.3 Assessment

THINK ABOUT IT

1. What is the difference between an explicit communicator and an implicit communicator?
2. Why do global marketers need to be aware of nonverbal communication?
3. Why might a company use the back translation process for an international advertisement?

MAKE ACADEMIC CONNECTIONS

4. **TECHNOLOGY**   Find an online translator, such as Google Translate. Enter five memorable advertising slogans or taglines and translate them to another language. Record the foreign slogans. Then using the same online translator or another, use the back translation process by translating the foreign slogans to English. Did the meanings change? (*Hint*: You may also ask a foreign language teacher to assist with the translation.)

5. **RESEARCH**   Conduct an online search to find a company that offers translation services. Create a company profile that describes the services it offers, the languages it translates, and the rates it charges. Include any other pertinent information an advertiser might need when trying to select a translation service.

6. **INTERNATIONAL**   Select a foreign country and conduct research to learn about its communication style. Address the verbal communication questions on page 392 and the nonverbal communication elements on pages 393–394. Present your findings to the class.

 Teamwork

Select a foreign country and perform a role-play of a meeting between businesspeople from the United States and the other country. (The foreign country researched in Number 6 above may be used.) The role-play should demonstrate the proper communication styles of both cultures.

Sharpen Your
21st CENTURY SKILLS

Digital Vision/Getty Images

Planning an International Career

As globalization increases, international careers are becoming more common. To succeed, businesses operating in an international marketplace need qualified employees who can work effectively with foreign businesspeople and customers. If you are interested in an international career, there are some steps you can take to prepare yourself.

1. *Understand yourself.* To determine if you are well suited for an international career, you need to understand your own values and beliefs and be open to the values and beliefs held by other cultures. You also need to determine if you are willing to live abroad for a period of time and pursue the necessary education and training for an international career.

2. *Strengthen your foundational skills.* Communication skills, problem-solving and critical-thinking skills, and leadership skills can help businesspeople overcome challenges that arise when working abroad.

3. *Improve your language skills.* English is widely used in international business. You must be able to convey messages in a way that both native and nonnative English speakers understand. In addition, you should become fluent in one or more foreign languages. This gives you access to information that may not be available in English and allows you to communicate directly with those who do

not speak English. It also shows respect for other cultures.

4. *Gain international experience.* Travel to other countries to interact with other cultures. If that's not possible, participate in local organizations that serve diverse ethnic groups. Or participate in a student-exchange program. It is important to expose yourself to other cultures.

5. *Network with international professionals.* Talk to people from other countries who live or work in your area. Visit a multinational company for which you'd like to work in the future and seek career advice. Join professional organizations and talk with people who have lived or worked abroad.

6. *Search for jobs in the global marketplace.* There are many websites dedicated to international careers. The U.S. government has a website that provides information about international internships and entry-level jobs.

Try It Out

Develop an international career plan based on a country in which you'd like to work. Describe how you will approach each of the steps above. Search online for an international job that is available in the country you selected. List the training, skills, and experience required for the job.

PARTNERSHIP FOR
21ST CENTURY SKILLS

© Yuri Arcurs/Shutterstock.com

Chapter 14 **Review**

SUMMARY

14.1 A Global Vision

- Globalization is the integration of different societies, cultures, and economies from around the world. It expands economic choices and raises the standard of living for consumers in many other countries.
- When creating an international promotional plan, marketers must consider a country's culture, demographics, economic conditions, and political environment.
- When learning about a country's culture, marketers should determine how it rates based on four factors: power distance, individualism/collectivism, uncertainty avoidance, and masculinity.
- Global marketing presents several challenges, including establishing a marketing mix, selecting media, and understanding international advertising regulations.

14.2 Diversity and Advertising

- Marketers are incorporating diversity into their advertising campaigns to more accurately reflect the changing population in the United States.
- The enormous growth of ethnic populations in the United States creates huge marketing opportunities for businesses. Marketers must be prepared to target ethnic groups with cross-cultural or culture-specific advertising campaigns.
- Three growing ethnic groups that have captured marketers' attention are African Americans, Asian Americans, and Hispanic Americans. Each of these ethnic groups has unique buying behaviors and preferences.

14.3 Cross-Cultural Communication

- To successfully enter the global market, marketers should understand the communication styles—both verbal and nonverbal—used in other countries.
  - Verbal communication among cultures differs based on conversational styles, the use of silence and humor, and the level of directness.
  - Elements of nonverbal communication include personal greetings, eye contact, facial expressions, personal space, gestures, personal appearance, colors, numbers, and symbols.
- When doing business globally, advertising campaigns need to be translated. The meaning of words and body language should be considered in the translation process.

WHAT DO YOU KNOW NOW?

Read Impact Advertising on page 377 again to review the global marketing strategy used for Barbie. Conduct research to learn how Mattel markets Barbie in other countries. What are Mattel's latest global marketing strategies for Barbie?

11Market

Vocabulary Builder

Match each statement with the term that best defines it. Some terms may not be used.

1. The coexistence of different ethnic, gender, racial, and socioeconomic groups
2. An interpreter who converts a message from one language to another
3. The process by which members of one cultural group adopt the beliefs and behaviors of another group
4. The tendency to view and value things based on one's own cultural beliefs
5. The sale of products and services to people in other countries
6. The process by which a company sells an exported product for a much lower price than the price charged for the same product in the home market of the exporter
7. Individuals who convey information in a concise, direct, and structured manner
8. Any method of conveying information without using words
9. A country's transportation, communication, and utility systems
10. The process of translating a message that has already been translated into a foreign language back to the original language

a. acculturation
b. back translation
c. cultural diversity
d. dumping
e. ethnocentrism
f. explicit communicators
g. globalization
h. implicit communicators
i. infrastructure
j. international trade
k. nonverbal communication
l. picturing
m. translator
n. visual diversity

Test Your Knowledge

11. The implicit communicator
    a. conveys information that is vague or has an implied meaning
    b. bases decisions on logic and facts
    c. uses a communication style common in the United States
    d. both a and c
12. Cultures in which there is a high degree of separation between social classes would have a high score in which of the following categories?
    a. collectivism   c. power distance
    b. individualism   d. masculinity
13. Cultures whose members are more self-centered would have a high score in which of the following categories?
    a. collectivism   c. power distance
    b. individualism   d. masculinity

14. ____ prevents marketers from seeing important cultural differences among markets.
    a. Visual diversity
    c. Infrastructure
    b. Ethnocentrism
    d. Globalization
15. Which of the following characteristics is evident in a newly industrialized country?
    a. high standard of living
    b. little economic wealth
    c. agriculture or mining industry emphasis
    d. improving educational systems
16. When marketers create a global marketing mix, questions to address include which of the following?
    a. Does the product have to be altered for the other country?
    b. What are the channels of distribution within the country?
    c. What is the overall standard of living in the country?
    d. all of the above
17. The two fastest-growing ethnic groups in the United States over the past decade are
    a. African-Americans and Hispanics
    b. African-Americans and Asians
    c. Asians and Hispanics
    d. Asians and Indians
18. All of the following consumer behaviors describe Asian Americans *except*
    a. they have the highest average family income of all ethnicities
    b. they spend more hours watching TV than do other ethnicities
    c. they are more likely to have newer technology
    d. they place a strong emphasis on family and education
19. Which of the following statements is false?
    a. The use of humor between businesspeople is acceptable in all cultures.
    b. In some cultures, long bouts of silence are expected before giving a response to the speaker.
    c. Implicit communicators base decisions on intuition and feelings.
    d. In some cultures, interactive communication, in which someone speaks and then someone else responds immediately, is offensive.
20. A ____ is *not* a type of nonverbal communication.
    a. smile
    c. pamphlet
    b. handshake
    d. symbol

Apply What You Learned

21. You have been asked by a marketer who works for a company in another country to describe nonverbal communication styles common among Americans. Describe at least ten behaviors using the following categories: eye contact, facial expressions, personal space, gestures, personal appearance, colors, numbers, and symbols.

22. Your company manufactures clothing for teenagers. You are considering selling your clothing in other countries. Before doing so, compile a list of questions regarding the marketing mix that would need to be answered.

23. You are the marketing manager for a company that has decided to sell its product internationally. Prepare a five-minute presentation that explains what the company should do before marketing globally. Outline the issues that must be considered and researched.

Make Academic Connections

24. **ECONOMICS**   Name a newly industrialized country. Learn more about the economic, educational, and technology changes that are occurring within the country. Based on what you learn, recommend a U.S. product that you think would sell well in that country. Create a print ad for the product.

25. **RESEARCH**   Conduct research to find two popular U.S. products that failed in other parts of the world. Explain why they failed. Describe how they might have succeeded by making some changes to the marketing mix.

26. **INTERNATIONAL**   Your company produces cookies that are sold throughout stores in the United States. You've decided that you want to sell the cookies in China. Study the Chinese culture and explain how the product would have to be altered to be marketed successfully to Chinese consumers.

27. **GEOGRAPHY**   Find a map of Europe. Select two European countries with which you are unfamiliar. Prepare a PowerPoint presentation about each country. Describe such things as the culture, economic conditions, political system, main imports, main exports, and other basic geographic information.

28. **TECHNOLOGY**   "Because of the Internet, going global is easier than it has ever been before." What do you think about this statement? Explain how the Internet has changed the way business is conducted globally. Then describe some of the challenges a business might encounter by trying to "go global" using the Internet.

You have discovered a cartoon in your community newspaper that pokes fun at another culture's beliefs and customs. You understand freedom of speech, but you believe the newspaper has shown disregard and disrespect for the other culture. The newspaper has a history of printing cultural-specific cartoons that you consider inappropriate. The neighborhood in which the newspaper is distributed is a highly culturally diverse community. This time, you think the newspaper has overstepped its boundaries.

What will you do? Will you take your complaints to the newspaper or will you make them public? What would be your message about cultural sensitivity?

Reality ✓

Intellectual Property at Risk

Intellectual property is the original, creative work of an artist or inventor. It may include songs, novels, inventions, and unique names, symbols, logos, or designs. It is protected by patents, trademarks, and copyrights. Intellectual property such as a brand name is an important part of a company's identity. Although there are many laws that serve to protect intellectual property rights, they may not be protected overseas.

Counterfeiting is a major problem in foreign countries, especially in China. *Counterfeiting* is the process of producing fake products that carry a well-known brand name. Prada handbags, Gillette razors, Nike shoes, Duracell batteries, True Religion jeans, and Callaway golf clubs are just a few of the counterfeit products manufactured and sold in China. In the United States, a set of Callaway golf clubs could cost as much as $3,000, but you can find them in China for as little as $275. Why are they so much cheaper in China? It's because they are not authentic. Chinese companies manufacture the golf clubs to look like the real thing and slap on the Callaway brand name. Callaway discovered the counterfeiting when customers began sending the broken clubs to the company for repair. Low-quality, inexpensive counterfeits can damage a company's reputation and reduce its revenues.

Numerous counterfeit products are shipped to the United States every day. The Internet and e-commerce sites like eBay have made it even easier to distribute counterfeit goods. The U.S. Customs and Border Protection is the federal agency in charge of enforcing intellectual property rights within the U.S. borders. It inspects shipments and seizes products that are in violation of copyrights, patents, and trademarks, but many shipments go undetected. Goods from China account for the majority of all seizures. Although Chinese authorities insist they are working on the problem, their actions say otherwise. The Chinese counterfeit market employs millions of factory workers and contributes to the country's economic growth, so local authorities often look the other way or charge offenders only small fines.

Think Critically

1. Why do you think counterfeiting has become such a big business?
2. What types of products do you think are prime targets for counterfeiters?
3. How is counterfeiting harmful to businesses and consumers?
4. Why is it important for the government to police counterfeiting activities?

You are the marketer for a large, international holiday lights business (Bright Lights) located along a busy interstate highway in New York. Although, Bright Lights predominantly sells outdoor lights for Christmas and other winter holidays, it is open for business throughout the entire year.

The owner of Bright Lights wants to increase sales. She would also like to diversify the products offered by the business to increase international sales throughout the year. The owner has asked you to recommend a more diversified product line, a new distribution strategy, a global advertising campaign, and special sales/promotion events throughout the year to increase international sales. You must present your plan to the business owner (judge).

You have ten minutes to determine how to approach and solve the problem presented above. During the preparation period, you may make notes to use during the presentation. You will have ten minutes to explain your plan of action and answer the business owner's questions. You must demonstrate the performance indicators listed below during your presentation.

Performance Indicators Evaluated
- Explain the nature and scope of distribution.
- Describe marketing functions and related activities.
- Explain the concept of product mix.
- Explain types of advertising media.
- Explain the importance of coordinating elements in advertisements.

Go to the DECA website for more detailed information.

Think Critically
1. Why would a company want to diversify its product line?
2. How can a seasonal business, such as one that predominantly caters to the Christmas holiday, market its product during other seasons?
3. What are some additional international distribution strategies for Bright Lights?
4. What kinds of special promotions could Bright Lights offer to increase sales?

www.deca.org

15

Planning Your Future in Advertising

© gary718/Shutterstock.com

Successful Advertising Careers

Throughout the years, many people have made a big impact on the advertising industry. Some of them are even referred to as legends because of the contributions they made.

The magazine *Advertising Age* places William Bernbach in the number one spot in its *Top 100 People of the Century* list. Many in the industry consider Bernbach as the single most influential creative force in advertising's history. He was one of the founders of the Doyle, Dane, Bernbach (DDB) Agency in 1949. In the early days of Bernbach's career, advertising agencies were afraid to say no to their clients, stifling the creative talents of the agencies. Bernbach realized that input from the client is vital, but emphasized that the ad agency bears ultimate responsibility for the message. He insisted on knowing how his client's products related to their users. He also wanted to know what human qualities and emotions came into play. Then he would determine the best way to communicate those elements, in TV and print ads, and capture the consumer's understanding and support. One of his best-remembered ad campaigns was for Avis, the car rental company. At the time, Hertz was the number one company in that industry. Knowing that the U.S. public loves an underdog, Bernbach came up with the tagline, "When you're No. 2, you try harder." The Avis ad campaign was directly responsible for increasing Avis's market share by 28 percent and closing the gap with frontrunner Hertz.

© Press Association via AP Images

Shirley Polykoff is also named in the *Advertising Age's* Top 100 list. Polykoff began her career at an early age selling coats in a Brooklyn department store. She wrote her first advertising copy as a teenage secretary for *Harper's Bazaar* magazine. She moved on to work at the Foote, Cone, & Belding advertising agency in 1955 as its lone female copywriter. She was assigned the new Clairol account because the agency felt only she could understand the product. During the mid-1950s, hair coloring among women was rare, with only 7 percent of U.S. women, mainly actresses and models, dying their hair. Polykoff believed that advertising should be a direct conversation with the consumer. She incorporated this philosophy in her Clairol advertising campaign and asked U.S. women, "Does she . . . or doesn't she?" Consumers were attracted by the slogan and the tagline, "Hair color so natural only her hairdresser knows for sure." Clairol sales increased by 413 percent in six years when more than 50 percent of U.S. women began using hair color. Polykoff's Clairol campaign has been recognized for its creativity as well as for its influence on changing attitudes about hair coloring.

1. **What common traits do Bernbach and Polykoff share?**

2. **What does the success of Bernbach's and Polykoff's advertising campaigns say about the importance of creativity in advertising?**

3. **What would you find most appealing about an advertising career?**

WHAT DO YOU KNOW?

15.1

A Career in Advertising

Goals
- Determine if a career in advertising is for you.
- Identify the skill set needed for a successful advertising career.

Terms
- skill set, p. 408
- soft skills, p. 408
- time management, p. 409
- hard skills, p. 411

FOCUS ON ADVERTISING

Reaching Consumers with Tryvertising

Creativity and problem solving are important skills for those working in the advertising industry. As more consumers tune out traditional advertising formats, such as TV commercials, businesses turn to advertisers to find innovative ways to reach consumers. Tryvertising is an example of thinking outside the box. It is a cross between advertising, product promotion, and marketing communication. Essentially, it integrates products into the daily life of consumers, giving them actual experience with the product. Car manufacturers like Mercedes-Benz, Porsche, and Mini Cooper partnered with luxury hotels to offer guests the use of a car with unlimited mileage during their stay. Some budget hotels were furnished with IKEA rooms for guests to try out. Gillette provided KLM Airlines with its Brush-Ups teeth wipes to distribute to passengers after their in-flight meals. Heinz used social media to open up a tryvertising store on Facebook. It made 3,000 bottles of its newest balsamic vinegar ketchup available to ketchup fans and encouraged them to talk about the new ketchup on Facebook. Companies who have participated in tryvertising have reported increased sales.

Work as a Team Why do you think creativity and problem-solving skills are crucial in the advertising industry? Why is tryvertising more effective than some of the other traditional forms of advertising?

Why Choose an Advertising Career?

The advertising industry is one of the most exciting fields in which to work. If you are creative with words and art and like creative problem solving, then an advertising career might be right for you. Those who enjoy commercials, magazine ads, radio spots, social media campaigns, and other creative advertising formats are often drawn to advertising careers. Advertising people also tend to love culture, movies, music, art, and books.

There are many job categories within the advertising industry from which to choose. You may start off as an administrative assistant or a junior copywriter. Perhaps you would rather work in the design department or provide media services. Maybe you are more interested in the marketing research aspect of advertising. There are jobs to suit most everyone's talents. Because of the numerous job categories in the advertising field, there is room for growth for those who choose a career in advertising. To determine if a career in advertising would interest you, consider the following.

- *Are you good at persuading and motivating people?* Advertising is all about persuading people to take some kind of action.
- *Do you like showing off your talents and being rewarded for it?* Writing the copy for an ad or creating the art for it allows you to showcase your skills. Knowing that the ad you helped create is being observed by thousands or even millions of people can be very rewarding and satisfying.
- *Do you like working with creative people from diverse backgrounds?* People working in the advertising industry often have unique, fun-loving personalities and come from diverse backgrounds and cultures, which makes working as part of a team exciting.
- *Do you enjoy staying on top of trends?* Are you always in touch with current trends in fashion, technology, music, and pop culture? Advertising must reflect what's happening in society right now.
- *Do you like working in a flexible, less structured environment?* It's never "another day at the office" in advertising because every day is different. Also, advertising agencies tend to be more flexible than traditional businesses when it comes to where or how the work gets done.
- *Do you enjoy social functions?* Many advertising campaigns are kicked off at special events. So those working in the advertising field must enjoy meeting and talking with new people in settings outside of work.
- *Are you interested in an international career?* The field of advertising is one of the most global business career options available. Large advertising agencies are opening offices all around the world. After years of experience, there is a possibility of working on global campaigns.
- *Are you technologically savvy?* The growing world of web advertising and e-commerce is injecting new, dynamic growth into the advertising field. The future of advertising offers huge opportunities in creating and maintaining online advertising campaigns.
- *Do you strive to make a good salary?* Advertising and marketing jobs are among the highest paid

Why is it important for those working in advertising to enjoy social functions?

jobs in most companies because effective advertising results in higher profits for a company. Those who stay in the advertising industry and perform well will be compensated well. The salary range varies widely depending on the position held. It also varies by region. Someone working in New York with big-name clients can earn more than someone working in a smaller city with smaller clients.

CHECKPOINT

How can you know if a career in advertising is for you?

Skills for Success

To succeed in the advertising industry, you will need a certain skill set. Your **skill set** includes the unique skills and abilities that you bring to the job market. It is comprised of soft skills and hard skills.

Soft Skills

Soft skills are a cluster of personal qualities, habits, attitudes, and social graces that enhance a person's job performance. Time management, organizational, problem solving, interpersonal, speaking, and listening skills are all considered soft skills. Although specialty skills, or core skills, that relate specifically to advertising are important, soft skills are just as important because of the nature of advertising jobs.

© NAN728/Shutterstock.com

How can good time management skills help you succeed professionally?

Time Management Skills Multiple projects and deadlines can make advertising a stressful career choice. The top professionals in the advertising industry spend well over 40 hours each week to complete projects on time. This type of schedule can take a heavy toll on individuals who have not learned how to manage time effectively. **Time management** is the act of budgeting time to increase efficiency and productivity. Tips for organizing your time more effectively include the following:

- Analyze how you spend your time and eliminate unnecessary activities that are time-wasters.
- Prioritize the tasks to be completed in order of importance.
- Create a schedule that allows time for each task.
- Use time management tools such as a day planner (a binder containing daily, weekly, or monthly calendars) or a scheduling software program.
- Learn to *delegate*, which involves transferring part of your workload to other people.

Organizational Skills There are few things that advertising professionals can do well without being organized. Poor organizational skills result in missed deadlines and lowered productivity. On the other hand, strong organizational skills result in tasks that are completed on time with fewer errors. Organizational skills are closely tied to time management skills. By keeping track of meetings, appointments, and deadlines, you'll know in advance what tasks need to be completed. This helps you stay ahead of the game, keeping you better organized.

Organizational skills also involve organizing your work area in a way where you can easily locate items that are needed. You should be able to quickly find what you need when you need it. Workers who know where to find notes or certain resources can save time and get more done. In advertising, nothing is more frustrating than not being able to locate important client

Making business feel less like work, one app at a time.

LinkedIn Free • Now you can take one of the top professional networking sites with you. Get status updates, find contact info, and connect with your clients from almost anywhere.

iXpenseIt £2.99 • Keep track of all your daily expenses and easily manage your monthly budget. Log your spending in real time – and even store pictures of your receipts.

LogMeIn £17.99 • With your iPhone, you can remotely view your computer desktop over the 3G network or Wi-Fi connection – and access files when you're away from the office.

Air Sharing £2.99 • Transform your iPhone into a portable storage device. Air Sharing lets you drag and drop a variety of common file formats, including PDFs, between your computer and phone.

Sudoku £1.79 • One of the most challenging and addictive logic games is now easy to play anywhere, with thousands of different grids and a variety of skill levels.

Keynote Remote £0.59 • Use your iPhone to wirelessly control the Apple Keynote presentations on your Mac. Advance your slides, see presentation notes, or preview your next slide – with the touch of your finger.

Timewerks £5.99 • Use this time-tracking and invoicing app to keep track of billable hours and materials spent on your various projects – then create reports and send invoices directly from your phone.

Flight Status £2.99 • Not sure when your plane is leaving? Stay up-to-date on thousands of flights and airports from all corners of the globe with the touch of your finger.

vCarder £1.19 • vCarder makes networking simple. Just select a contact from your address book, customise the information and send it via email, straight from your iPhone.

Quicksheet® £7.49 • Create, edit and save spreadsheets on your iPhone. And with support for over 125 spreadsheet functions, you can make last-minute changes wherever you happen to be.

Bloomberg Free • Staying on top of the world's markets is easier when you have one of the most respected sources for financial news and analysis right on your phone.

SpeakEasy £1.19 • Easily make quality audio recordings with your iPhone's built-in mic. From voice memos to lectures, recording is as simple as tapping a button.

Qype Radar Free • If you're not sure where to entertain your clients, just use your iPhone. With a tap of a finger, you'll instantly have thousands of local reviews of bars, clubs, restaurants, hotels and shops.

Currency Free • Need to know how sterling compares to the dollar, or any of over 90 other currencies around the world? Now the latest exchange rates are right at your fingertips.

Print n Share £3.99 • Wirelessly access email attachments, photos and other documents that are on your computer, and send them to print from your iPhone.

National Rail £4.99 • Need to catch a train for a meeting? With the National Rail Enquiries app, you can get live timetable information with updates on arrivals, departures, delays, cancellations and engineering works, direct to your iPhone.

The amazing iPhone 3G is now even more amazing, with over 35,000 apps on the App Store. iPhone users worldwide have already downloaded over 1 billion, across every category from games to business.

Only on O₂ | 🍎 iPhone 3G

How can electronic devices such as the iPhone help you improve your time management and organizational skills?

documents during crucial stages of developing an advertising campaign. Going back to the client to get missing information can result in a lack of confidence on the part of the client.

Problem-Solving Skills Creating advertising campaigns and sales promotions requires advertising professionals to analyze the objectives of the advertiser and to develop strategies to achieve each of the objectives. Those working in advertising are called upon to solve problems by thinking creatively and by coming up with ideas that are fresh and new. Alternative solutions or approaches to advertising and sales promotions must be developed. Then logic and reasoning are used to identify the strengths and weaknesses of each alternative before choosing the most appropriate one.

Interpersonal Skills Advertising careers require strong interpersonal skills, which influence your interactions with other people. They are often referred to as social skills or people skills. Advertising professionals work closely with many other people on the advertising team, some of whom can be difficult and demanding. Good interpersonal skills will go a long way in developing positive working relationships with others. Individuals who have good interpersonal skills generally are cheerful, cooperative, considerate, empathetic, respectful, and good communicators. They also are good at resolving conflicts and recognizing others for a job well done.

Speaking Skills When working in advertising, you must know how to give an effective presentation to clients and coworkers. You often will have to present advertising and sales promotion ideas to others. Public speaking is a fine art that improves with practice. Good speakers are knowledgeable about their topic, making them more credible. For example, an individual who is presenting an advertising campaign must know everything there is to know about the product being advertised. Speakers are also confident, which comes from knowing they have worthy ideas to share with others. They are able to develop a presentation that is interesting, informative, relevant, and concise. They communicate their message in a clear, easy-to-understand format. They invite members of the audience to ask questions and are at ease in answering those questions. All the while, they demonstrate energy and enthusiasm throughout their presentation.

Listening Skills Careers in advertising and sales promotion require active listening skills. Hearing is a physical ability while listening is an active process that assigns meaning to what another person is saying. Advertising professionals must be able to listen to their client's needs to develop the best campaign to meet those needs. Good listeners do the following:

- stop what they are doing and pay attention to what the speaker is saying

What is the difference between hearing and listening?

- use body language, such as facial expressions, eye contact, or nod-ding, to express interest in what the speaker is saying
- encourage the speaker with positive verbal responses that invite him or her to provide more information
- listen to the whole message before deciding how to respond
- empathize by trying to understand the speaker's point of view
- avoid criticizing the speaker
- restate what they have heard and ask meaningful questions to clarify

Hard Skills

In all advertising careers, certain hard skills are required. **Hard skills** are technical skills that are learned through training. They include reading, writing, and computer-related skills. It is understood that writing is an important skill for advertising professionals. You must be able to express your ideas clearly both orally and in writing. If you are involved in the artistic side of advertising, you may also need graphic design skills.

SPOTLIGHT ON SUCCESS

Photo Courtesy of CCL

SEAN CAHEE

Dillard's Department Store

When Sean Cahee graduated from Westbury High School in Houston, Texas, he was not sure what career path he would pursue. Serving as vice president of his school's DECA chapter sparked Sean's interest in the retail clothing industry, leading to a career at Target. Today, Sean is a Ralph Lauren clothing specialist/sales associate in the men's department at Dillard's in Sugar Land, Texas. Sean's successful career at Dillard's can be attributed to his strong people skills, sense for fashion, and knowledge of the latest clothing trends. Sean has a friendly personality that makes him a favorite sales associate among customers.

Dillard's philosophy is that "every life has a style and every style, a life." Dillard's "Style of Your Life" promotional campaign has been instrumental in solidifying Dillard's as an upscale department store that offers better prices and more enticing fashion assortments. Sean has incorporated this philosophy into his work. He views customers as individuals with different needs and styles and has the unique capability of meeting those needs whether the customer is 13 years old or 80 years old. Sean has regularly earned the Pace Setter status at Dillard's for selling at least $300,000 of merchandise during the year. Dillard's CAD (Clienteling at Dillard's) program helps Sean connect with his customers. The CAD is a sophisticated computer program that allows sales associates to keep track of guest preferences, including preferred clothing styles and sizes, birthdays, and other pertinent information. Sean uses this valuable database of information to maintain contact with customers on a continuous basis. This type of follow-up further enhances Sean's image as a caring sales associate who strives to provide the best customer service possible.

Sean is the perfect role model for Dillard's "Style of Your Life" promotional campaign. Not only does he help customers find their style but he also showcases his own impeccable clothing style every day at work. Because fashion is a big part of his career, it is important that Sean dress the part.

Think Critically

What skills do you think are most important for a career in the retail industry? Do you think soft skills or hard skills are more important? Explain your answers. Why do you think Sean has succeeded in this industry? What makes him a favorite among customers?

In today's business world, computer-related skills are crucial. Those working in the advertising field may need to know how to use desktop publishing, graphic design, or web design software. Being technologically savvy is important because much of today's advertising is done online or over wireless devices. You need to have an understanding of the latest technological mediums used to deliver advertising messages, such as Facebook, Twitter, and YouTube. Keeping current in the advertising industry may involve attending classes and seminars to update your technology skills.

///////// CHECKPOINT \\\\\\\\\

What are some soft skills required of those working in advertising?

15.1 Assessment

THINK ABOUT IT

1. Answer the questions on page 407 to determine if an advertising career would interest you. What job traits do you find appealing or unappealing?

2. What is the difference between soft skills and hard skills? Which do you think are more important in the advertising industry? Why?

3. Why are problem-solving skills essential for an advertising career?

MAKE ACADEMIC CONNECTIONS

4. **SPEECH** Your guidance counselor has asked you to participate in the school's career day by speaking about advertising careers. Prepare a five-minute speech describing what it would be like to work in advertising. Discuss the skills required of individuals working in this field. PowerPoint slides can be used to enhance the speech.

5. **MANAGEMENT** Time management and organizational skills are essential for those working in the advertising industry. It is important to develop these skills while in school to be better prepared for college and the workplace. Make a list of all the responsibilities you have involving school, work, home, sports, and extracurricular activities over the next two weeks. Prioritize them and create a schedule for completing all activities. Use day planners, calendars, or scheduling software.

6. **PROBLEM SOLVING** Think back over the past several weeks about some of the problems you've had to resolve. Choose one and describe how you might approach it differently if the same problem occurs again. List new ideas and options for tackling the problem.

 Teamwork

Good interpersonal skills are crucial to a successful advertising career. As a team, create four short skits that demonstrate interpersonal skills in the workplace. Two skits should demonstrate poor interpersonal skills. Then the same skits should be redone to demonstrate proper interpersonal skills.

15.2

The Workplace

Goals

- Describe employer expectations for employees.
- Identify employees' rights in the workplace.

Terms

- corporate culture, p. 414
- punctual, p. 414
- initiative, p. 415
- multifaceted, p. 415
- discrimination, p. 417
- harassment, p. 417
- workplace bullying, p. 417

FOCUS ON ADVERTISING

Selling Employer Expectations

Employers have certain expectations of their employees. For example, employees are expected to budget wisely and save the company money whenever possible. The U.S. Postal Service (USPS) created a series of advertisements based on these expectations. The TV commercials emphasized the savings generated by using USPS's Priority Mail Flat Rate program. Using the tagline, "If it fits, it ships," an actor posing as a postal worker explains to employees at various companies that whatever they can fit in the flat rate box or envelope (up to 70 pounds) ships for one rate to anywhere in the United States. In one commercial, as an employee is busy preparing envelopes for a large mailing, the postal worker explains how the company can save money using the flat rate program. The worker states aloud that he doesn't care about saving the company money. Unbeknownst to the employee, his boss is standing behind him with a scowl on his face. This USPS ad conveys the message that employers expect employees to use company resources efficiently and that USPS can lend a hand in doing so.

Work as a Team Why do you think the USPS chose to focus on employer expectations in its advertising campaign? Do you think this is an effective approach? Why or why not? Name other ads that use the same approach.

Employer's Expectations

High school and college students have a good understanding of teacher expectations. Show up on time ready to learn and put forth your best effort to earn good grades. The real world is not that simple. During the first few weeks or perhaps months on the job,

How can the corporate culture affect the working environment?

individuals may feel very unsure of how they will succeed in this new environment. They must adjust to the **corporate culture**, which refers to an organization's values, beliefs, and behaviors. In many ways, the corporate culture defines an organization's personality. It influences the employer's expectations of its workers. It affects the way things are done and how people work, behave, and make decisions. Some corporate cultures may be more relaxed and flexible, while others may be more rules-oriented and rigid. Regardless of the corporate culture, however, all employers have certain expectations of their employees.

Be Dependable

Great employees show up for work every day and do what they say they will do every time. They have good attendance, meaning others do not have to step in to do their work. They are also **punctual**, meaning they are exactly on time or a little ahead of schedule. Dependable employees can be counted on to always follow directions and to always have their work done right, when it is supposed to be done.

Be Honest and Trustworthy

Employers expect employees to be truthful with customers, clients, coworkers, and supervisors. They also expect employees to make an honest effort to complete their work to the best of their abilities. Being honest means admitting your mistakes and not making excuses or blaming others. Employees must be trustworthy when it comes to a company's money, equipment, and other valuables. They also have to be trusted to follow company policies.

Have a Good Attitude

An employee's attitude reflects his or her state of mind. Your attitude affects the way you respond to people and the way you approach your work. Workers who have positive attitudes tend to be optimistic, enthusiastic, and friendly. They are pleasant to be around and show respect for others. As a worker, they are more willing to accept change, listen to opposing viewpoints, and accept responsibility for their mistakes. On the other hand, a worker with a negative attitude finds fault with everything and everyone, complains about his or her job, is not open to change, and is inconsiderate of others. Negative attitudes can be contagious and spread among others, creating a stressful working environment.

Take Initiative

Taking **initiative** means taking action without being asked to do so. Employees who have initiative are often described as go-getters. They get the ball rolling on their own. Instead of sitting around and waiting to be told what to do, they jump in and get the job done. These workers look for more efficient ways of performing tasks, come up with new ideas that benefit the company, and find solutions to problems. Not surprisingly, those who show initiative often take on leadership roles. They may also be **multifaceted**, meaning they have more skills than those required for their specific position. They enthusiastically apply these skills to a variety of tasks and are willing to learn new skills.

Work Well with Others

Working cooperatively with others is key to long-term career success. Good working relationships make the work environment more pleasant. At various times throughout your career, you may find that you have to rely on others to get the job done. The support and respect of your coworkers is needed to help you succeed. Chances are, some of your coworkers will come from different cultural backgrounds. Employers expect employees to relate and work well with a diverse group of people. In today's workplace, people often work together in teams. Achieving team goals requires the cooperation of all team members. In addition, employees must work well with customers or clients and provide them with the best service possible.

© Stephen Coburn/Shutterstock.com

Why is cooperation among coworkers an important concern for businesses?

Employees' Rights

Just as employers have certain expectations, employees have certain rights in the workplace. They have a right to a safe working environment, fair and equal treatment in the workplace, and protection from discrimination and harassment.

Safe Working Conditions

Employees working in construction zones or factories often can be seen wearing hard hats and safety glasses. This equipment helps protect employees from injury. By law, employers must provide this equipment to their employees. The Occupational Safety and Health Administration (OSHA) is the government agency that sets and enforces standards for safe and healthful working conditions. Although hard hats and safety glasses generally are not needed in an office environment, there are still other safety issues in the workplace that must be addressed. For example, work areas must be well lit to avoid harm to eyes. Meal times and breaks must be provided to employees under certain circumstances. All exits and aisles must be kept clear and doors must be unlocked from the inside. Employers need to correct any safety problems that employees call to their attention.

Equality in the Workplace

There are many employment equality laws that help level the playing field for employees. The Equal Pay Act of 1963 outlaws different wage scales for equal work, meaning workers doing the same job must

What kinds of safety hazards might pose a threat to office workers?

receive the same pay. The Civil Rights Act of 1964 paved the way for equal employment opportunity. The law prohibits discrimination by employers. **Discrimination** is the act of treating one person less favorably than another person because of race, color, religion, gender, or national origin. It often results in the loss of job or promotion opportunities for those discriminated against.

The Age Discrimination Act of 1967 extended protection against discrimination to include people between the ages of 40 and 70. The Americans with Disabilities Act of 1990 provides equal opportunity for individuals with disabilities. Employers are obliged to make reasonable accommodations for employees with disabilities, and disabled employees must be given a fair chance for possible employment and promotion opportunities. The Family and Medical Leave Act of 1993 protects against discrimination of employees who must take time off to care for a new baby or for an ill family member. This law requires employers with 50 or more workers to grant up to 12 weeks of unpaid leave a year.

NET Bookmark

The problem of workplace bullying is not new. Millions of working adults say they have been bullied at some point in their working lives. Legislation called the Healthy Workplace Bill (HWB) would make bullying illegal and has been introduced in more than 20 states since 2003. Access www.cengage.com/school/advertising and click on the link for Chapter 15. Read about workplace bullying and the Healthy Workplace Bill. What are the terms of the HWB? Do you believe such a law is needed? Why or why not?

www.cengage.com/school/advertising

Protection from Harassment

Harassment is unwelcome verbal or physical conduct. In the workplace, harassment that is based on gender, marital status, religion, age, disability, race, and sexual orientation is illegal. This type of harassment is often referred to as workplace bullying. **Workplace bullying** refers to repeated, unreasonable actions of an individual (or a group) directed toward an employee (or a group of employees) for the purpose of intimidating, degrading, humiliating, or undermining the employee. It can take the form of belittling or offensive remarks, exclusion from outings, false accusations, criticism of work, or stolen possessions. It can lead to a hostile working environment, which has a negative effect on an employee's work performance. Bullying has become an increasingly more common issue due to the growing use of social media, such as Facebook. Workplace bullying can result in dismissal from the company and possible legal action.

Corporate/institutional bullying occurs when bullying is entrenched in an organization and becomes accepted as part of the workplace culture. It is the result of unreasonable expectations of employees, where failure to meet those expectations means making life unpleasant. Individuals are less likely to engage in bullying behavior when it is understood that the organization does not tolerate such behavior and

What would you do if confronted by a bully in the workplace?

© Piotr Marcinski/Shutterstock.com

that the "bully" is likely to be punished. Because victims of bullying can suffer from significant physical and mental health problems that can affect work performance, it is in the best interest of an organization not to tolerate bullying. The victim or any witnesses of bullying should be encouraged to report such incidences.

It is important to remember that bullying involves repeated attacks against the targeted person, creating an ongoing pattern of bad behavior. "Tough" or "demanding" bosses are not necessarily bullies as long as they are respectful and fair, and their primary motivation is to obtain the best performance by setting high, reasonable expectations.

///////// CHECKPOINT ◥◥◥◥◥◥◥◥

What are some basic employee rights?

15.2 Assessment

THINK ABOUT IT

1. What is a multifaceted employee? Why is this type of employee valuable to a company?
2. Why do companies prefer employees that take initiative? Provide an example of how an employee can take initiative.
3. Why should a company discourage workplace bullying?

MAKE ACADEMIC CONNECTIONS

4. **WRITING**   Your school has expectations of its students just as an employer does of its employees. Review the employer expectations described on pages 414–415. Use these same expectations to create a student handbook that describes appropriate student behavior.

5. **COMMUNICATION**   As part of a company's safety policies, it generally creates a fire safety evacuation plan to be used in case of emergencies. Conduct research to learn more about creating an evacuation plan. Then develop one for your home, school, or workplace.

6. **HISTORY**   Select one of the employment equality laws described in this lesson. Learn more about the history of the law. Prepare a classroom presentation that explains the background of the law and its stipulations. In addition, describe a lawsuit that was based on the equality law and explain the outcome of it.

Teamwork

Bullying often starts at a young age and can continue into adulthood. To help prevent bullying at your school, develop a bully awareness and prevention campaign. Create posters, flyers, videos, or other items containing general information about bullying and ways to prevent it that can be shown or distributed to students at your school.

Leadership, Career Development, and Team Building

Goals

- Identify leadership qualities and leadership tasks.
- Describe career development techniques.
- Explain the importance of teams and describe how they function.

Terms

- leadership, p. 419
- empowering, p. 421
- networking, p. 421
- informational interview, p. 422
- internship, p. 423
- career portfolio, p. 423
- mentor, p. 423
- team, p. 424

Beginning a Career in Advertising

FOCUS ON ADVERTISING

Because there is keen competition for entry-level advertising jobs, students interested in a career in this field are encouraged to gain experience through internships or other work-related programs. Gannett, the nation's largest print, broadcast, and digital information company, has a Talent Development Program that enables it to train and develop employees. It is a ten-week training program and a full-time employment opportunity. Participants are paid an entry-level salary during those ten weeks. They work with a mentor, who meets with them on a regular basis, giving participants the opportunity to inquire and learn about the various aspects of the media profession. Upon successful completion of the program, participants will be offered a full-time position. College students must apply for admittance to this program, meet GPA requirements, and demonstrate strong business skills, such as time management, organizational, problem-solving, communication, and multimedia skills.

Work as a Team Why do you think companies such as Gannett are willing to invest time and money into training students? How does this benefit both the company and the student?

What Is Leadership?

At some point throughout your career, you may be expected to take a leadership role. **Leadership** is the ability to motivate and direct a group of people to achieve a common goal. In the advertising industry, there are many opportunities to act as a leader. You may lead the team that is developing a new advertising campaign. Or perhaps you may lead the

group that is in charge of one of the many components of the advertising campaign, such as media, copywriting, art, marketing research, or production. You may even own an advertising agency and be responsible for leading your employees. Regardless of the leadership role, leaders must have certain qualities and perform specific tasks to succeed.

Leadership Qualities

Is there one type of person who makes the best leader? Generally, the answer is "no." Leadership comes in all shapes and sizes. However, research has shown that effective leaders have certain traits that set them apart from others. The greatest leaders have strong people skills. They understand the differences that make people unique and incorporate those individual skills to achieve goals. Leaders also have a positive attitude. They motivate people to achieve through encouragement, recognition, and rewards. Although they expect high-quality performance, they tolerate honest mistakes.

Effective leaders must have good communication skills. They must be able to share information in large meetings or in one-on-one discussions. As communicators, leaders are knowledgeable, persuasive, and good listeners. Planning is another important skill for leaders. They must set goals and develop strategies for achieving the goals. A plan of action helps guide the group as its members work toward the goals. Finally, a true leader has integrity and is reliable, trustworthy, and fair.

Leadership Tasks

Leadership involves rising to the challenge, making decisions, and motivating others to achieve goals. In addition, leaders take on many other roles. Typically, leaders perform the following tasks as they tackle their many roles.

- *Communicate goals.* Whether the goal is to create a dynamic advertising campaign, develop a new exciting product, or set sales strategies, the leader always has a clear target in mind and helps others understand it.

Why do leaders need good communication skills to succeed?

- *Establish a positive work environment.* A leader is responsible for setting the tone and establishing a positive working climate that shows commitment and gives support to all group members. Those who perform well are recognized and rewarded for their accomplishments.
- *Set a good example.* Leading by example can be very effective. If a leader is honest, listens well, and shows respect for others, followers are likely to adopt the same behaviors. Leaders should act as role models.
- *Direct the completion of tasks.* To accomplish goals, a leader will have to develop a schedule and delegate tasks to others. As others work to complete their tasks, the leader provides guidance and support as needed and monitors their progress to ensure deadlines are met.
- *Empower others.* **Empowering** means giving others substantial responsibility and the freedom to make their own decisions. This gives people a sense of importance and improves their performance. Leaders should encourage others to provide input.
- *Handle conflict.* Leaders will work with people from diverse backgrounds with diverse opinions. As a result, conflict will likely arise on occasion. An effective leader will encourage others to openly express their ideas and to compromise or collaborate on a solution.

CHECKPOINT

What are three leadership qualities?

Career Development

Career development is a planning method used to meet a person's career goals. It is an ongoing, life-long process that involves learning new skills and making improvements to help you achieve more in your career. Career development can help you succeed in making a career change or moving up within a company. Establishing professional contacts and gaining work experience are two of the most important components in career development. These can be achieved through networking and internships.

Professional Networking

"Who you know" has a major impact on your career success. This can sometimes be as important as "what you know." **Networking** is the process of developing a broad list of contacts with other people, groups, or organizations. You may establish contacts through social and business functions. *Professional networks* include individuals who are willing to assist you with career development. People in your professional network can answer questions, give advice, and provide valuable information about career opportunities. They may also introduce you to others, resulting in an expanded network. Having the right connection increases your chance of achieving your career goals.

Who can you include in your network?

Developing a Network Building your network is an ongoing process. It begins with family, friends, teachers, and acquaintances. Your network will expand as you meet and interact with other people. When you begin working, you can add coworkers to your network. Today, it is easier than ever to establish contacts online through websites, blogs, and social networking sites. The members of your network can be valuable as you grow professionally.

As you continue on your career path, you may need to target individuals for your network. To do this, you need to focus on what you want to achieve in your career and determine who can help you. For example, you can conduct an **informational interview**, which involves talking to a human resource representative or manager of a company where you might like to work to obtain general information and advice about the company. You should not be afraid to ask about career opportunities, typical career paths within the company, and desirable employee traits. This helps you establish contacts at the company and may increase your chances of being hired when job opportunities become available.

Successful networking involves staying in touch with all of your professional contacts. You should make a point periodically to contact individuals in your network. Keep detailed contact information, including names, job titles, addresses, e-mails, and telephone numbers.

How can student organizations help you prepare for a career?

Student and Professional Organizations Networking can begin at an early age. Actively participating in student organizations like DECA, FBLA, and BPA are good examples of professional networking for young people interested in business and marketing careers. Students can participate in leadership conferences and competitive events. The competitive events provide students with the experience of developing creative ideas, implementing a plan of action, and presenting the plan to others in a professional manner. These are daily tasks required in many industries, including the advertising industry.

Professional networking is strengthened by joining and actively participating in professional organizations directly related to the career field. Advertising professionals can participate in the following professional organizations: American Marketing Association, American Advertising Federation, and the Advertising Research Foundation. The Ad Council provides educational resources to help professionals enhance their advertising careers.

The Value of an Internship

Competition for entry-level advertising jobs is intense. There are many more candidates than advertising positions. Individuals involved in advertising must be willing to start at the bottom and work their way up. An internship in the advertising field can give you a competitive edge. Many employers (77.3 percent) said that they use their internship programs as a tool for recruiting entry-level employees. An **internship** is a hands-on learning experience related to career goals and interests. Paid and unpaid internships are available to high school and college students while they are completing their education. Internships provide students with the opportunity to

- acquire practical work experience relating to the student's career choice
- learn more about a specific industry/field
- identify interests, skills, and talents
- determine whether their interests match their skills
- develop professionalism and experience
- learn and improve specific skills such as communication, problem solving, teamwork, and leadership
- increase their marketability and value to employers
- build their professional network

Overall, an internship will enhance an individual's **career portfolio**, which is a collection of projects, work experiences, awards, a resume, and other items that applicants present to prospective employers to validate their value to the company. Personal accomplishments at an internship are an important part of the portfolio.

Choosing an Internship Internships provide a unique exploratory opportunity for students. They help students determine if they have selected a career that matches their interests and talents. Thus, choosing the internship program that is right for you is an important decision. Cooperative (Co-op) education coordinators can provide information about internship experiences available to high school students. University career centers can also provide valuable information regarding the availability of internships. In addition, there are many websites dedicated to internships and cooperative education experiences.

The Internship Sponsor The internship sponsor is the company that employs the intern. Companies that offer internships are responsible for providing a valuable learning experience for the intern. Oftentimes while interning, the student will work with a mentor. A **mentor** is an individual who acts as a role model and provides training and advice. The mentor is also a resource when the intern has questions related to the career or industry. The value of internships depends on the sincere interest demonstrated by the intern, sponsoring company, and mentor.

Working on Teams

In today's workplace, more decisions are being made by teams of employees rather than a single supervisor or manager. Teamwork is ranked as one of the most desirable skills by employers. In the workplace, a **team** is a small group of employees who work together to achieve a specific goal. There are several benefits to teams. Generally, the problem-solving process is quicker because more people are responsible for solving a particular problem. In addition, the various experiences and backgrounds of the team members result in a greater number of creative and innovative ideas and solutions. Teams build stronger employee relationships as team members collaborate and develop respect and trust for one another. Perhaps the biggest benefit for a company is that teamwork results in improved productivity.

How a Team Functions

The members of a team take on various roles. The team leader directs the group's efforts, runs meetings, and provides guidance and support as needed. The team leader may be appointed by a company executive or elected by the team. The team leader should work with the team members to assign each of them a formal role and clearly state the responsibilities of the role. Strengths and talents should be considered when assigning roles. On advertising teams, the team leader must be careful not to hinder the individual creativity of each member. Although team members are responsible for completing certain tasks, they should not feel restricted by their roles and should be encouraged to make contributions in all areas.

© Andresr/Shutterstock.com

Why are teams generally more productive than employees who work alone?

Often, team members will take on informal roles themselves. For example, one team member may act as a coordinator by taking the lead in organizing activities. Another team member may take on the mediator role and work to resolve disagreements among team members. The team member who acts as the clarifier will interpret and summarize what has been said and done. Another team member may be known as the cheerleader because he gives pep talks when morale is low. Although team members have not been asked to take on these informal roles, others know they can be counted on to do so.

Types of Teams

Throughout your career, you may participate on different types of teams. In the advertising industry, you are likely to work on a *functional team*, which is associated with a specific functional department within a company, such as the marketing or advertising department. Specialized functional teams can often address certain tasks more efficiently because they are uniquely qualified. People working in the marketing department of a company participate in functional teams that create advertising campaigns for the company's products. A *problem-solving team* is established to resolve a specific problem or complete a specific task. For example, a problem-solving team consisting of marketers may be assembled to determine how to promote a product at an upcoming special event. A *cross-functional team* brings members from various departments together to solve problems or complete tasks. A marketer may work on a team that includes company executives, financial officers, the client, artists, photographers, media specialists, and production personnel to carry out the advertising plan.

Measuring and Recognizing Team Performance

Teams need to measure their performance. Although individual performance is important, the advertising team as a whole should be evaluated for its effectiveness. This makes it essential to be an active team member who makes a positive contribution to the team. When evaluating performance, a company will consider many factors. An advertising team could be evaluated based on its strategic ability, creativity, and communication of the advertising campaign. Its ability to meet deadlines and stay within budget will also be assessed. Most importantly, the team's goals and its progress in accomplishing those goals will be evaluated. For example, if an advertising team's goal is to increase product awareness among teenagers by 20 percent, the actual results of the advertising campaign will be measured against this goal.

Clients and their advertising agencies must regularly evaluate what's working, what's not, and why. Rather than wait until the end of a project, it is best to conduct a formal, ongoing evaluation at various points throughout the project to ensure everything is on target. Continual feedback will result in the most effective advertising campaign.

When a team has performed well, it should be rewarded. Recognition of a job well done is an important motivator for team performance. Praise or a simple thank you from management can go a long way. Management also can arrange team events, such as a luncheon or special outing. When an advertising team completes its work on a major advertising campaign, a special event can be held to roll out the campaign and to recognize the individual and team efforts that went into it. If the budget allows, bonuses can be used to reward a team that has achieved or exceeded its goals. If an advertising campaign results in increased sales, the team responsible for it may be deserving of a bonus. Regardless of the kind of reward system used, it is important for management to establish a clear link between team performance and rewards. In other words, management must clearly communicate what actions will be rewarded.

CHECKPOINT

Why are teams popular in today's workplace?

15.3 Assessment

THINK ABOUT IT

1. Why is it important for a team leader to empower team members?
2. Why is networking a valuable component of career development?
3. What makes an internship a good learning experience for students?
4. What is the difference between formal roles and informal roles on a team?

MAKE ACADEMIC CONNECTIONS

5. **PROBLEM SOLVING**   You have just learned that your advertising agency will be laying off several workers, including you. You have worked in the advertising industry for ten years and have developed an extensive professional network during that time. Explain how you can use your professional network to find a new job during a poor economy.

6. **MATH**   A student who is interested in a marketing career is offered $9.50 an hour to intern for an advertising agency over the summer. The same student is offered $10.75 an hour to work as a sales clerk in a department store. How much would the student make weekly at each job? What would be the difference in yearly earnings? (Hint: There are 40 hours in a week and 52 weeks in a year.) Besides income, what other factors might the student consider in choosing between the jobs?

7. **RESEARCH**   Conduct research to learn about internship opportunities in the advertising and sales promotion industries. Prepare a short PowerPoint presentation that describes four internship opportunities. Include the name of each company, its location, a job description, job requirements, salary (if it's a paid position), and other important details.

Teamwork

Form a team of five or six students and define a goal your team will accomplish. For example, the goal may be to complete a school project or to plan a school event. Select a leader and then assign roles to the other team members. Then develop a plan for achieving your goal. Create a written document that states the team's goal, the team members, the specific responsibilities of the team leader and each team member, and the team's plan of action for achieving the goal.

Sharpen Your
21st CENTURY SKILLS

Digital Vision/Getty Images

Interviewing Strategies

The job interview is one of the most important stages in the job-seeking process. It gives you the opportunity to showcase your qualifications to an employer. Most employers make a hiring decision based on how you perform during the interview. The job applicant who is well prepared and has effective interviewing skills is more likely to be hired. The following interviewing strategies can help you get the job.

1. *Learn about the company in advance.* Research the company to learn about its mission, objectives, and future plans. Be prepared to answer the question, "Why do you want to work for the company?" It is also a good idea to learn the name of the interviewer so that you can greet him or her by name.

2. *Practice an interview with a friend or relative.* Have responses prepared for commonly asked interview questions. Be ready to provide actual examples or accomplishments that display your skills. Know your career goals in case you're asked where you want to be professionally in a few years.

3. *Be on time.* Better yet, be five to ten minutes early. Being late makes a bad impression on the interviewer. It's a good idea to drive to the company ahead of time so you know exactly where you are going and how long it takes to get there.

4. *Bring the appropriate materials.* Bring a notepad to take notes. This makes you stand out from other job candidates. Also, bring extra copies of your resume to have handy during the interview and to make available to others who may join the interview. Have contact information for three references in case you are asked for it.

5. *Remain calm and in control during the interview.* Try to relax and stay as calm as possible. Maintain eye contact and do not stare at the floor, ceiling, or wall when speaking or listening to avoid appearing disinterested. Don't babble, use slang, or make jokes. Be cooperative and enthusiastic. Show interest by asking questions about the job and the company.

6. *Follow up after the interview.* Send a short thank-you letter that expresses your interest in the job and reminds the interviewer of the special skills you can bring to the company. A thank-you letter will help keep you in the interviewer's mind.

Try It Out

Choose a career that interests you. Develop a list of ten interview questions that you think could be asked during an interview for your selected career. Prepare answers to each question. Work with a partner to role-play the interview. After the interview, write a follow-up, thank-you letter.

© Gina Sanders/Shutterstock.com

PARTNERSHIP FOR
21st CENTURY SKILLS

SUMMARY

15.1 A Career in Advertising

- Those who choose a career in advertising commonly have specific traits. They are good at persuading people; like showing off their talents; like working with people from diverse backgrounds; enjoy staying on top of trends; prefer working in a flexible, less structured environment; enjoy social events; and are technologically savvy.

- To succeed in the advertising industry, certain soft skills (personal qualities) are required, including time management skills, organizational skills, problem-solving skills, interpersonal skills, speaking skills, and listening skills.

- Hard skills (technical skills) required in the advertising industry include good reading, writing, and computer-related skills. Artistic or graphic design skills may also be needed.

15.2 The Workplace

- Employers expect their employees to be dependable, honest, and trustworthy; have a good attitude; take initiative; and work well with others.

- Employees have certain rights in the workplace. They are entitled to equality in the workplace, free from discrimination based on race, color, religion, gender, or national origin.

- Harassment often takes the form of workplace bullying. This involves repeated, unreasonable actions of an individual directed toward an employee for the purpose of intimidating, degrading, humiliating, or undermining the employee.

15.3 Leadership, Career Development, and Team Building

- Leadership is the ability to motivate and direct a group of people to achieve a common goal. Leadership tasks include communicating goals, establishing a positive work environment, setting a good example, directing the completion of tasks, empowering others, and handling conflict.

- Career development is a planning method used to meet a person's career goals. Establishing professional contacts and gaining work experience are important components of career development. Networking and internships are excellent ways to help grow your career.

- Teams offer many benefits, such as quicker problem solving, more creative and innovative solutions and ideas, stronger employee relationships, and improved productivity.

WHAT DO YOU KNOW Now?

Read Impact Advertising on page 405 again to review the careers of two early pioneers in the advertising industry. Conduct research to learn about other influential people in the advertising industry. What impact did they have? Select one and prepare a short presentation on what you learned.

Chapter 15 Assessment

Vocabulary Builder

Match each statement with the term that best defines it. Some terms may not be used.

1. Giving others substantial responsibility and freedom to make their own decisions
2. A cluster of personal qualities, habits, attitudes, and social graces that enhance a person's job performance
3. The process of developing a broad list of contacts with other people, groups, or organizations
4. An organization's values, beliefs, and behaviors
5. A hands-on learning experience related to career goals and interests
6. Unwelcome verbal or physical conduct
7. The act of budgeting time to increase efficiency and productivity
8. Technical skills that are learned through training
9. The act of treating one person less favorably than another person
10. A collection of projects, work experiences, awards, a resume, and other items that applicants present to prospective employers

a. career portfolio
b. corporate culture
c. discrimination
d. empowering
e. harassment
f. hard skills
g. informational interview
h. initiative
i. internship
j. leadership
k. mentor
l. multifaceted
m. networking
n. punctual
o. skill set
p. soft skills
q. team
r. time management
s. workplace bullying

Test Your Knowledge

11. Which of the following traits is *not* common among those working in the advertising industry?
    a. stays on top of trends
    b. is creative
    c. avoids socializing with others
    d. is persuasive
12. A multifaceted employee
    a. can apply his/her skills to a variety of tasks
    b. has more skills than those required for a specific position
    c. is willing to learn new skills
    d. all of the above
13. Which of the following statements about workplace bullying is false?
    a. It refers to a single incident in the workplace.
    b. It is intended to intimidate or humiliate an employee.
    c. It can involve belittling or offensive remarks.
    d. It can have a negative effect on work performance.

14. Taking initiative means
    a. being exactly on time or ahead of schedule
    b. taking action without being asked to do so
    c. budgeting time to increase productivity
    d. giving others substantial responsibility
15. Which type of team would most likely be assembled to plan a party for the launch of a new product?
    a. functional   c. problem-solving
    b. cross-functional   d. collaborative
16. Which of the following is *not* a soft skill?
    a. time management   c. problem-solving
    b. listening   d. graphic design
17. Equality in the workplace laws do *not* make it illegal to discriminate based on _____.
    a. job qualifications   c. gender
    b. race   d. age
18. A good leader does all of the following *except*
    a. acts as a role model for team members
    b. discourages differing opinions to avoid conflict
    c. clearly communicates the team's goals
    d. develops a schedule and delegates tasks
19. _____ are part of your network.
    a. Friends   c. Coworkers
    b. Family members   d. all of the above
20. Which of the following statements is false?
    a. Internships help you identify your interests and skills.
    b. Internships may be paid or unpaid positions.
    c. Internships will not increase your value to employers.
    d. Internships can enhance your career portfolio.

Apply What You Learned

21. Visit an online career site and search for jobs in the advertising or promotions field. Select two of the jobs and review the job qualifications. What types of soft skills and hard skills are required?
22. Conduct research to learn more about organizational skills. Prepare a list of ten tips for staying organized in the workplace.
23. Employers expect employees to be dependable. In one or two paragraphs, describe what being dependable in the workplace means to you. Describe behaviors and actions that demonstrate dependability.

Make Academic Connections

24. **CAREERS** Interview someone currently working in an advertising position to learn why the person chose a career in advertising and what he or she considers the benefits of an advertising career. Create a list of questions in advance. The interview may be conducted in person, by phone, or by e-mail. Compile your interview in a written format.

25. **ETHICS**   You are the human resource director for an advertising agency. The president of your company has asked you to prepare a short, five-minute PowerPoint presentation about harassment and bullying in the workplace. Describe behaviors and actions that would be considered harassment or workplace bullying, reasons it will not be tolerated, and likely consequences of such actions.

26. **WRITING**   Write a two-page report titled "The Importance of Career Development." The essay should explain the benefits of career development and provide helpful career development tips.

27. **COMMUNICATION**   You have conducted an informational interview with the human resource director of an advertising agency where you would like to work. Write a follow-up, thank-you letter to the HR director to remind him of your interest in the company. The letter should also reflect key points you learned about the company during the interview. The HR director's name and address are Robert Smith, Dynamic Advertising, 1500 University Avenue, Sugar Land, Texas 77479.

28. **RESEARCH**   Participating in a student organization has many benefits, including enhancement of leadership, teamwork, and communication skills. Conduct research to learn about five student organizations that students can join. Write a short description of each organization and share your findings with the class. Which organization would interest you the most? Why? For those interested in a career in advertising, which organization would be the most beneficial? Why?

29. **PROBLEM SOLVING**   As the owner of an advertising agency, you must evaluate the effectiveness of the advertising teams that are assembled to work on various advertising campaigns. Create a performance evaluation form to be used for teams. List at least ten criteria on which the teams will be evaluated. You may want to search the Internet for a sample performance evaluation form to use as a model.

You were recently hired as an account planner for an advertising agency. Although you have made an attempt to get along with all of your coworkers, one of them has been extremely unfriendly. During team meetings, this coworker refers to you as "the youngster" and discredits your ideas because of your inexperience. She has arranged several lunch meetings to discuss various projects but has always excluded you. You have caught her talking with other coworkers about you on several occasions. Because she is the senior account planner, you must run all of your work by her first. You prepared an advertising plan for a new client and gave it to her to review. You later discovered that she had presented your ideas as her own to upper management.

What would you do? Do you think this is a case of workplace bullying? Why or why not? What would be your recommendations for resolving this issue?

Reality ✔

Leadership Styles

Throughout your career, you will encounter many leadership styles. A leadership style is the manner and approach of providing direction, implementing plans, and motivating people. Three major leadership styles have been identified: autocratic, democratic, and laissez-faire.

Autocratic leaders, also known as authoritarian leaders, tell their employees what needs to be done and how it should be done. They make decisions independently with little or no input from their employees. There is a clear division between the leader and the employees. Employee performance is closely supervised. This leadership style is often viewed as controlling. Research has shown that autocratic leadership discourages creativity and initiative on the part of the employee. This style of leadership works best with new employees who are just learning the job or when there is little time for group decision making.

Democratic leaders, also known as participative leaders, involve employees in the decision-making process but retain the final decision-making authority. Although they provide guidance, supervision is minimal, and employees are responsible for their performance. Employees are encouraged to express their ideas and make suggestions. Generally, this is the most effective leadership style. It works well with a team of workers who know their job. It promotes greater job satisfaction and improves morale.

Laissez-faire leaders, also known as delegative leaders, offer little or no guidance to employees and leave decision making to them. Because leaders cannot do everything, they delegate certain tasks. Laissez-faire leadership works well when employees are highly qualified in a specific area of expertise. However, it can lead to poorly defined goals and a lack of direction for employees.

Good leaders change their leadership styles to fit the circumstances. They may use an autocratic style to implement a new procedure that replaces the current one that is not working. By asking for the employees' ideas and input on the new procedure, they are using the democratic style. If they delegate tasks to others to develop and implement the new procedure, they are using the laissez-fair style.

Think Critically

1. What are the advantages and disadvantages of each leadership style?
2. What might influence which leadership style is used?
3. Which leadership style would you prefer? Why?

Human resource management is an organizational function that deals with employee-related issues such as compensation, hiring, performance, safety, wellness, benefits, employee motivation, communication, administration, and training. Any problems related to these issues can cause major problems for a business unless they are addressed. This is the responsibility of the human resource manager.

TOPIC   You are the human resource manager for a home improvement store that employs 200 full-time employees who earn salaries ranging from $30,000 to $58,000 a year. Your store has experienced a 19 percent dip in sales compared to sales last year. You realize that the sluggish economy may be partially responsible for the decline in sales; however, you are also aware that employees are not always effective at making sales. You believe this can be contributed to poor selling skills as well as a lack of motivation. You have decided that the store should implement a base salary and sales commission plan ($20,000 plus 6 percent on personal sales) for employees and offer training to help them improve their sales skills.

Many full-time employees have voiced their concern with your proposed salary/sales commission plan. They believe that low sales during weekdays when customer traffic is much lower will affect their commissions and overall salary. You must convince upper management (judges) why your proposed wage and salary plan is good for the company and employees.

You have 30 minutes to develop the presentation. You will have one note card on which to take notes for your presentation. You will have five to seven minutes to present your ideas to upper management. Management has an additional three minutes to ask questions about your presentation.

Performance Indicators Evaluated
* Demonstrate knowledge of human resources management event and management concepts.
* Apply critical thinking skills to interpret personnel policies.
* Demonstrate effective oral communication skills.
* Demonstrate successful evaluation techniques.
* Demonstrate effective persuasive and informative communication and presentation skills.

Go to the BPA website for more detailed information.

Think Critically
1. Why do you think employees might object to changing from a straight salary compensation plan to a salary plus commission plan?
2. How can a human resources manager help employees feel less anxious about a salary plus commission plan?
3. Why do you think it is important to implement a training program in combination with the new compensation plan?

www.bpa.org

Glossary

A

acculturation the process by which members of one cultural group adopt the beliefs and behaviors of another group

advertiser the client (persons, organizations, companies, and manufacturers of products and services) that needs creative messages (advertisements) and advertising campaigns to reach target markets

advertising a paid form of communication intended to inform, persuade, and remind an audience to take some kind of action

advertising agency a marketing business that plans, creates, and manages the advertising for other businesses (clients)

advertising campaign a series of related advertisements with a common theme or idea that focuses on a specific product, service, brand, or message

advertising plan a description of the goals of an advertising campaign, methods to use to accomplish those goals, and ways to evaluate whether those goals are achieved

aerial advertising advertising in the sky

affirmative disclosure the act of including material facts that were not disclosed in a previous ad in all future ads

agenda a list of topics to be discussed at a meeting

Alcohol and Tobacco Tax and Trade Bureau (TTB) the government agency that implements and enforces a broad range of provisions to ensure that alcohol products are created, labeled, and advertised in accordance with federal laws and regulations

approach the first contact that the salesperson makes with the customer

attitude study a survey that measures consumer attitudes before and after exposure to an ad

B

back translation the process of translating a message that has already been translated into a foreign language back to the original language

balance sheet a financial statement that summarizes a company's assets, liabilities, and owner's equity (net worth) as of a specific date.

banner ad a small, rectangular advertisement that usually appears at the top or side of a web page and contains a link to the advertiser's site

benefit segmentation the segmentation of consumers based on specific benefits they expect to receive from a product or service

blog a website maintained by an individual or business where entries (posts) that are intended for public access are made on a regular basis

boutique advertising agency a small, specialized advertising company that outsources many of its services; also referred to as a virtual ad agency

boycott an organized effort to avoid purchasing goods and services from a particular company

brainstorming an organized approach of generating a large number of ideas in a group setting

brand the combination of unique qualities of a company, product, or product line

brand advertising a form of advertising that is used to build an image based on the set of values held by the company

brand awareness the extent to which a brand is recognized and associated with a specific product or service

brand equity the value that a company realizes from having a product with a recognizable name

brand extension a marketing strategy that allows a business to use one of its well-known brand names in a new product category

brand image the consumer's impression of a brand

brand loyalty the consumer's commitment to purchase one brand over all other brands

branding a marketing strategy used to build brand recognition

business-to-business marketing the process by which businesses purchase products or services from other businesses

buying motives the driving forces that cause consumers to buy products and services

C

career portfolio a collection of projects, work experiences, awards, a resume, and other items that applicants present to prospective employers to validate their value to the company

cease-and-desist order a legal order to discontinue a deceptive ad

change agents people who bring about meaningful changes that add value to their lives and other's

channel of distribution the path on which products and services flow from the producer to the final consumer

cinema advertising ads that run in movie theaters before the start of movies

close the step in the sales process when the customer decides to buy a product or service

commission system a payment method by which an advertising agency is compensated based on the amount of money a business (advertiser) spends on advertising media

communication the exchange of meaningful information between two or more people

communication channel the medium used to distribute a message

comparison advertising ads that promote the superiority of a brand by comparing its features to those of a competitive brand

competition-matching method an advertising budgeting method that is based on the amount of money spent by competitors on advertising

consumer the end user of a product or service

consumer behavior the way consumers make buying decisions, choose among alternatives, and use products

consumer credit financing made available by retailers to assist consumers in making purchases

consumerism the organized effort of consumers to influence business practices

consumer-oriented advertising ads created from the customer's perspective to make the message more appropriate and significant for customers

consumer-oriented sales promotions a variety of incentives designed to encourage customers to buy a specific brand

context the situation in which communication occurs

convenience products types of products that are purchased regularly without much planning

copywriting the process of using words to express creative ideas and concepts

corporate advertising a form of advertising that is intended to enhance a company's reputation or build goodwill

corporate culture an organization's values, beliefs, and behaviors

corrective ad an ad that rectifies any false impressions created by deceptive advertising

cost of living the average cost of the basic necessities of life such as housing, food, clothing, utilities, transportation, health care, and other miscellaneous expenses

coupon a certificate that entitles the buyer to a price reduction on a product or service

creative brief a description of what the advertising campaign is to accomplish

creative strategy a description of who the target market is, what the advertising message should be, and how the message will be communicated

cross-selling a direct marketing program aimed at customers who already purchase other products from the company

cultural diversity the coexistence of different ethnic, gender, racial, and socioeconomic groups

culture the shared attitudes and behaviors of a specific social group

customer profile a description of the characteristics exhibited by an individual who is likely to buy a business's products or services

D

deal loader a premium given by a manufacturer to a retailer for ordering a certain quantity of a product

deception the act of making false or misleading statements in an advertisement

decoding the interpretation of the language and symbols to uncover the meaning of a message

defamation the act of making a false or derogatory statement that gives a negative impression about a competing business or product

demographics consumer characteristics such as age, gender, race, marital status, income, education level, and occupation

demonstration a personalized presentation that shows how a product can benefit and provide value to the customer

direct channel distribution method by which producers sell directly to final consumers

direct marketing a promotional technique used to get consumers to buy products or services from a nonretail setting

direct retailing the process of selling products through representatives who work door-to-door or at home sales parties

disclaimer a statement that outlines the limitations of a product

discretionary income the amount of money remaining for spending and saving after taxes and other essential expenses are paid

discrimination the act of treating one person less favorably than another person because of race, color, religion, gender, or national origin

distribution the methods used by businesses to get their products to customers

distribution center a large facility that offers a variety of supply chain services to help move a product to the marketplace more efficiently

dumping a pricing practice by which a company sells an exported product for a much lower price than the price charged for the same or similar product in the home market of the exporter

E

elastic demand occurs when the demand for a product is affected by its price

electronic data interchange (EDI) the electronic exchange of information between the purchaser and supplier

emotional motives reasons to make a purchase based on feelings, beliefs, or attitudes

empowering giving others substantial responsibility and the freedom to make their own decisions

encoding the conversion of ideas or thoughts into a message

endorsement a public expression of approval or support for a product or service

ethics moral principles that guide the actions and behaviors of a person or group

ethnocentrism the tendency to view and value things based on one's own cultural beliefs

explicit communicators people who convey information in a concise, direct, and structured manner

exports   products and services sold to another country

extensive decision making   the methodical consumer decision-making process used to buy an infrequently purchased product

F

Federal Communications Commission (FCC)   the government agency that monitors and regulates interstate and international communications by radio, television, wire, satellite, and cable

Federal Trade Commission (FTC)   the government agency that regulates unfair methods of competition and unfair or deceptive acts that may affect competition

fee system   a payment method by which an advertising agency is paid an hourly rate for different services provided

feedback   the receiver's response to a message

focus group   a small number of people recruited to discuss a topic being studied

follow-up   the act of contacting the customer after the sale to ensure satisfaction

Food and Drug Administration (FDA)   the government agency that ensures food, cosmetics, drugs, and medical devices are safe and effective

4Cs Model   a communication model that includes four components: comprehension, connection, credibility, and contagiousness

frequency   the number of times a person is exposed to an advertisement

G

generic brand   a no-name product that competes with brand-name products

geographic segmentation   the segmentation of consumers based on where they live

globalization   the integration of different societies, cultures, and economies from around the world

green marketing   the use of advertising to support and improve the environment

gross domestic product (GDP)   the total dollar value of all products and services produced by a country within a certain time period

H

harassment   unwelcome verbal or physical conduct

hard skills   technical skills that are learned through training

hedonic needs   needs that focus on enjoyment and pleasure

I

illustration   the actual drawing, photography, or other type of art used in an advertisement

image advertising   ads that promote the general perception of a product or service rather than its function or purpose

implicit communicators   people who convey information that is vague or has an implied meaning

imports   products and services purchased from another country

incentive-based system   a payment method by which an advertising agency's fee is based on the achievement of agreed-upon performance objectives

income statement   a financial statement that reports a company's revenues, expenses, and net loss or profit for a specific period of time

indirect channel   distribution method that involves *intermediaries*, or individuals and businesses that move a product from the producer to the consumer

industry trade groups   trade associations that are founded and funded by businesses operating in a specific industry and that are responsible for public relations activities such as advertising, education, political donations, lobbying, and publishing

inelastic demand   occurs when a change in price has very little effect on the demand for a product

inflation an increase in the general level of prices for products and services and a decrease in purchasing power

infomercial a lengthy paid advertisement that showcases the benefits of a product

informational interview a meeting with a human resource representative or manager of a company where you might like to work to obtain general information and advice about the company

infrastructure a country's transportation, communication, and utility systems

initiative taking action without being asked to do so

integrated marketing communication (IMC) a strategy used to plan, execute, and monitor all promotional messages about a product to ensure consistency among all those messages

intensive distribution a marketing strategy to sell a product at as many locations as possible

international trade the sale of products and services to people in other countries

internship a hands-on learning experience related to career goals and interests

interpersonal communication communicating "one on one" with another person

invoice an itemized bill for products and services that states the terms of payment

involuntary attention the kind of attention a consumer gives an advertising message that uses various attention-gaining techniques

K

kiosk a small, free-standing booth containing a computer or display screen that distributes product information

L

layout a drawing of the print advertisement showing where all the elements in the ad are positioned

lead time the amount of time required to produce and place an advertisement

leadership the ability to motivate and direct a group of people to achieve a common goal

licensed brand a well-known brand owned by one company that is sold for use by another company

limited decision making the consumer decision-making process in which a moderate amount of time is spent collecting and comparing information about an unfamiliar product or brand

logistics the physical distribution process that involves transporting, storing, and delivering products throughout the supply chain

M

markdown a reduction from the original selling price

market response model an advertising budgeting method that examines the number of sales generated in relation to the dollar amount spent on advertising

market segmentation the process of dividing a large group of consumers into meaningful subgroups based on identifiable and similar characteristics and needs

market share a business's portion of the total sales generated by all of the businesses operating in the same market

marketing all of the processes used to identify, create, and maintain exchange relationships that satisfy individuals and organizations

marketing concept identifying and satisfying the needs of customers during the development and marketing of a product or service

marketing database a collection of names, addresses, and behavioral information gathered from individual customers

marketing functions related activities that must be completed to accomplish an important marketing goal

marketing mix the combination of four marketing elements—product, price, distribution, and promotion—used by a business

marketing plan a written description of the marketing objectives and the planned marketing strategies and activities required to meet those objectives

marketing-information system an organized method of collecting, storing, processing, and reporting information that is needed to make marketing decisions

mass communication communicating a message to a large, diversified audience using mass media

mass marketing a marketing strategy used to appeal to a large, general group of consumers

media the channels of communication used to send a message to the target market

mentor an individual who acts as a role model and provides training and advice

mobile advertising ads directed to consumers' Internet-enabled mobile devices, such as smartphones, MP3 players, and digital tablets like the iPad

multifaceted having more skills than those required for an employee's specific position

N

need anything you require for survival

networking the process of developing a broad list of contacts with other people, groups, or organizations

niche market a smaller market that has a unique set of needs

noise any distraction or interference that acts as a barrier to a message

nonprice competition a pricing strategy by which a company tries to distinguish its product or service from competing products based on factors other than price, such as design, quality, and workmanship

nonverbal communication any method of conveying information without using words

O

objective-and-task method an advertising budgeting method that estimates the cost of achieving advertising objectives

obsolescence occurs when a product is out of date, no longer wanted, or unusable

online advertising a form of promotion that uses the Internet and World Wide Web as the advertising medium to deliver marketing messages that attract customers

P

patronage motives reasons to make a purchase based on loyalty

penetration pricing a pricing strategy in which a low price is set for new products to gain a larger market share rapidly

percentage-of-sales method an advertising budgeting method that sets the budget as a fixed percentage of past or projected sales

personal selling face-to-face communication between the buyer and seller that attempts to influence the buying decision

phishing an Internet scam by which an e-mail falsely claims to be a legitimate business or other organization in an attempt to get personal information

picturing the use of pictures to communicate a message

point-of-sale (POS) system a computerized system that updates inventory records as each sale occurs

pop-up ad an online advertisement that opens on top of the current web page being viewed

positioning the process of creating a unique image or identity for a brand to distinguish it from competing brands

preapproach the process of researching prospective customers before initially contacting them

premium an item offered to consumers for free or at a reduced price with the purchase of another item

press release a written statement to inform the media about a new product or special event

price competition a pricing strategy by which a company tries to distinguish its product or service from competing products based on low price

price equilibrium the point at which demand and supply are equal

price skimming a pricing strategy in which a high price is set to emphasize the uniqueness of a product and to recover the product development costs quickly

primary market research the process of collecting data for the first time to use in solving a specific problem

product advertising a form of advertising that uses rational arguments to communicate why consumers need a specific product by highlighting the benefits associated with the use of that product

product life cycle the sequence of stages that a product goes through during its time on the market; there are four stages—introduction, growth, maturity, and decline

product line a group of closely related products with slight variations developed by the same business

product mix the product assortment, which includes all of the different products a business sells

product placement a form of advertising in which a business's product, service, or name is used in a television show, movie, video game, or other form of entertainment

product usage the amount of a product purchased and used by a consumer

promotion all communications used by a business to create a favorable impression of its products or services

promotional mix a combination of advertising, public relations, personal selling, and sales promotion used by businesses to reach their target market

promotional plan an outline of how all of the elements in the promotional mix will work together to reach the target market

psychographics a description of consumers' interests, attitudes, opinions, and lifestyles

public relations activities and events that create goodwill for a business or other organization

publicity any nonpaid form of communication designed to arouse public interest about a product, service, business, or event

puffery an exaggeration or a subjective opinion used to sell products

punctual being exactly on time or a little ahead of schedule

purchase order a form listing the types, quantities, and prices of products ordered

purchasing power the value of a dollar (or other unit of currency) as measured by the amount of products and services it can buy

push money a bonus given by manufacturers to salespeople for selling a specific brand

R

rational motives reasons to make a purchase based on facts or logic

reach the total number of people who will be exposed to an advertisement over a period of time

rebate a refund of money offered to consumers who purchase a specific product

recall test a test that measures how much an audience remembers about an advertising message

recession a period of time when the economy experiences a downturn

recognition test a test that measures a lower level of brand awareness by determining whether audience members remember seeing an ad

reference group an organization or group of people that an individual identifies with and admires

resonance test a test that measures the extent to which an advertising message resonates or strikes a chord with the target audience

return on investment (ROI) the amount earned as a result of money invested, expressed as a percentage

RFM analysis an analysis that calculates the value of each customer based on *r*ecency, *f*requency, and *m*onetary factors

routine decision making the consumer decision-making process for frequently purchased, low-cost products that require little thought

S

sales promotion the use of marketing activities that provide extra value and buying incentives for customers

sample a smaller group that is representative of the target market

sampling providing consumers with the opportunity to use a product on a risk-free trial basis

search engine ad an ad for which an advertiser pays the search engine to place it near relevant search results based on keywords; also known as a *paid search*

secondary market research the process of collecting and analyzing data previously gathered for other purposes

self-regulation the advertising industry's attempt to regulate and control its actions

share of voice a company's portion (percentage) of overall advertising in a specific product category

shopping products types of products that consumers want to own after they meet personal needs

situational analysis a description of the environment in which a business is operating

skill set the unique skills and abilities that an individual brings to the job market

slogan a short, memorable phrase that establishes an identity for a brand

social media websites where users create and share information

soft skills a cluster of personal qualities, habits, attitudes, and social graces that enhance a person's job performance

spam an unwanted online communication that is sent out in mass

specialty products types of products that have a strong brand loyalty

sponsorship a company's support of an issue, cause, or event that is consistent with company objectives

stereotype a generalization about the "typical" characteristics of a specific group of individuals

storyboard a sketch that provides the play-by-play sequence of visual scenes and ad copy used in a television advertisement

subliminal message information that your subconscious, or unconscious mind, receives without you fully realizing that you're receiving it

suggestion selling offering customers related products and services that could enhance the use of their purchased product

supply chain all of the businesses involved in the flow of products, services, resources, and information from the producer to the consumer

survey a list of questions used to obtain facts, opinions, and attitudes

SWOT analysis an examination of a business's strengths, weaknesses, opportunities, and threats

synergy the sum of the results produced by a team

T

target market a specific group of consumers to whom the business wants to sell its products or services

team a small group of employees who work together to achieve a specific goal

tie-in promotion a joint promotion of two or more products or services

time management the act of budgeting time to increase efficiency and productivity

trade allowance a reward offered by manufacturers to retailers in exchange for supporting the manufacturer's brand by performing various marketing activities; also called a *trade deal*

trade credit financing offered by one business to another business

trademark a company's exclusive right to use a brand name, symbol, or design

transit advertising ads that appear on the interior or exterior of public transportation (buses, taxis, subways) and other vehicles

translator an interpreter who converts a message from one language to another

U

unique selling proposition an advertisement that emphasizes a unique quality or significant consumer benefit

unsought products types of products that are not actively sought out by consumers

V

value the consumer's perception of how much satisfaction a product provides beyond the price paid for the product

visual diversity an advertising technique by which advertisements show Americans of different races and ethnicities interacting in schools, workplaces, homes, and other venues while consuming the advertised product

visual merchandising the process of displaying products in a way that makes them appealing and enticing to customers

voluntary attention the kind of attention a consumer devotes to an advertising message that meets his or her current purchasing goals

W

want something that is desired

warehouse a building designed to store large quantities of products safely

workplace bullying repeated, unreasonable actions of an individual (or a group) directed toward an employee (or a group of employees) for the purpose of intimidating, degrading, humiliating, or undermining the employee

Index